# Mathematical Problems in Rock Mechanics and Rock Engineering

# Mathematical Problems in Rock Mechanics and Rock Engineering

Editors

**Shaofeng Wang**
**Linqi Huang**
**Xin Cai**
**Zhengyang Song**

MDPI • Basel • Beijing • Wuhan • Barcelona • Belgrade • Manchester • Tokyo • Cluj • Tianjin

*Editors*
Shaofeng Wang
Central South University
China

Linqi Huang
Central South University
China

Xin Cai
Central South University
China

Zhengyang Song
University of Science and Technology Beijing
China

*Editorial Office*
MDPI
St. Alban-Anlage 66
4052 Basel, Switzerland

This is a reprint of articles from the Special Issue published online in the open access journal *Mathematics* (ISSN 2227-7390) (available at: https://www.mdpi.com/si/mathematics/Mathematical_Problems_Rock_Mechanics_Rock_Engineering).

For citation purposes, cite each article independently as indicated on the article page online and as indicated below:

LastName, A.A.; LastName, B.B.; LastName, C.C. Article Title. *Journal Name* **Year**, *Volume Number*, Page Range.

**ISBN 978-3-0365-6091-5 (Hbk)**
**ISBN 978-3-0365-6092-2 (PDF)**

© 2023 by the authors. Articles in this book are Open Access and distributed under the Creative Commons Attribution (CC BY) license, which allows users to download, copy and build upon published articles, as long as the author and publisher are properly credited, which ensures maximum dissemination and a wider impact of our publications.

The book as a whole is distributed by MDPI under the terms and conditions of the Creative Commons license CC BY-NC-ND.

# Contents

**Linqi Huang, Shaofeng Wang, Xin Cai and Zhengyang Song**
Mathematical Problems in Rock Mechanics and Rock Engineering
Reprinted from: *Mathematics* **2023**, *11*, 67, doi:10.3390/math11010067 . . . . . . . . . . . . . . . 1

**Jiajun Wang, Linqi Huang, Xibing Li, Yangchun Wu and Huilin Liu**
Effect of Particle Size Distribution on the Dynamic Mechanical Properties and Fractal Characteristics of Cemented Rock Strata
Reprinted from: *Mathematics* **2022**, *10*, 2078, doi:10.3390/math10122078 . . . . . . . . . . . . . . 5

**Diyuan Li, Junjie Zhao and Jinyin Ma**
Experimental Studies on Rock Thin-Section Image Classification by Deep Learning-Based Approaches
Reprinted from: *Mathematics* **2022**, *10*, 2317, doi:10.3390/math10132317 . . . . . . . . . . . . . . 27

**Qi Li, Zhen Li, Peng Li, Ruikai Pan and Qingqing Zhang**
Characterization of 3D Displacement and Stress Fields in Coal Based on CT Scans
Reprinted from: *Mathematics* **2022**, *10*, 2512, doi:10.3390/math10142512 . . . . . . . . . . . . . . 55

**Xianglong Li, Yongbo Wu, Lihua He, Xiaohua Zhang and Jianguo Wang**
Research on Dynamic Properties of Deep Marble Influenced by High Temperature
Reprinted from: *Mathematics* **2022**, *10*, 2603, doi:10.3390/math10152603 . . . . . . . . . . . . . . 71

**Naseer Muhammad Khan, Kewang Cao, Muhammad Zaka Emad, Sajjad Hussain, Hafeezur Rehman, Kausar Sultan Shah, Faheem Ur Rehman and Aamir Muhammad**
Development of Predictive Models for Determination of the Extent of Damage in Granite Caused by Thermal Treatment and Cooling Conditions Using Artificial Intelligence
Reprinted from: *Mathematics* **2022**, *10*, 2883, doi:10.3390/math10162883 . . . . . . . . . . . . . . 87

**Daolong Chen, Changgen Xia, Huini Liu, Xiling Liu and Kun Du**
Research on *b* Value Estimation Based on Apparent Amplitude-Frequency Distribution in Rock Acoustic Emission Tests
Reprinted from: *Mathematics* **2022**, *10*, 3202, doi:10.3390/math10173202 . . . . . . . . . . . . . . 109

**Jiangjiang Yin, Jianyou Lu, Fuchao Tian and Shaofeng Wang**
Pollutant Migration Pattern during Open-Pit Rock Blasting Based on Digital Image Analysis Technology
Reprinted from: *Mathematics* **2022**, *10*, 3205, doi:10.3390/math10173205 . . . . . . . . . . . . . . 127

**Junbo Qiu, Xin Yin, Yucong Pan, Xinyu Wang and Min Zhang**
Prediction of Uniaxial Compressive Strength in Rocks Based on Extreme Learning Machine Improved with Metaheuristic Algorithm
Reprinted from: *Mathematics* **2022**, *10*, 3490, doi:10.3390/math10193490 . . . . . . . . . . . . . . 145

**Jiadong Qiu and Fan Feng**
Effect of Different Tunnel Distribution on Dynamic Behavior and Damage Characteristics of Non-Adjacent Tunnel Triggered by Blasting Disturbance
Reprinted from: *Mathematics* **2022**, *10*, 3705, doi:10.3390/math10193705 . . . . . . . . . . . . . . 163

**Xin Xiong, Feng Gao, Keping Zhou, Chun Yang and Jielin Li**
Mechanical Properties and Strength Evolution Model of Sandstone Subjected to Freeze–Thaw Weathering Process: Considering the Confining Pressure Effect
Reprinted from: *Mathematics* **2022**, *10*, 3841, doi:10.3390/math10203841 . . . . . . . . . . . . . . 183

**Niaz Muhammad Shahani, Barkat Ullah, Kausar Sultan Shah, Fawad Ul Hassan, Rashid Ali, Mohamed Abdelghany Elkotb, Mohamed E. Ghoneim and Elsayed M. Tag-Eldin**
Predicting Angle of Internal Friction and Cohesion of Rocks Based on Machine Learning Algorithms
Reprinted from: *Mathematics* **2022**, *10*, 3875, doi:10.3390/math10203875 . . . . . . . . . . . . . . . 203

**Shuang Gong, Chaofei Wang, Furui Xi, Yongqiang Jia, Lei Zhou, Hansong Zhang, Jingkuo Wang, Xingyang Ren, Shuai Wang, Shibin Yao and Juan Liu**
Dynamic Tensile Mechanical Properties of Outburst Coal Considering Bedding Effect and Evolution Characteristics of Strain Energy Density
Reprinted from: *Mathematics* **2022**, *10*, 4120, doi:10.3390/math10214120 . . . . . . . . . . . . . . . 221

*Editorial*

# Mathematical Problems in Rock Mechanics and Rock Engineering

Linqi Huang [1], Shaofeng Wang [1,*], Xin Cai [1] and Zhengyang Song [2]

[1] School of Resources and Safety Enginerring, Central South University, Changsha 410083, China
[2] School of Civil and Resource Engineering, University of Science and Technology Beijing, Beijing 100083, China
* Correspondence: sf.wang@csu.edu.cn

**MSC:** 74R10

---

**Citation:** Huang, L.; Wang, S.; Cai, X.; Song, Z. Mathematical Problems in Rock Mechanics and Rock Engineering. *Mathematics* **2023**, *11*, 67. https://doi.org/10.3390/math11010067

Received: 9 November 2022
Accepted: 30 November 2022
Published: 25 December 2022

**Copyright:** © 2022 by the authors. Licensee MDPI, Basel, Switzerland. This article is an open access article distributed under the terms and conditions of the Creative Commons Attribution (CC BY) license (https://creativecommons.org/licenses/by/4.0/).

With the increasing requirements for energy, resources and space, numerous rock engineering projects (e.g., mining, tunnelling, underground storage, geothermal energy, petroleum, water conservancy and hydropower) are more often being constructed and operated in large-scale environments with complex geology. Meanwhile, rock failures and rock instabilities (e.g., rockbursts, large-scale collapse, slabbing, zonal disintegration and microseism) occur more frequently, severely threatening the safety and stability of rock engineering projects. It is well-recognized that rock has multi-scale structures, from minerals, particles, fractures, fissures, joints and stratification to fault, and involves multi-scale fracture processes. Meanwhile, rocks are commonly subjected simultaneously to complex static stress and strong dynamic disturbance, providing a hotbed for the occurrence of rock failures. In addition, there are many multi-physics coupling processes in a rock mass, such as the coupled thermo–hydromechanical interaction in fractured porous rocks. It is still difficult to understand these rock mechanics and characterize rock behavior during complex stress conditions, multi-physics processes and multi-scale changes. Therefore, our understanding of rock mechanics and the prevention and control of failure and instability in rock engineering needs to be furthered. This Special Issue, "Mathematical Problems in Rock Mechanics and Rock Engineering", aims to bring together original research discussing innovative efforts regarding in situ observations, laboratory experiments and theoretical, numerical and big-data-based methods to overcome the mathematical problems related to rock mechanics and rock engineering. It includes 12 manuscripts that illustrate the valuable efforts for addressing mathematical problems in rock mechanics and rock engineering.

The article by Wang et al. [1] aims to investigate the dynamic mechanics and post-failure characteristics of fault-cemented rock strata by Split Hopkinson pressure bar (SHPB) dynamic impact tests on cemented rock samples with various particle size distributions (PSDs). The results show that the breakage ratio and fractal dimension have a linear relationship regardless of the PSD or strain, and the dynamic strength is negatively linearly related to the fractal dimension under the PSD effect but positively linearly related to the fractal dimension under the strain rate effect.

The article by Li et al. [2] aims to analyze the impact of optimizers (Adam, SGD, RMSprop) and learning rate (lambda and cosine decay modes) on the performance of deep learning-based algorithms for rock thin-section image classification by using 2634 rock thin-section images including three rock types—metamorphic, sedimentary and volcanic rocks. The investigation shows that the cosine learning-rate decay mode is the better option for learning-rate adjustment during the training process, and the capabilities of the model using Adam and RMSprop optimizers were more robust than that of SGD.

The study proposed by Li et al. [3] aimed to quantify the degree of coal macroscopic deformation under different loads using Computed tomography (CT) scans. The results illustrate that fractures and minerals significantly affect the stress state and displacement field distribution features, the maximum principal stresses and shear stresses in different matrices differ significantly, and the presence of minerals and fractures induce prevalent shear stress in coal and make coal prone to stress concentration.

Li et al. [4] investigated the effect of temperature on the dynamic properties of marble using the dynamic and static combined SHPB test device, considering that deep rock will be impacted by different temperatures and varied disturbance degrees. The results revealed that the diameter and height of the specimen increased, and the mass and longitudinal wave velocity dropped as the temperature climbed. The variation laws of the total stress–strain curves after varied high temperatures are substantially the same, and the peak stress was negatively correlated with the action temperature.

Khan et al. [5] propose a new predictive model based on artificial intelligence to quantify the damage factor of rock by thermal treatment followed by subsequent cooling conditions (slow and rapid). The results show that an ANN-based predictive model is the most efficient model for quantifying the rock damage factor based on porosity compared to other models based on multilinear regression (MLR) and the adoptive neural-fuzzy inference system (ANFIS).

Chen et al. [6] developed a method to obtain the size distribution characteristics of the real source from the apparent amplitude in doubly truncated distribution using rock acoustic emission (AE) tests. The results indicate that mineral grains of different sizes and compositions and different types of discontinuities of rock specimens determine the rock fracture characteristics and the AE $b$ value. The dynamic $b$ values decreased linearly during the loading process, which confirms that variations in the $b$ value also depend on the stress.

Yin et al. [7] proposed a pollution evaluation system based on the fractal dimension theory (Dbox(P)) and the grayscale average algorithm (Ga) in digital image-processing technology to recognize and analyze the distributions of the smoke–dust cloud and subsequently determine the pollution degrees. The results obviously denote three diffusion stages of the pollutants, mainly including the generation stage, cloud-formation stage and the diffusion stage during open-pit rock blasting.

Qiu et al. [8] developed a dataset of 734 samples from previous studies on different countries' magmatic, sedimentary and metamorphic rocks to estimate uniaxial compressive strength (UCS) using three main factors of point load index, P-wave velocity and the Schmidt hammer rebound number based on an extreme learning machine improved with a metaheuristic algorithm. The results show that the extreme learning machine with the whale optimization algorithm (WOA-ELM model) has high accuracy and reliability, which means that it has broad application potential for estimating the UCS of different rocks.

Qiu et al. [9] aimed to analyze the effect of tunnel distribution on the dynamic response characteristics of a remote non-adjacent tunnel. The results show that the stress wave amplitude of the non-adjacent tunnel is closely related to the tunnel distribution, but only near the sidewalls of the non-adjacent tunnel is the stress wave waveform sensitive to the tunnel distribution.

Xiong et al. [10] analyze the evolution characteristics of freeze-and-thaw (F&T) damage based on the $T_2$ spectrum distribution curves of sandstone specimens before and after F&T weathering cycles. The results show that the quantity of F&T weathering cycles and confining pressure can significantly influence the pre-peak and post-peak deformation behaviors of sandstone specimens.

Shahani et al. [11] developed four advanced machine learning (ML)-based intelligent prediction models, namely Lasso regression (LR), ridge regression (RR), decision tree (DT) and support vector machine (SVM), to predict $c$ in (MPa) and $\varphi$ in (°) of rock, with P-wave velocity in (m/s), density in (gm/cc), UCS in (MPa) and tensile strength in (MPa) as the input parameters. The results show that UCS and tensile strength were the most influential parameters in predicting $c$ and $\varphi$.

Gong et al. [12] studied the dynamic tensile mechanical properties, layered effect and density evolution characteristics of strain energy for coal using the split Hopkinson pressure bar (SHPB) technique. The results show that the bedding orientation of the coal has a significant effect on its deformation and damage features. The presence of weak planes, microcracks and laminae causes its shear damage zone to behave with more complexity.

The guest editors hope that the selected papers will help scholars and researchers to push forward the progress in dealing with the mathematical problems in rock mechanics and rock engineering.

**Author Contributions:** Conceptualization, S.W. and L.H.; writing—original draft preparation, S.W., L.H., X.C. and Z.S.; writing—review and editing, S.W., L.H., X.C. and Z.S.; supervision, S.W. and L.H.; project administration, S.W. All authors have read and agreed to the published version of the manuscript.

**Data Availability Statement:** Not applicable.

**Conflicts of Interest:** The authors declare no conflict of interest.

## References

1. Wang, J.; Huang, L.; Li, X.; Wu, Y.; Liu, H. Effect of Particle Size Distribution on the Dynamic Mechanical Properties and Fractal Characteristics of Cemented Rock Strata. *Mathematics* **2022**, *10*, 2078. [CrossRef]
2. Li, D.; Zhao, J.; Ma, J. Experimental Studies on Rock Thin-Section Image Classification by Deep Learning-Based Approaches. *Mathematics* **2022**, *10*, 2317. [CrossRef]
3. Li, Q.; Li, Z.; Li, P.; Pan, R.; Zhang, Q. Characterization of 3D Displacement and Stress Fields in Coal Based on CT Scans. *Mathematics* **2022**, *10*, 2512. [CrossRef]
4. Li, X.; Wu, Y.; He, L.; Zhang, X.; Wang, J. Research on Dynamic Properties of Deep Marble Influenced by High Temperature. *Mathematics* **2022**, *10*, 2603. [CrossRef]
5. Khan, N.M.; Cao, K.; Emad, M.Z.; Hussain, S.; Rehman, H.; Shah, K.S.; Rehman, F.U.; Muhammad, A. Development of Predictive Models for Determination of the Extent of Damage in Granite Caused by Thermal Treatment and Cooling Conditions Using Artificial Intelligence. *Mathematics* **2022**, *10*, 2883. [CrossRef]
6. Chen, D.; Xia, C.; Liu, H.; Liu, X.; Du, K. Research on b Value Estimation Based on Apparent Amplitude-Frequency Distribution in Rock Acoustic Emission Tests. *Mathematics* **2022**, *10*, 3202. [CrossRef]
7. Yin, J.; Lu, J.; Tian, F.; Wang, S. Pollutant Migration Pattern during Open-Pit Rock Blasting Based on Digital Image Analysis Technology. *Mathematics* **2022**, *10*, 3205. [CrossRef]
8. Qiu, J.; Yin, X.; Pan, Y.; Wang, X.; Zhang, M. Prediction of Uniaxial Compressive Strength in Rocks Based on Extreme Learning Machine Improved with Metaheuristic Algorithm. *Mathematics* **2022**, *10*, 3490. [CrossRef]
9. Qiu, J.; Feng, F. Effect of Different Tunnel Distribution on Dynamic Behavior and Damage Characteristics of Non-Adjacent Tunnel Triggered by Blasting Disturbance. *Mathematics* **2022**, *10*, 3705. [CrossRef]
10. Xiong, X.; Gao, F.; Zhou, K.; Yang, C.; Li, J. Mechanical Properties and Strength Evolution Model of Sandstone Subjected to Freeze–Thaw Weathering Process: Considering the Confining Pressure Effect. *Mathematics* **2022**, *10*, 3841. [CrossRef]
11. Shahani, N.M.; Ullah, B.; Shah, K.S.; Hassan, F.U.; Ali, R.; Elkotb, M.A.; Ghoneim, M.E.; Tag-Eldin, E.M. Predicting Angle of Internal Friction and Cohesion of Rocks Based on Machine Learning Algorithms. *Mathematics* **2022**, *10*, 3875. [CrossRef]
12. Gong, S.; Wang, C.; Xi, F.; Jia, Y.; Zhou, L.; Zhang, H.; Wang, J.; Ren, X.; Wang, S.; Yao, S.; et al. Dynamic Tensile Mechanical Properties of Outburst Coal Considering Bedding Effect and Evolution Characteristics of Strain Energy Density. *Mathematics* **2022**, *10*, 4120. [CrossRef]

**Disclaimer/Publisher's Note:** The statements, opinions and data contained in all publications are solely those of the individual author(s) and contributor(s) and not of MDPI and/or the editor(s). MDPI and/or the editor(s) disclaim responsibility for any injury to people or property resulting from any ideas, methods, instructions or products referred to in the content.

Article

# Effect of Particle Size Distribution on the Dynamic Mechanical Properties and Fractal Characteristics of Cemented Rock Strata

Jiajun Wang, Linqi Huang *, Xibing Li, Yangchun Wu and Huilin Liu

School of Resources & Safety Engineering, Central South University, Changsha 410083, China; jjwang@csu.edu.cn (J.W.); xbli@csu.edu.cn (X.L.); wuyangchun1995@csu.edu.cn (Y.W.); lhlblack@csu.edu.cn (H.L.)
* Correspondence: huanglinqi@csu.edu.cn; Tel.: +86-134-6905-9806

**Abstract:** To investigate the dynamic mechanics and post-failure characteristics of fault-cemented rock strata, broken rock particles were reshaped to obtain cemented rock samples with various particle size distributions (PSDs). Split Hopkinson pressure bar (SHPB) dynamic impact tests were performed on the cemented rock samples under different strain rates. The test results show that plastic deformation occurs in the cemented rock sample as a result of its porous structure. Therefore, there is no linear phase in the dynamic stress–strain curves. With an increase in the Talbot index and mixture type, more large particles were contained inside the cemented rock sample, and the dynamic strength gradually increased. A power function can effectively describe the relationship between the strain rate and dynamic strength for various Talbot indices. After dynamic impact, the fragments of the cemented rock samples exhibit evident fractal laws, and the breakage of the samples includes breakage of the original rock particle itself and breakage between the rock particles and cementations. The breakage ratio and fractal dimension both decrease with the increase in the number of mixture type and Talbot index but increase with the increase in strain rate. It is worth noting that the breakage ratio and fractal dimension have a linear relationship regardless of the PSD or strain. The relationship between the dynamic strength and fractal dimension has different response laws for the PSD and strain rate effects. The dynamic strength is negatively linearly related to the fractal dimension under the PSD effect but positively linearly related to the fractal dimension under the strain rate effect. This research work can provide foundation support for investigating the instability mechanism of fault cemented rock strata under dynamic stress.

**Keywords:** cemented rock sample; SHPB impact; PSD; fractal dimension

**MSC:** 74R10

## 1. Introduction

Faults are common geological structures [1,2] encountered in underground mining activities. As shown in Figure 1, the roadway advance faces a hidden fault: the fault rock strata may be in cemented states because the fault zone includes silicate, lime minerals, mineral water, and broken rock and other components [3]. The dynamic stress induced by the disturbance of excavation is inevitably loaded onto fault-cemented strata and may cause failure of the fault's geological structure. Therefore, investigating the dynamic mechanical properties of fault-cemented rock strata is vital for understanding fault instability mechanisms.

Cemented rock strata widely exist in various engineering geological conditions [4,5], and there is much research [3,6–9] on their physical and mechanical properties. Fall et al. [10,11] studied the strength characteristics of cemented paste backfill (CPB), and suggested that the uniaxial compression strength (UCS) has an exponential relationship with the solid-phase mass fraction and a linear relationship with the cement–sand ratio. Jiang et al. [12] investigated the influence of sodium chloride on the yield stress and strength law of cemented tailings material, and found that the UCS of CPB decreases with an increase in

Citation: Wang, J.; Huang, L.; Li, X.; Wu, Y.; Liu, H. Effect of Particle Size Distribution on the Dynamic Mechanical Properties and Fractal Characteristics of Cemented Rock Strata. *Mathematics* **2022**, *10*, 2078. https://doi.org/10.3390/math10122078

Academic Editors: Andrey Jivkov and Manuel Pastor

Received: 17 May 2022
Accepted: 13 June 2022
Published: 15 June 2022

**Publisher's Note:** MDPI stays neutral with regard to jurisdictional claims in published maps and institutional affiliations.

**Copyright:** © 2022 by the authors. Licensee MDPI, Basel, Switzerland. This article is an open access article distributed under the terms and conditions of the Creative Commons Attribution (CC BY) license (https://creativecommons.org/licenses/by/4.0/).

the initial NaCl concentration. Xu et al. [13,14] conducted triaxial compression experiments on CPB samples, and their results showed that the brittleness and failure pattern change with increasing cement content. Through acoustic emissions (AE) and computed tomography (CT) scanning [15], shear cracks have been observed inside rock specimens, and tensile cracks observed along rock/backfill interfaces. The laboratory testing strength of CPB material is determined by many factors such as the binder proportion [16], curing age [17], concentration [18] and cement-tailings ratio [19], whereas the load characteristics of cemented rock strata under geotechnical engineering conditions are highly complex. Therefore, investigating the static mechanical properties of cemented rock strata is insufficient to reveal the instability mechanism.

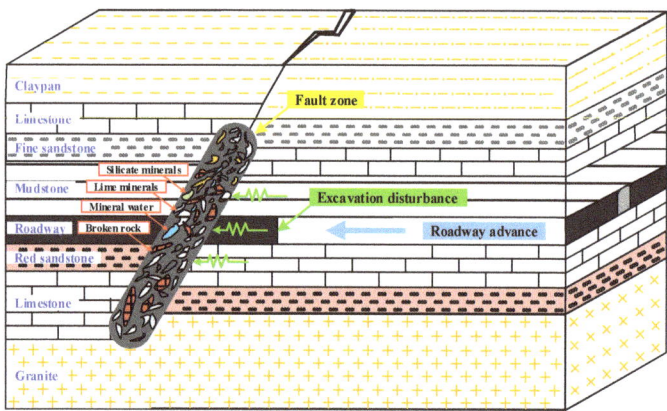

**Figure 1.** Cemented rock strata in fault zone: excavation for a roadway is shown, with an example of possible adjacent layering.

A dynamic load [20] is inevitable for cemented rock strata in underground engineering activities, and much attention [21–24] has been paid to the dynamic mechanical properties of cemented materials. Cao et al. [25] investigated the effect of the strain rate on the dynamical mechanical response and failure patterns of cemented tailings composite specimens; the dynamic strength increases exponentially and the fractal dimension increases linearly with the average strain rate. Tan et al. [26] reported that the dynamic strength has a power-function relationship with the average strain rate; the failure pattern shows tensile failure and X-shaped shear failure. When cemented tailings backfill was reinforced by polyester fiber, the dynamic stress–strain curves exhibited a "double-peak" phenomenon [27]. Yang et al. [28] proposed that cemented tailings backfill (CTB) experience shear failure and tensile failure with an increase in the confining pressure. The compression strength and ultrasonic pulse velocity (UPV) [29] of cemented rock samples increase linearly with increasing curing time, and the UPV can be applied to the prediction of the UCS of cemented rock samples. Chen et al. [30] established an exponential correlation between the dynamic strength and strain rate. The interface shear strength between CPB and rock were investigated by direct shear tests, which indicated that the strength is time-dependent [31]. Zheng et al. [32] discussed the energy dissipation law of CTB samples after split Hopkinson pressure bar (SHPB) tests, and the results suggest that the absorbed energy first increases and then decreases with increasing average strain rate. Wang et al. [33] reported that the dynamic tensile and shear strengths increase by 72% and 127%, respectively, relative to static loading strengths. However, these achievements focused on the strength characteristics and failure patterns of cemented rock materials. In actuality, cemented rock is likely to have fragmented under impact loading. The fragmentation of partial surrounding rock is a key factor affecting the stability of the rock strata. Therefore, it is necessary to study and analyze the fragmentation characteristics of cemented rock strata under impact load.

The state of cemented rock materials after failure can indicate the instability mechanism in the cemented rock strata [34,35]. In the present study, fault-broken red sandstone rocks were cemented and reshaped into specimens for dynamic impact tests. The choice of the particle fractions in the mixture was considered; we investigated the influence of the particle size distribution (PSD) on the dynamical mechanical properties of cemented rock samples and their fractal characteristics. Finally, the functional relationship between the dynamic strength and the fractal dimension was established, and the influences of the PSD and strain rate on this relationship were analyzed.

## 2. Materials and Scheme

### 2.1. Materials

Broken red sandstones were collected from the fault zone of the Sima coal field in the Shanxi province of China. The material collected was subjected to a secondary crushing before manufacturing the cemented rock samples; the sample preparation process is shown in Figure 2.

**Figure 2.** Sample preparation process (**a–e**): Sieved red sandstone particles; maximum sizes in each group are 2, 3, 5, 8 and 10 mm. (**f**) Cementation material. (**g**) Specimen molds. (**h**) Samples for strength tests: diameter, 50 mm; height, 25 mm.

(a) Rock particle preparation

Rock particles of different sizes were obtained by sieving the crushed granular red sandstone. In the natural accumulation state of broken rock in the fault zone, the size of the broken rock pieces follows a continuous distribution. To simulate the continuous nature of the PSD in the cemented rock samples prepared for testing, the sieved rock particles were divided into five groups (0–2 mm, 2–3 mm, 3–5 mm, 5–8 mm and 8–10 mm) (Figure 2a–e).

(b) Component proportion

Rock particles of a single size and mixtures of particles of various sizes were used for specimen preparation. For the mixtures, the PSD of each group in the cemented sample was described using Talbot's [36] grading method:

$$P_i = \left(\frac{d_i}{d_m}\right)^T \times 100\% \tag{1}$$

where $P_i$ is the mass percentage of rock particles whose size is smaller than $d_i$, $d_m$ is the largest particle size ($d_m$ = 10 mm) and $T$ is the Talbot index characterizing the distribution.

(c) Cementing reshaped sample

After measuring the raw material quantities for specimens of various Talbot indices (particle size fractions) and cement fractions, the cementation materials (Figure 2f) and red sandstone particles were mixed with water and stirred, and the slurry mixture was then injected into molds (Figure 2g). To reduce the number of gas holes in the preparation process and obtain a uniform distribution of fine particles, the slurry mixture specimens were vibrated and tamped. After the molds were removed, the cemented rock samples were cured for 28 days. The finished cemented samples, with a diameter of 50 mm and a height of 25 mm after manufacturing, are shown in Figure 2h.

## 2.2. Test Scheme

To investigate the effect of the PSD on the dynamic mechanical properties of cemented rock samples, the Talbot index and mixture type were varied to realize different PSDs. In the series of cemented rock samples designated $S_3$, three of the five particle mass groups (maximum size 2, 3, 5, 8, 10 mm) are chosen in a sequence (i.e., {2, 3, 5}, {3, 5, 8} and {5, 8, 10}) with mass ratios selected to produce three distinct Talbot indices (0.5, 1.0, 2.0); there are nine $S_3$ sample types in total. Specimens denoted by $S_4$ have four components (i.e., {2, 3, 5, 8} and {3, 5, 8, 10}) to create two mixture types with three Talbot indices; there are six sample types. In the $S_5$ series, only one mixture type is possible {2, 3, 5, 8, 10}, and with three Talbot indices, there are only three types of cemented rock sample. The masses of each component were calculated for the various Talbot indices and mixture types and are listed in Table 1.

Table 1. Experimental design for different particle size distributions (PSDs).

| Sample Number | Talbot Index T | Particle Mass (g) | | | | | Total Mass (g) |
|---|---|---|---|---|---|---|---|
| | | 0–2 mm | 2–3 mm | 3–5 mm | 5–8 mm | 8–10 mm | |
| $S_{3-0.5-I}$ | 0.5 | 44.27 | 9.95 | 15.78 | / | / | 70.00 |
| $S_{3-0.5-II}$ | | / | 42.87 | 12.47 | 14.66 | / | 70.00 |
| $S_{3-0.5-III}$ | | / | / | 49.50 | 13.11 | 7.39 | 70.00 |
| $S_{3-1.0-I}$ | 1.0 | 28.00 | 14.00 | 28.00 | / | / | 70.00 |
| $S_{3-1.0-II}$ | | / | 26.25 | 17.50 | 26.25 | / | 70.00 |
| $S_{3-1.0-III}$ | | / | / | 35.00 | 21.00 | 14.00 | 70.00 |
| $S_{3-2.0-I}$ | 2.0 | 11.20 | 14.00 | 44.80 | / | / | 70.00 |
| $S_{3-2.0-II}$ | | / | 9.84 | 17.50 | 42.66 | / | 70.00 |
| $S_{3-2.0-III}$ | | / | / | 17.50 | 27.30 | 25.20 | 70.00 |
| $S_{4-0.5-I}$ | 0.5 | 35.00 | 7.87 | 12.47 | 14.66 | / | 70.00 |
| $S_{4-0.5-II}$ | | / | 38.34 | 11.16 | 13.11 | 7.39 | 70.00 |
| $S_{4-1.0-I}$ | 1.0 | 17.50 | 8.75 | 17.50 | 26.25 | / | 70.00 |
| $S_{4-1.0-II}$ | | / | 21.00 | 14.00 | 21.00 | 14.00 | 70.00 |
| $S_{4-2.0-I}$ | 2.0 | 4.38 | 5.47 | 17.50 | 42.65 | / | 70.00 |
| $S_{4-2.0-II}$ | | / | 6.30 | 11.20 | 27.30 | 25.20 | 70.00 |
| $S_{5-0.5-I}$ | 0.5 | 31.30 | 7.04 | 11.16 | 13.11 | 7.39 | 70.00 |
| $S_{5-1.0-I}$ | 1.0 | 14.00 | 7.00 | 14.00 | 21.00 | 14.00 | 70.00 |
| $S_{5-2.0-I}$ | 2.0 | 2.80 | 3.50 | 11.20 | 27.30 | 25.20 | 70.00 |

The total mass of the rock particles in each sample was 70 g and the mass of cement was 25 g. In addition, Figure 3a–c shows the relationship between the mass percentage and particle size of the $S_3$, $S_4$ and $S_5$ series samples, respectively. The cemented rock samples were composed of rock particles of at least three sizes, for a total of 18 types. To explore the PSD effect, 18 cemented rock samples were subjected to dynamic impact tests at the same strain rate. To explore the strain rate effect, the $S_5$ series of cemented rock samples were subjected to impact tests under five different strain rates.

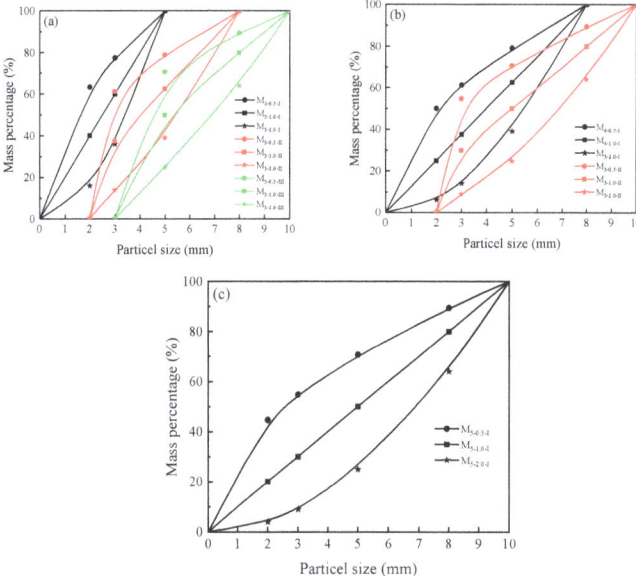

**Figure 3.** Particle size distribution (PSD) in cemented rock samples. (**a**) $S_3$ series (3 component rock mixture); (**b**) $S_4$ series (4 components); (**c**) $S_5$ series (5 components). Mass percentages are cumulative, showing total mass below the indicated size.

## 3. Test System and Measurement Principles

### 3.1. SHPB Experimental Setup

Dynamic impact tests were performed using a modified SHPB system [37]. As shown in Figure 4, the impact device is composed of a gas cavity, cone-shaped striker, incident bar, transmitted bar, absorption bar and fixed tailstock. The data acquisition subsystem includes an acquisition computer, oscilloscope, dynamic strain meter, Wheatstone bridges, strain gauges and a data line.

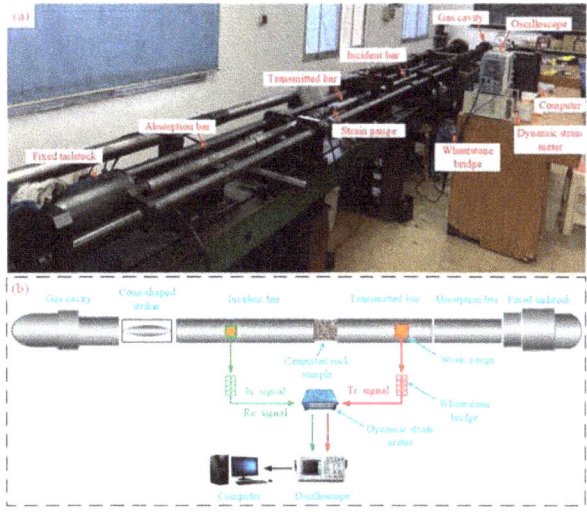

**Figure 4.** Testing system: (**a**) equipment layout; (**b**) apparatus schematic.

The rock sample is placed between the incident and transmitted bars. Strain gauges are installed on both the incident and transmitted bars. During testing, a slowly rising half-sine wave is generated when the cone-shaped striker impacts the front end of the incident bar; this wave is generated when high-pressure gas drives the cone-shaped striker against the incident bar. When the incident wave arrives at the bar–sample interface, part of the wave amplitude is reflected back into the incident bar (reflected wave), while the remainder passes through the sample and propagates in the transmitted bar (transmitted wave). As a result of the time difference between the incident and reflected waves passing the strain gauges on the incident bar, the incident and reflected wave signals may be distinguished and recorded. A strain gauge on the transmitted bar also records the transmitted wave signal. The two sets of strain gauges are connected to Wheatstone bridges, and the pulse signals are monitored with a dynamic strain gauge and an oscilloscope and passed to the acquisition computer. The pulse signal set contains primarily the incident strain $\varepsilon_I(t)$, reflected strain $\varepsilon_R(t)$ and transmitted strain $\varepsilon_T(t)$. Based on one-dimensional stress wave theory [38], the axial stress $\sigma(t)$, strain $\varepsilon(t)$ and strain rate $\dot{\varepsilon}(t)$ of the cemented rock sample are expressed as:

$$\begin{cases} \sigma(t) = \dfrac{A_b E_b}{2A_s}[\varepsilon_I(t) + \varepsilon_R(t) + \varepsilon_T(t)] \\ \varepsilon(t) = \dfrac{C_b}{L_s}\int_0^t [\varepsilon_I(t) - \varepsilon_R(t) - \varepsilon_T(t)]dt \\ \dot{\varepsilon}(t) = \dfrac{C_b}{L_s}[\varepsilon_I(t) - \varepsilon_R(t) - \varepsilon_T(t)] \end{cases} \quad (2)$$

where $A_b$, $C_b$ and $E_b$ are the cross-sectional area, P-wave velocity and Young's modulus of the three bars. $A_S$ and $L_S$ are the cross-sectional area and length of the cemented rock sample, respectively.

### 3.2. Measurement Principles

#### 3.2.1. Fractal Dimension

The concept of a fractal was used in geophysics by Turcotte [39]; the number of fragments $N_{(r)}$ with a particle size larger than $r$ exhibits a power-function relationship with $r$ as follows:

$$N_{(r)} = cr^{-D_f} \quad (3)$$

where $c$ is the proportionality coefficient, and $D_f$ is the fractal dimension.

The probability density distribution function [40] of fragments with sizes smaller than $r$ can be expressed as:

$$P_{(r)} = 1 - \left(\dfrac{r_{min}}{r}\right)^{D_f} \quad (4)$$

where $P_{(r)}$ is the probability of fragments smaller than $r$ and $r_{min}$ is the minimum fragment size.

The total volume of the fragments can be calculated by integrating fragments of various sizes.

$$V = \int_{r_{min}}^{r_{max}} N_t \left(\dfrac{4}{3}\pi r^3\right) dP_{(r)} \approx \dfrac{4}{3}\pi N_t \dfrac{D_f}{3-D_f} r_{min}^{D_f} r_{max}^{3-D_f} \quad (5)$$

where $N_t$ is the total number of fragments of various sizes and $r_{max}$ is the maximum size of the fragments.

From Equation (5), the mass of rock fragments with sizes smaller than $r_i$ can be obtained as:

$$M_{(r<r_i)} = \dfrac{4}{3}\pi N_t \rho \dfrac{D_f}{3-D_f} r_{min}^{D_f} r_{max}^{3-D_f} \quad (6)$$

where $M_{(r<r_i)}$ is the mass of rock fragments with sizes smaller than $r_i$ and $\rho$ is the rock density. The mass ratio is expressed as follows:

$$\dfrac{M_{(r<r_i)}}{M_t} = \left(\dfrac{r_i}{r_{max}}\right)^{3-D_f} \quad (7)$$

where $M_t$ is the total mass of rock fragments.

Taking the logarithm of Equation (6), a linear form is obtained:

$$Ln\left(\frac{M_{(r<r_i)}}{M_t}\right) = (3 - D_f) Ln\left(\frac{r_i}{r_{max}}\right) \quad (8)$$

The fractal dimension $D_f$ can be calculated by fitting $Ln\left(\frac{M_{(r<r_i)}}{M_t}\right)$ and $Ln\left(\frac{r_i}{r_{max}}\right)$ linearly.

#### 3.2.2. Crushing Ratio

The crushing ratio is a significant parameter for the failure of geological features. Ma et al. proposed a quantitative method to measure the particle breakage degree, and the breakage ratio ($B_M$) is defined as the variation in all PSD after a dynamic impact, which is calculated as follows:

$$B_M = \sum_{i=1}^{N} \left(w_i^d - w_i^o\right) \quad (9)$$

where $N$ is the component range appropriate to the increased particle content after dynamic impact, $w_i^o$ is the original particle content within a certain range and $w_i^d$ is the corresponding particle content after the dynamic impact.

### 4. Test Results

#### 4.1. Dynamic Mechanical Characteristics

The one-dimensional stress wave propagation theory and stress equilibrium in cemented rock samples should be confirmed during SHPB tests [41]. The strain gauge attached to the incident bar recorded the incident and reflected signals, which were used for the calculation of the incident and reflected waves. The strain gauge attached to the transmitted bar recorded the transmitted signal, which was used to calculate the transmitted wave. As shown in Figure 5, the sum of the incident and reflected waves is approximately equal to that of the transmitted wave. This indicated that the two ends of the cemented rock sample in the dynamic impact experiment reached a stressed equilibrium condition.

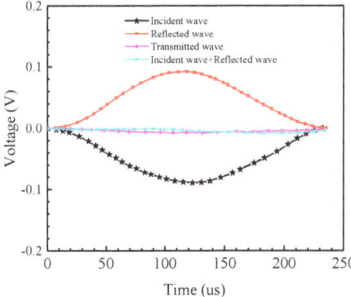

**Figure 5.** Stress equilibrium diagram.

Figure 6 shows the dynamic stress–strain curves of cemented rock samples with different PSDs; Figure 6a–c shows the $S_3$, $S_4$ and $S_5$ series individually. The curves show that the dynamic stress first increases and then decreases with strain, which conforms to a typical dynamic stress evolution law [42]. The dynamic stress curves have no obvious linear stage, which can be attributed to the abundant pore structures in the cemented rock sample. Damage and plastic deformation can easily occur in a porous medium, resulting in a stress that nonlinearly varies with strain under a dynamic load. Figure 7 shows the dynamic stress–strain curves of the $S_5$ series samples with different strain rates for different Talbot indices. Comparing Figure 7a–c, the dynamic strength increases with increasing Talbot index; this suggests that the large particles in the skeleton structure mainly contributed to the dynamic strength.

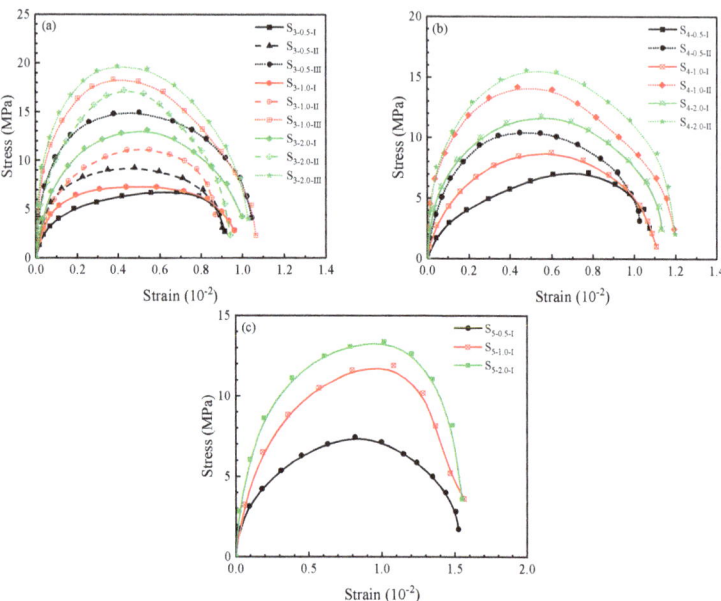

**Figure 6.** Dynamic stress–strain curves for different PSDs: (**a**) $S_3$ series; (**b**) $S_4$ series; (**c**) $S_5$ series.

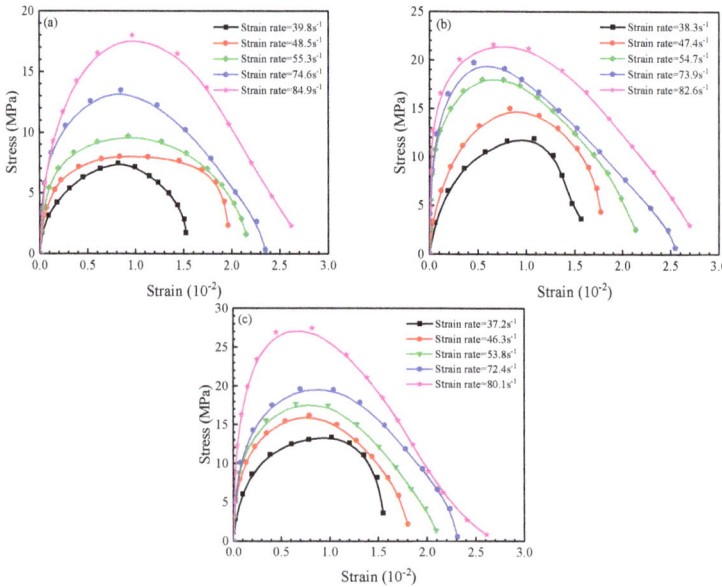

**Figure 7.** Dynamic stress–strain curves of $S_5$ series samples (i.e., 5 particle size components) under different strain rates. Talbot indices for the particle size distributions are: (**a**) T = 0.5; (**b**) T = 1.0; (**c**) T = 2.0.

## 4.2. Variation of Fractal Characteristics of Cemented Rock Samples

Under the dynamic impact in the SHPB apparatus, the cemented rock samples broke into granular particles. The fractal behavior of cemented rock samples can effectively reflect the fracture characteristics under the dynamic stress, which is an important basis for the instability mechanism of cemented rock strata. As shown in Figure 8, the cemented rock samples exhibited a high degree of fragmentation. Nevertheless, intuitively describing the fragmentation degree of cemented rock samples through fragments is challenging. Therefore, we classified the fragments and analyzed their fractal characteristics to determine the fragmentation degree of the cemented rock samples. After sieving and weighing the fragments, the fractal laws for the cemented rock samples were obtained.

**Figure 8.** Failure and fractal nature of impact fragments of cemented rock samples for different PSDs. Original samples had Talbot indices 0.5, 1.0, and 2.0. 3-component samples.

Figures 9–11 show the fractal laws describing the fragments from the $S_3$, $S_4$ and $S_5$ series of cemented rock samples, respectively. Table 2 lists the linear fitting formulas and their $R^2$ values for the fragments from different PSD samples; the $R^2$ of all curves is greater than 0.9, indicating that the fragments exhibit obvious fractal characteristics after dynamic impact. When considering the effect of strain rate on the fragmentation degree, the fragment size decreases with the increase in strain rate, as shown in Figure 12. Figure 13 shows the fractal laws of the $S_5$ series, and Table 3 lists the linear fitting formulas and goodness-of-fit ($R^2$) for the fragments under different strain rates. The goodness-of-fit of the linear fitting formulas is credible, which suggests that the fractal phenomenon is a universal law under different strain rates.

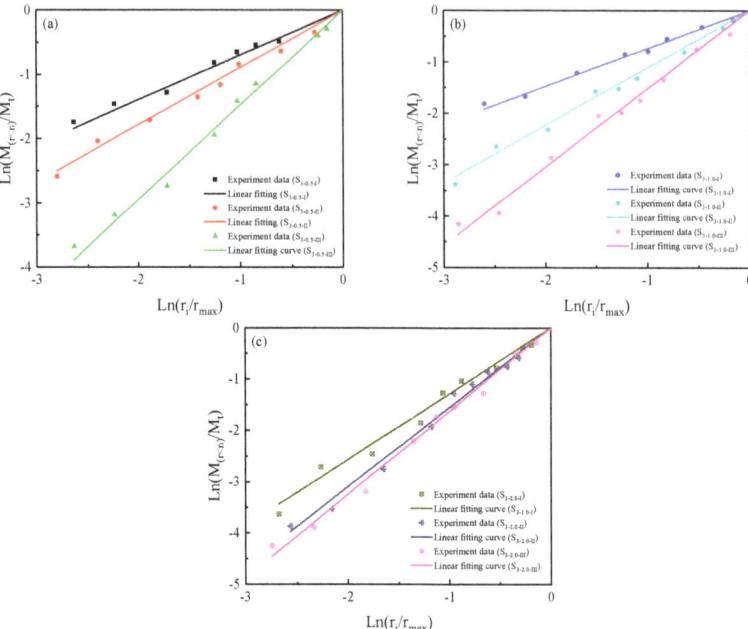

**Figure 9.** Fractal characteristics of fragments from $S_3$ series samples: (**a**) T = 0.5; (**b**) T = 1.0; (**c**) T = 2.0.

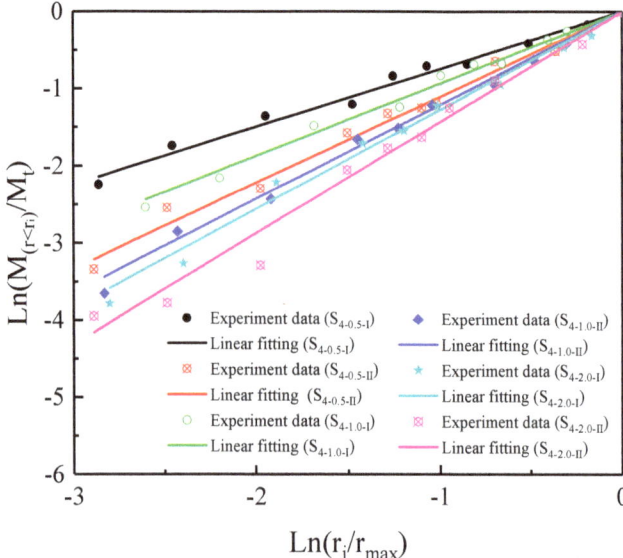

**Figure 10.** Fractal characteristics of fragments from $S_4$ series samples.

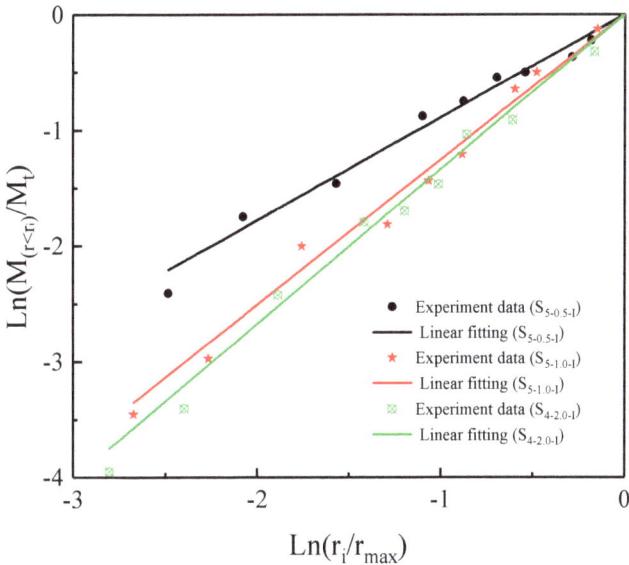

**Figure 11.** Fractal characteristics of fragments from $S_5$ series samples.

**Table 2.** Fractal fitting of cemented rock samples with different PSDs.

| Sample No. | Linear Fitting Formula | $R^2$ |
|---|---|---|
| $S_{3-0.5-I}$ | $Ln(M_{(r<r_i)}/M_t) = 0.699 Ln(r_i/r_{max}) + 2.311 \times 10^{-3}$ | 0.901 |
| $S_{3-0.5-II}$ | $Ln(M_{(r<r_i)}/M_t) = 0.891 Ln(r_i/r_{max}) + 3.456 \times 10^{-4}$ | 0.913 |
| $S_{3-0.5-III}$ | $Ln(M_{(r<r_i)}/M_t) = 1.473 Ln(r_i/r_{max}) + 3.124 \times 10^{-4}$ | 0.924 |
| $S_{3-1.0-I}$ | $Ln(M_{(r<r_i)}/M_t) = 0.738 Ln(r_i/r_{max}) + 4.747 \times 10^{-4}$ | 0.935 |
| $S_{3-1.0-II}$ | $Ln(M_{(r<r_i)}/M_t) = 1.114 Ln(r_i/r_{max}) + 3.698 \times 10^{-3}$ | 0.927 |
| $S_{3-1.0-III}$ | $Ln(M_{(r<r_i)}/M_t) = 1.521 Ln(r_i/r_{max}) + 7.845 \times 10^{-4}$ | 0.906 |
| $S_{3-2.0-I}$ | $Ln(M_{(r<r_i)}/M_t) = 1.284 Ln(r_i/r_{max}) + 9.874 \times 10^{-4}$ | 0.918 |
| $S_{3-2.0-II}$ | $Ln(M_{(r<r_i)}/M_t) = 1.547 Ln(r_i/r_{max}) + 2.311 \times 10^{-3}$ | 0.904 |
| $S_{3-2.0-III}$ | $Ln(M_{(r<r_i)}/M_t) = 1.623 Ln(r_i/r_{max}) + 9.456 \times 10^{-5}$ | 0.911 |
| $S_{4-0.5-I}$ | $Ln(M_{(r<r_i)}/M_t) = 0.748 Ln(r_i/r_{max}) + 6.235 \times 10^{-4}$ | 0.935 |
| $S_{4-0.5-II}$ | $Ln(M_{(r<r_i)}/M_t) = 1.112 Ln(r_i/r_{max}) + 7.112 \times 10^{-5}$ | 0.907 |
| $S_{4-1.0-I}$ | $Ln(M_{(r<r_i)}/M_t) = 0.937 Ln(r_i/r_{max}) + 4.789 \times 10^{-4}$ | 0.929 |
| $S_{4-1.0-II}$ | $Ln(M_{(r<r_i)}/M_t) = 1.214 Ln(r_i/r_{max}) + 6.341 \times 10^{-4}$ | 0.956 |
| $S_{4-2.0-I}$ | $Ln(M_{(r<r_i)}/M_t) = 1.278 Ln(r_i/r_{max}) + 6.231 \times 10^{-5}$ | 0.919 |
| $S_{4-2.0-II}$ | $Ln(M_{(r<r_i)}/M_t) = 1.438 Ln(r_i/r_{max}) + 5.587 \times 10^{-4}$ | 0.922 |
| $S_{5-0.5-I}$ | $Ln(M_{(r<r_i)}/M_t) = 0.889 Ln(r_i/r_{max}) + 7.654 \times 10^{-4}$ | 0.914 |
| $S_{5-1.0-I}$ | $Ln(M_{(r<r_i)}/M_t) = 1.254 Ln(r_i/r_{max}) + 4.478 \times 10^{-5}$ | 0.903 |
| $S_{5-2.0-I}$ | $Ln(M_{(r<r_i)}/M_t) = 1.337 Ln(r_i/r_{max}) + 6.214 \times 10^{-4}$ | 0.917 |

**Figure 12.** Failure and fractal nature of $S_{5\text{-}1.0\text{-}I}$ cemented rock samples under different strain rates.

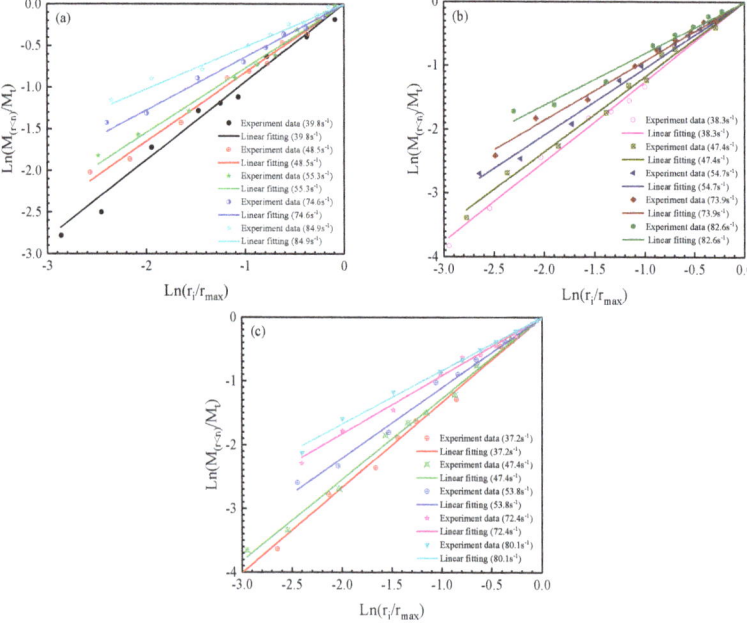

**Figure 13.** Fractal characteristics of $S_5$ series samples fragments under different strain rates: (**a**) T = 0.5; (**b**) T = 1.0; (**c**) T = 2.0.

Table 3. Fractal fitting of cemented rock samples with different strain rates.

| Sample No. | Strain Rate | Linear Fitting Formula | $R^2$ |
|---|---|---|---|
| $S_{5-0.5-I}$ | 39.5 s$^{-1}$ | $Ln(M_{(r<r_i)}/M_t) = 0.937Ln(r_i/r_{max}) + 4.799 \times 10^{-3}$ | 0.934 |
| | 48.5 s$^{-1}$ | $Ln(M_{(r<r_i)}/M_t) = 0.825Ln(r_i/r_{max}) + 7.245 \times 10^{-4}$ | 0.921 |
| | 55.3 s$^{-1}$ | $Ln(M_{(r<r_i)}/M_t) = 0.772Ln(r_i/r_{max}) + 5.719 \times 10^{-4}$ | 0.925 |
| | 74.6 s$^{-1}$ | $Ln(M_{(r<r_i)}/M_t) = 0.637Ln(r_i/r_{max}) + 8.742 \times 10^{-5}$ | 0.902 |
| | 84.9 s$^{-1}$ | $Ln(M_{(r<r_i)}/M_t) = 0.511Ln(r_i/r_{max}) + 2.171 \times 10^{-3}$ | 0.945 |
| $S_{5-1.0-I}$ | 38.3 s$^{-1}$ | $Ln(M_{(r<r_i)}/M_t) = 1.254Ln(r_i/r_{max}) + 8.445 \times 10^{-4}$ | 0.925 |
| | 47.4 s$^{-1}$ | $Ln(M_{(r<r_i)}/M_t) = 1.178Ln(r_i/r_{max}) + 9.824 \times 10^{-5}$ | 0.931 |
| | 54.7 s$^{-1}$ | $Ln(M_{(r<r_i)}/M_t) = 1.045Ln(r_i/r_{max}) + 6.631 \times 10^{-3}$ | 0.951 |
| | 73.9 s$^{-1}$ | $Ln(M_{(r<r_i)}/M_t) = 0.928Ln(r_i/r_{max}) + 7.741 \times 10^{-4}$ | 0.916 |
| | 82.6 s$^{-1}$ | $Ln(M_{(r<r_i)}/M_t) = 0.811Ln(r_i/r_{max}) + 1.123 \times 10^{-3}$ | 0.912 |
| $S_{5-2.0-I}$ | 37.2 s$^{-1}$ | $Ln(M_{(r<r_i)}/M_t) = 1.337Ln(r_i/r_{max}) + 3.214 \times 10^{-4}$ | 0.925 |
| | 47.4 s$^{-1}$ | $Ln(M_{(r<r_i)}/M_t) = 1.274Ln(r_i/r_{max}) + 6.321 \times 10^{-4}$ | 0.933 |
| | 53.8 s$^{-1}$ | $Ln(M_{(r<r_i)}/M_t) = 1.105Ln(r_i/r_{max}) + 6.341 \times 10^{-5}$ | 0.904 |
| | 72.4 s$^{-1}$ | $Ln(M_{(r<r_i)}/M_t) = 0.914Ln(r_i/r_{max}) + 6.539 \times 10^{-4}$ | 0.926 |
| | 80.1 s$^{-1}$ | $Ln(M_{(r<r_i)}/M_t) = 0.836Ln(r_i/r_{max}) + 5.117 \times 10^{-2}$ | 0.938 |

### 4.3. Variation of Breakage Ratio of Cemented Rock Samples

After the broken rock particles are cemented and reshaped, an integral structure has been formed. Dynamic impact damages not only the cementation structure between rock particles but also the rock particles themselves [43]. As shown in Figure 14, many breakages occur in the individual rock particles, which implies that rock particle breakage is a common behavior during dynamic impact. Breakage ratio is a method applied for calculation of the particle broken of cemented rock samples, which is of great significance for investigating the secondary broken of cemented rock samples. Therefore, it is necessary to explore the breakage law of cemented rock samples.

Figure 14. Breakage behavior of rock particles: (a) broken sample after dynamic impact; (b) area 1; (c) area 2; (d) area 3.

The breakage ratio was calculated using Equation (8) and the results are shown in Figure 15. As for the effect of PSD on breakage behavior, the breakage ratio $B_M$ (indicating a change in the PSD) appears to decrease with an increase in the Talbot index in the $S_3$ and $S_4$ series of cemented rock samples, except for the $S_5$ series of cemented rock samples (as shown in Figure 15a). A high Talbot index corresponds to more large rock particles in the cemented rock sample, which verifies that large particles contribute to the formation of the solid structure of the cemented rock sample. As for the effect of strain rate on breakage behavior, $B_M$ obviously increases with an increase in strain rate (as shown in Figure 15b).

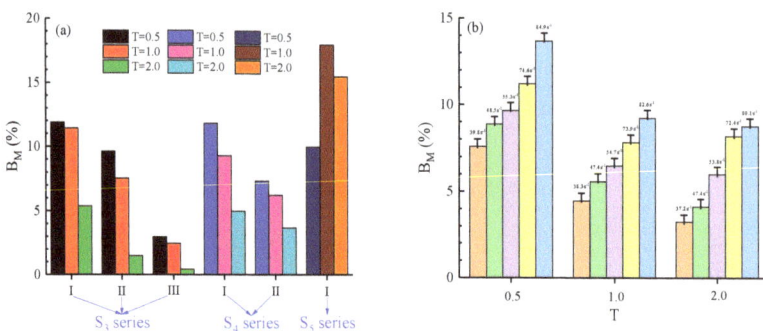

**Figure 15.** Breakage ratio $B_M$ of cemented rock samples: (**a**) various PSD; (**b**) various strain rates.

## 5. Discussion

*5.1. Effects of PSD and Strain Rate on Dynamic Strength*

5.1.1. Effect of PSD on Dynamic Strength

From the test results in Section 4.1, the PSD has a remarkable influence on the dynamic strength of cemented rock samples. Figure 16a shows the dynamic strength variation of the $S_3$ series with the PSD, which indicates that the dynamic strength increases with an increase in both the Talbot index and mixture type; these indicate cemented rock samples containing more large rock particles, which can create dynamic strength. This behavior is also seen in the $S_4$ and $S_5$ series (Figure 16b,c).

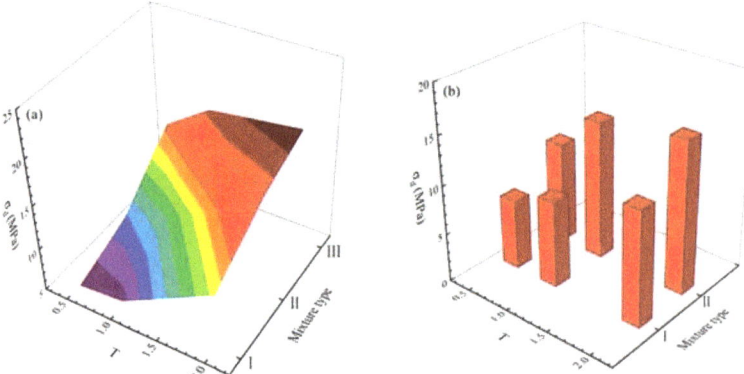

**Figure 16.** *Cont.*

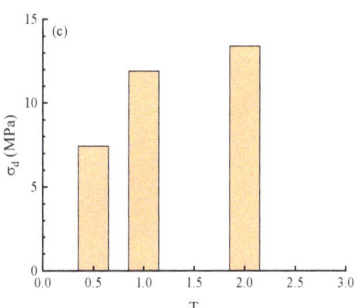

**Figure 16.** Dynamic strength dependence on PSD (Talbot Index) and component mixture type: (**a**) $S_3$ series; (**b**) $S_4$ series; (**c**) $S_5$ series.

5.1.2. Effect of Strain Rate on Dynamic Strength

Under the action of dynamic impact, the dynamic strength of the rock material follows the rate effect [44]. Figure 17 shows the variation of dynamic strength with strain rate in the S5 series of cemented rock samples; Figure 17a–c corresponds to the different Talbot indices (T = 0.5, 1.0 and 2.0) that denote different PSDs. The dynamic strength and strain rate in the experimental data are well fitted by the power function.

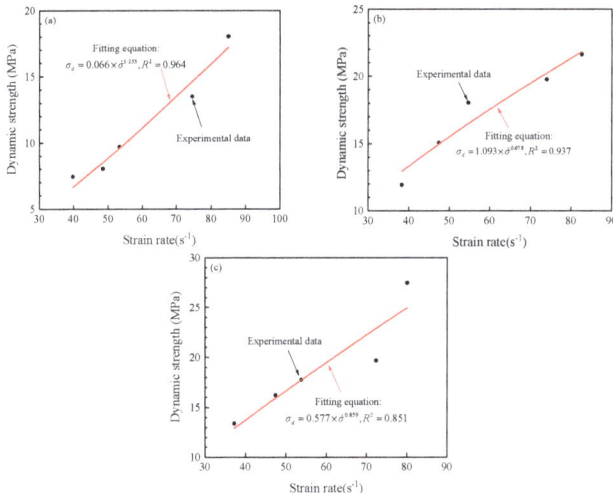

**Figure 17.** Dynamic strength dependence on strain rate in the $S_5$ series samples with different particle size distributions: Talbot indices (**a**) T = 0.5; (**b**) T = 1.0; (**c**) T = 2.0.

## 5.2. Effects of PSD and Strain Rate on Fractal Characteristics
5.2.1. Effects of PSD on Fractal Dimension

Figure 18a shows the variation of the fragmentation fractal dimension with PSD of the $S_3$ series of cemented rock samples, indicating that the fractal dimension decreases with an increase in the Talbot index and mixture type. Figure 18b,c show the fractal dimension variation of the $S_4$ and $S_5$ series of cemented rock samples, and the variation law is consistent with that of the $S_3$ series of cemented rock samples. Compared with the strength variation, the fractal dimension variation shows an opposite response to the PSD effect.

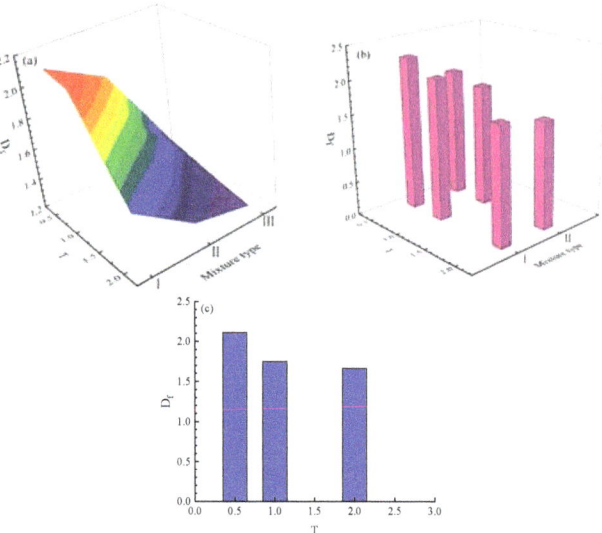

**Figure 18.** Dependence of the fragmentation fractal dimension on the particle size distribution (Talbot Index) and component mixture type: (**a**) Series 3; (**b**) Series 4; (**c**) Series 5.

5.2.2. Effect of Strain Rate on Fractal Dimension

In the experimental data, the fractal dimension is seen to increase with strain rate. Linear fitting functions can describe the relationship between the strain rate and the fractal dimension of fragmentation products from cemented rock samples. As shown in Figure 19, the goodness of fit is relatively high for the three types of Talbot index, which suggests the validity of these linear fittings.

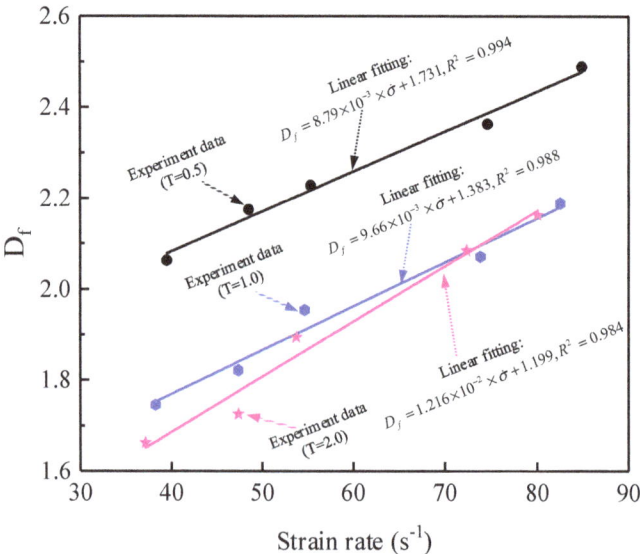

**Figure 19.** Dependence of fractal dimension on strain state in the $S_5$ series samples. Particle size distributions are represented by Talbot indices T = 0.5, 1.0, and 2.0.

## 5.3. Relationship between Dynamic Strength and Fractal Dimension

### 5.3.1. Relationship between Crush Ratio and Fractal Dimension

The breakage ratio reflects the change in the size distribution of rock particles following the dynamic impact, which can comprehensively reflect the breakage of the original rock particle itself and the breakage between the rock particles and cement. The fractal dimension directly reflects the relationship between the fragment mass and fragment size of cemented rock samples. Therefore, both are related to the breaking characteristics of cemented rock samples. For variations in either the sample PSDs or the strain rate, the fractal dimension of fragmentation products increases with the breakage ratio (Figure 20). It is found that the fractal dimension and breakage ratio are well fitted by linear functions. It is noteworthy that the slopes of the two fitted curves are equal. This indicates that neither the change in the internal structure of the cemented rock sample nor the change in the external dynamic load conditions will change this linear relationship, which further shows that the breakage ratio and fractal dimension are intrinsically linked and not affected by other factors.

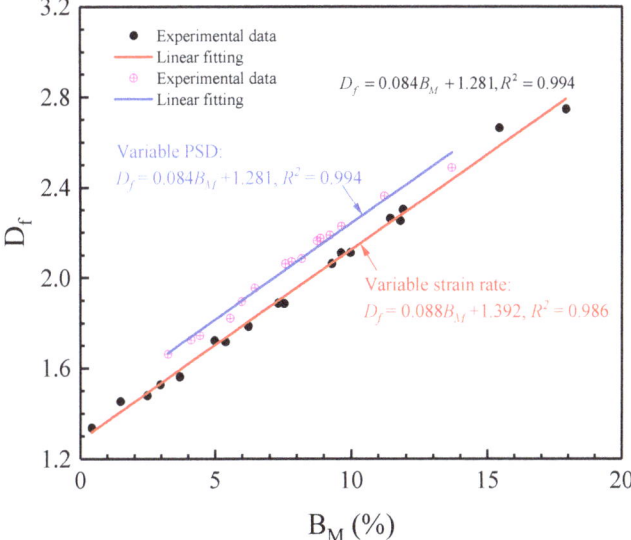

**Figure 20.** Relationship between breakage ratio and fractal dimension following fragmentation. Breakage ratio $B_M$ indicates change in PSD of original rock particles. Blue curve arises from samples having different initial PSDs; red curve is from different strain rates being applied.

### 5.3.2. Relationship between Dynamic Strength and Fractal Dimension

Figure 21 shows the effect of the PSD on the relation between dynamic strength and fractal dimension; the experimental data (Table 2) show that the dynamic strength decreases as the fractal dimension increases. When the strain rate remains unchanged and only the PSD of the cemented rock sample is changed, the fractal dimension is negatively correlated with the dynamic strength, as measured by linear fitting. This phenomenon indicates that when the external dynamic load conditions remain unchanged, the change in the internal structure mainly affects the dynamic strength and fractal characteristics of cemented rock samples. The change in the PSD mainly causes a change in the proportion of large particles, which directly determines the dynamic strength. The crushing degree of the cemented rock sample with a high strength was small, corresponding to a low fractal dimension. Therefore, there is a negative linear correlation between the dynamic strength and the fractal dimension.

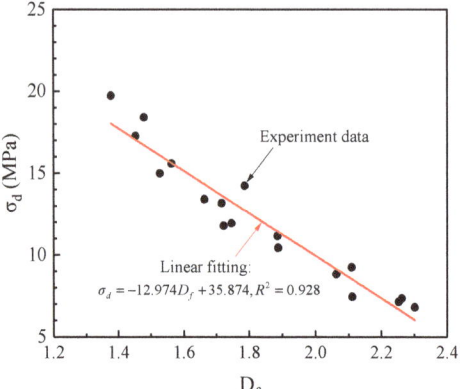

**Figure 21.** Relation between dynamic strength and fractal dimension following fragmentation. Constant strain rate is used, while samples have different PSDs—based on Table 2.

Figure 22 shows the effect of strain rate on the relation between dynamic strength and the fractal dimension for samples with different Talbot indices; the experimental data (Table 3) show that the dynamic strength increases with increasing fractal dimension for sample sets with different Talbot indices (as shown in Figure 22a–c). When the PSD remains unchanged and only the strain rate is changed, the fractal dimension is positively correlated with the dynamic strength, as seen through linear fitting. This phenomenon indicates that for the same values of the PSD, the strain rate directly determines the dynamic strength and fractal characteristics of the cemented rock sample, with both exhibiting the same response characteristics as the strain rate effect. Therefore, a positive linear correlation exists between dynamic strength and fractal dimension.

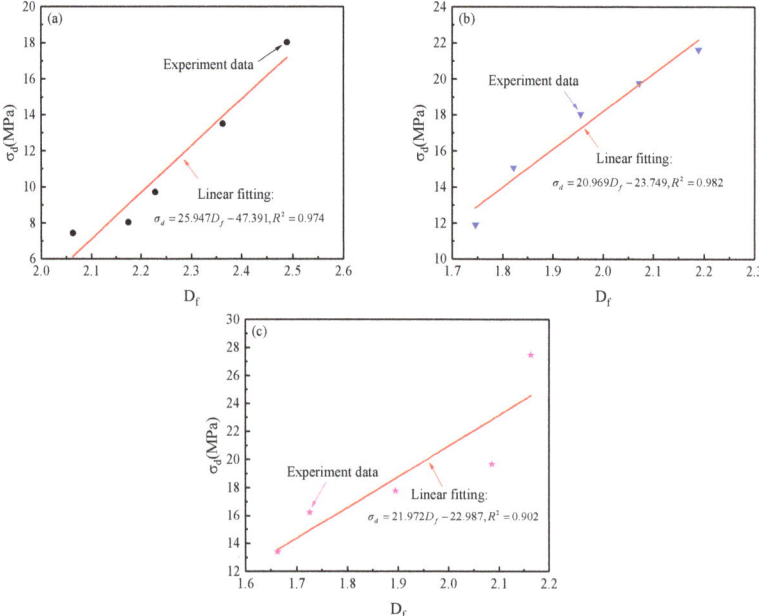

**Figure 22.** Relation between dynamic strength and fractal dimension: effect of strain rate. (a) T = 0.5; (b) T = 1.0; (c) T = 2.0.

## 6. Conclusions

This study focuses on the dynamic mechanics and fractal characteristics of fault-cemented rock strata. The broken rock particles were reshaped to obtain cemented rock samples with variable particle size distributions, and split Hopkinson pressure bar dynamic impact tests were carried out on the cemented rock samples under different strain rates. The following conclusions were drawn.

(1) The stress–strain curves show that the dynamic stress first increases and then decreases with increasing strain. This indicates that plastic deformation occurs because of the porous structure of the cemented rock sample. Therefore, the stress nonlinearly changes with strain through the entire dynamic stress–strain curve. The cemented rock sample with a high Talbot index and mixture type contains more large particles, and its dynamic strength increases gradually. A power function effectively describes the relationship between the strain rate and the dynamic strength for various Talbot indices.

(2) By analyzing the relationship between fragment mass and fragment size, it is found that the fragments of cemented rock samples follow obvious fractal laws after dynamic impact. The breakage of cemented rock samples includes the breakage of the original rock particle itself and the breakage between the rock particles and cementations. The fractal dimension and breakage ratio both decrease with the increase in mixture type and the Talbot index but increase with the increase in strain rate. It is worth noting that the breakage ratio and fractal dimension have a linear relationship regardless of the PSD or strain rate.

(3) The PSD and strain rate effects influence the internal structure of the cemented rock sample and the response to an external load, respectively. The relationship between the dynamic strength and fractal dimension has different response laws for the PSD and strain rate effects. The dynamic strength is linearly related to the fractal dimension in a negative sense under differences in PSD but linearly related positively to the fractal dimension under differences in strain rate.

**Author Contributions:** J.W. is responsible for the experimental part, data processing and the paper writing; L.H. and X.L. are responsible for the conceptualization and article review; H.L. and Y.W. are responsible for experimental setup and part of data processing. All authors have read and agreed to the published version of the manuscript.

**Funding:** The study was supported by the National Natural Science Foundation of China (Grant Nos. 51904335, 51927808 and 52174098). The authors would like to acknowledge the editor and anonymous reviewers for their valuable comments for the improvement of this paper.

**Institutional Review Board Statement:** Not applicable.

**Informed Consent Statement:** Not applicable.

**Data Availability Statement:** The data presented in this study are available on request from the corresponding author.

**Conflicts of Interest:** The authors declare no conflict of interest.

## References

1. Islam, M.R.; Shinjo, R. Mining-induced fault reactivation associated with the main conveyor belt roadway and safety of the Barapukuria Coal Mine in Bangladesh: Constraints from BEM simulations. *Int. J. Coal Geol.* **2009**, *79*, 115–130. [CrossRef]
2. Wang, H.; Xue, S.; Shi, R.; Jiang, Y.; Gong, W.; Mao, L. Investigation of Fault Displacement Evolution During Extraction in Longwall Panel in an Underground Coal Mine. *Rock Mech. Rock Eng.* **2020**, *53*, 1809–1826. [CrossRef]
3. Ma, D.; Kong, S.; Li, Z.; Zhang, Q.; Wang, Z.; Zhou, Z. Effect of wetting-drying cycle on hydraulic and mechanical properties of cemented paste backfill of the recycled solid wastes. *Chemosphere* **2021**, *282*, 131163. [CrossRef] [PubMed]
4. Wang, Z.; Li, W.; Chen, J. Application of Various Nonlinear Models to Predict the Uniaxial Compressive Strength of Weakly Cemented Jurassic Rocks. *Nat. Resour. Res.* **2022**, *31*, 371–384. [CrossRef]
5. Demirdag, S. Effects of freezing-thawing and thermal shock cycles on physical and mechanical properties of filled and unfilled travertines. *Constr. Build. Mater.* **2013**, *47*, 1395–1401. [CrossRef]
6. Yin, Q.; Jing, H.; Su, H.; Zhao, H. Experimental Study on Mechanical Properties and Anchorage Performances of Rock Mass in the Fault Fracture Zone. *Int. J. Geomech.* **2018**, *18*, 04018067. [CrossRef]

7. Zhu, W.; Hughes, J.J.; Bicanic, N.; Pearce, C.J. Nanoindentation mapping of mechanical properties of cement paste and natural rocks. *Mater. Charact.* **2007**, *58*, 1189–1198. [CrossRef]
8. Huang, L.; Guo, Y.; Li, X. Failure characteristics of shale after being subjected to high temperatures under uniaxial compression. *Bull. Eng. Geol. Environ.* **2021**, *81*, 33. [CrossRef]
9. Wang, J.; Ma, D.; Li, Z.; Huang, Y.; Du, F. Experimental investigation of damage evolution and failure criterion on hollow cylindrical rock samples with different bore diameters. *Eng. Fract. Mech.* **2022**, *260*, 108182. [CrossRef]
10. Fu, J.-X.; Song, W.-D.; Tan, Y.-Y. Study on Microstructural Evolution and Strength Growth and Fracture Mechanism of Cemented Paste Backfill. *Adv. Mater. Sci. Eng.* **2016**, *2016*, 8792817. [CrossRef]
11. Fall, M.; Benzaazoua, M.; Ouellet, S. Experimental characterization of the influence of tailings fineness and density on the quality of cemented paste backfill. *Miner. Eng.* **2005**, *18*, 41–44. [CrossRef]
12. Jiang, H.; Fall, M. Yield stress and strength of saline cemented tailings materials in sub-zero environments: Slag-paste backfill. *J. Sustain. Cem.-Based Mater.* **2017**, *6*, 314–331. [CrossRef]
13. Xu, W.-b.; Liu, B.; Wu, W.-l. Strength and deformation behaviors of cemented tailings backfill under triaxial compression. *J. Cent. South Univ.* **2020**, *27*, 3531–3543. [CrossRef]
14. Weilv, W.; Xu, W.; Jianpin, Z. Effect of inclined interface angle on shear strength and deformation response of cemented paste backfill-rock under triaxial compression. *Constr. Build. Mater.* **2021**, *279*, 122478. [CrossRef]
15. Yu, X.; Kemeny, J.; Li, J.; Song, W.; Tan, Y. 3D Observations of Fracturing in Rock-Backfill Composite Specimens Under Triaxial Loading. *Rock Mech. Rock Eng.* **2021**, *54*, 6009–6022. [CrossRef]
16. Yin, S.; Wu, A.; Hu, K.; Wang, Y.; Zhang, Y. The effect of solid components on the rheological and mechanical properties of cemented paste backfill. *Miner. Eng.* **2012**, *35*, 61–66. [CrossRef]
17. Fang, K.; Fall, M. Chemically Induced Changes in the Shear Behaviour of Interface Between Rock and Tailings Backfill Undergoing Cementation. *Rock Mech. Rock Eng.* **2019**, *52*, 3047–3062. [CrossRef]
18. Zhou, N.; Zhang, J.; Ouyang, S.; Deng, X.; Dong, C.; Du, E. Feasibility study and performance optimization of sand-based cemented paste backfill materials. *J. Clean. Prod.* **2020**, *259*, 120798. [CrossRef]
19. Zhou, X.; Hu, S.; Zhang, G.; Li, J.; Xuan, D.; Gao, W. Experimental investigation and mathematical strength model study on the mechanical properties of cemented paste backfill. *Constr. Build. Mater.* **2019**, *226*, 524–533. [CrossRef]
20. Lu, G.; Fall, M. Modeling Postblasting Stress and Pore Pressure Distribution in Hydrating Fill Mass at an Early Age. *Int. J. Geomech.* **2018**, *18*, 04018090. [CrossRef]
21. Liu, Z.-y.; Gan, D.-q.; Gan, Z. Dynamic regimes of cemented backfill at early-age. *J. Cent. South Univ.* **2021**, *28*, 2079–2090. [CrossRef]
22. Dikonda, R.K.; Mbonimpa, M.; Belem, T. Specific Mixing Energy of Cemented Paste Backfill, Part II: Influence on the Rheological and Mechanical Properties and Practical Applications. *Minerals* **2021**, *11*, 1159. [CrossRef]
23. Cao, S.; Yilmaz, E.; Song, W.; Yilmaz, E.; Xue, G. Loading rate effect on uniaxial compressive strength behavior and acoustic emission properties of cemented tailings backfill. *Constr. Build. Mater.* **2019**, *213*, 313–324. [CrossRef]
24. Wu, Y.; Huang, L.; Li, X.; Guo, Y.; Liu, H.; Wang, J. Effects of Strain Rate and Temperature on Physical Mechanical Properties and Energy Dissipation Features of Granite. *Mathematics* **2022**, *10*, 1521. [CrossRef]
25. Cao, S.; Xue, G.; Song, W.; Teng, Q. Strain rate effect on dynamic mechanical properties and microstructure of cemented tailings composites. *Constr. Build. Mater.* **2020**, *247*, 118537. [CrossRef]
26. Tan, Y.-y.; Yu, X.; Elmo, D.; Xu, L.-h.; Song, W.-d. Experimental study on dynamic mechanical property of cemented tailings backfill under SHPB impact loading. *Int. J. Miner. Metall. Mater.* **2019**, *26*, 404–416. [CrossRef]
27. Xue, G.; Yilmaz, E.; Feng, G.; Cao, S.; Sun, L. Reinforcement effect of polypropylene fiber on dynamic properties of cemented tailings backfill under SHPB impact loading. *Constr. Build. Mater.* **2021**, *279*, 122417. [CrossRef]
28. Yang, L.; Xu, W.; Yilmaz, E.; Wang, Q.; Qiu, J. A combined experimental and numerical study on the triaxial and dynamic compression behavior of cemented tailings backfill. *Eng. Struct.* **2020**, *219*, 110957. [CrossRef]
29. Xu, S.; Suorineni, F.T.; Li, K.; Li, Y. Evaluation of the strength and ultrasonic properties of foam-cemented paste backfill. *Int. J. Min. Reclam. Environ.* **2017**, *31*, 544–557. [CrossRef]
30. Chen, X.; Shi, X.; Zhou, J.; Li, E.; Qiu, P.; Gou, Y. High strain rate compressive strength behavior of cemented paste backfill using split Hopkinson pressure bar. *Int. J. Min. Sci. Technol.* **2021**, *31*, 387–399. [CrossRef]
31. Nasir, O.; Fall, M. Shear behaviour of cemented pastefill-rock interfaces. *Eng. Geol.* **2008**, *101*, 146–153. [CrossRef]
32. Zheng, D.; Song, W.; Cao, S.; Li, J.; Sun, L. Investigation on Dynamical Mechanics, Energy Dissipation, and Microstructural Characteristics of Cemented Tailings Backfill under SHPB Tests. *Minerals* **2021**, *11*, 542. [CrossRef]
33. Wang, C.-l.; Ren, Z.-z.; Huo, Z.-k.; Zheng, Y.-c.; Tian, X.-p.; Zhang, K.-f.; Zhao, G.-f. Properties and hydration characteristics of mine cemented paste backfill material containing secondary smelting water-granulated nickel slag. *Alex. Eng. J.* **2021**, *60*, 4961–4971. [CrossRef]
34. Wu, J.; Yin, Q.; Gao, Y.; Meng, B.; Jing, H. Particle size distribution of aggregates effects on mesoscopic structural evolution of cemented waste rock backfill. *Environ. Sci. Pollut. Res.* **2021**, *28*, 16589–16601. [CrossRef]
35. Liu, H.; Zhang, J.; Zhou, N.; Guo, Y.; Li, B.; Yan, H.; Deng, X. Investigation of spatial stratified heterogeneity of cemented paste backfill characteristics in construction demolition waste recycled aggregates. *J. Clean. Prod.* **2020**, *249*, 119332. [CrossRef]

36. Ma, D.; Duan, H.; Li, X.; Li, Z.; Zhou, Z.; Li, T. Effects of seepage-induced erosion on nonlinear hydraulic properties of broken red sandstones. *Tunn. Undergr. Space Technol.* **2019**, *91*, 102993. [CrossRef]
37. Li, X.B.; Lok, T.S.; Zhao, J. Dynamic Characteristics of Granite Subjected to Intermediate Loading Rate. *Rock Mech. Rock Eng.* **2005**, *38*, 21–39. [CrossRef]
38. Li, X.; Zhou, T.; Li, D. Dynamic Strength and Fracturing Behavior of Single-Flawed Prismatic Marble Specimens Under Impact Loading with a Split-Hopkinson Pressure Bar. *Rock Mech. Rock Eng.* **2017**, *50*, 29–44. [CrossRef]
39. Turcotte, D.L. Fractals and fragmentation. *J. Geophys. Res. Solid Earth* **1986**, *91*, 1921–1926. [CrossRef]
40. Deng, Y.; Chen, M.; Jin, Y.; Zou, D. Theoretical analysis and experimental research on the energy dissipation of rock crushing based on fractal theory. *J. Nat. Gas Sci. Eng.* **2016**, *33*, 231–239. [CrossRef]
41. Li, X.; Zhou, T.; Li, D.; Wang, Z. Experimental and Numerical Investigations on Feasibility and Validity of Prismatic Rock Specimen in SHPB. *Shock. Vib.* **2016**, *2016*, 7198980. [CrossRef]
42. Li, X.; Gu, H.; Tao, M.; Peng, K.; Cao, W.; Li, Q. Failure characteristics and meso-deterioration mechanism of pre-stressed coal subjected to different dynamic loads. *Theor. Appl. Fract. Mech.* **2021**, *115*, 103061. [CrossRef]
43. Huang, L.-q.; Wang, J.; Momeni, A.; Wang, S.-f. Spalling fracture mechanism of granite subjected to dynamic tensile loading. *Trans. Nonferrous Met. Soc. China* **2021**, *31*, 2116–2127. [CrossRef]
44. Li, X.; Zou, Y.; Zhou, Z. Numerical Simulation of the Rock SHPB Test with a Special Shape Striker Based on the Discrete Element Method. *Rock Mech. Rock Eng.* **2014**, *47*, 1693–1709. [CrossRef]

Article

# Experimental Studies on Rock Thin-Section Image Classification by Deep Learning-Based Approaches

Diyuan Li *, Junjie Zhao and Jinyin Ma

School of Resources and Safety Engineering, Central South University, Changsha 410083, China; junjie-zhao@csu.edu.cn (J.Z.); majinyin@csu.edu.cn (J.M.)
* Correspondence: diyuan.li@csu.edu.cn

**Abstract:** Experimental studies were carried out to analyze the impact of optimizers and learning rate on the performance of deep learning-based algorithms for rock thin-section image classification. A total of 2634 rock thin-section images including three rock types—metamorphic, sedimentary, and volcanic rocks—were acquired from an online open-source science data bank. Four CNNs using three different optimizer algorithms (Adam, SGD, RMSprop) under two learning-rate decay schedules (lambda and cosine decay modes) were trained and validated. Then, a systematic comparison was conducted based on the performance of the trained model. Precision, f1-scores, and confusion matrix were adopted as the evaluation indicators. Trials revealed that deep learning-based approaches for rock thin-section image classification were highly effective and stable. Meanwhile, the experimental results showed that the cosine learning-rate decay mode was the better option for learning-rate adjustment during the training process. In addition, the performance of the four neural networks was confirmed and ranked as VGG16, GoogLeNet, MobileNetV2, and ShuffleNetV2. In the last step, the influence of optimization algorithms was evaluated based on VGG16 and GoogLeNet, and the results demonstrated that the capabilities of the model using Adam and RMSprop optimizers were more robust than that of SGD. The experimental study in this paper provides important practical value for training a high-precision rock thin-section image classification model, which can also be transferred to other similar image classification tasks.

**Keywords:** rock; rock thin-section image; image classification; convolutional neural network; deep learning

**MSC:** 68T07

## 1. Introduction

Rock type classification, a valuable task, is extremely important in geological engineering, rock mechanics, mining engineering, and resource exploration. While the characteristics of rocks' appearance under outdoor conditions often show diversity due to illumination, shading, humidity, shape, etc., the main way of classifying rock types in situ is to distinguish rock apparent features with the utilization of auxiliary tools, such as a magnifying glass and a knife. In contrast, owing to the presence of different mineral compositions in the rock, the features of color, grain size, shape, internal cleavage, structure, and other information are visible in rock thin-section images, which can represent specific rock petrographic information. In any case, it is challenging for geologists to classify both image formats mentioned above based on their experiences, and it is also time-consuming and costly. Therefore, it is necessary for researchers to study how to classify rocks efficiently and accurately.

In the past, many scholars have studied different methods to identify rock types, which can be summarized into the following categories: physical test methods, numerical statistical analysis, and intelligent approaches.

X-ray diffraction (XRD) is a common method of physical testing that can quickly obtain rock mineral fractions, and rock types can then be classified based on rock mineral-fraction information. Shao et al. [1] used X-ray powder crystal diffraction to accurately recognize gneiss rock feldspar, albite, and quartz but could not identify metallic minerals, such as tourmaline, sphene, etc. Chi et al. [2] analyzed the whole-rock chemical composition by XRD and then calculated the rock impurity factor, magnesium factor, and calcium factor based on chemical compositions to make the final classification of marble. However, due to the limitations of the XRD mineral semiquantitative analysis technique, such as inaccurate quantification of mineral components, it is still necessary to rely on other methods to verify the identification results of the XRD mineral semiquantitative method.

Zhang et al. [3,4] utilized a mathematics statistics theory to extract rock lithology features, Sr and Yb are considered as the classification characteristics of granite rock. Shaaban and Tawfik [5] adopted a rough-set mathematical theory to classify six types of volcanic rock, and the proposed model prioritizes computation times and cost. Yin et al. [6] combined means of image processing and pattern recognition, investigated features of rock structures in FMI image format, and developed a classification system with 81.11% accuracy. The rock thin-section image classification effect of four pattern recognition methods was evaluated by Młynarczuk et al. [7], and finally, the nearest-neighbor algorithm and CIELab data format were confirmed as the best scheme. The methods mentioned above have good results for rock classification, but the model performance differs depending on the level of knowledge of different people. With the convenience of digital image acquisition, it is possible to accumulate a large dataset. Thus, intelligent algorithms based on large datasets are widely applied to the classification of rock types. Unlike physical and numerical analysis methods, intelligent methods involve less or no human interaction and achieve better generalization.

Marmo et al. [8] introduced image-processing technology and an artificial neural network (ANN) to identify carbonate thin sections; the model showed 93.5% accuracy. Singh et al. [9] followed the same method as Marmo: 27-dimensional numerical parameters were extracted as the neural network input, and the model reached 92.22% precision for classifying basaltic thin-section images. A support vector machine (SVM) algorithm was developed by Chatterjee et al. [10]. A total of 40 features were selected out of the original 189 features as the model input, and six types of limestone were identified with 96.2% performance. Patel et al. [11] developed a robust model based on a probabilistic neural network (PNN) and nine color histogram features, and the overall error rate of classification was below 6% on seven limestone rock types. Tian et al. [12] proposed an SVM identification model with the combination of Principal Component Analysis (PCA) and obtained 97% classification accuracy. Khorram et al. [13] presented a limestone classification model in which six features were obtained from segmentation images and used as the input of the neural network, and the model achieved a higher $R^2$ value. Intelligent methods show advantages in rock type classification. However, it is worth noting that they heavily rely on the quality of numerical features extracted by researchers, which directly determines the final performance of the model.

Convolutional neural networks (CNNs), another intelligent approach, also have great advantages in image-processing fields. The earliest application of a CNN was designed to solve the problem of classifying handwritten digital numbers [14], which obtained remarkable success, and afterward, the achievements of CNNs are blooming everywhere, including in object detection [15–19], face recognition [20], natural language processing [21,22], remote sensing [23,24], autonomous driving [25], and intelligent medicine [26–28].

Recently, many researchers have made great breakthroughs in transferring computer-based methods to rock class identification and classification. Li et al. [29] used an enhanced TradaBoost algorithm to recognize microscopic sandstone images collected in different areas. Polat et al. [30] transferred two CNNs to automatically classify six types of volcanic rocks and evaluated the effect of four different optimizers. Anjos et al. [31] proposed four CNN models to identify three kinds of Brazilian presalt carbonate rocks using microscopic thin-section images. Samet et al. [32] presented an image segmentation method based on the fuzzy rule, which used rock thin sections as input and returned mineral segmentation regions. Yang et al. [33] employed a ResNet50 neural network to classify five scales of rock thin-section images, and finally, the model obtained excellent performance. Xu et al. [34] studied petroleum exploration and deep learning algorithms; the ResNet-18 convolutional neural network was selected to classify four types of rock thin-section images. Su et al. [35] innovatively proposed a method that consisted of three CNNs, and the final prediction label was the combination of three CNN results. The proposed model performs well in classifying thirteen types of rock thin-section images. Gao et al. [36] comprehensively compared shallow neural networks and deep neural networks on the classification of rock thin-section images, and the results show that deep neural networks outperform shallow networks. According to three main types of rock—metamorphic, sedimentary, and volcanic rock—Ma et al. [37] studied an enhanced feature extraction CNN model based on SeNet [38], and the model achieved 90.89% accuracy on the test dataset. Chen et al. [39] introduced ResNet50 and ResNet101 neural networks to construct a classifier to complete the identification of rock thin-section images, reaching 90.24% and 91.63% performance, respectively. In addition, some other researchers have studied rock type classification based on datasets obtained by digital cameras instead of microscopic images [40–42].

Of course, all the methods mentioned above provide great theoretical support for the automatic classification of rocks, while many focus on only a small number of rock classes or the subclasses of the three major rocks. To the best of our knowledge, most existing studies have focused on the neural network's classification accuracy of rock types instead of considering how to train networks to enhance the effect of the model. Additionally, compared to the general images that could be easily distinguished by a CNN, thin-section images of rocks are special; the composition of mineral crystals in the rock thin-section image is not uniform in proportion, and there is no clear definition of semantic-level feature information, such as particle size and shape contour of mineral crystals. Meanwhile, mineral crystals fill the whole image so that there is no exact distinction between background and foreground in the rock thin-section image. Thus, it is essential to study the training methodologies of the CNN models.

Therefore, in this paper, three kinds of main rocks and their subclasses were selected as the research objects, not only for systematically evaluating the classification precision of four kinds of CNN model for three types of rock but also for discussing the influence of the optimization algorithms (RMSprop, SGD, and Adam optimizers) and learning-rate decay modes (cosine and lambda learning-rate decay schedules) on the model's accuracy during the network training process. Finally, the optimal neural network model and the best training skills are summarized, which provides a reliable reference for the better realization of automatic rock class classification.

The structure of this study is as follows: the Section 2 introduces detailed information about the dataset, theoretical knowledge of four CNN algorithms, and learning-rate adjustment methods. The Section 3 depicts model training requirements and the results analysis of the trained model. The Section 4 evaluates the performance of four algorithms, optimizers, and the learning-rate decay modes. Furthermore, experimental verification on another database is carried out to validate the effect of the best-trained model. Finally, the optimum model, optimization algorithms, and learning-rate adjustment mode are obtained.

## 2. Materials and Methods

### 2.1. Dataset

Rock is a geological body formed by a regular combination of one or more minerals under geotectonic movement according to its formation causes and chemical constituents. It can be divided into three categories: metamorphic, sedimentary, and volcanic rocks. Metamorphic rocks are mainly formed by internal forces; in addition to the mineral components of the original rocks, there are also some prevalent metamorphic minerals, such as sericite and garnet. The effect of external forces forms sedimentary rocks, and secondary minerals also account for a considerable amount, including calcite, dolomite, kaolinite, etc. Volcanic rocks are primary minerals formed by the effect of Earth's internal force and have more complex compositions (quartz, feldspar, amphibole, pyroxene, olivine, biotite, etc.). Granite and basalt are the two most widely distributed kinds of volcanic rocks.

The dataset used in this study is a photomicrograph rock dataset acquired from Nanjing University of China [43] that includes three rock types—metamorphic, sedimentary, and volcanic rocks, which contain 40 subclasses, 28 subclasses, and 40 subclasses, respectively—and a total of 2634 microscopic images, Figure 1 shows the three types of rock thin section images.

**Figure 1.** Three types of microscopic thin-section images: (**a**,**b**) metamorphic rocks; (**c**,**d**) sedimentary rocks; (**e**,**f**) volcanic rocks.

Table 1 shows the detailed descriptions of the dataset 1. The thin-section images were photographed under both single-polarized light and cross-polarized light. First, a representative field of view was selected, and two images, including a single-polarization photo and cross-polarization photo, were then taken at the position of 0°, and other microscopic images were taken every 15° under the transmission cross-polarization. Thus, there are a total of eight or nine images for a single rock thin section, and all photomicrographs are shown in RGB format with a resolution of 1280 × 1024 or 4908 × 3264 pixels.

*2.2. Deep Learning-Based Approaches*

Artificial intelligence (AI) technologies have been rapidly developed and widely applied in many areas in recent years. There is no doubt that they represent a new technological revolution. Throughout the wave of AI, algorithms play the dominant role, and the inherent relationships are shown in Figure 2. As a branch of machine learning, deep learning algorithms have the superiority of powerful self-learning and feature extraction abilities compared to other machine learning methods.

Table 1. Detailed descriptions of the dataset.

| Class | Subclass | Numbers | | |
|---|---|---|---|---|
| | | Subclass Number | Total Number | Microscopic Image Number |
| Metamorphic Rock | Mylonite | 2 | 40 | 972 |
| | Hornstone | 3 | | |
| | Skarn | 3 | | |
| | Marble | 3 | | |
| | Serpentine | 1 | | |
| | Dolomite | 1 | | |
| | Slate | 1 | | |
| | Phyllite | 2 | | |
| | Schist | 9 | | |
| | Gneiss | 6 | | |
| | Granulite | 3 | | |
| | Amphibole | 1 | | |
| | Eclogite | 1 | | |
| | Migmatite | 1 | | |
| | Cataclasite | 1 | | |
| | Others | 2 | | |
| Sedimentary Rock | Clastic rock | 5 | 28 | 699 |
| | Sandstone | 6 | | |
| | Shale | 6 | | |
| | Limestone | 5 | | |
| | Dolomite | 1 | | |
| | Siliceous rock | 1 | | |
| | Evaporative rock | 1 | | |
| | Others | 3 | | |
| Volcanic Rock | Ultrabasic rock | 7 | 40 | 963 |
| | Basic rock | 7 | | |
| | Neutral rock | 7 | | |
| | Acidic rock | 11 | | |
| | Others | 8 | | |
| | | | 108 | 2634 |

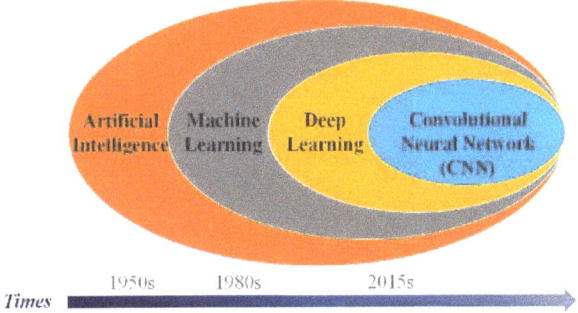

Figure 2. The connection between deep learning and AI [44].

CNNs, which are the main part of deep learning algorithms, were introduced by Fukushima [45] for the first time. Usually, a convolutional neural network consists of three parts: convolutional layers, activation layers, and pooling layers. Convolutional layers are similar to filters, mainly in charge of extracting image features, and the convolutional layer is also the module with the largest number of parameters. The nonlinearity property is of great importance for CNNs; otherwise, the forward process could be viewed as a simple linear operation, which is useless for model convergence and the final model accuracy. Therefore, activation layers are a necessary module of CNNs, regarded as a kind of nonlinearity function. Generally, pooling layers, which aim to reduce the feature map size, are placed behind the activation layers. The four types of typical activation functions are as follows:

$$\sigma(z) = \max(0, z) \quad (1)$$

$$\sigma(z) = \frac{1}{(1 + e^{-z})} \quad (2)$$

$$\sigma(z) = \frac{e^z - e^{-z}}{e^z + e^{-z}} \quad (3)$$

$$\sigma(z) = \begin{cases} z, & z \geq 0 \\ \frac{z}{a}, & z < 0 \end{cases} \quad (4)$$

Note: Equations (1)–(4) are the ReLU, sigmoid, tanh, and leaky ReLU activation functions, respectively.

Four classical and well-performed CNN algorithms (VGG16, GoogLeNet, MobileNetV2, ShuffleNetV2) were used for rock microscopic thin-section classification in this paper, and the contents of each are depicted in the following sections.

2.2.1. GoogLeNet

GoogLeNet was proposed by the research team at Google Co., Ltd. Mountain View, CA, USA. [46] and named the champion of the ImageNet competition in 2014, a global vision challenge competition. In GoogLeNet, the inception network structure, the main highlight of the work, was first presented and optimized. The architecture of the inception module is shown in Figure 3a. There are three kinds of convolutional layers with corresponding kernel sizes (1 × 1, 3 × 3, 5 × 5) and a max pooling layer with a 3 × 3 slide window. The former feature maps are used as the input of the inception structure, and the final output equals the concatenation of the result computed by four branches separately. GoogLeNet is regularly composed of the inception structure, and the prediction step is completed by the final fully connected layer, which not only ensures the model performance but also considers the computations of the network. Figure 3b shows the overall architecture of GoogLeNet.

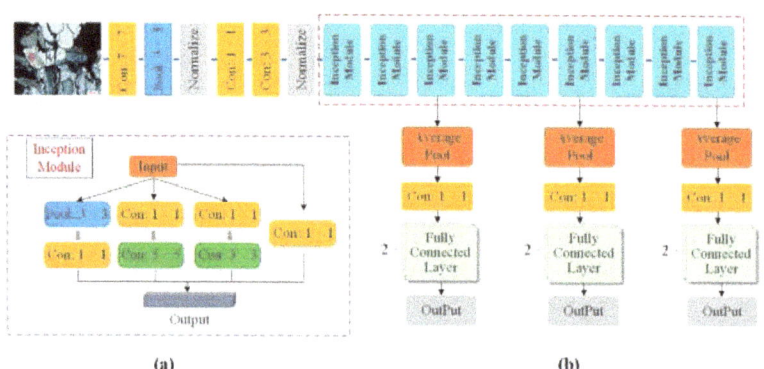

Figure 3. Network structure: (a) GoogLeNet architecture; (b) inception module structure.

2.2.2. VGG16

VGGNet was proposed by the visual geometry group of Oxford University [47]. Furthermore, Qassim et al. [48] discussed the model speed and size of VGG16 by proposing a compressed VGG16 network. There are a total of five subnetworks of VGGNet (VGG11, VGG11-LRN, VGG13, VGG16, VGG19), with numbers 11, 13, etc., indicating the number of convolutional layers in the VGGNet except for pooling layers, and the VGG16 network was used in our paper for comparison. Figure 4 shows the architecture of the VGG16 network. The structure is very simple and easily understandable. Sixteen convolutional layers are divided into five blocks and then directly connected to each other. Meanwhile, five pooling layers are interspersed in the middle, and all convolutional layers have the same convolutional kernel size (3 × 3). Furthermore, multiple 3 × 3 convolution layers connected in series increase the depth of the network, which guarantees the performance of the model to some extent, and compared with the use of large convolution kernels, it has fewer parameters and better nonlinearity.

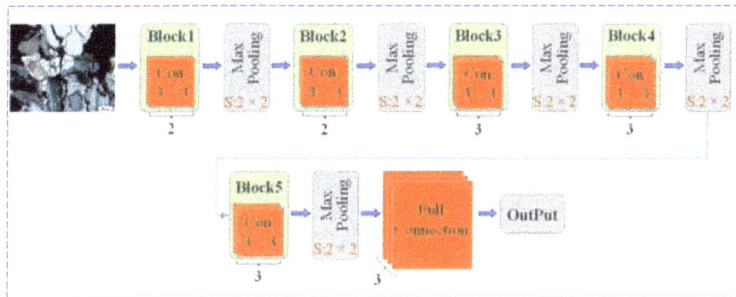

**Figure 4.** VGG16 architecture.

### 2.2.3. MobilenetV2

MobileNet, a lightweight convolutional neural network focused on model compression compared to the two networks mentioned above, aims to balance accuracy and latency and its application in mobile devices. MobileNetV1 and MobileNetV2 are the two versions of MobileNet, and the latter is improved and optimized. Thus, it was selected as the research method in the present paper. Similar to the MobileNetV1 network, MobileNetV2 [49] still uses the depth-wise separable convolution unit module, as shown in Figure 5. Additionally, a bottleneck residual module was developed, which has the same effect as the residual module in the Residual Network (ResNet [50]). The bottleneck residual module contains three convolutional layers, as shown in Figure 6b, but the difference is that the middle convolutional layer of the bottleneck residual module is a depth-wise separable convolution, and the last layer is a linear convolution operation without an activation layer to avoid missing much semantic information [49]. Similarly, multiple bottleneck blocks are connected in an orderly manner in the structure of MobileNetV2, as shown in Figure 6a.

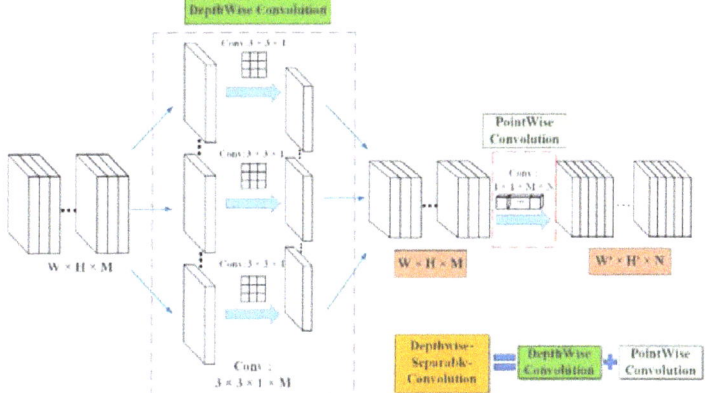

**Figure 5.** Depth-wise separable convolution structure.

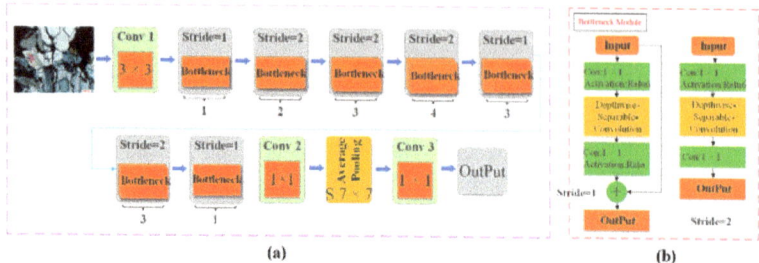

**Figure 6.** Network structure. (**a**) MobileNetV2 architecture; (**b**) bottleneck module structure.

2.2.4. ShuffleNetV2

Floating-point operations per second (FLOPs) are usually adopted as the evaluation index of network model efficiency. As mentioned in ShuffleNetV2 [51], it is not good enough to only consider FLOPs since computer memory access cost (MAC), as well as the platform (such as ARM or GPU), also have an obvious influence on the model running speed. Hence, four experiments were carried out in ShuffleNetV2 to analyze the factors affecting the efficiency of the neural network. The experimental results demonstrate that an efficient network structure should include the following points: (1) Keep the same channel depth of input and output in convolutional layers; (2) the groups of group convolution should be well controlled; (3) the number of branches in the neural network structure should be reduced as much as possible; and (4) element-add operations should also be avoided properly. Accordingly, two kinds of optimized block units are proposed in ShuffleNetV2, as shown in Figure 7a, and the architecture of ShuffleNetV2 was formed by regularly connecting the block units shown in Figure 7b.

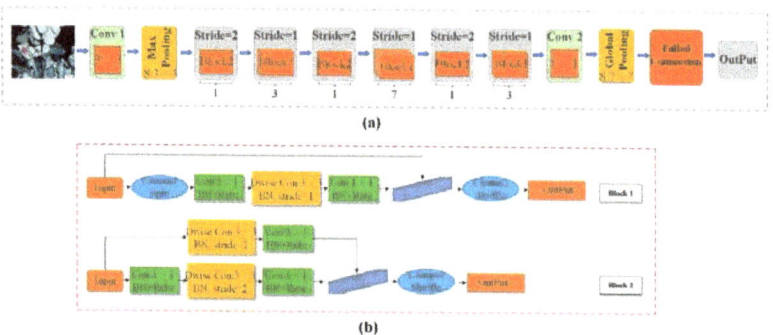

**Figure 7.** Network structure: (**a**) ShuffleNetV2 architecture; (**b**) block module structure.

2.3. Learning-Rate Decay Schedules

An appropriate learning-rate decay method is beneficial to the convergence of model training as well as the final accuracy of the model. Consequently, this paper employed and analyzed two commonly used learning-rate decay schedules in the deep learning field: cosine decay and lambda decay modes. The cosine learning-rate decay schedule was first proposed by Loshchilov et al. [52], and the main theoretical idea is that the learning rate decreases from the initial value to zero according to the cosine function, as shown in Equation (5). The lambda learning-rate decay schedule means that the later learning rate equals the initial learning rate multiplied by a coefficient $\gamma$, and $\gamma$ is the function of training steps or epochs. The calculation formula is shown in Equation (6).

$$L_t = \frac{1}{2}\left(1 + \cos\frac{t\pi}{T}\right)L_0 \tag{5}$$

$$new_l = initial_l \times \gamma$$
$$\gamma = 1.0 - \frac{epoch}{300} \tag{6}$$

Note: $L_0$ is the initial learning rate; $T$ is the total number of training steps or epochs; and t is the number of training steps or epochs.

The learning rate setting is important to the convolutional neural network learning process. For cosine decay and lambda decay (Equations (5) and (6)), if the learning rate is too low, the learning speed of the neural network will be severely affected, and the training period will be increased. In contrast, it is not easy to achieve good convergence in the model training if the learning rate is high enough. Hence, dynamic adjustment strategies for updating the learning rate are usually adopted. A learning rate warm-up method, proposed in ResNet, mainly includes two steps: at the beginning of training, the learning rate is started from a smaller value and changed to the initial learning rate after some iterations or epochs, and it is then gradually decreased along with the training process. In this paper, gradual warm-up, a modified warm-up method proposed by Goyal et al. [53], was selected as the learning-rate adjustment method for the cosine and lambda learning-rate decay schedules; this method started from a smaller value and gradually increased with each iteration or epoch until reaching the initial learning rate, instead of always keeping a small value and then decreasing step-by-step. Figure 8 shows the learning-rate attenuation process of the cosine and lambda modes. The learning rates of both modes tend to increase first and then decrease; however, the attenuation process of the cosine decay mode is smoother than that of the lambda decay schedule.

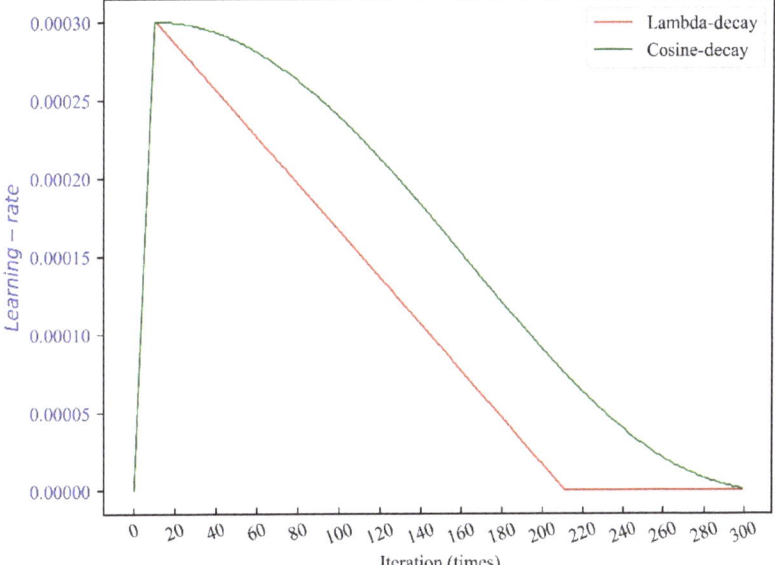

**Figure 8.** Gradual warm-up learning-rate curves of cosine and lambda decay schedules.

## 3. Results

Four methods—GoogLeNet, VGG16, MobileNetV2, and ShuffleNetV2—were all trained and validated with the same dataset. Three types of deep learning optimizers and two learning-rate decay schedule modes were employed during the training process. Finally, the following sections systematically compare and analyze the experimental results of the four algorithms under different training skills.

## 3.1. Training

PyTorch, one of the deep learning algorithm frameworks, was selected as the model training framework. The total images were divided into training and testing datasets at a ratio of 8:2. First, the unified default hyperparameters of the four algorithms were as follows: the input image size was 224 × 224, the total number of training epochs was 300, and the batch size was 64. The parameters of the optimizer were set as follows: the Adam optimizer was set with an initial learning rate of 0.0003; the momentum and weight decay were set at 0.9 and 0.005 for the SGD optimizer; and the initial learning rate and the alpha of the RMSprop optimizer were 0.0003 and 0.99, respectively. The initial learning rate was 0.0003, and the warm-up epoch was 10. All experiments were trained on an RTX3090 GPU with 32 GB GDDR GPU memory and an Intel i7-11700 CPU.

## 3.2. Analysis of the Results

The performance of the model on rock microscopic thin-section images classification was compared based on three evaluation indices: precision, f1-scores, and confusion matrix. Precision ($P$) indicates the proportion of samples in the true positive class among all the samples that were predicted to be positive classes and is computed as Equation (7). Recall ($R$) equals the proportion of all positive samples correctly predicted by the model, shown as Equation (8). The $F1\_scores$, which consider a balance between precision and recall, are distributed between 0~1. The closer to 1, the better the model is, as shown in Equation (9). The confusion matrix, also known as the error matrix, is a standard format for expressing accuracy represented by an $n \times n$ matrix. Each column of the confusion matrix represents a predicted class, and the sum of the values in this column equals the number of samples classified as that category. The values on the diagonal line indicate the number of samples accurately predicted by the model, and the other two remaining values in each column indicate the number of other classes of rocks that were misidentified.

$$P = \frac{TP}{TP + FP} \qquad (7)$$

$$R = \frac{TP}{TP + FN} \qquad (8)$$

$$F1\_scores = 2 \times \frac{P \times R}{P + R} \qquad (9)$$

### 3.2.1. Results of GoogLeNet

The GoogLeNet classification model was trained with three optimizers (Adam, SGD, and RMSprop) with the utilization of the cosine learning-rate decay schedule and lambda decay schedule. In this section, we will analyze and discuss the performance of the trained model.

1. Cosine learning-rate decay schedule

In this part, the learning-rate adjustment during training was fixed as the cosine decay mode for all models. Figure 9 shows the training loss curves and the model classification precision for the three types of rock. Figure 9a shows that the training loss exhibited obvious gaps for different optimizers. The loss of the model trained under the Adam optimizer descended the fastest but, finally, had a value closer to RMSprop. In contrast, SGD was the slowest and had a larger convergence value at the end of training. Figure 9b–d show the GoogLeNet model's classification precision for the three types of rock with the use of the three optimization algorithms. For metamorphic rock, as shown in Figure 9b, the classification model with the RMSprop optimizer had the highest precision, followed by Adam and SGD; for sedimentary and volcanic rock, as shown in Figure 9c,d, the model with the RMSprop and Adam optimizers maintained almost the same precision, while SGD had the lowest accuracy. In summary, the RMSprop optimizer performed slightly better than Adam, and SGD was the worst.

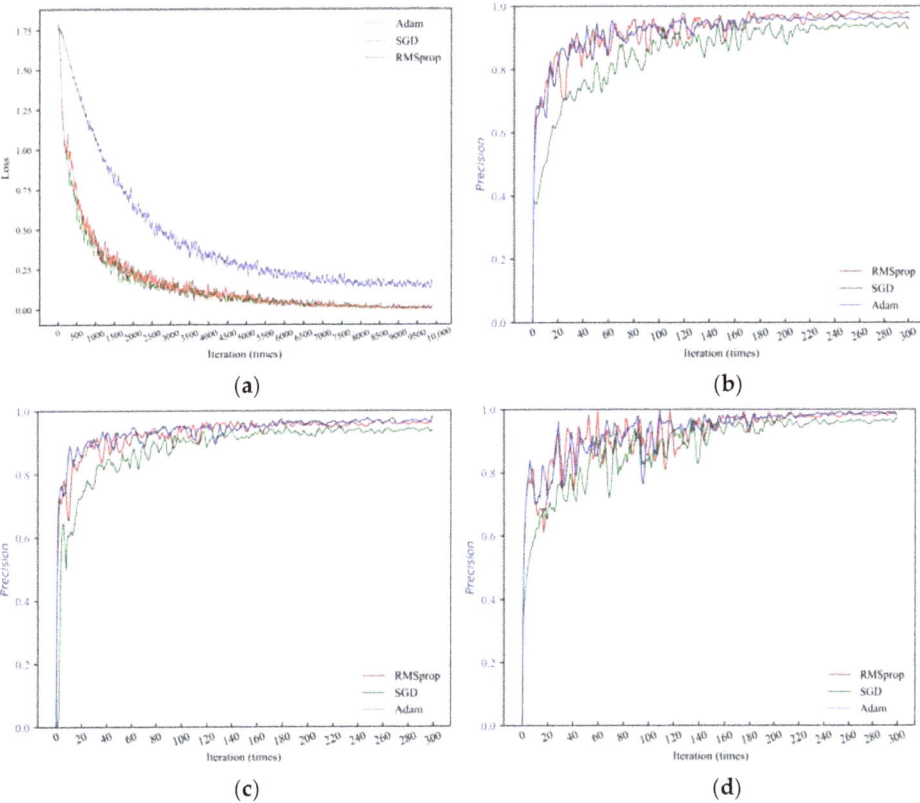

**Figure 9.** (a) Training loss of GoogLeNet under three optimizers; (b) classification precision of metamorphic rock under three optimizers; (c) classification precision of sedimentary rock; and (d) classification precision of volcanic rock.

Additionally, performance was further evaluated based on confusion matrixes, as shown in Figure 10. The confusion matrix clearly revealed the detailed classification results of the three types of rock for the models trained under different optimizers. Model training with the RMSprop optimizer obtained the best precision of 97.9% for metamorphic rock classification, as shown in Figure 10a. Model training with the Adam optimizer obtained 97.8% accuracy for sedimentary rock. For volcanic rock recognition, model training with the RMSprop and Adam optimizers had the same precision of 98.4%.

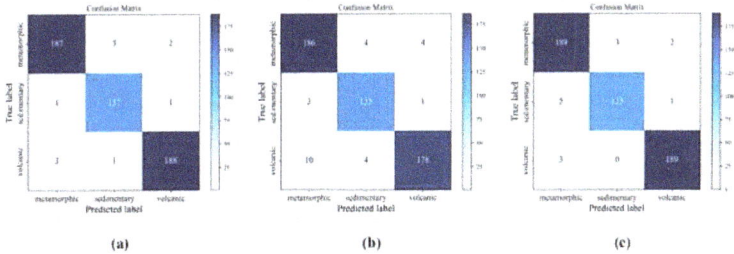

**Figure 10.** Confusion matrixes: (a) RMSprop optimizer; (b) SGD optimizer; (c) Adam optimizer.

The detailed results are displayed in Table 2. Model training with the SGD optimizer performed slightly worse than RMSProp and Adam, which is reflected in the conclusions obtained in Figure 9.

Table 2. Detailed classification results for all rock types.

| Rock Types | Evaluation | Cosine Decay Schedule | | |
| --- | --- | --- | --- | --- |
| | | Adam | SGD | RMSprop |
| Metamorphic | P | 96% | 93% | 98% |
| | F1-scores | 0.97 | 0.95 | 0.97 |
| Sedimentary | P | 98% | 94% | 96% |
| | F1-scores | 0.97 | 0.96 | 0.97 |
| Volcanic | P | 98% | 97% | 98% |
| | F1-scores | 0.98 | 0.95 | 0.98 |

2. Lambda learning-rate decay schedule

This part of the trial was carried out under the lambda learning-rate decay schedule, which aims to compare with the cosine learning-rate decay mode, and the results are shown as follows. Figure 11a shows the result of the model training loss; Figure 11b indicates the model classification accuracy of metamorphic rock trained under the three optimizers; Figure 11c shows the sedimentary rock identification result; and Figure 11d shows volcanic.

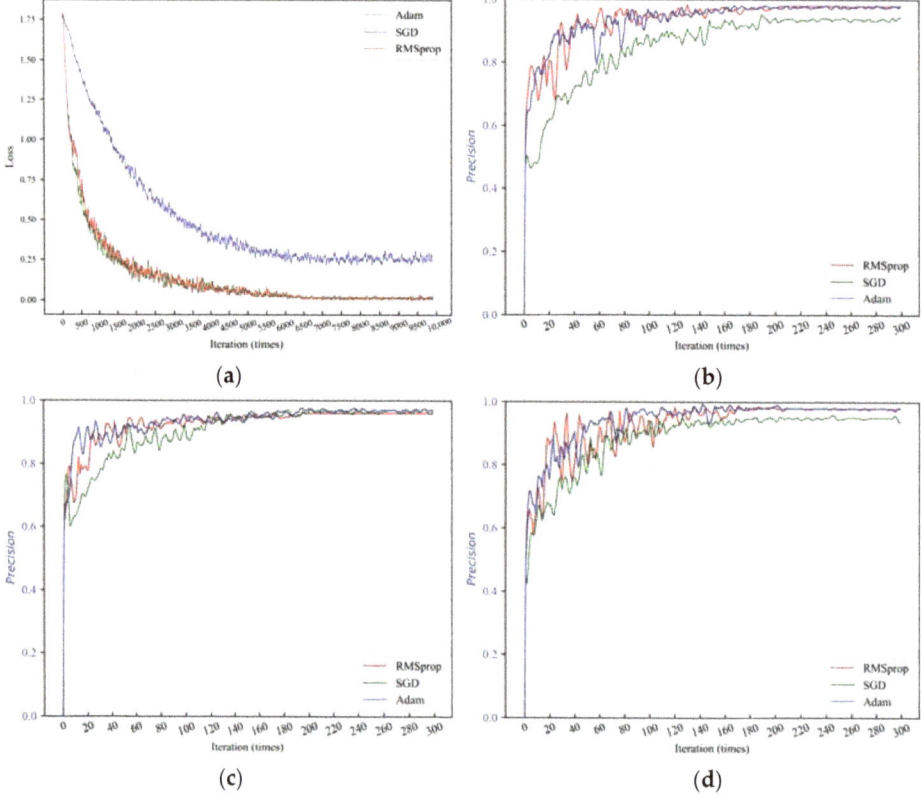

**Figure 11.** (a) Training loss of GoogLeNet under three optimizers; (b) classification precision of metamorphic rock under three optimizers; (c) classification precision of sedimentary rock; and (d) classification precision of volcanic rock.

Figure 12 is the confusion matrix of the classification result on the validation dataset. Figure 12a shows the result of the GoogLeNet model trained under RMSprop optimization algorithms; the number of rocks predicted to be metamorphic was 196, of which 188 were truly metamorphic rock, and 4 were incorrectly predicted (2 belonged to sedimentary, and the other 2 were volcanic). For sedimentary rocks, the truly predicted number was 136, and the number of prediction errors was 6 (4 were metamorphic, and 2 were volcanic). There were 188 samples correctly identified as volcanic rock, and 3 other classes were misclassified. Similarly, Figure 12b,c show the result of the model trained with the SGD and Adam optimizers.

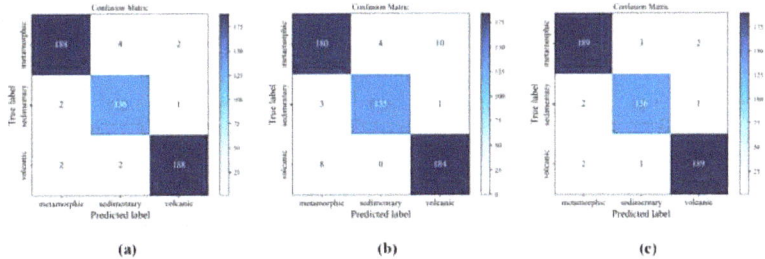

**Figure 12.** Confusion matrixes: (**a**) RMSprop optimizer; (**b**) SGD optimizer; (**c**) Adam optimizer.

According to Figures 11 and 12 and Table 3, it can be summarized, with the same conclusion compared to the cosine learning-rate decay schedule, that the RMSprop and Adam optimizers achieved better performance than SGD. In addition, the comparison result between the two learning-rate decay schedules can also be obtained from Table 3. The average classification accuracy of the two learning-rate decay modes for the three types of rock is approximately 96%, and the gap is negligible.

**Table 3.** Detailed classification results for all rock types.

| Rock Types | Evaluation | Lambda Decay Schedule | | |
|---|---|---|---|---|
| | | Adam | SGD | RMSprop |
| Metamorphic | P | 98% | 94% | 98% |
| | F1-scores | 0.98 | 0.94 | 0.97 |
| Sedimentary | P | 97% | 97% | 96% |
| | F1-scores | 0.97 | 0.97 | 0.97 |
| Volcanic | P | 98% | 94% | 98% |
| | F1-scores | 0.98 | 0.95 | 0.98 |

Thus, for GoogLeNet, the influence of the optimization algorithms on the classification of rock types is more evident compared to learning-rate decay modes.

### 3.2.2. Results of VGG16

The VGG16 neural network was selected as the method to classify rock microscopic thin-section images, and the last fully connected layer of the VGG16 structure was changed to three. The model optimizers and learning-rate decay schedules remained the same as for GoogLeNet, and the experimental result could also be obtained from the perspective of two learning-rate decay modes.

1. Cosine learning-rate decay schedule

Likewise, the cosine learning-rate decay mode was adopted in this section. Figures 13 and 14 and Table 4 show the capabilities of the trained models in the classification of three types of rock microscopic thin-section images. Figure 13 shows the results of the VGG16 model trained under the three optimizers: (a) is the loss curve during the training iteration, and (b–d) are the prediction accuracy curves of the three models for metamorphic, sedimentary, and volcanic, respectively.

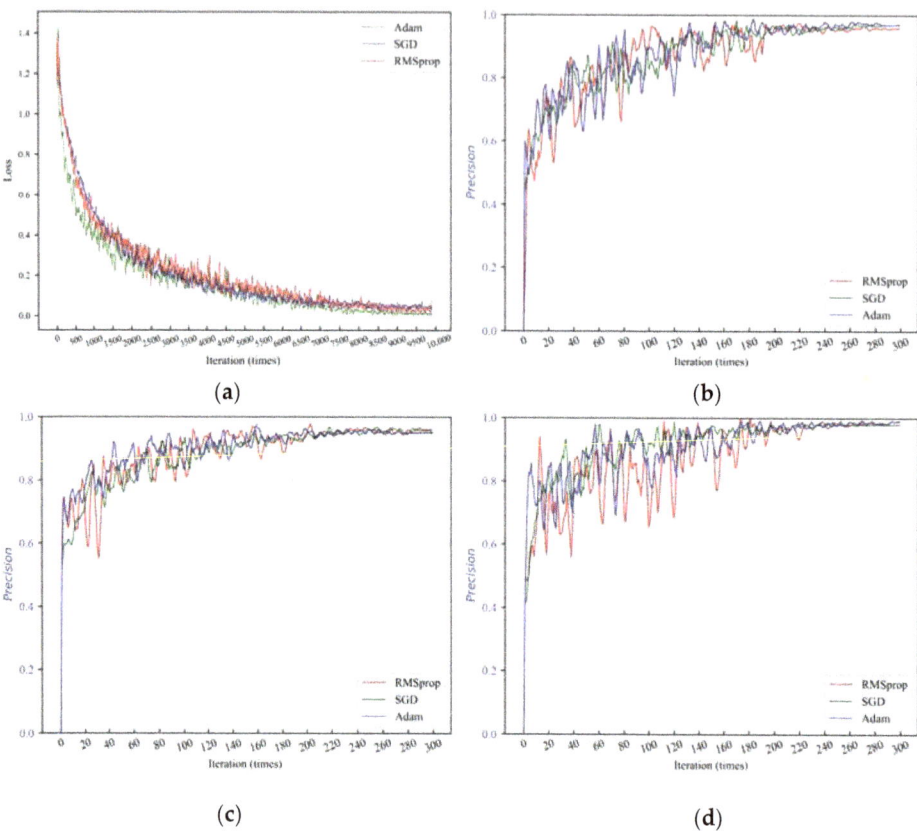

**Figure 13.** (a) Training loss of VGG16 under three optimizers; (b) classification precision of metamorphic rock under three optimizers; (c) classification precision of sedimentary rock; and (d) classification precision of volcanic rock.

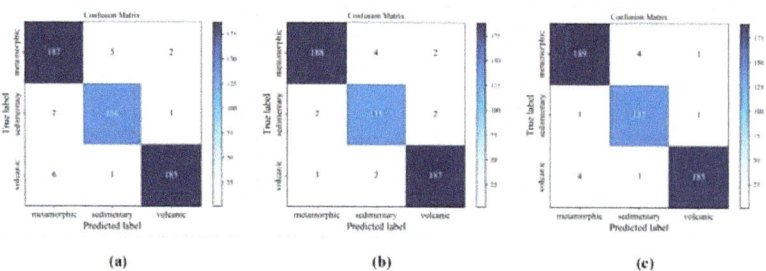

**Figure 14.** Confusion matrixes: (a) RMSprop optimizer; (b) SGD optimizer; (c) Adam optimizer.

**Table 4.** Detailed classification results for all rock types.

| Rock Types | Evaluation | Cosine Decay Schedule | | |
|---|---|---|---|---|
| | | Adam | SGD | RMSprop |
| Metamorphic | P | 97% | 97% | 96% |
| | F1-scores | 0.97 | 0.97 | 0.96 |
| Sedimentary | P | 95% | 95% | 96% |
| | F1-scores | 0.97 | 0.96 | 0.97 |
| Volcanic | P | 99% | 98% | 98% |
| | F1-scores | 0.98 | 0.97 | 0.97 |

Figure 14 exhibits the confusion matrix. It could be concluded that the performance of the trained models under the three optimizers using the cosine learning-rate decay mode was almost equivalent, and the average precision over the three types of rock all reached 97% of the model trained with the three optimizers, as shown in Table 4.

2. Lambda learning-rate decay schedule

For the lambda decay mode, the models of VGG16 with the use of the RMSprop and Adam optimizers achieved higher accuracy than SGD in the classification of metamorphic and sedimentary rock, while for volcanic rock, the result of the trained model with the SGD optimizer was better than that of RMSprop and Adam, as shown in Figure 15.

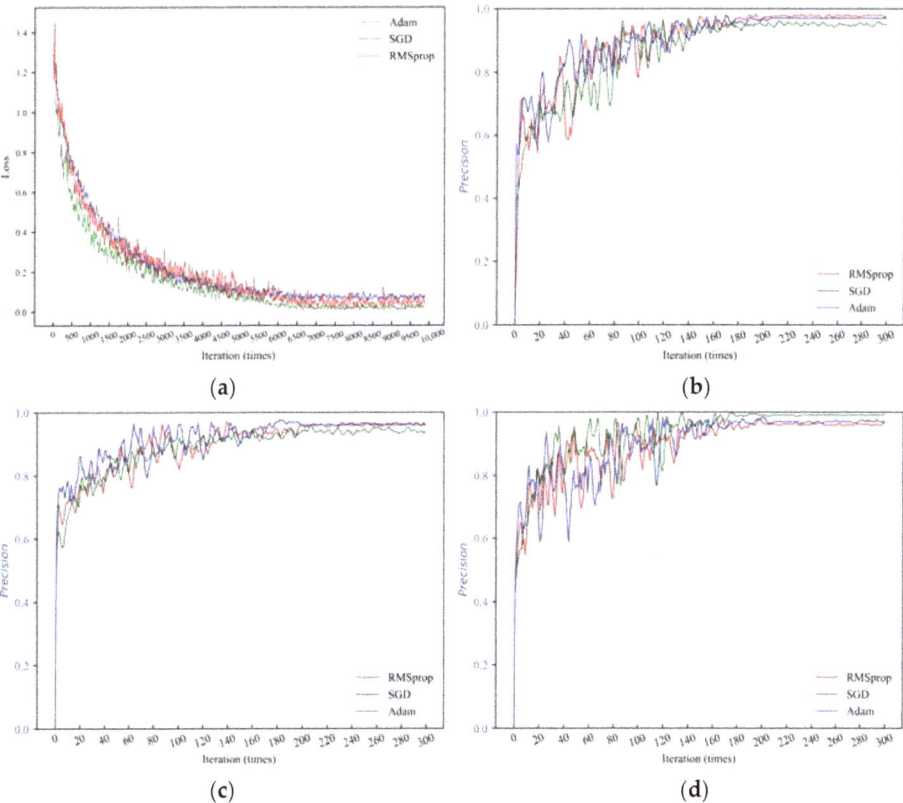

**Figure 15.** (a) Training loss of VGG16 under three optimizers; (b) classification precision of metamorphic rock under three optimizers; (c) classification precision of sedimentary rock; and (d) classification precision of volcanic rock.

Figure 16 is the confusion matrix. For volcanic rock, it is clear that the classification precision of the model trained with the SGD optimization algorithm was higher than that of the RMSprop and Adam optimizers. A total of 183 samples were predicted as volcanic rocks, and only 1 was misclassified.

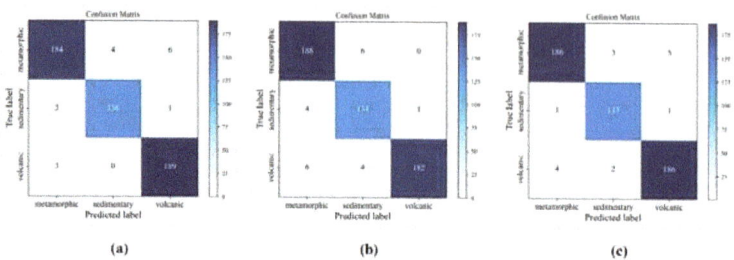

**Figure 16.** Confusion matrixes: (**a**) RMSprop optimizer; (**b**) SGD optimizer; (**c**) Adam optimizer.

Additionally, the average classification accuracy of the VGG16 model under the two learning-rate decay modes for the three types of rock was 96.6%, 95.8%, and 98.3% and 96.7%, 95.3%, and 97.6%, respectively, and the difference is small, as shown in Table 5.

**Table 5.** Detailed classification results for all rock types.

| Rock Types | Evaluation | Lambda Decay Schedule | | |
|---|---|---|---|---|
| | | Adam | SGD | RMSprop |
| Metamorphic | P | 97% | 95% | 98% |
| | F1-scores | 0.97 | 0.96 | 0.96 |
| Sedimentary | P | 96% | 94% | 96% |
| | F1-scores | 0.98 | 0.95 | 0.97 |
| Volcanic | P | 97% | 99% | 97% |
| | F1-scores | 0.97 | 0.97 | 0.98 |

Finally, according to the above conclusions, both the optimization algorithms and learning-rate decay schedules had little effect on the accuracy of the VGG16 model.

### 3.2.3. Results of MobileNetV2

Similarly, the MobileNetV2 neural network was used and trained with the methods adopted in the aforementioned networks. The results of the cosine and lambda learning rate decay modes were analyzed in the following sections.

1. Cosine learning-rate decay schedule

According to Figure 17, it is clear that the classification model using the RMSprop optimizer obtained the best effect, followed by the Adam and SGD optimizers.

In addition, the specific experimental results are summarized in Figure 18 and Table 6. Model training with the Adam optimizer achieved an accuracy of 94% in classifying metamorphic rocks, and RMSProp obtained 94% and 98% performances for sedimentary and volcanic rocks, respectively. While it can be seen that SGD had an obvious gap among the three optimizers, the precision was 3~7% lower than that of the RMSprop and Adam optimizers.

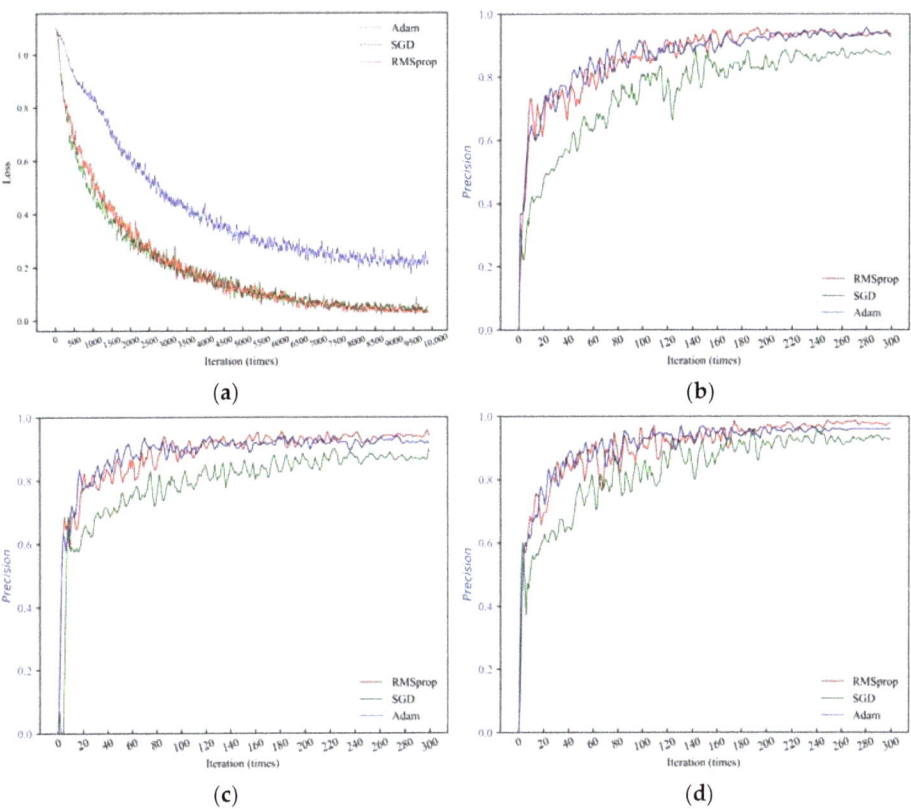

**Figure 17.** (a) Training loss of MobileNetV2 under three optimizers; (b) classification precision of metamorphic rock under three optimizers; (c) classification precision of sedimentary rock; and (d) classification precision of volcanic rock.

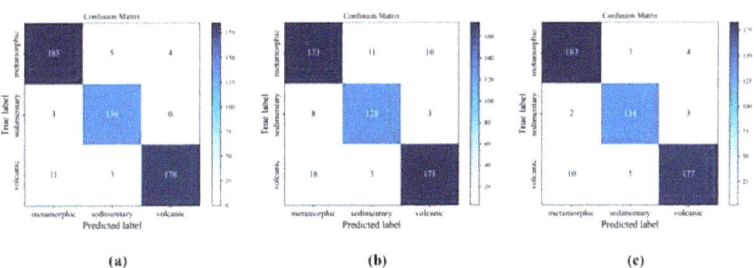

**Figure 18.** Confusion matrixes: (a) RMSprop optimizer; (b) SGD optimizer; (c) Adam optimizer.

Table 6. Detailed classification results for all rock types.

| Rock Types | Evaluation | Cosine Decay Schedule | | |
| --- | --- | --- | --- | --- |
| | | Adam | SGD | RMSprop |
| Metamorphic | P | 94% | 87% | 93% |
| | F1-scores | 0.94 | 0.88 | 0.94 |
| Sedimentary | P | 92% | 90% | 94% |
| | F1-scores | 0.94 | 0.91 | 0.96 |
| Volcanic | P | 96% | 93% | 98% |
| | F1-scores | 0.94 | 0.91 | 0.95 |

2. Lambda learning-rate decay schedule

The classification models utilizing lambda learning-rate decay were also trained. Figure 19 exhibits the training loss and the precision of the test data along with the training process. It is apparent that the Adam and RMSprop optimizers had a better tendency than SGD, whether on loss convergence or precision.

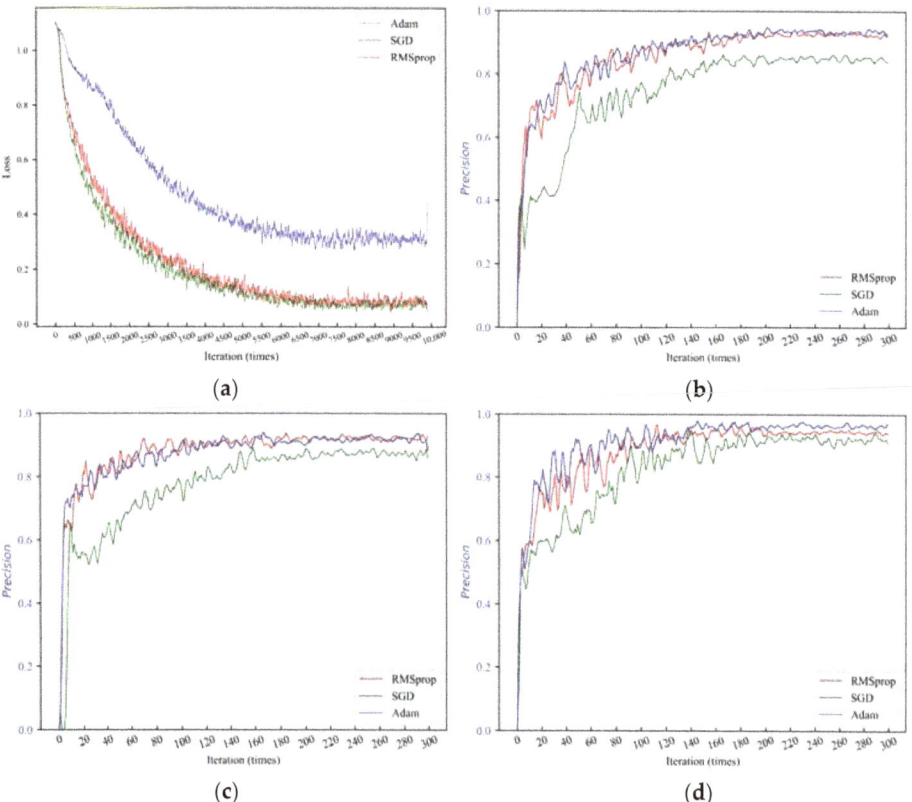

Figure 19. (a) Training loss of MobileNetV2 under three optimizers; (b) results of metamorphic rock under three optimizers; (c) results of sedimentary rock; and (d) results of volcanic rock.

Figure 20 indicates the ability of the classification models. The exact evaluation index value of the models with the application of the three optimizers could be calculated using Equations (7)–(9), and the results are shown in Table 7. The RMSprop optimizer achieved 93% accuracy for both metamorphic and sedimentary rocks. The highest precision of volcanic classification was the model using Adam, which achieved 97% performance.

However, the SGD optimizer had a large gap between the RMSprop and Adam optimizers for all types of rock. In particular, the accuracy was 84% for metamorphic rock, which was 9% lower than that of RMSprop.

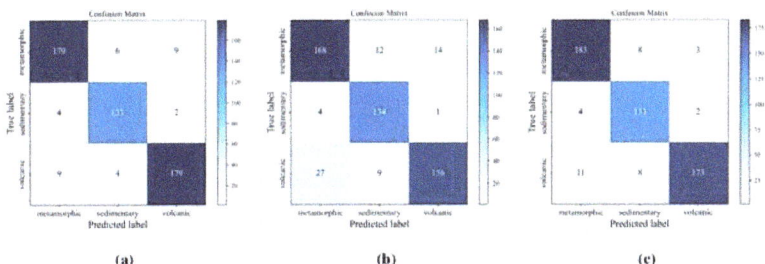

**Figure 20.** Confusion matrixes: (**a**) RMSprop optimizer; (**b**) SGD optimizer; (**c**) Adam optimizer.

**Table 7.** Detailed classification results for all rock types.

| Rock Types | Evaluation | Lambda Decay Schedule | | |
|---|---|---|---|---|
| | | Adam | SGD | RMSprop |
| Metamorphic | P | 92% | 84% | 93% |
| | F1-scores | 0.93 | 0.85 | 0.93 |
| Sedimentary | P | 89% | 86% | 93% |
| | F1-scores | 0.92 | 0.91 | 0.94 |
| Volcanic | P | 97% | 91% | 94% |
| | F1-scores | 0.94 | 0.86 | 0.94 |

According to Table 7, the average classification accuracy of the MobileNetV2 model with the employment of two learning-rate decay modes for the three types of rock was 91.3%, 92.0%, and 95.6% and 90.3%, 89.3%, and 94.0%, respectively. Obviously, learning-rate decay modes had a certain impact on MobileNetV2. For sedimentary rock, the classification accuracy of the model using the lambda decay method was almost 3% lower than that of the cosine. In addition, whether it was the cosine learning-rate decay method or the lambda decay method, the optimizer greatly influenced the model.

### 3.2.4. Results of ShuffleNetV2

For comprehensive comparison, the ShuffleNetV2 neural network was employed and trained following the same methods used in the three above algorithms, and the trial results are depicted in the next sections.

1. Cosine learning-rate decay schedule

As shown in Figure 21, the ShuffleNetV2 model using the SGD optimizer achieved poor accuracy in classifying the three types of rock microscopic images. Meanwhile, the loss was also at a higher value at the end of training. Overall, the performance of SGD was worse than that of the other two optimizers.

Figure 22 and Table 8 show that the metamorphic rock class was accurately classified with 95% precision by the model using the RMSprop and Adam optimizers. The model with the RMSprop optimizer achieved 95% precision for sedimentary rock, while in terms of volcanic rock type, the best result was using Adam, with 98% performance. However, the model using the SGD optimizer performed worse in the classification of all three types of rocks. The worst result was for metamorphic rocks, with an accuracy of only 75%, which was 20% lower than that of RMSprop and Adam.

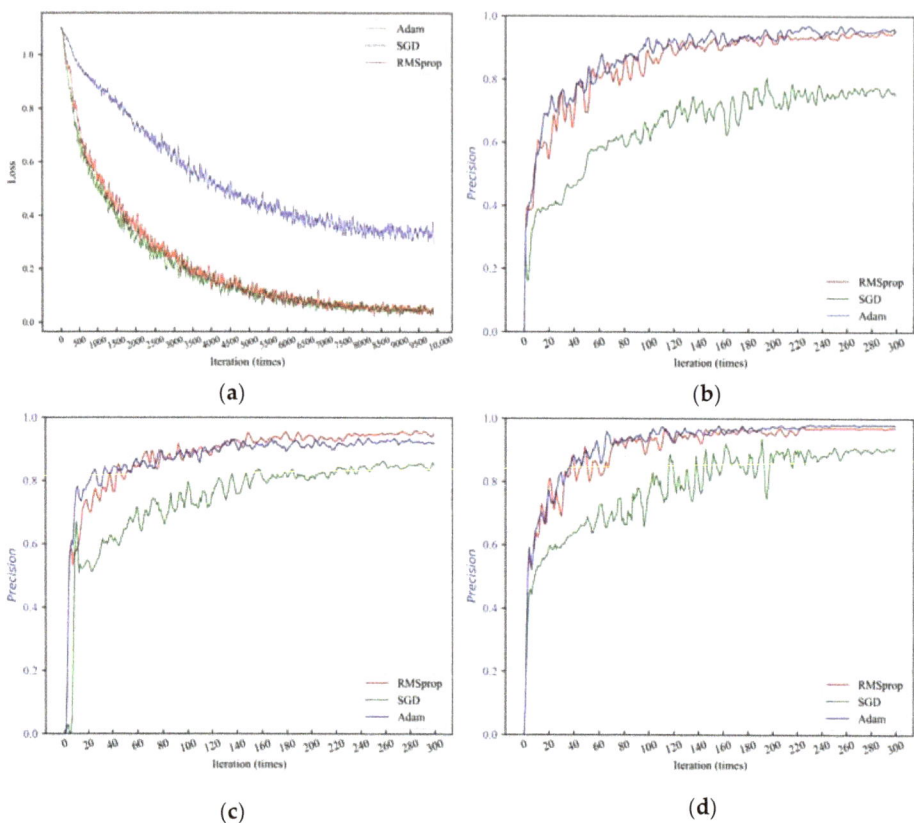

**Figure 21.** (**a**) Training loss of ShuffleNetV2 under three optimizers; (**b**) results of metamorphic rock under three optimizers; (**c**) results of sedimentary rock; and (**d**) results of volcanic rock.

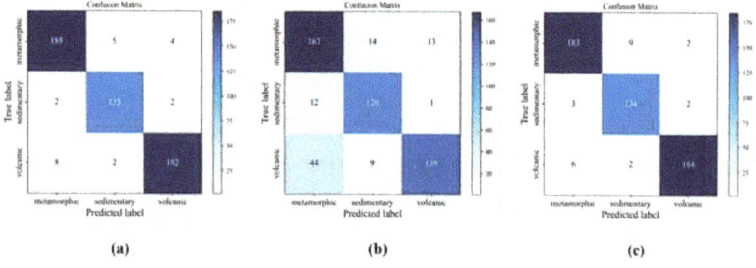

**Figure 22.** Confusion matrixes: (**a**) RMSprop optimizer; (**b**) SGD optimizer; (**c**) Adam optimizer.

**Table 8.** Detailed classification results for all rock types.

| Rock Types | Evaluation | Cosine Decay Schedule | | |
|---|---|---|---|---|
| | | Adam | SGD | RMSprop |
| Metamorphic | P | 95% | 75% | 95% |
| | F1-scores | 0.95 | 0.80 | 0.95 |
| Sedimentary | P | 92% | 85% | 95% |
| | F1-scores | 0.94 | 0.88 | 0.96 |
| Volcanic | P | 98% | 91% | 97% |
| | F1-scores | 0.97 | 0.81 | 0.96 |

2. Lambda learning-rate decay schedule

According to Figure 23, it can be concluded that the training loss and the accuracy of the test dataset during the training process remained the same as those of the model under the cosine learning-rate decay mode. The performance from excellent to poor ranked as follows: RMSprop, Adam, and SGD.

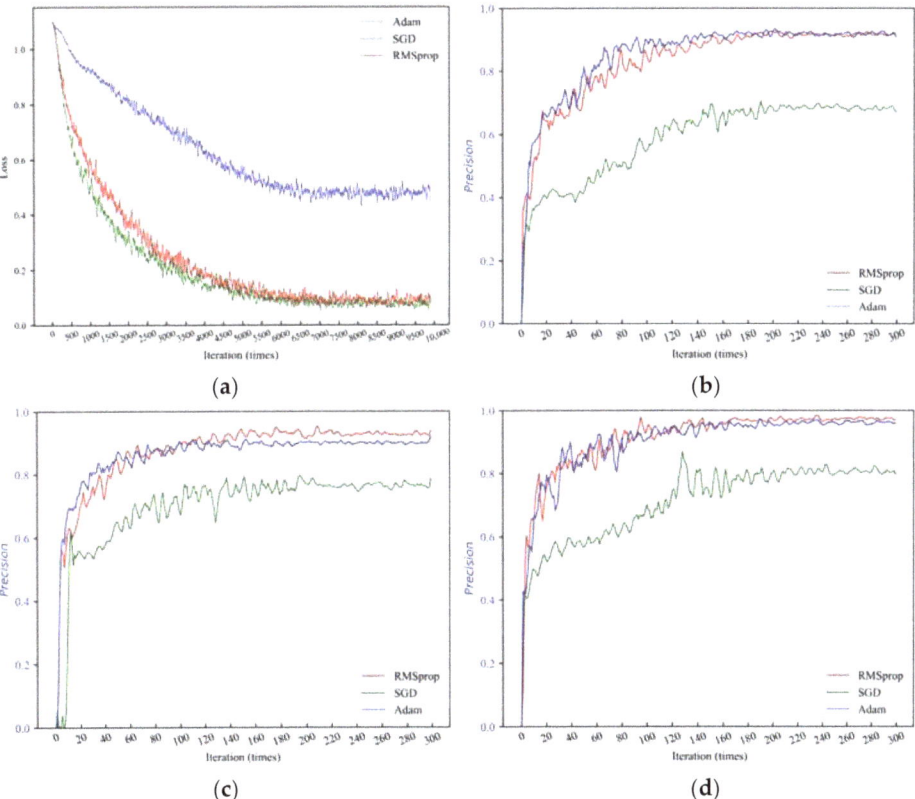

**Figure 23.** (a) Training loss of ShuffleNetV2 under three optimizers; (b) results of metamorphic rock under three optimizers; (c) results of sedimentary rock; and (d) results of volcanic rock.

As stated in Figure 24, regarding the SGD optimizer, the number of samples identified as metamorphic rocks was 206, of which a total of 22 samples were sedimentary rocks and 46 samples were volcanic rocks. Hence, the accuracy for the classification of metamorphic rocks was only 67%, as listed in Table 9. Furthermore, the precision of the other two types of rock was also not good enough based on the confusion matrix result for the SGD optimizer.

In contrast, the RMSprop and Adam optimizers showed the same effect with an average accuracy higher than 90%.

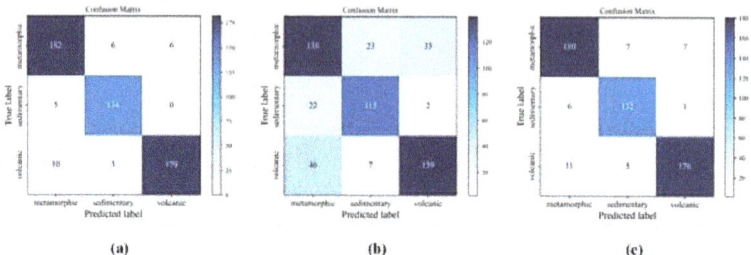

Figure 24. Confusion matrixes: (a) RMSprop optimizer; (b) SGD optimizer; (c) Adam optimizer.

Table 9. Detailed classification results for all rock types.

| Rock Types | Evaluation | Lambda Decay Schedule | | |
|---|---|---|---|---|
| | | Adam | SGD | RMSprop |
| Metamorphic | P | 91% | 67% | 92% |
| | F1-scores | 0.92 | 0.69 | 0.93 |
| Sedimentary | P | 92% | 79% | 94% |
| | F1-scores | 0.93 | 0.81 | 0.95 |
| Volcanic | P | 96% | 80% | 97% |
| | F1-scores | 0.94 | 0.76 | 0.95 |

Likewise, according to Table 9, the average classification accuracy of the ShuffleNetV2 model with the employment of two learning-rate decay modes for three types of rock was 88.3%, 90.7% and 95.3% and 83.3%, 88.3%, and 91.0%, respectively. The maximum difference was the result for metamorphic rock, which exhibited a 5% gap, followed by volcanic rock (4.3%) and sedimentary rock (2.4%). Therefore, the performance of the ShuffleNetV2 model was sensitive to the learning-rate decay modes. Additionally, it is worth noting that the choice of optimizer greatly impacted the model accuracy for the ShuffleNetV2 network.

## 4. Discussion

Based on the above experiments, it is worth affirming that CNNs achieve excellent performance in image classification. Second, the average classification precision of the model with three optimizers using the cosine learning-rate decay method was better than that of the lambda decay mode, as shown in Figure 25. The circular dotted line represents the results of models with the utilization of the cosine learning-rate decay schedule, and the square solid line shows the lambda decay method. It is clear that the circular dotted lines are almost always above the solid lines.

However, the performance of the four models also varied. GoogLeNet and VGG16 were more robust than the latter two networks. From our perspective, both the MobileNetV2 and ShuffleNetV2 networks consist of a depth-wise separable convolution module, which has a weak ability to extract features from microscopic images, which then affects the model's performance. Therefore, GoogLeNet and VGG16 were considered the best models in our research.

Additionally, Figure 26 shows GoogLeNet and VGG16's classification precision for the three types of rock with the use of Adam, SGD and RMSprop. It could be concluded that the classification effect of the model trained with the SGD optimizer was worse than that of the other two optimizers for both GoogLeNet and VGG16, which is also basically consistent with the conclusion of [30].

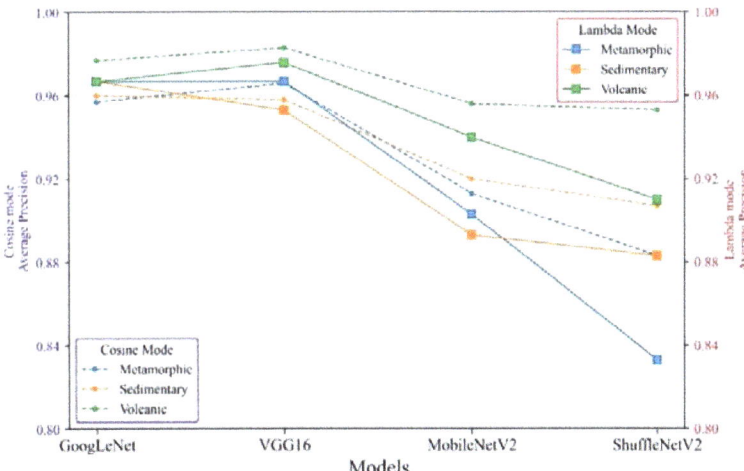

**Figure 25.** Model average precision under two learning-rate decay modes. The left dotted line indicates cosine learning-rate decay result, and the right solid line is the result of lambda.

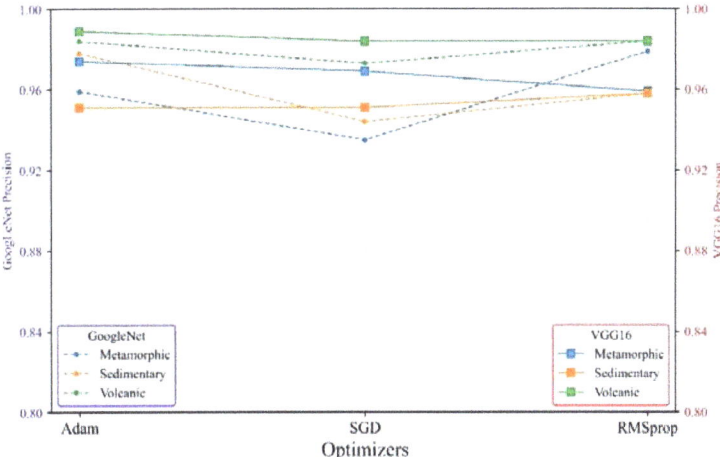

**Figure 26.** Model precision under three optimizers. The dotted line is GoogLeNet, and the solid line is VGG16.

In summary, the best options for the intelligent classification of rock thin-section images are the cosine decay mode, RMSprop optimizer, and VGG16 classification model. The classification accuracies of VGG16 for the three types of rock were 96.7%, 95.3%, and 98.6%, which are higher than that of Harinie et al. [54] (the average accuracy for the three types of rock is 87%) and He et al. [37] (the average precision of the model is 90.89%). Thus, the training guidelines proposed in this paper are proven to be practical and effective.

## 5. Experimental Verification

This section presents supplementary quantitative evaluation results of the best classification model on another dataset. A total of 14 images were collected from an identification report made by the Changsha Research Institute of Mining and Metallurgy (CRIMM) of China, which did not exist in our training dataset. Specific information about the data is listed in Table 10.

Table 10. Detailed descriptions of the validated datasets.

| Class | Subclass | Numbers | |
|---|---|---|---|
| | | Subclass Number | Microscopic Image Number |
| Metamorphic Rock | Dolomite Marble | 2 | 4 |
| | Marble | 2 | |
| Sedimentary Rock | Quartz Sandstone | 2 | 4 |
| | Feldspar Sandstone | 2 | |
| Volcanic Rock | Biotite Granite | 2 | 6 |
| | Basalt | 2 | |
| | Quartz Diorite | 2 | |
| | | | 14 |

Figure 27 shows the model classification results of some samples. It could be concluded that the confidence scores for the overall classification were relatively high, as shown in Figure 27. Figure 28 indicates the confusion matrix of the final classification results for all datasets. Five images were identified as metamorphic rock (four were truly classified, and one volcanic rock image was misidentified). Another volcanic rock was classified as sedimentary rock, and the remaining four volcanic rock images were correctly classified. Therefore, two images were misclassified among fourteen images, and the accuracy was 85.7%. It is indicated that the trained model also generalizes well to the other dataset.

**Figure 27.** Classification results of other data: (**a**,**e**) metamorphic rock classification results; (**b**,**d**) sedimentary rock classification results; (**c**,**f**) volcanic rock classification results.

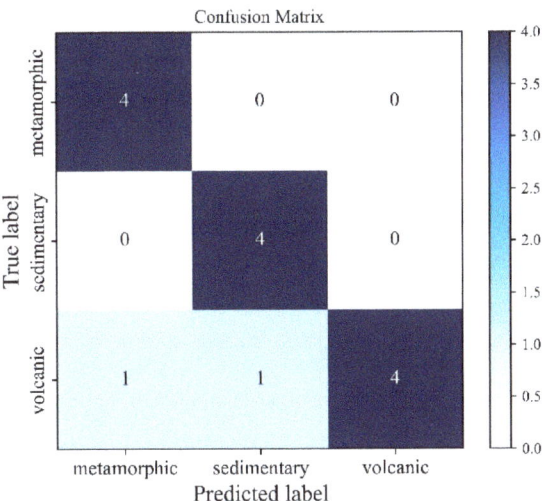

**Figure 28.** Confusion matrix of the final classification results.

## 6. Limitations and Future Studies

Accurate rock thin-section image classification for various datasets is important in geotechnical engineering. However, in this paper, only a small number of samples from the dataset were evaluated, and the experimental studies were conducted only in terms of comparing accuracy, without analyzing the differences in size and speed of the different models [55,56]. In the future, more data should be considered in the database. Moreover, the efficiency of the model should be comprehensively evaluated, and technologies related to model compression could be studied.

## 7. Conclusions

In this paper, comprehensive experimental studies on the robustness of deep learning-based algorithms for the classification of rock thin-section images was carried out, and the conclusions are summarized as follows:

(1) Four CNN models for rock thin-section image classification were trained under two learning-rate decay schedules. The differences in the average classification precision between GoogLeNet and VGG16 were within one percent in both learning-rate decay modes. For MobileNetV2, the average identification precision for three types of rock using the cosine learning-rate decay mode were higher than that of lambda: 1%, 2.7%, and 1.6%, respectively. In addition, the difference for ShuffleNetV2 was the most obvious. The classification results for three types of rock with the cosine decay mode were 5%, 2.4%, and 4.3% higher than that of lambda decay mode. Thus, the cosine learning-rate decay mode is the best option.

(2) GoogLeNet and VGG16 exhibited a more stable performance and achieved a classification precision higher than 96%. The average precision of MobileNetV2 was 2~7% lower than that of GoogLeNet and VGG16. In addition, the result of ShuffleNetV2 was unacceptable, especially for metamorphic and sedimentary rocks. The maximum accuracy difference for the classification of the two kinds of rocks was up to 13.3% and 8.4% compared to GoogLeNet.

(3) The importance of optimizers during the neural network training process was evaluated. In general, the RMSprop and Adam optimizers had a better effect on model training. For GoogLeNet, the final model precision with the use of the RMSprop and Adam optimizers was 1~3% higher than that of SGD. The VGG16 network maintained almost the same result for the three optimization algorithms.

(4) The best options for the intelligent classification of rock thin-section images are the cosine decay mode, RMSprop optimizer, and VGG16 classification model, which could provide an alternative program for similar image classification tasks.

(5) The trained model generalizes well to another dataset, which could reach 85.7% classification precision.

**Author Contributions:** Conceptualization, D.L. and J.Z.; methodology, J.Z.; software, J.Z.; validation, J.M.; investigation, J.M.; resources, D.L.; writing—original draft preparation, J.Z. and D.L.; writing—review and editing, D.L. and J.M.; visualization, J.Z.; supervision, D.L.; project administration, D.L.; funding acquisition, D.L. All authors have read and agreed to the published version of the manuscript.

**Funding:** This research was supported by the National Natural Science Foundation of China (Grant No.:52074349).

**Institutional Review Board Statement:** Not applicable.

**Informed Consent Statement:** Not applicable.

**Data Availability Statement:** Not applicable.

**Acknowledgments:** We are also very grateful to XM, Hu of Nanjing University, China for sharing these valuable data.

**Conflicts of Interest:** The authors declare no conflict of interest.

# References

1. Shao, J.; Chi, G.; Shi, Y. Application of X-ray powder crystal diffraction method in the identification and classification of gneiss. *Geol. Resour.* **2020**, *29*, 490–496+453.
2. Chi, G.; Wu, Y.; Wang, H.; Chen, Y.; Wang, D. The application of X-ray fluorescence spectrometry in the identification and classification of marble. *Rock Miner. Test.* **2018**, *37*, 43–49.
3. Zhang, Q.; Jin, W.; Li, C.; Wang, Y. Revisiting the new classification of granitic rocks based on whole-rock Sr and Yb contents: Index. *Acta Petrol. Sin.* **2010**, *26*, 985–1015.
4. Zhang, Q.; Jin, W.; Li, C.; Wang, Y. On the classification of granitic rocks based on whole-rock Sr and Yb concentrations III: Practice. *Acta Petrol. Sin.* **2010**, *26*, 3431–3455.
5. Shaaban, S.M.; Tawfik, S.Z. Classification of volcanic rocks based on rough set theory. *Eng. Technol. Appl. Sci. Res.* **2020**, *10*, 5501–5504. [CrossRef]
6. Yin, X.; Liu, Q.; Hao, H.; Wang, Z.; Huang, K. FMI image based rock structure classification using classifier combination. *Neural Comput. Appl.* **2011**, *20*, 955–963. [CrossRef]
7. Młynarczuk, M.; Górszczyk, A.; Ślipek, B. The application of pattern recognition in the automatic classification of microscopic rock images. *Comput. Geosci.* **2013**, *60*, 126–133. [CrossRef]
8. Marmo, R.; Amodio, S.; Tagliaferri, R.; Ferreri, V.; Longo, G. Textural identification of carbonate rocks by image processing and neural network: Methodology proposal and examples. *Comput. Geosci.* **2005**, *31*, 649–659. [CrossRef]
9. Singh, N.; Singh, T.; Tiwary, A.; Sarkar, K. Textural identification of basaltic rock mass using image processing and neural network. *Comput. Geosic.* **2010**, *14*, 301–310. [CrossRef]
10. Chatterjee, S. Vision-based rock-type classification of limestone using multi-class support vector machine. *Appl. Intell.* **2013**, *39*, 14–27. [CrossRef]
11. Patel, A.K.; Chatterjee, S. Computer vision-based limestone rock-type classification using probabilistic neural network. *Geosci. Front.* **2016**, *7*, 53–60. [CrossRef]
12. Tian, Y.; Guo, C.; Lv, L.; Li, F.; Gao, C.; Liu, Y. Multi-color space rock shin-section image classification with SVM. In Proceedings of the 2019 IEEE 8th Joint International Information Technology and Artificial Intelligence Conference (ITAIC), Chongqing, China, 24–26 May 2019; pp. 571–574.
13. Khorram, F.; Memarian, H.; Tokhmechi, B.; Soltanianzadeh, H. Limestone chemical components estimation using image processing and pattern recognition techniques. *J. Min. Env.* **2011**, *2*, 49–58.
14. Lecun, Y.; Bottou, L.; Bengio, Y.; Haffner, P. Gradient-based learning applied to document recognition. *Proc. IEEE* **1998**, *86*, 2278–2324. [CrossRef]
15. Bochkovskiy, A.; Wang, C.-Y.; Liao, H.-Y.M. Yolov4: Optimal speed and accuracy of object detection. *arXiv* **2020**, arXiv:2004.10934.
16. Farhadi, A.; Redmon, J. Yolov3: An incremental improvement. *arXiv* **2018**, arXiv:1804.02767.
17. Liu, W.; Anguelov, D.; Erhan, D.; Szegedy, C.; Reed, S.; Fu, C.-Y.; Berg, A.C. SSD: Single shot MultiBox detector. In *Computer Vision—ECCV 2016, Proceedings of the European Conference on Computer Vision, Amsterdam, The Netherlands, 11–14 October 2016*; Springer International Publishing: Cham, Switzerland, 2016; pp. 21–37.

18. Redmon, J.; Divvala, S.; Girshick, R.; Farhadi, A. You only look once: Unified, real-time object detection. In Proceedings of the IEEE Conference on Computer Vision and Pattern Recognition (CVPR), Las Vegas, NV, USA, 27–30 June 2016; pp. 779–788.
19. Ren, S.; He, K.; Girshick, R.; Sun, J. Faster r-cnn: Towards real-time object detection with region proposal networks. *Adv. Neural Inf. Process. Syst.* **2015**, *28*, 91–99. [CrossRef]
20. Schroff, F.; Kalenichenko, D.; Philbin, J. Facenet: A unified embedding for face recognition and clustering. In Proceedings of the 2015 IEEE Conference on Computer Vision and Pattern Recognition (CVPR), Boston, MA, USA, 8–12 June 2015; pp. 815–823.
21. Chowdhury, G.G. Natural language processing. *Annu. Rev. Inf. Sci. Technol.* **2003**, *37*, 51–89. [CrossRef]
22. Hirschberg, J.; Manning, C.D. Advances in natural language processing. *Science* **2015**, *349*, 261–266. [CrossRef]
23. Khelifi, L.; Mignotte, M. Deep learning for change detection in remote sensing images: Comprehensive review and meta-analysis. *IEEE Access* **2020**, *8*, 126385–126400. [CrossRef]
24. Zhu, X.X.; Tuia, D.; Mou, L.; Xia, G.-S.; Zhang, L.; Xu, F.; Fraundorfer, F. Deep learning in remote sensing: A comprehensive review and list of resources. *IEEE Geosci. Remote Sens. Mag.* **2017**, *5*, 8–36. [CrossRef]
25. Huang, Y.; Chen, Y. Autonomous driving with deep learning: A survey of state-of-art technologies. *arXiv* **2020**, arXiv:2006.06091.
26. Albarqouni, S.; Baur, C.; Achilles, F.; Belagiannis, V.; Demirci, S.; Navab, N. Aggnet: Deep learning from crowds for mitosis detection in breast cancer histology images. *IEEE Trans. Med. Imaging* **2016**, *35*, 1313–1321. [CrossRef] [PubMed]
27. Yang, L.; Zhang, Y.; Chen, J.; Zhang, S.; Chen, D.Z. Suggestive annotation: A deep active learning framework for biomedical image segmentation. In Proceedings of the International Conference on Medical Image Computing and Computer-Assisted Intervention, Quebec City, QC, Canada, 10–14 September 2017; pp. 399–407.
28. Zhu, W. *Deep Learning for Automated Medical Image Analysis*; University of California: Irvine, CA, USA, 2019.
29. Li, N.; Hao, H.; Gu, Q.; Wang, D.; Hu, X. A transfer learning method for automatic identification of sandstone microscopic images. *Comput. Geosci.* **2017**, *103*, 111–121. [CrossRef]
30. Polat, O.; Polat, A.; Ekici, T. Automatic classification of volcanic rocks from thin section images using transfer learning networks. *Neural Comput. Appl.* **2021**, *33*, 11531–11540. [CrossRef]
31. Anjos, C.; Avila, M.; Vasconcelos, A.; Neta, A.; Landau, L. Deep learning for lithological classification of carbonate rock micro-CT images. *Comput. Geosci.* **2021**, *25*, 971–983. [CrossRef]
32. Samet, R.; Amrahov, S.E.; Ziroglu, A.H. Fuzzy Rule-Based Image Segmentation technique for rock thin section images. In Proceedings of the 2012 3rd International Conference on Image Processing Theory, Tools and Applications (IPTA), Istanbul, Turkey, 15–18 October 2012; pp. 402–406.
33. Yang, H.Z.; Xu, D.Y. Research and Analysis of Image Enhancement Algorithm in the Classification of Rock Thin Section Images. In Proceedings of the 2021 3rd International Conference on Intelligent Control, Measurement and Signal Processing and Intelligent Oil Field (ICMSP), Xi'an, China, 23–25 July 2021; pp. 125–128.
34. Xu, Y.; Dai, Z.; Luo, Y. Research on Application of Image Enhancement Technology in Automatic Recognition of Rock Thin Section. *IOP Conf. Ser. Earth Environ. Sci.* **2020**, *605*, 012024. [CrossRef]
35. Su, C.; Xu, S.-j.; Zhu, K.-y.; Zhang, X.-c. Rock classification in petrographic thin section images based on concatenated convolutional neural networks. *Earth Sci. Inform.* **2020**, *13*, 1477–1484. [CrossRef]
36. Gao, R.; Ji, C.; Qiang, X.; Cheng, G.; Liu, Y. Rock Thin Section Image Classification Research from Shallow Network to Deep Neural Network. In Proceedings of the 2016 International Conference on Education, Management and Computer Science (EMCS 2016), Shenyang, China, 1–3 January 2016; pp. 620–625.
37. Ma, H.; Han, G.; Peng, L.; Zhu, L.; Shu, J. Rock Thin Sections Identification Based on Improved Squeeze-and-Excitation Networks Model. *Comput. Geosci.* **2021**, *152*, 104780. [CrossRef]
38. Hu, J.; Shen, L.; Sun, G. Squeeze-and-Excitation Networks. In Proceedings of the IEEE Conference on Computer Vision and Pattern Recognition, Providence, RI, USA, 18–21 June 2018.
39. Chen, G.J.; Li, P.S. Rock thin-section image classification based on residual neural network. In Proceedings of the 2021 6th International Conference on Intelligent Computing and Signal Processing (ICSP), Xi'an, China, 9–11 April 2021; pp. 521–524.
40. Li, D.; Zhao, J.; Liu, Z. A Novel Method of Multitype Hybrid Rock Lithology Classification Based on Convolutional Neural Networks. *Sensors* **2022**, *22*, 1574. [CrossRef]
41. Liu, X.; Wang, H.; Jing, H.; Shao, A.; Wang, L. Research on intelligent identification of rock types based on faster R-CNN method. *IEEE Access* **2020**, *8*, 21804–21812. [CrossRef]
42. Xu, Z.; Ma, W.; Lin, P.; Shi, H.; Pan, D.; Liu, T. Deep learning of rock images for intelligent lithology identification. *Comput. Geosci.* **2021**, *154*, 104799. [CrossRef]
43. Lai, W.; Jiang, J.; Qiu, J.; Yu, J.; Hu, X. A photomicrograph dataset of rocks for petrology teaching at Nanjing University. Science Data Bank. Available online: https://www.scidb.cn/en/ (accessed on 10 May 2022).
44. Goodfellow, I.; Bengio, Y.; Courville, A. *Deep Learning*; MIT Press: Cambridge, MA, USA, 2016; pp. 216–261.
45. Fukushima, K. Artificial vision by deep CNN neocognitron. *IEEE Trans. Syst. Man Cybern. Syst.* **2021**, *51*, 76–90. [CrossRef]
46. Szegedy, C.; Liu, W.; Jia, Y.; Sermanet, P.; Reed, S.; Anguelov, D.; Erhan, D.; Vanhoucke, V.; Rabinovich, A. Going Deeper With Convolutions. In Proceedings of the IEEE Conference on Computer Vision and Pattern Recognition (CVPR), Boston, MA, USA, 7–12 June 2015; pp. 1–9.
47. Simonyan, K.; Zisserman, A. Very Deep Convolutional Networks for Large-Scale Image Recognition. In Proceedings of the 3rd.International Conference on Learning Representations (ICLR), San Diego, CA, USA, 7–9 May 2015.

48. Qassim, H.; Verma, A.; Feinzimer, D. Compressed residual-VGG16 CNN model for big data places image recognition. In Proceedings of the 2018 IEEE 8th Annual Computing and Communication Workshop and Conference (CCWC), Las Vegas, NV, USA, 8–10 January 2018; pp. 169–175.
49. Sandler, M.; Howard, A.; Zhu, M.; Zhmoginov, A.; Chen, L.C. MobileNetV2: Inverted Residuals and Linear Bottlenecks. In Proceedings of the IEEE Conference on Computer Vision and Pattern Recognition (CVPR), Salt Lake City, UT, USA, 18–23 June 2018; pp. 4510–4520.
50. He, K.; Zhang, X.; Ren, S.; Sun, J. Deep residual learning for image recognition. In Proceedings of the IEEE Conference on Computer Vision and Pattern Recognition (CVPR), Las Vegas, NV, USA, 26 June–1 July 2016; pp. 770–778.
51. Ma, N.; Zhang, X.; Zheng, H.-T.; Sun, J. ShuffleNet V2: Practical Guidelines for Efficient CNN Architecture Design. In Proceedings of the European Conference on Computer Vision (ECCV), Munich, Germany, 8–14 September 2018; pp. 122–138.
52. Loshchilov, I.; Hutter, F. Sgdr: Stochastic gradient descent with warm restarts. In Proceedings of the International Conference on Learning Representations (ICLR-2017), Toulon, France, 24–26 April 2017.
53. Goyal, P.; Dollár, P.; Girshick, R.; Noordhuis, P.; Wesolowski, L.; Kyrola, A.; Tulloch, A.; Jia, Y.; He, K. Accurate, Large Minibatch SGD: Training ImageNet in 1 Hour. *arXiv* **2017**, arXiv:1706.02677.
54. Harinie, T.; Janani, C.I.; Sathya, B.S.; Raju, S.; Abhaikumar, V. Classification of rock textures. In Proceedings of the International Conference on Information Systems Design and Intelligent Applications, Visakhapatnam, India, 5–7 January 2012; pp. 887–895.
55. Zejia, Z.; Zhu, L.; Nagar, A.; Kyungmo, P. Compact deep neural networks for device based image classification. In Proceedings of the 2015 IEEE International Conference on Multimedia and Expo Workshops (ICMEW), Turin, Italy, 29 June–3 July 2015; pp. 1–6.
56. Arie, W.; Choong, J.; Kaushalya, M.; Tsuyoshi, M. Towards robust compressed convolutional neural networks. In Proceedings of the 2019 IEEE International Conference on Big Data and Smart Computing (BigComp), Kyoto, Japan, 27 February–2 March 2019; pp. 1–8.

*Article*

# Characterization of 3D Displacement and Stress Fields in Coal Based on CT Scans

Qi Li [1], Zhen Li [2,*], Peng Li [1], Ruikai Pan [1] and Qingqing Zhang [3]

[1] Department of Mining Engineering, Shanxi Institute of Energy, Jinzhong 030600, China; liq@sxie.edu.cn (Q.L.); lipeng@sxie.edu.cn (P.L.); panrk@cqu.edu.cn (R.P.)
[2] College of Safety and Emergency Management Engineering, Taiyuan University of Technology, Taiyuan 030024, China
[3] State Key Laboratory of Coal Mine Safety Technology, CCTEG Shenyang Research Institute, Fushun 113000, China; zhangqingqing@syccri.com
* Correspondence: lizhen@tyut.edu.cn; Tel.: +86-183-3470-6610

**Abstract:** Computed tomography (CT) scans were performed on samples of an outburst-prone coal seam at different loading stages. The area and roundness of the CT images were used to quantify the degree of the coal macroscopic deformation under different loads. A spatial matching algorithm was used to calculate the three-dimensional (3D) displacement fields of different regions of interest (ROIs, containing primary fractures, minerals, and only coal) under different loads. The presence of fractures and minerals were found to promote and inhibit displacement, respectively, and the 3D displacement field data followed a normal distribution. A meshfree numerical simulation was used to determine the 3D maximum principal stress, shear stress and displacement fields under different loads. The following results were obtained: fractures and minerals significantly affect the stress state and displacement field distribution features, the maximum principal stresses and shear stresses in different matrices differ significantly, and the presence of minerals and fractures induce a prevalent shear stress in coal and make coal prone to stress concentration.

**Keywords:** CT scan; 3D displacement field; 3D stress field; meshfree numerical simulation

**MSC:** 74-05

## 1. Introduction

Coal is typically anisotropic, and high sample dispersion makes it challenging to determine the deformation features and stress field patterns of raw coal samples. Considering the importance of the stress and deformation fields in analysing coal stability, a computed tomography (CT) scan with a loading function was used to determine the deformation features of coal under different loads in this study. A novel numerical simulation method was applied to a three-dimensional (3D) CT model to analyse the coal stress state.

A variety of experimental and theoretical methods have been used to investigate the internal structure and deformation features of coal over the past few years [1–7], which has advanced the prevention and control of related hazards. CT scans enable the noncontact nondestructive testing of samples and can be combined with 3D reconstruction techniques to quantitatively analyse the coal mesostructure. Kawakata et al. [8] first used CT to scan the damage state of rock after triaxial loading but the samples were not loaded during the scanning process. Cao et al. [9] analysed the fracture evolution and seismic response features of hydraulic fracturing under triaxial loading conditions and performed CT scans to quantitatively characterise pre-existing and hydraulic fractures. Fan et al. [10] performed threshold segmentation on CT scan data and statistically analysed the pore size distribution, throat radius, throat length, and coordination number of the pore network model. Li et al. [11] experimentally analysed the pore features of coal samples

with different bursting proneness by low-temperature nitrogen adsorption and desorption, scanning electron microscopy (SEM) and CT. The results showed that stress exacerbates the complexity of the pore structure. Li et al. [12] used CT to visualize the evolution of the fracture features of coal samples under uniaxial and triaxial loading conditions. Quantitative characterisation of the fractures demonstrated that the grey value, fracture volume and CT porosity can be used to quantitatively evaluate the degree of damage to coal. Lu et al. [13] found using CT scans on coal samples under different load conditions that the expansion of primary fractures and the development of new fractures increase the coal connectivity. Liu et al. [14] analysed the porosity of coal through CT scans and NMR experiments and quantitatively characterised the fractal dimension. Tao et al. [15] analysed the porosity and fracture heterogeneity of coal using a variety of experimental methods (SEM, carbon dioxide and nitrogen adsorption, and CT scans) and proposed an index to quantitatively predict coal macrolithotypes. Wang et al. [16–18] used CT scans to analyse the pore structure and seepage features of coal, which were then used to conduct a dynamic water injection simulation analysis. Wu et al. analysed the fractal features of a coal fracture network to find that the porosity is exponentially related to fractal dimension. Zhang et al. [19] used various experimental methods to perform a multiscale characterisation of coal samples of different ranks. The results of the aforementioned studies have revealed the variation features of fractures under stress and the corresponding influence on gas migration.

Wang et al. [20] analysed two-dimensional (2D) CT scan images of coal samples as well as 3D reconstruction models to find that the confining pressure and presence of minerals have significant effects on the features of fracture propagation. Mao et al. [21] compared digital volumetric speckle photographs with the deformation results obtained from CT images to determine the deformation features of coal at different loading stages. Sampath et al. [22] generated a 2D fracture network from CT imaging to study the gas flow and coal deformation process. Roslin et al. [23] used SEM and CT to analyse pore structure and carried out numerical simulation based on the reconstruction model.

The 3D deformation features of coal during different loading processes are investigated in this study. A feature point spatial matching algorithm is used to calculate and analyse the displacement field. A meshfree numerical simulation of the 3D reconstruction model is performed to analyse the 3D stress field and the stress states of different matrices (coal, minerals, and regions near fractures).

## 2. Materials and Methods

### 2.1. Sample Preparation

The studied coal samples were taken from the no. 3 coal seam of the Sihe coal mine in Shanxi Province, China. The coal seam is located at the southern end of the Qinshui coalfield and presents an outburst risk. The coal samples were cut into $\varphi 25$ mm $\times$ h50 mm cylinders, of which the end faces were polished to ensure parallelism.

### 2.2. Experimental Device and Methods

The experimental device consists of a microfocus CT scan system and a triaxial stress-displacement test system. A Vtomex L300 CT scan system with an observation resolution of up to 500 nm was used. The triaxial stress-displacement test system can perform uniaxial and triaxial loading tests on $\varphi 25$ mm $\times$ h50 mm samples, with a maximum axial compression of 100 kN, a maximum confining pressure of 30 MPa, and a loading rate range of 0.1–3 mm/min. The attenuation coefficient of the X-ray intensity and the density of the material satisfy the following equation [24]:

$$I' = I_o \exp(-\mu x) \quad (1)$$

$$\mu x = \ln(I_o / I') \quad (2)$$

$$\int \mu \mathrm{d}l = \ln(I_o / I') \quad (3)$$

where $I_o$ is the initial intensity of the X-ray; $I'$ is the intensity of the X-ray after passing through the material; $\mu$ is the attenuation coefficient of the material; and $x$ is the penetration distance of the ray.

Three sets of phased CT scan tests were performed on the Sihe coal samples under the loading process, with an axial loading rate of 0.2 mm/min and a CT scan resolution of 30 μm. The axial stress–strain data were recorded, and the axial compression was maintained constant during the CT scan.

### 2.3. Boundary Delineation of 3D CT Model

Figure 1 presents CT images showing highly discernible minerals inside the coal. Using the minerals as feature points, the Z-axis position in the CT images was recorded to delineate the upper and lower boundaries of the 3D model. Threshold segmentation was performed on the CT data to determine the boundaries of the 3D model, thus accurately delineating the range of the 3D CT model at each stage.

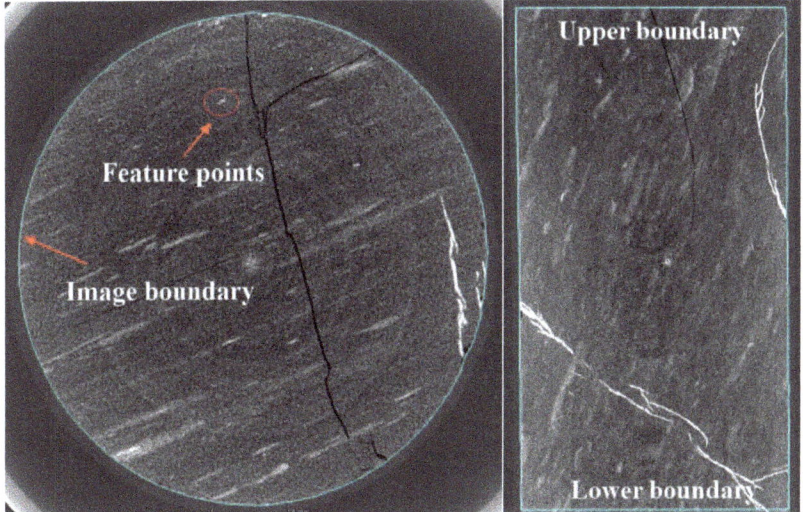

**Figure 1.** Boundary determination of 3D model.

### 2.4. Displacement Field Algorithm and ROI Delineation

The feature points were used to select a region of interest (ROI) for the 3D model at each stage, and the 3D displacement field was calculated. A spatial image matching algorithm was used to measure the displacement field of the 3D ROI under different loading conditions with high precision. The ROI was determined to be a cuboid of size 4 mm × 4 mm × 2 mm, considering the computational burden, the size of the fractures and minerals and the excessive number of voxels (more than 1 billion) in the 3D model. Figure 2 shows the selected ROIs, where ROI1, ROI2, and ROI3 correspond to regions containing primary fractures, coal only, and minerals, respectively.

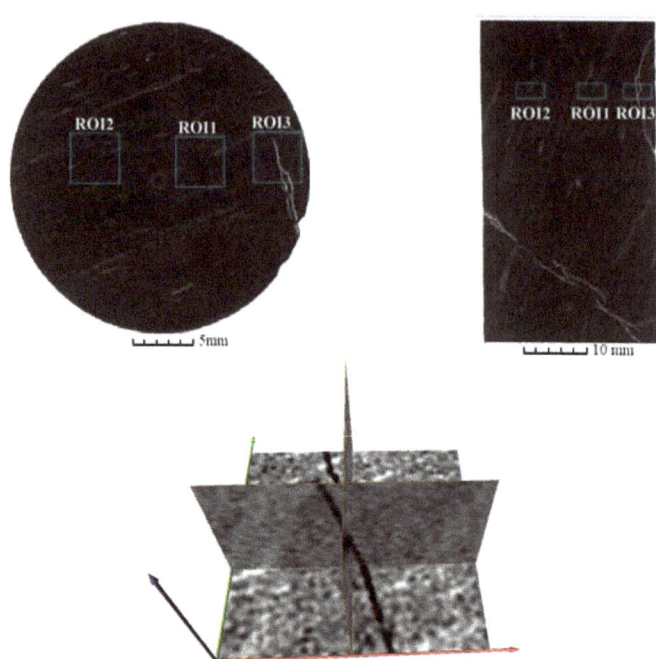

**Figure 2.** Positions of ROI1, ROI2, and ROI3 (**top left**: top view of CT image; **top right**: side view of CT image) and slices in 3 dimensions of ROI1 (**bottom**).

## 3. Results

### 3.1. Deformation and Failure Features

Considering the large volume of data, Sihe sample 1 was analysed in this study.

Figure 3 shows clear anisotropic features for the failure of the sample along the Z-axis at the post-peak stage. Figure 4 shows that the distribution of primary fractures and minerals in the sample had a determining effect on the failure features. Considering the post-peak 3D model in conjunction with the CT images in Figures 3 and 4 shows that a slip instability occurred in the sample along the mineral region. The yellow circles in Figure 4 show the damage in the range containing minerals.

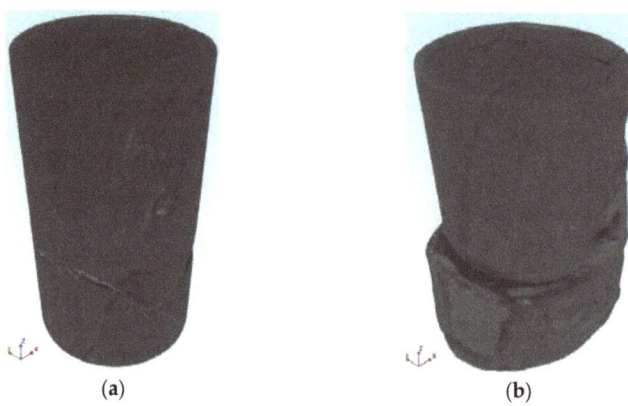

**Figure 3.** 3D reconstruction model at the initial (**a**) and post-peak stages (**b**).

**Figure 4.** Vertical CT slice at the initial (a) and post-peak (stage 8) stages (b).

Figure 5 shows the stress–strain curve of Sihe sample 1 at the loading stages corresponding to CT scans and the red numbers correspond to the stages of CT scans.

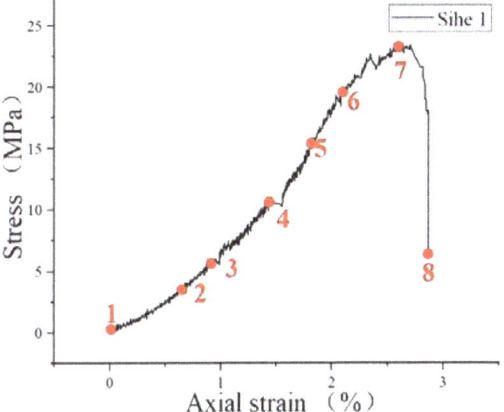

**Figure 5.** Stress–strain curve and corresponding stage of CT scan.

The CT images of the upper and lower end faces and the middle position at each stage were analysed to determine the changes in area and roundness.

The roundness is calculated as follows:

$$R = \frac{4S}{\pi \times L_{major}^2} \qquad (4)$$

where $S$ is the image area and $L_{major}$ is the length of the major axis of the smallest circumscribed ellipse fitted to the image.

The roundness quantifies the change in the shape of a CT image, indicating the degree of closeness to a perfect circle. A roundness of unity indicates that the image is a perfect circle. In Figure 6, the points of each curve correspond to the loading stage (red dots) in Figure 5.

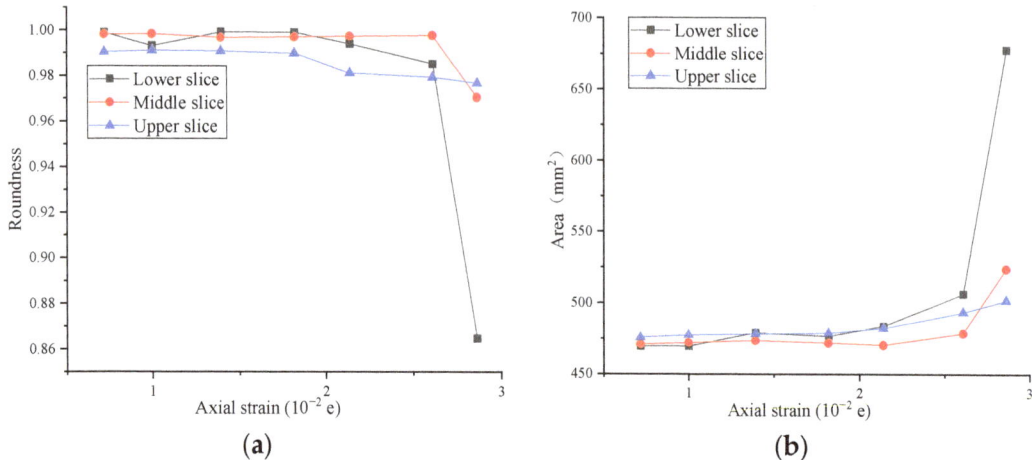

**Figure 6.** Relationship between axial strain and roundness (**a**) and area (**b**) of CT slice.

The calculated roundness was a monotonically decreasing function, and the change in the roundness was generally consistent with the change in the area. The shape and area of each part exhibited a large degree of variation during the instability. The coefficient of variation of the image roundness was calculated to be 0.0473, 0.0097, and 0.0061 for the three slices, that is, the roundness of the lower slice was significantly larger than those of the middle and upper slices. The anisotropy of the deformation and failure features of the sample were very pronounced at the macroscopic scale.

*3.2. Results for 3D Displacement Field*

The ROIs for each scanning stage were compared with that of the initial state by using the digital volume correlation module of the Avizo software (i.e., scanning stage 1). Seven sets of calculation results were obtained for each ROI, as shown in Figure 7. Figure 7a corresponds to the displacement field of the second loading stage, and so on.

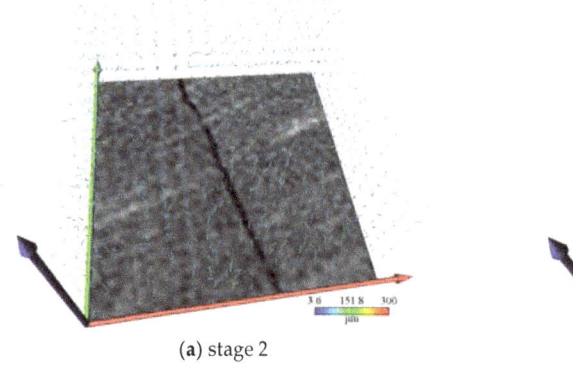
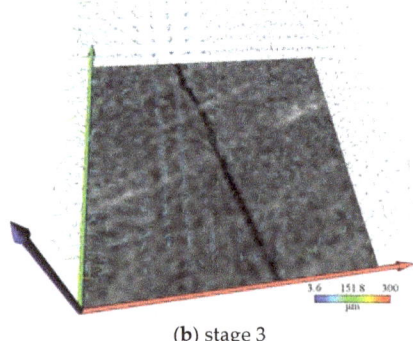

(**a**) stage 2   (**b**) stage 3

**Figure 7.** *Cont.*

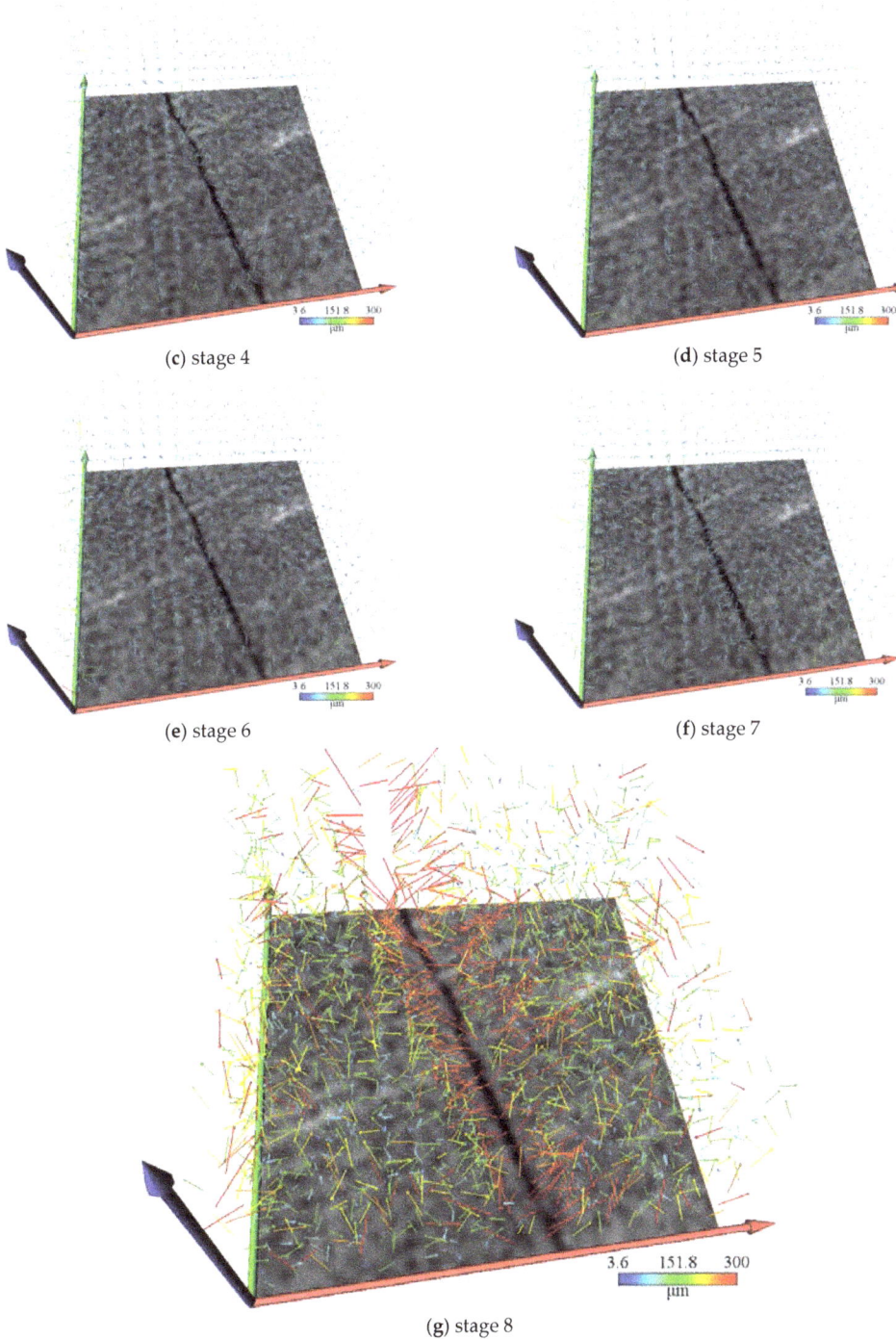

**Figure 7.** Calculated 3D displacement field at different stages of ROI1.

Figure 7a shows the displacement field at the compaction stage: the overall displacement was low, and an analysis of the vector direction shows that the transverse displacement was larger than the longitudinal displacement. Comparing Figure 7b with Figure 7a show that the vector angle was closer to the longitudinal direction than the transverse direction, indicating a significant compression effect of the load. Compared to the displacement field in Figure 7a,b, the results in Figure 7c,d show little change, whereas those in Figure 7e show a pronounced change. The norm of the vector in and near the fracture region is significantly larger than that in fracture-free regions, indicating a significant increase in the displacement in the fracture region. Figure 7f corresponds to the peak stress state: a large displacement was distributed over a significantly wide range, including regions near the fractures and at the boundary. This result shows that under the peak strength loading, the internal displacement of the coal sample increased and was distributed over a wide range. The most significant change in the vector field is shown in Figure 7g: the norm of the vector field increases dramatically, especially over the fracture region and the nearby area, where the displacement generally exceeds 300 µm. The displacement in fracture-free regions generally remains larger than 150 µm.

The displacement fields of ROI2 and ROI3 were calculated, and the post-peak displacement fields were comparatively analysed. Figure 8 shows significant differences among the post-peak displacement field features of the different ROIs. The displacement field of ROI2 (basically coal) was most uniform, with a displacement of approximately 150 µm and large displacements in only small well-defined regions. The distribution features of the displacement field of ROI3 (containing minerals) were similar to those of ROI1 at the corresponding stages: the displacement was large over the region near the minerals, and smaller in the nearby coal region.

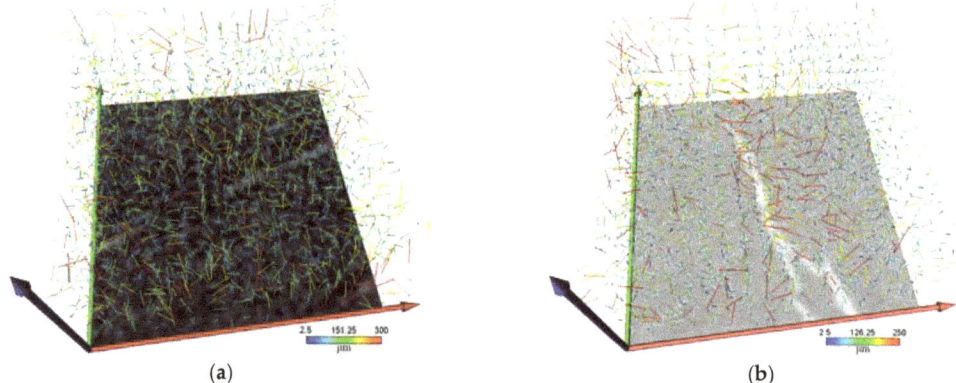

**Figure 8.** Calculated 3D displacement field at the post-peak stage (stage 8 in Figure 5) for ROI2 (a) and ROI3 (b).

Figures 9–11 are the statistical results of the displacement at each stage of ROI1, ROI2, and ROI3.

A statistical analysis showed that the displacement field of each ROI follows a normal distribution. The displacement fields for ROI1-3 were fitted to obtain the following equation:

$$y = y_0 + \frac{Ae^{\frac{-4\ln(2)(x-x_c)^2}{w^2}}}{w\sqrt{\frac{\pi}{4\ln(2)}}} \qquad (5)$$

where $x$ is the position parameter for the normal distribution and corresponds to the mean displacement, and $w$ describes the dispersion of the data. The fitting parameters $x$ and $w$ of the displacement field of ROI1-3 were statistically calculated at each stage (stage 2 to 8), and the results are presented in Figure 12.

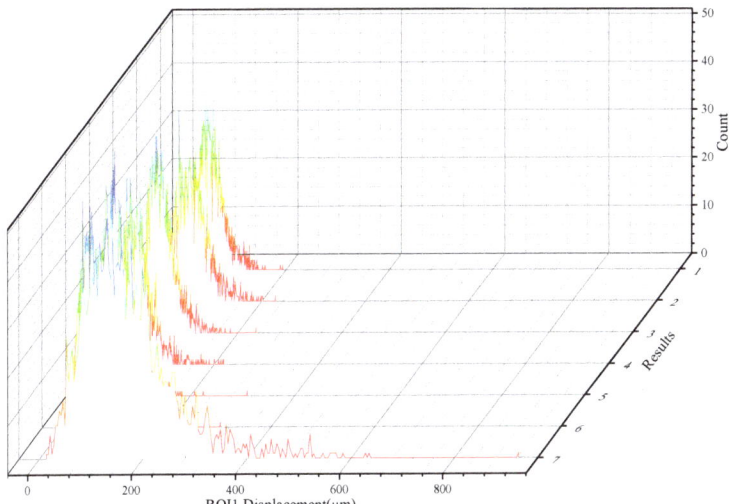

**Figure 9.** Statistical results for the ROI1 displacement field at different stages (stage 2 to 8).

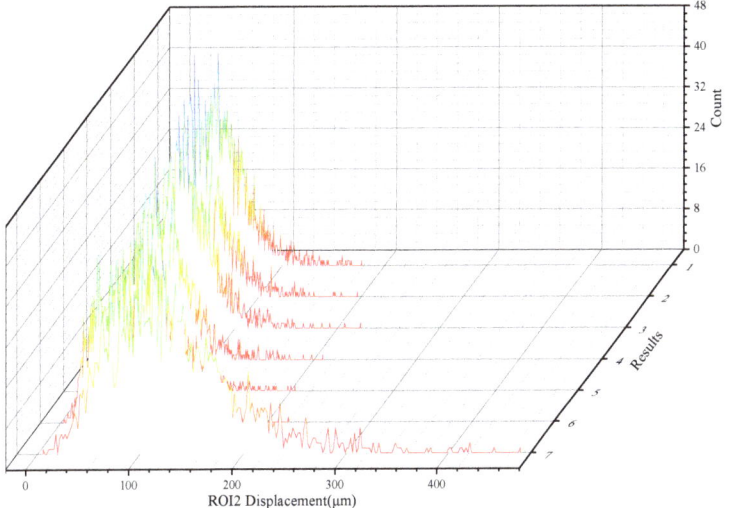

**Figure 10.** Statistical results for the ROI2 displacement field at different stages (stage 2 to 8).

Table 1 lists the mean displacements for the post-peak stage and the full stress–strain process of ROI1-3.

**Table 1.** Mean displacements of different ROIs.

| Item | Stage | ROI1 | ROI2 | ROI3 |
|---|---|---|---|---|
| Mean displacement | All stages (μm) | 76.887 | 73.613 | 66.089 |
| | Post-peak stage (μm) | 148.336 | 136.263 | 117.470 |

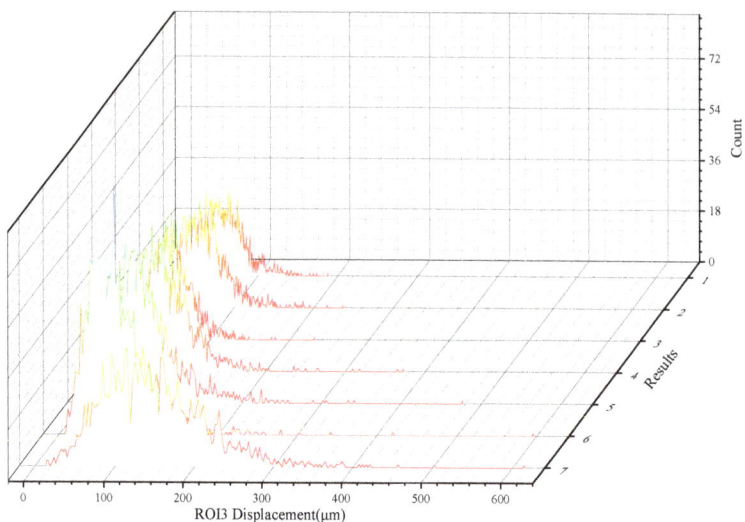

**Figure 11.** Statistical results for the ROI3 displacement field at different stages (stage 2 to 8).

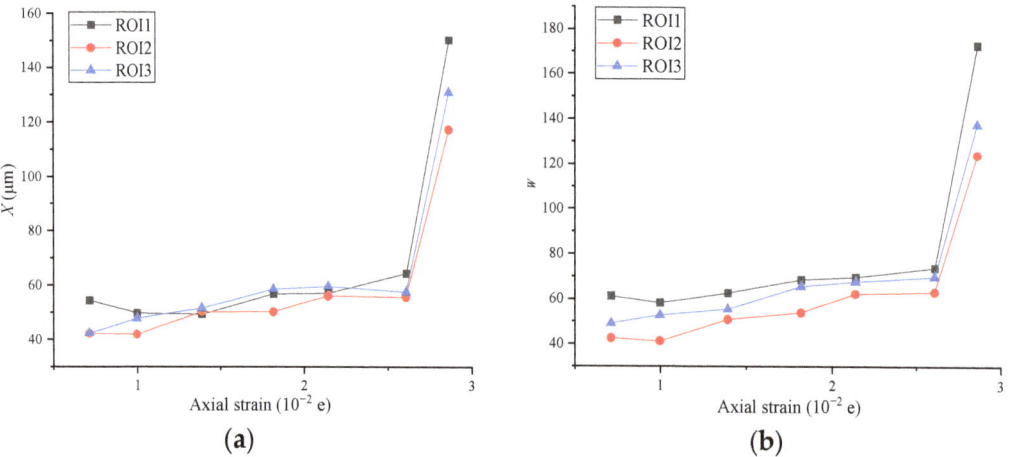

**Figure 12.** Variation curves of characteristic parameters $x$ (**a**) and $w$ (**b**) of the fitted normal distributions for ROI1-3.

Figure 12 shows the mean and dispersion of the displacement field versus the axial strain for ROI1-3. Considering these results in conjunction with those presented in Table 1 shows that (1) there is a turning point in the statistics (i.e., the mean and dispersion) of the displacement field at the compaction stage; (2) the displacement increases monotonically with the load after the compaction stage; (3) the dispersion in the statistical results of the displacement field increases steadily with the loading, reflecting an increase in the number of extreme displacements in the sample; and (4) the displacement fields of different ROIs at the same stage differ significantly.

### 3.3. Analysis of Simulation Results

Mechanical tests using the MTS816 rock test system were used to measure the Young's modulus and Poisson's ratio of each sample. The grey value ranges for different matrices (coal, minerals, and fractures) were determined, and the mechanical test results were used to set the variable physical parameters (Young's modulus and Poisson's ratio) for different matrices, as shown in Figure 13. A meshfree numerical simulation of the 3D CT model under mechanical loading (with stress values corresponding to stages 2–7 in Figure 5) was carried out by using VG software.

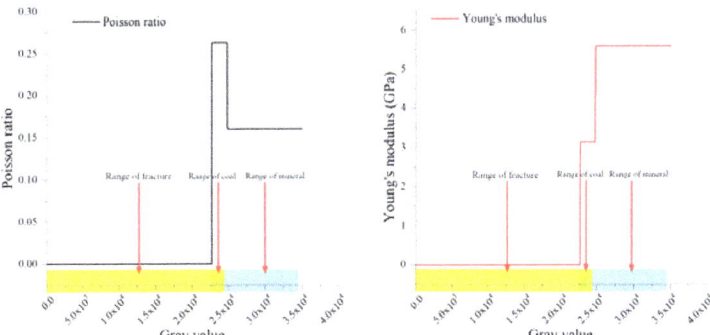

**Figure 13.** Setting the simulation parameters for different matrices.

The 3D CT model was directly simulated to obtain the 3D shear stress, principal stress, and displacement fields under different loads, as shown in Figures 14–16. Combining these results with those presented in Figure 17 clearly shows that the mineral distribution had a significant effect on the stress field.

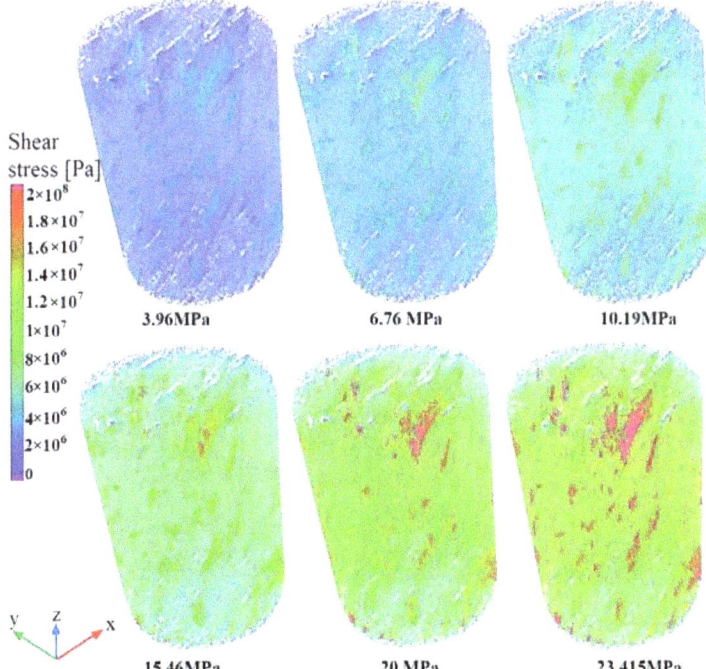

**Figure 14.** Simulated 3D shear stress field under different loads.

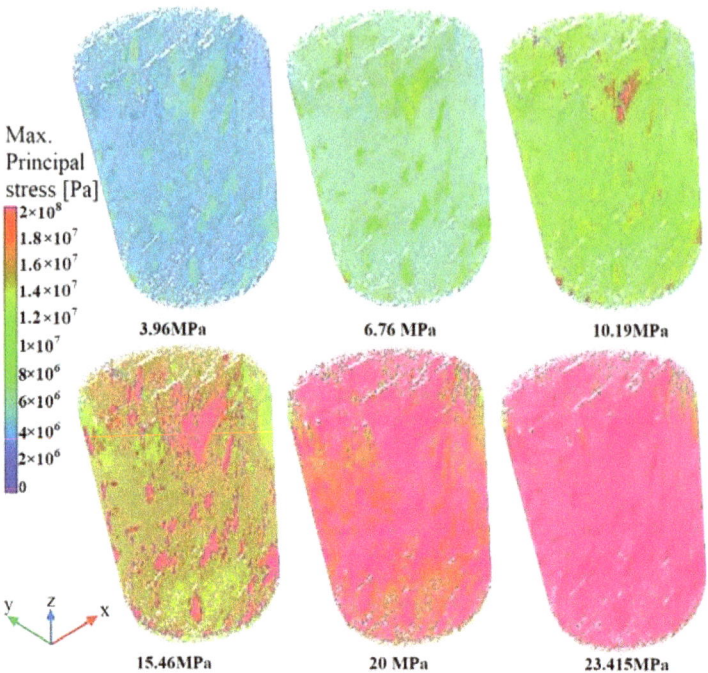

**Figure 15.** Simulated 3D maximum principal stress field under different loads.

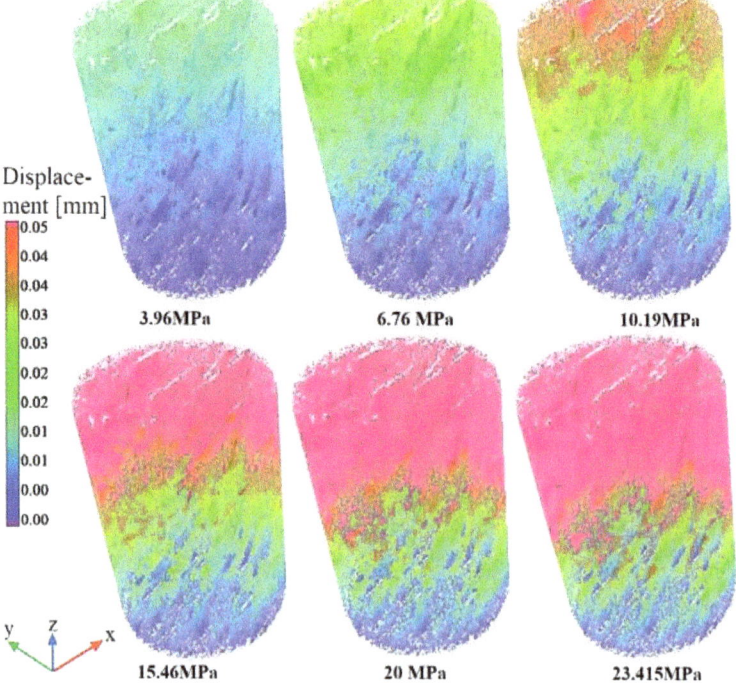

**Figure 16.** Simulated 3D displacement field under different loads.

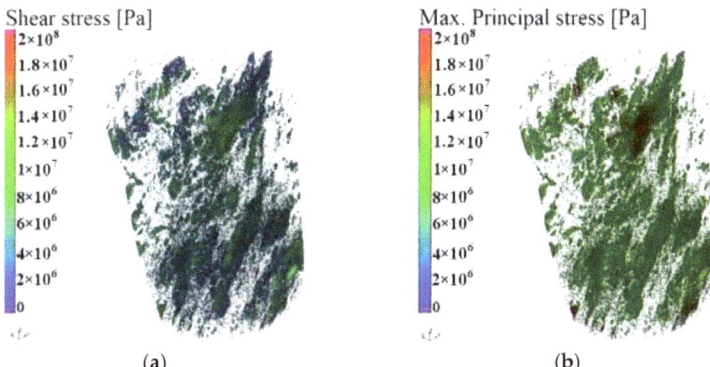

**Figure 17.** Stress state in mineral regions under a load of 10.19 MPa: (**a**) shear stress (**b**) maximum principal stress.

The simulated principal stress and shear stress of the sample under a stress of 10.19 MPa are shown in Figure 18.

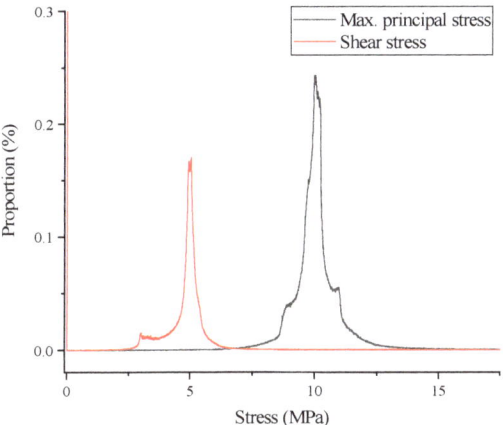

**Figure 18.** Distribution of maximum principal stress and shear stress under a 10.19-MPa load.

Figure 18 shows a very complex coal stress state in the presence of minerals and fractures. The presence of fractures resulted in both the maximum principal stress and shear stress being 0 MPa in 0.6984% of the regions in the sample. The influence of the mineral distribution features resulted in a prevalent shear stress state, where most of the shear stresses were in the 5-MPa range.

The shear stress distribution was bimodal (except in the fracture region): the minimum shear stress was 2.517 MPa, and 2.3% of the shear stress ranged between 2.517 and 3 MPa. More than 95% of the shear stresses were between 3 and 6.4 MPa, and only 1.6% of the shear stresses were greater than 6.4 MPa, with the maximum shear stress being 11.6 MPa.

The maximum principal stress followed a trimodal distribution. Only 0.89% of the maximum principal stresses were below 6 MPa, and 3.57% of the principal stresses were between 6 and 8.57 MPa. The percentage of maximum principal stresses between 8.5 and 8.9 MPa increased rapidly, and 79.5% of the maximum principal stresses were between 8.9 and 10.7 MPa. The maximum principal stresses in 14.34% of the regions were between 10.7 and 12.87 MPa, whereas the maximum principal stresses were higher than 12.87 MPa in only 1.67% of the regions.

The changes in the proportions of the maximum principal stress and shear stress between 10 and 20 MPa and above 20 MPa for each stress state were statistically analysed. Figure 19 shows that the proportions of the maximum principal stress and the shear stress above 20 MPa in the sample increased monotonically with the load. For loads above 15.46 MPa, the proportion of the maximum principal stresses higher than 20 MPa increased rapidly from 1.628% to 51.683%. At the peak stress, the maximum principal stress exceeded 20 MPa in 96.35% of the regions. The proportion of regions with shear stresses above 20 MPa increased rapidly for loads above 15.46 MPa, but the proportion itself remained very low. The proportion of the shear stresses between 10 and 20 MPa increased significantly with the load from 1.5% to 43.457% to 82.739%.

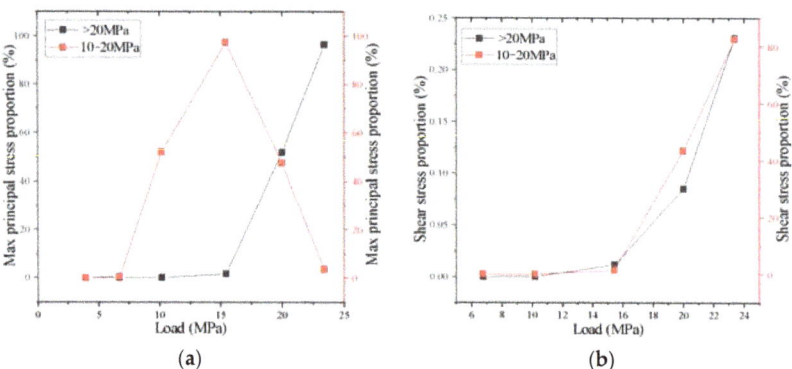

**Figure 19.** Proportion of maximum principal stress (**a**) and shear stress (**b**) at different pressures.

Two points in the 3D model were selected for each matrix (coal, minerals, and near fractures), and Figure 20 shows the corresponding maximum principal stress and shear stress. The different matrices within the sample exhibited significantly different stress states. The maximum principal stresses in the mineral matrix were higher than those in the coal matrix, indicating stress concentration in the mineral regions. By comparison, the stresses in the regions near the fractures were all low.

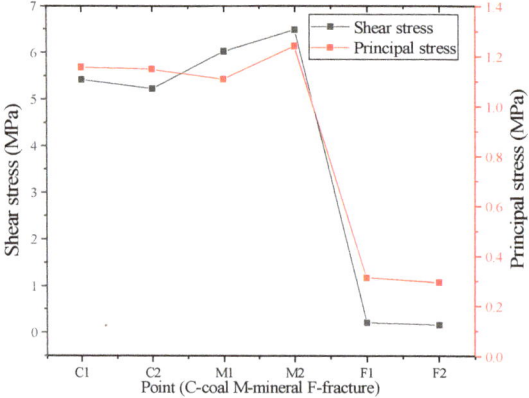

**Figure 20.** Shear stresses and principal stresses in different matrices (C—coal, M—mineral, and F—fracture).

## 4. Conclusions

The deformation features of coal under stress at macro- and mesoscales was investigated, and a meshless simulation was performed using a 3D CT model to obtain the 3D principal stress, shear stress, and displacement fields. The main conclusions are given below.

1. Primary fractures and minerals have a determining influence on the deformation and failure features of coal and are the key factors producing anisotropic coal deformation. The primary fractures propagate as compression increases and crisscross new fractures.
2. The ROI displacement field data of different matrices in the coal sample follow a normal distribution, and the differences in the corresponding deformations under load are statistically significant. The deformation at the primary fractures increases substantially with stress, and the mineral region is also prone to large deformation from stress concentration. The increase in the displacement is promoted by the presence of fractures and inhibited in the presence of minerals.
3. A highly complex coal stress state forms under an applied stress, and the distribution of minerals and fractures significantly affects the stress field distribution. The presence of minerals and fractures produces a prevalent shear stress in the coal that is mainly concentrated in the vicinity of where these entities are located and is highly unfavourable for sample stability.
4. To ensure safe field operation, the mineral distribution features in coal seams and the development level and distribution features of primary fractures should be determined. Targeted measures can then be taken to improve the stress state and enhance the safety level.

**Author Contributions:** Conceptualization, Q.L. and Z.L.; methodology, Z.L.; software, Q.L.; validation, Z.L., P.L. and R.P.; formal analysis, Q.L.; investigation, Z.L.; resources, Q.L.; data curation, P.L. and Q.Z.; writing—original draft preparation, Q.L.; writing—review and editing, Z.L.; visualization, Z.L.; supervision, Q.L.; project administration, Z.L.; funding acquisition, Z.L. All authors have read and agreed to the published version of the manuscript.

**Funding:** This research was funded by the National Natural Science Foundation of China, grant number 51904198, the Science Foundation for Youths of Shanxi Province, grant number 201901D211036 and grant number 202103021223392, and Natural Science Research of Shanxi Province (202103021224334) and the APC was funded by the National Natural Science Foundation of China, grant number 51904198.

**Institutional Review Board Statement:** Not applicable.

**Informed Consent Statement:** Not applicable.

**Data Availability Statement:** Not applicable.

**Conflicts of Interest:** The authors declare no conflict of interest.

# References

1. Sobczyk, J. A comparison of the influence of adsorbed gases on gas stresses leading to coal and gas outburst. *Fuel* **2014**, *115*, 288–294. [CrossRef]
2. Sobczyk, J. The influence of sorption processes on gas stresses leading to the coal and gas outburst in the laboratory conditions. *Fuel* **2011**, *90*, 1018–1023. [CrossRef]
3. Lu, X.; Armstrong, R.T.; Mostaghimi, P. High-pressure X-ray imaging to interpret coal permeability. *Fuel* **2018**, *226*, 573–582. [CrossRef]
4. Tan, J.; Xie, J.; Li, L.; Lyu, Q.; Han, J.; Zhao, Z. Multifractal analysis of acoustic emissions during hydraulic fracturing experiments under uniaxial loading conditions: A Niutitang shale example. *Geofluids* **2020**, *2020*, 8845292. [CrossRef]
5. Nie, B.; Fan, P.; Li, X. Quantitative investigation of anisotropic characteristics of methane-induced strain in coal based on coal particle tracking method with X-ray computer tomography. *Fuel* **2018**, *214*, 272–284. [CrossRef]
6. Zhang, Z.; Xie, H.; Zhang, R.; Gao, M.; Ai, T.; Zha, E. Size and spatial fractal distributions of coal fracture networks under different mining-induced stress conditions. *Int. J. Rock Mech. Min.* **2020**, *132*, 104364. [CrossRef]
7. Feng, Z.; Cai, T.; Zhou, D.; Zhao, D.; Zhao, Y.; Wang, C. Temperature and deformation changes in anthracite coal after methane adsorption. *Fuel* **2017**, *192*, 27–34. [CrossRef]
8. Kawakata, H.; Cho, A.; Yanagidani, T.; Shimada, M. The observations of faulting in westerly granite under triaxial compression by X-ray CT scan. *Int. J. Rock Mech. Min. Sci. Geomech.* **1997**, *34*, 375. [CrossRef]
9. Cao, W.; Yildirim, B.; Durucan, S.; Wolf, K.; Cai, W.; Agrawal, H.; Korre, A. Fracture behaviour and seismic response of naturally fractured coal subjected to true triaxial stresses and hydraulic fracturing. *Fuel* **2021**, *288*, 119618. [CrossRef]

10. Fan, N.; Wang, J.; Deng, C.; Fan, Y.; Wang, T.; Guo, X. Quantitative characterization of coal microstructure and visualization seepage of macropores using CT-based 3D reconstruction. *J. Nat. Gas Sci. Eng.* **2020**, *81*, 103384. [CrossRef]
11. Li, Y.T.; Jiang, Y.D.; Zhang, B.; Song, H.H.; Dong, W.B.; Wang, P.P. Investigation on the pore characteristics of coal specimens with bursting proneness. *Fuel* **2019**, *9*, 16518. [CrossRef] [PubMed]
12. Li, Y.Y.; Cui, H.Q.; Zhang, P.; Wang, D.K.; Wei, J.P. Three-dimensional visualization and quantitative characterization of coal fracture dynamic evolution under uniaxial and triaxial compression based on CT scanning. *Fuel* **2020**, *262*, 116568. [CrossRef]
13. Lu, W.; Wei, G.; Wang, Z.; Jia, T.; Sun, S.; Ju, Y. Micro-nano fine characterization of coal fracture evolution during the triaxial compression creep. *Fuel* **2021**, *21*, 495–504. [CrossRef] [PubMed]
14. Liu, W.; Wang, G.; Han, D.; Xu, H.; Chu, X. Accurate characterization of coal pore and fissure structure based on CT 3D reconstruction and NMR. *J. Nat. Gas Sci. Eng.* **2021**, *96*, 104242. [CrossRef]
15. Tao, S.; Pan, Z.J.; Chen, S.D.; Tang, S.L. Coal seam porosity and fracture heterogeneity of marcolithotypes in the Fanzhuang Block, southern Qinshui Basin, China. *J. Nat. Gas Sci. Eng.* **2019**, *66*, 148–158. [CrossRef]
16. Wang, G.; Han, D.; Qin, X.; Liu, Z.; Liu, J. A comprehensive method for studying pore structure and seepage characteristics of coal mass based on 3D CT reconstruction and NMR. *Fuel* **2020**, *281*, 118735. [CrossRef]
17. Wang, G.; Qin, X.; Han, D.; Liu, Z. Study on seepage and deformation characteristics of coal microstructure by 3D reconstruction of CT images at high temperatures. *Fuel* **2021**, *31*, 175–185. [CrossRef]
18. Wang, G.; Han, D.Y.; Jiang, C.H.; Zhang, Z.Y. Seepage characteristics of fracture and dead-end pore structure in coal at micro- and meso-scales. *Fuel* **2020**, *266*, 117058. [CrossRef]
19. Zhang, G.; Ranjith, P.G.; Fu, X.; Li, X. Pore-fracture alteration of different rank coals: Implications for $CO_2$ sequestration in coal. *Fuel* **2021**, *289*, 119081. [CrossRef]
20. Wang, D.; Zeng, F.; Wei, J.; Zhang, H.; Wu, Y.; Wei, Q. Quantitative analysis of fracture dynamic evolution in coal subjected to uniaxial and triaxial compression loads based on industrial CT and fractal theory. *J. Pet. Sci. Eng.* **2021**, *196*, 108051. [CrossRef]
21. Mao, L.; Lian, X.; Hao, N.; Wei, F.; An, L. 3D strain measurement in coal using digital volumetric speckle photography. *J. China Coal Soc.* **2015**, *40*, 65–72.
22. Sampath, K.H.S.M.; Perera, M.S.A.; Elsworth, D.; Matthai, S.K.; Ranjith, P.G.; Li, D. Discrete fracture matrix modelling of fully-coupled $CO_2$ flow-Deformation processes in fractured coal. *Int. J. Rock Mech. Min.* **2021**, *138*, 104644. [CrossRef]
23. Roslin, A.; Pokrajac, D.; Zhou, Y. Cleat structure analysis and permeability simulation of coal samples based on micro-computed tomography (micro-CT) and scan electron microscopy (SEM) technology. *Fuel* **2019**, *254*, 115579. [CrossRef]
24. Wu, Y.; Yang, D.; Wei, J.; Yao, B.; Zhang, H.; Fu, J.; Zeng, F. Damage constitutive model of gas-bearing coal using industrial CT scanning technology. *J. Nat. Gas Sci. Eng.* **2022**, *101*, 104543. [CrossRef]

*Article*

# Research on Dynamic Properties of Deep Marble Influenced by High Temperature

Xianglong Li [1,2], Yongbo Wu [1,2], Lihua He [3], Xiaohua Zhang [1,2] and Jianguo Wang [1,2,*]

1. Faculty of Land Resources Engineering, Kunming University of Science and Technology, Kunming 650093, China; lxl00014002@163.com (X.L.); 20202101092@stu.kust.edu.cn (Y.W.); sunset830@163.com (X.Z.)
2. New Blasting Technology Engineering Research Center of Yunnan Provincial Education Department, Kunming 650093, China
3. Faculty of Mining Industry, Kunming Metallurgy College, Kunming 650033, China; lxiangning2022@163.com
* Correspondence: wangjg0831@163.com

**Abstract:** Deep rock will be influenced by the excavation disturbances of different degrees, which seriously affects the safety production of underground mines. Considering that deep rock will be impacted by different temperatures and varied disturbance degrees, this work analyzes the effect of temperature on the dynamic properties of marble by means of the dynamic and static combined SHPB test device. The results reveal that as the temperature climbed, the diameter and height of the specimen increased and the mass and longitudinal wave velocity dropped. The variation laws of total stress–strain curves after varied high temperatures are substantially the same; the peak stress was negatively correlated with the action temperature. At 25 °C~400 °C, the failure mode of specimens is less affected by temperature. When the temperature is higher than 400 °C, the failure degree of specimens increases with the growth of temperature. At 25~400 °C, the above energy varies minimally. At 400~800 °C, with the increase in temperature, the incident energy, transmitted energy and absorption energy decrease, and the reflection energy increases gradually.

**Keywords:** high-temperature marble; SEM; dynamic properties; crack propagation

**MSC:** 74H99

## 1. Introduction

With the depletion of shallow resources, the development of mineral resources has migrated to depth. The mining depth worldwide is more than 1000 m. In South Africa, the depth of gold mines greater than 5000 m is obtained [1–4]. Deep surrounding rock is in a specified temperature field in practical engineering. Its mechanical properties may alter under the influence of temperature field. This can have a significant impact on the development of underground mines [5–10]. Blasting or non-explosive mining disturbance is extremely vulnerable to the accumulation of brittle rock in a sudden release of elastic strain energy, which can produce a rock explosion, a loss of mine property, and endanger the staff safety. Therefore, the examination into marble properties and energy distribution law of rocks under different disturbance intensities after high temperature can provide a valuable reference for the identification of rock burst in a deep extraction process.

Extensive research studies have been conducted on rocks subjected to high temperatures in order to investigate the impact of temperature on the mechanical properties of rocks. Chen et al. [11] studied the peak stress, peak strain, and elastic modulus of marble specimens in response to high temperature. By examining the change in ultrasonic velocity and porosity of sandstone following thermal treatment, Zhao et al. [12] identified the temperature influence on sandstone damage. Zhai et al. [13] investigated the influence of temperature on the peak stress and elastic modulus of marble using the MTS810 test system and found that after 800 °C, the mechanical properties of marble deteriorated precipitously. Ni et al. [14] used rock uniaxial compression test to study the mechanical properties of marble samples after 100 °C, 300 °C, 450 °C, 600 °C and 1, 10, 20 different temperature cycles. It is found that with the increase of temperature and cycles, the failure mode of the specimen gradually changes from typical brittle failure to brittle plastic failure. Taking marble as the research object, Huang et al. [15] carried out uniaxial compression test and acoustic wave test on high temperature rock samples after water cooling and natural cooling, analyzed and compared the changes of peak strength, elastic modulus, attenuation coefficient, longitudinal wave velocity and main frequency of rock samples under different conditions. Zeng et al. [16] used polarized light microscopy to investigate fine-grained marble after numerous high-temperature cycles, quantified the length, openness, and number of microcracks, and discussed the crack expansion pattern of specimens after various thermal cycles. Li et al. [17] used uniaxial compression test to analyze and study the physical and mechanical properties of jointed sandstone after experiencing different temperatures, and obtained the variation law of stress-strain curve, peak strength, peak strain and elastic modulus of jointed sandstone after high temperature with temperature. To investigate the effect of temperature on rock impact propensity, Zhang et al. [18] conducted uniaxial compression and fracture electron microscope scanning tests on granite samples under real-time high temperature (25~850 °C) and after high-temperature heat treatment (25~1200 °C).

Using a large-diameter SHPB setup, Xu et al. [19] investigated and analyzed the dynamic mechanical properties of marble at various temperatures and loading rates in rock dynamics. They found that the peak strain and peak stress of specimens exhibited various degrees of loading rate strengthening. Yin et al. [20] conducted an impact test on sandstone subjected to various high-temperature treatments using a SHPB equipment and evaluated the influence of temperature on the mechanical properties of sandstone from a fine perspective. Ping et al. [21] The impact test of sandstone and limestone after high temperature treatment was carried out by variable cross-section SHPB test system. The influence of temperature field on rock dynamic properties was studied. Yin et al. [22] used a self-developed temperature-pressure coupling and dynamic disturbance test system to study the impact test of sandstone samples under four temperature levels (20 °C, 100 °C, 200 °C, 300 °C) and four axial static pressure levels (0, 20, 60, 80 MPa). Based on the principle of energy dissipation, the energy dissipation law of rock specimen under dynamic-static combined loading at different temperatures is calculated. Liu et al. [23] carried out rock impact compression tests at room temperature under different impact pressures (0.8, 1.0, 1.2 MPa) and under different temperatures (200 °C, 400 °C, 600 °C, 800 °C) using a split Hopkinson pressure bar device to study the high temperature dynamic behavior of deep skarn. Using MTS652.02 and SHPB test system, Li et al. [24] carried out uniaxial impact compression test on sandstone samples heated at 800 °C, and analyzed the variation of dynamic characteristics of sandstone in the strain rate range of 17.904~62.600 s$^{-1}$. Using SHPB device, Zhang et al. [25] studied the dynamic failure characteristics of sandstone after treatment at −15 °C~1000 °C, and analyzed the influence of temperature on the damage degree and energy dissipation in the failure process of deep sandstone.

In summary, there are extensive studies on the physical and mechanical properties of high-temperature marble under static and dynamic loading conditions. However, the effect of temperature on the mechanical characteristics of rocks under combined dynamic and static conditions is given little attention in the available literature. In order to study the effect of temperature on the physical and dynamic properties of marble under dynamic and static combination, the basic physical parameters of marble after different temperature treatments were measured. At the same time, the stress—strain SHPB test device was used to study the stress-strain curve, crushing characteristics and the relationship between energy evolution and temperature of marble specimens.

## 2. Specimen Preparation and Test Procedures

The rock specimens were collected at the Dahongshan copper mine in Yuxi, Yunnan, China. Samples were gathered from the same compacted and homogenous rock block specimen. The size of the marble sample was determined to be Φ 50 × 50 mm in size in accordance with the stress uniformity theory and SHPB test sample size reference [26]. Using the SC-200 automatic coring machine, SCQ-300 automatic cutting machine, and SHM-200 double end grinder, rock samples were cored, cut, and ground for testing. The vertical error is less than 0.25° and both ends of the control specimen are uneven by less than 0.05 mm. The marble specimen has a compressive strength of 60.75 MPa, a modulus of elasticity is 38.71 GPa with a density of 2.70 g/cm$^3$.

First, all the marble specimens were separated into 5 groups and the specimens in each group were numbered for the convenience of recording. Next, the specimen mass, height, diameter, and longitudinal wave velocity were measured. Subsequently, each group of samples was placed in an XH7L-12 box resistance furnace with temperatures set to 200 °C, 400 °C, 600 °C, and 800 °C, respectively. After reaching the specified temperature, the samples were maintained at a steady temperature for two hours. Before and after high temperature, the mass, height, diameter, and longitudinal wave velocity of samples were measured after natural cooling. Finally, the uniaxial impact compression test of the specimen was carried out and the crack propagation information was recorded using a high-speed camera.

### 2.1. Experimental System and Experimental Principle

The test adopts the SHPB test apparatus of the Rock Mechanics Laboratory at Kunming University of Science and Technology to conduct a dynamic and static combined impact test on the marble specimen. As depicted in Figure 1, the system consists primarily of three components: the main equipment, the launch system, and the test system, including power source, the bullet, the elastic pressure bar, the axial loading device, the support frame, and the test analysis instrument. The elastic pressure bars consist of both incident and transmitted bars. The length of the incidence bar is 2000 mm, the length of the transmitted bar is 1500 mm, the diameter of the elastic bar is 50 mm, the longitudinal wave velocity is 5190 m/s, and the elastic modulus is 210 GPa.

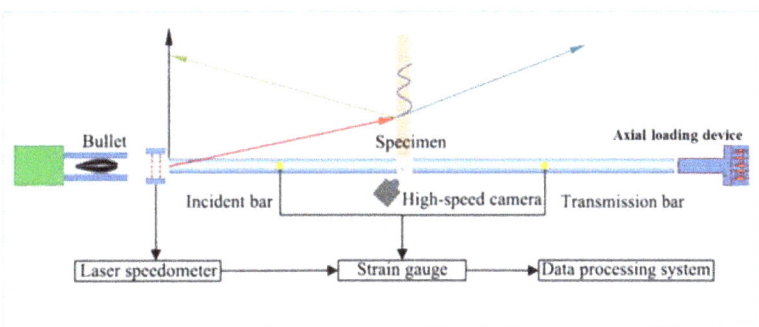

**Figure 1.** SHPB test equipment.

The motion equation has a decisive influence on the axial motion of particles in the bar, so it is necessary to discuss the motion equation. The cross-sectional area of incident bar and transmitted bar is $A_0$, the elastic modulus is $E_0$, and the density is $\rho_0$. Figure 2 shows the schematic diagram of a micro-element before bar deformation.

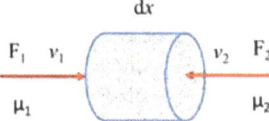

**Figure 2.** Diagram of the differential element before the deformation of bar.

As shown in the above figure, it is assumed that the length of the differential element is dy and the cross-sectional area is $A_0$. The whole compression bar is in a static equilibrium state before the impact. When the punch strikes the bar, the bar deforms, and the particles in the differential element are subject to the left force $F_1$ and the right force $F_2$. The forces $F_1$ and $F_2$ operating on the differential element are proportional to the stress acting on the cross-section of the compression bar. In the elastic range, the connection between the stress and strain of the compression bar follows Hooke's law, and the strain caused by the compression bar can be obtained. This strain can be expressed by the particle's displacement of the particle, that is, the resistance in the differential element can be expressed by the particle's displacement. Let the left end face displacement of the micro element be $\mu_1$ and the right end face displacement be $\mu_2$. Then, a stress equation exists [27]:

$$\begin{cases} F_1 = A_0 E_0 \dfrac{\partial \mu_1}{\partial x} \\ F_2 = A_0 E_0 \dfrac{\partial \mu_2}{\partial x} \end{cases} \quad (1)$$

According to Newton's second law, we can obtain the following pressure pulse motion equation:

$$A_0 E_0 \dfrac{\partial \mu_1}{\partial x} - A_0 E_0 \dfrac{\partial \mu_2}{\partial x} = A_0 dx \rho_0 \dfrac{\partial^2 \mu_1}{\partial t^2} \quad (2)$$

Assuming that the particle acceleration in the differential element is a constant, the equation can be simplified as follows:

$$C_0^2 \left( \dfrac{\partial \mu_1}{\partial x} - \dfrac{\partial \mu_2}{\partial x} \right) = \dfrac{\partial^2 \mu_1}{\partial t^2} dx \quad (3)$$

where $C_0$ is the wave velocity of stress wave in bar, which can be calculated by the following formula:

$$C_0 = \sqrt{E_0/\rho_0} \quad (4)$$

where $E_0$ and $\rho_0$ are elastic modulus and density of elastic bar, respectively.

Since the differential element displacement $\mu_1$ and $\mu_2$ have the following relationship:

$$C_0^2 \dfrac{\partial^2 \mu_1}{\partial x^2} = \dfrac{\partial^2 \mu_1}{\partial t^2} \quad (5)$$

Based on the basic theory of wave dynamics, the wave equation in one-dimensional elastic compression bar is derived.

When the bullet hits the incident bar at a certain impact velocity, a compression strain pulse $\varepsilon_1(t)$ will be produced in the incident bar. Under the condition of one-dimensional stress propagation, the stress pulse, also known as the elastic stress wave, propagates forward with velocity $C_0$ in the incident bar. When the incident wave propagates to the interface between the incident bar and the rock specimen, because the wave impedance of the rock is less than that of the incident bar, part of the pulse is reflected into the incident bar to form a reflection unloading strain pulse $\varepsilon_R(t)$, and the remaining part generates a transmitted compression strain pulse $\varepsilon_T(t)$ in the transmitted bar [28]. Strain gauges adhered to the incident bar and transmitted bar can measure three types of strain pulses $\varepsilon_1(t)$, $\varepsilon_R(t)$ and $\varepsilon_T(t)$.

The displacement of the left and right ends of the specimen is $\mu_1$ and $\mu_2$, respectively. The velocities of the incident wave, reflection wave, and transmitted wave on the end surface are $v_I$, $v_R$, and $v_T$, respectively. The velocities of the left and right ends are $v_1$ and $v_2$, respectively. According to the theoretical derivation formula:

$$\begin{cases} v_1 = v_I + v_R = -C_0\varepsilon_I + C_0\varepsilon_R = C_0(\varepsilon_R - \varepsilon_I) \\ v_2 = v_T = -C_0\varepsilon_T \end{cases} \quad (6)$$

Displacements are:

$$\begin{cases} \mu_1 = \int_0^t v_1 dt = C_0 \int_0^t (\varepsilon_R - \varepsilon_I) dt \\ \mu_2 = \int_0^t v_2 dt = C_0 \int_0^t \varepsilon_T dt \end{cases} \quad (7)$$

Assuming that the original length of the specimen is $L_S$, the average strain of the specimen is:

$$\varepsilon_S = \frac{\mu_1 - \mu_2}{L_S} = \frac{C_0}{L_S} \int_0^t (\varepsilon_I - \varepsilon_R - \varepsilon_T) dt \quad (8)$$

Then, the force $F_1$ and $F_2$ of sample face 1 and face 2 are:

$$\begin{cases} F_1 = A_0 E_0 (\varepsilon_I + \varepsilon_R) \\ F_2 = A_0 E_0 \varepsilon_T \end{cases} \quad (9)$$

When the cross-sectional area of the specimen is the same as the area of the elastic compression bar, the stress at both ends of the specimen is:

$$\begin{cases} \sigma_1 = E_0(\varepsilon_I + \varepsilon_R) \\ \sigma_2 = E_0 \varepsilon_T \end{cases} \quad (10)$$

The average stress $\sigma_S$ in the sample is:

$$\sigma_S = \frac{(\sigma_1 + \sigma_2)}{2} = \frac{E_0(\varepsilon_I + \varepsilon_R + \varepsilon_T)}{2} \quad (11)$$

In summary, the stress, strain, and strain rate of the specimen are obtained [29]:

$$\begin{cases} \sigma_S(t) = \frac{1}{2} E_0 (\varepsilon_I(t) + \varepsilon_R(t) + \varepsilon_T(t)) \\ \varepsilon_S(t) = \int_0^t (\varepsilon_I(t) - \varepsilon_R(t) - \varepsilon_T(t)) dt \\ \dot{\varepsilon}_S(t) = \frac{C_0}{L_S} (\varepsilon_I(t) - \varepsilon_R(t) - \varepsilon_T(t)) \end{cases} \quad (12)$$

The energy carried by incident wave, reflected wave, and transmitted wave can be calculated by integrating the measured strain. The integral formula is as follows:

$$W = A_0 \rho_0 C_0 \int_0^t \varepsilon^2(t) dt \quad (13)$$

The energy carried by incident wave, reflected wave, and transmitted wave is as follows:

$$\begin{cases} W_I = A_0 \rho_0 C_0 \int_0^t \varepsilon_I^2 dt \\ W_R = A_0 \rho_0 C_0 \int_0^t \varepsilon_R^2 dt \\ W_T = A_0 \rho_0 C_0 \int_0^t \varepsilon_T^2 dt \end{cases} \quad (14)$$

According to the law of conservation of energy, the energy loss in the impact process can be obtained, and the energy absorbed by the specimen can be expressed as:

$$W_A = W_I - W_R - W_T \tag{15}$$

where $W_I$ represents the energy carried by the incident wave; $W_R$ is the energy carried by the reflected wave; $W_T$ is the energy carried by the transmitted wave; and $W_A$ is the energy dissipated in the test, that is, the energy absorbed by the failure of the specimen.

## 2.2. Model and Principle of One-Dimensional Static and Dynamic Combination Loading

Before the one-dimensional static and dynamic combined loading test, it is necessary to analyze whether the bar and specimen under axial compression meet the stress wave transmitted theory on which the device depends.

As shown in Figure 3, deep rock mass under one-dimensional stress is often subjected to both static stress and dynamic load. Sample micro-force of static and dynamic combination is shown in Figure 4. According to the assumption of one-dimensional stress wave in the bar [30], the force–deformation relationship of the micro-element under combined loading can be obtained:

**Figure 3.** Schematic diagram of static and dynamic combination.

$$P_s + P_d \quad\quad P_s + P_d + \frac{\partial(P_s + P_d)}{\partial x}\Delta x$$

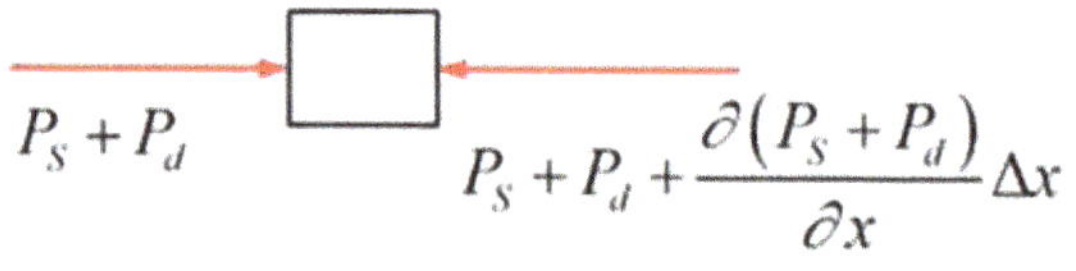

**Figure 4.** Sample micro-force of static and dynamic combination.

$$-\frac{\partial(P_s + P_d)}{\partial x}\Delta x = \rho_0 A_0 \Delta x \frac{\partial^2 u}{\partial t^2} \tag{16}$$

$A_0$ and $\rho$ are the cross-sectional area and density of the elastic bar, respectively; $u$ is the displacement of the micro-element after being stressed; and $P_S$ and $P_d$ are the static and dynamic loading of the sample, respectively.

According to stress, strain, and Hooke's Law:

$$\begin{cases} \sigma = \dfrac{P_S + P_d}{A_0} \\ \sigma = E_0 \varepsilon \\ \varepsilon = -\dfrac{\partial u}{\partial x} \end{cases} \tag{17}$$

Combining the above equations yields:

$$\rho_0 \frac{\partial^2 u}{\partial t^2} = E_0 \frac{\partial^2 u}{\partial x^2} \qquad (18)$$

The velocity of incident stress wave in compression bar can be expressed by Formula (4), then Formula (18) can be expressed as:

$$\frac{\partial^2 u}{\partial t^2} - C^2 \frac{\partial^2 u}{\partial x^2} = 0 \qquad (19)$$

The same fluctuation equations derived from the combined dynamic and static loading experimental system and the conventional SHPB test system illustrate the applicability of the one-dimensional stress wave theory to the one-dimensional combined dynamic and static loading experimental system.

### 2.3. Experimental Procedure

In this experiment, the loading axial pressure of marble was determined to be 6 MPa, or 10% of its uniaxial compressive strength, based on its uniaxial compressive strength. The impact of velocity was determined by conducting pre-tests on specimens at room temperature. The pre-test results show that when the impact pressure is 0.4 MPa, the specimen is damaged after three times of impact. Therefore, the impact pressure was set as 0.5 MPa, 0.55 MPa, 0.6 MPa, 0.65 MPa in this experiment. The corresponding average impact velocities were 15.32 m/s, 18.17 m/s, 21.83 m/s and 23.49 m/s, respectively. The corresponding average impact velocities were 15.32 m/s, 18.17 m/s, 21.83 m/s, and 23.49 m/s, while the temperature gradients were 25 °C, 200 °C, 400 °C, 600 °C, and 800 °C, respectively. For this reason, this experiment was separated into four groups, with five pieces in each group undergoing an impact test at a different temperature. Three parallel tests were designed for each temperature, totaling 60 pieces.

## 3. Physical Properties of Marble before and after High Temperature

### 3.1. Apparent Morphological Characteristics of Specimens before and after High Temperature

The apparent diagram of marble specimens treated at different temperatures (25~800 °C) is shown in Figure 5. The diagram shows that the apparent color of marble specimen heated at 200 °C is deepened. When the temperature exceeds 400 °C, the color of marble specimen surface gradually becomes lighter, that is, from light gray to milky white, and a large number of black spots appear on the specimen surface [31]. At 600 °C, the surface of marble becomes very rough, and many microcracks appear on the surface, indicating that the mineral composition of marble has undergone phase transformation, which destroys the original microstructure of the rock. When the temperature reaches 81,000 °C, the color of the specimen becomes white, the volume expansion decreases obviously, and the internal structure of marble has been seriously damaged.

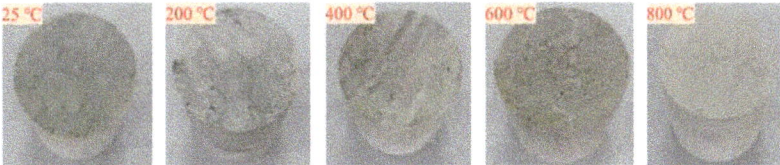

**Figure 5.** Apparent morphology of marble specimens after high-temperature treatment.

### 3.2. Variation in Specimen Mass and Longitudinal Wave Velocity

Figure 6a–d shows the changes in geometric size and physical properties of marble before and after high-temperature treatment. Figure 6a depicts the relationship between marble sample height and temperature. The specimen height increases with the increase in temperature on the whole. When heated to 200 °C~400 °C, the specimen height changed little. When heated to 600 °C~800 °C, the height of the specimen changes noticeably. When the temperature was 800 °C, the height of the specimen increased from 50.23 mm before heating to 51.34 mm, with an increase of 2.2%. The fluctuation curve of marble sample diameter with temperature is shown in Figure 6b The variation in the diameter with temperature is similar to that of the diameter with temperature. The diameter of a specimen increases as the temperature rises. At a room temperature of 200 °C, the height of the specimen changed little. At 200 °C, the diameter of the specimen increased by only 0.23 mm. When heated to 400 °C, 600 °C, and 800 °C, the diameter of the specimen changed drastically. After a high temperature of 800 °C, the diameter increased from 52.03 mm before heating to 54.96 mm, with an increase of 5.6%. This is primarily due to the irreversible thermal expansion of the internal part of the specimen at high temperature. Therefore, the specimen size will not return to its original state after cooling. Due to the decomposition of carbonates when the temperature reaches 800 °C, the rock strength rapidly declines, and $CO_2$ gas is emitted during the decomposition process, causing the expansion of the height and diameter of high-temperature marble and loose particles [32]. Figure 6c illustrates the variation curve of sample mass and temperature. Between the room temperature and high temperature of 600 °C, the mass change in the sample was not obvious, the loss rate was less than 1%. At 800 °C, the mass decreased from 243.59 g to 234.82 g, reduced by 3.6%. Due to the thermal decomposition of some minerals in marble caused by the high temperature, the specimen mass changes significantly [33]. The fluctuation curve of marble longitudinal wave velocity with temperature is depicted in Figure 6d The longitudinal wave velocity of the sample decreases with the increase in the overall temperature of the sample. The longitudinal wave velocity of the sample heated to 400 °C changed little, only reducing by 8.6%. When heated to 600 °C and 800 °C, the longitudinal wave velocity decreased significantly by 41.27% and 70.62%, respectively. There are two main reasons for the decrease in rock longitudinal wave velocity after high temperature. On the one hand, when the rock is subjected to high temperature, the free water in the pore evaporates to water vapor and the volume of the pore increases. The pore has a blocking effect on the propagation of longitudinal wave velocity, resulting in a decrease in wave velocity. On the other hand, there are a large number of cracks in the rock, which will lead to the further expansion of cracks and the generation of new cracks under the action of temperature. The higher the temperature, the higher the number of cracks, so the wave velocity of rock samples decreases significantly after high temperature [34]. The above result shows that temperature has a significant impact on the physical properties of marble, and the greater the temperature, the more obvious the impact.

*3.3. Influence of High Temperature on the Microstructure of Marble*

The change in the internal microstructure of rock can be observed by scanning electron microscope images. Figure 7 illustrates typical SEM images of granite samples subjected to varying temperatures. For comparison purposes, all images have the same magnification (Mag = 500). Even at room temperature (25 °C), marble retains its natural cracks. When marble samples were heated to 200 °C, the number of microcracks did neither increase nor decrease. Compared to the marble at room temperature, the crack width and number of specimens increased marginally following heat treatment at 400 °C, but the increase was minimal. In the specimens of marble subjected to heat treatments at 600 °C and 800 °C, the number and width of cracks rose dramatically. At 800 °C, cracks even penetrated the specimens, and the thermal damage of specimens was serious.

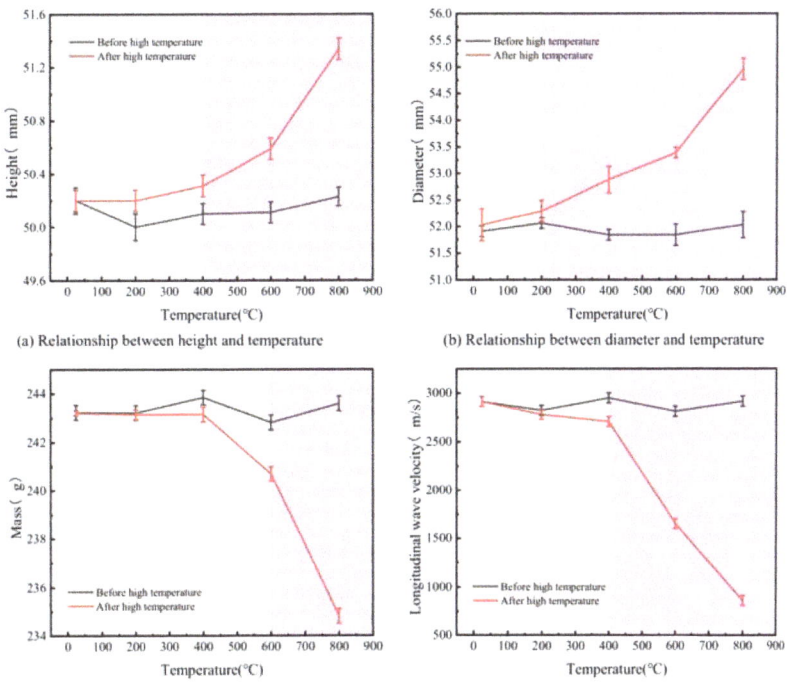

(a) Relationship between height and temperature
(b) Relationship between diameter and temperature
(c) Relationship between mass and temperature
(d) The relationship between longitudinal wave velocity and temperature

**Figure 6.** Changes of physical properties of marble samples after different temperatures.

**Figure 7.** SEM micrograph of marble after high-temperature treatment.

## 4. Dynamic Compressive Mechanical Properties of Marble after High Temperature

*4.1. Stress–Strain Properties*

The total stress–strain curves of marble specimens under different loading speeds at room temperature and after different high temperatures are shown in Figure 8.

It can be seen from Figure 8 that the total stress–strain curves of marble specimens treated at different temperatures ($T$) under different loading rates ($v$) can be roughly divided into four stages, namely fissure compaction stage, elastic deformation stage, plastic deformation stage, and failure stage. In the initial compaction stage, the microcracks in marble tend to close under external dynamic load. Therefore, in this stage, the stress-strain curve slightly upward bending, curve slope increases gradually. Under dynamic load, the stress-strain curves of concave stage are not obvious, but it do exist [35,36]. In the elastic deformation stage, the strain grows as the stress increases, and their correlation is approximately linear. At varying temperatures, the slopes of marble specimens vary. In the plastic deformation stage, as stress increases, the slope of the curve gradually reduces, and the rate of slope reduction for marble at different temperatures varies. When peak stress is attained, the slope of the curve becomes zero. In the failure stage, the stress-strain curve decreases rapidly, and the slope of the curve is negative. At this time, the bearing capacity of marble decreases.

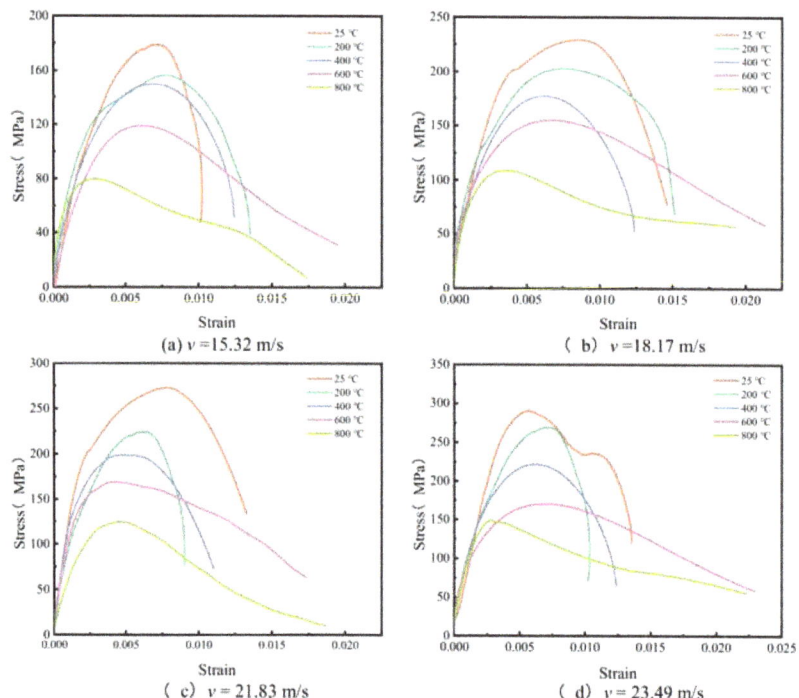

Figure 8. Stress–strain curves in marble after high-temperature treatment.

When the impact velocity is constant, the stress-strain curves of marble vary at different temperatures. Specifically, before 400 °C, the stress-strain curves of marble had little difference. At this time, the failure stage curve of the specimen has a "drop" phenomenon, indicating that the brittleness of the specimen is obvious within this temperature range. When the temperature exceeds 400 °C, the stress-strain curve of the specimen gradually shifts to the right, and the slope of the curve slows down in the failure stage, indicating that the mechanical properties of marble change from brittleness to plasticity. When the temperature is constant, the stress and strain of marble are similar under different impact velocities. With the increase of impact velocity, the specimen shows the strengthening effect of impact velocity, that is, the peak stress increases with the increase of impact velocity.

### 4.2. The Variation Pattern of Peak Stress

Figure 9 shows the relationship between the peak stress, impact velocity, and temperature of the sample. At the same temperature, the peak stress of the marble specimen increases as the impact velocity increases, indicating that the impact velocity has a significant strengthening effect. The dynamic peak stress ($\sigma_P$) increases linearly with the impact velocity ($v$), and the fitting relationship is:

$$\sigma_P = av + b \qquad (20)$$

where $a$ and $b$ are the fitting parameters. The values of marble specimens at different temperatures are shown in Table 1.

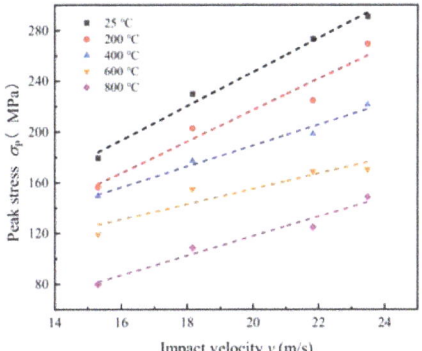

**Figure 9.** Relationship between the dynamic peak stress and the impact velocity.

**Table 1.** Fitting parameters for the peak stress and the impact velocity.

| Temperature $T/°C$ | a | b | $R^2$ |
|---|---|---|---|
| 25 | 13.48 | −22.42 | 0.98 |
| 200 | 12.41 | −31.01 | 0.94 |
| 400 | 8.24 | 24.52 | 0.98 |
| 600 | 6.09 | 33.49 | 0.87 |
| 800 | 7.73 | −36.62 | 0.96 |

Figure 9 demonstrates that, at the same temperature, the peak stress of the specimen increases progressively with increasing impact velocity. When the impact velocity remains unchanged, the specimen's peak stress steadily falls as the temperature rises.

There are two primary reasons for the analysis: first, the high temperature causes the expansion stress inside the marble specimen to increase, resulting in the expansion of the original micro-cracks and the generation of new micro-cracks [37]. Due to the fact that the primary components of marble are calcite ($CaCO_3$) and dolomite ($MgCa(CO_3)_2$), high temperature will lead to the degradation and decomposition of dolomite structure, thereby reducing the ability of marble to resist external load damage.

The relationships between dynamic peak stress and the impact velocity of marble specimens at various temperatures are listed in Table 1. It can be seen from Table 1 that the minimum fitting correlation coefficient $R^2$ between dynamic peak stress and the impact velocity of marble specimens at different temperatures is 0.87, indicating that the correlation between them is obvious. In the fitting formula, coefficient a represents the rate of peak stress rise with impact velocity. The greater the value of a, the more pronounced the strengthening effect of impact velocity. In general, with the gradual increase in temperature, the strengthening effect of impact velocity on marble peak stress is lower.

### 4.3. Crack Extension Process and Damage Mode

Figure 10 illustrates the axial damage process of marble at a speed of 18.17 m/s and a temperature of 400 °C using a high-speed camera.

**Figure 10.** Failure process of specimen taken by high-speed camera.

During the early loading stage of the stress wave, no cracks are detected on the specimen surface. At 50 µs, as a result of the reciprocating propagation of the stress wave in the specimen, an obvious crack, referred to as the major crack, appears on the side of the specimen. At 100~150 µs, the crack length and width gradually expand with time due to the ongoing action of the stress wave. At 200~300 µs, cracks begin to gather and penetrate the whole specimen. At 400 µs, the specimen became unstable, and its bearing capacity drastically dropped. The formation of cracks is mainly due to the dynamic loading induced stress concentration at the crack tip, such that the stress value at the crack tip exceeds the tensile strength of the specimen.

Figure 11 depicts the failure modes of marble specimens at 25~800 °C under four impact velocities. At the same impact velocity, the crushing degree at 600~800 °C is greater than that at 25~400 °C. It shows that temperature has a significant effect on the fracture characteristics of the specimen. When the impact velocity is low (15.32 m/s $\leq v \leq$ 618.17 m/s), the specimen can still maintain a certain bearing capacity at temperatures between 25 ~600 °C. At 800 °C, the specimen is unstable. At a higher impact velocity (21.83 m/s $\leq v \leq$ 23.49 m/s), at 25 °C $\leq T \leq$ 400 °C, the bulk rate of the specimen is higher and the average particle size is larger. When 600 °C $\leq T \leq$ 800 °C, the specimen suffered from crushing failure, with small particle size and relatively uniform distribution.

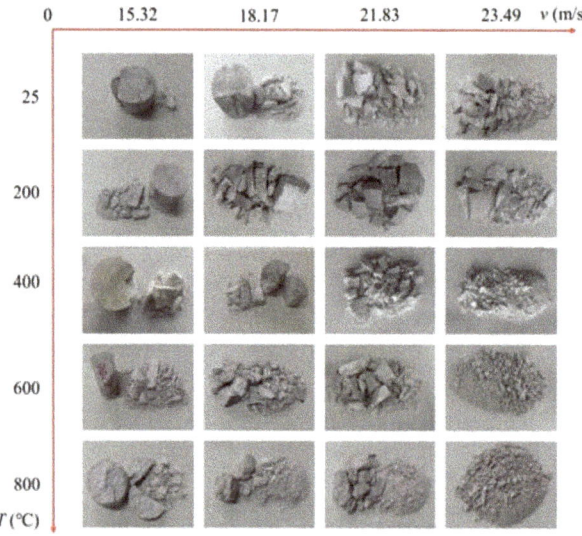

**Figure 11.** Failure mode of marble after high temperatures.

At the same temperature, with the increase in impact velocity, the fracture surface of the specimen gradually expands, the degree of fragmentation increases, and the fragment size decreases [21].

*4.4. Energy Analysis of Rocks under Combined Dynamic and Static Loading*

In rock engineering, the excavation, fragmentation, and disturbance of rock mass inevitably involve the inflow, accumulation, dissipation, and outflow of energy, and the energy changes throughout the entire rock deformation and failure process. Therefore, it is crucial to examine the failure deformation of rock from the perspective of energy [38]. In the SHPB test, The incident energy ($W_I$), absorption energy ($W_A$), transmitted energy ($W_T$), and reflection energy ($W_R$) can be calculated using Formulas (14) and (15). Figure 12 depicts the relationship between incident energy, absorbed energy, transmitted energy, reflected energy, and temperature at various impact velocities.

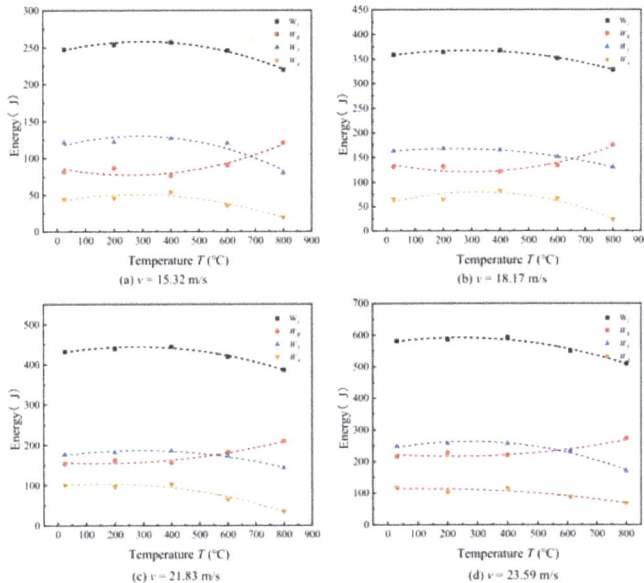

**Figure 12.** Change of energy with temperature under different impact velocity.

Figure 12a–d shows the relationship between the energy and temperature of the specimen under different impact velocities. When the impact velocity is constant, the incident energy increases first and then decreases with the increase of temperature, and reaches the maximum at 400 °C. The reflected energy first decreases and then increases with the increase of temperature, and the two are quadratic functions with an upward opening. The transmission energy and absorption energy first increase and then decrease with the increase of temperature, and the two are quadratic functions with an open downward direction. With the increase of impact velocity, the incident energy, reflection energy, transmission energy and absorption energy of the specimen increase. The fitting relationship between temperature and energy at different impact velocities is listed in Table 2.

**Table 2.** Fitting relationship between temperatures and energies at different impact velocities.

| Impact Velocity $v$ (m/s) | Fitting Relationship | $R^2$ |
| --- | --- | --- |
| 15.32 | $W_I = 244.30 + 0.09T - 1.51 \times 10^{-4}T^2$ | 0.98 |
|  | $W_R = 87.51 - 0.08T + 1.44 \times 10^{-4}T^2$ | 0.90 |
|  | $W_T = 115.35 + 0.10T - 1.96 \times 10^{-4}T^2$ | 0.91 |
|  | $W_A = 41.43 + 0.07T - 1.18 \times 10^{-4}T^2$ | 0.92 |
| 18.17 | $W_I = 356.28 + 0.08T - 1.44 \times 10^{-4}T^2$ | 0.98 |
|  | $W_R = 138.41 - 0.12T + 2.03 \times 10^{-4}T^2$ | 0.91 |
|  | $W_T = 161.91 + 0.05T - 1.15 \times 10^{-4}T^2$ | 0.98 |
|  | $W_A = 55.95 + 0.15T - 2.32 \times 10^{-4}T^2$ | 0.88 |
| 21.83 | $W_I = 427.99 + 0.12T - 2.10 \times 10^{-4}T^2$ | 0.98 |
|  | $W_R = 157.64 - 0.04T + 1.31 \times 10^{-4}T^2$ | 0.95 |
|  | $W_T = 172.91 + 0.09T - 1.62 \times 10^{-4}T^2$ | 0.98 |
|  | $W_A = 97.44 + 0.06T - 1.79 \times 10^{-4}T^2$ | 0.94 |
| 23.59 | $W_I = 577.06 + 0.13T - 2.67 \times 10^{-4}T^2$ | 0.95 |
|  | $W_R = 223.99 - 0.07T + 1.54 \times 10^{-4}T^2$ | 0.87 |
|  | $W_T = 239.89 + 0.17T - 3.22 \times 10^{-4}T^2$ | 0.99 |
|  | $W_A = 113.18 + 0.02T - 9.95 \times 10^{-4}T^2$ | 0.86 |

## 5. Conclusions

At room temperature and high temperatures (25~800 °C), the fundamental physical properties of marble were determined. SHPB impact compression test was used to measure the effect of temperature on the dynamic characteristics of marble.

(1) Temperature has a great influence on the physical properties and geometric size of marble. As the temperature increases, the color of marble specimens gradually changes from light gray to milky white. The length and diameter of marble samples increase with the increase of temperature, while the mass and longitudinal wave velocity decrease with the increase of temperature. From room temperature to 200 °C, the change of physical properties and geometric size of marble is not obvious, but the change is more obvious at 400~800 °C. The higher the temperature, the more obvious the change.

(2) At the same temperature, the stress-strain curves of marble specimens under different impact velocities are similar. When the impact velocity is constant, with the increase of temperature, the curve gradually shifts to the right, the brittleness of the specimen decreases and the plasticity increases.

(3) The crack propagation of the specimen is completed within 200 µs, and the failure mode is tensile stress splitting failure. Temperature has significant influence on the failure mechanism of specimens. In general, when the impact velocity is constant, when $25\ °C \leq T \leq 400\ °C$, the crushing degree of the specimen is higher than $600\ °C \leq T \leq 800\ °C$. When the temperature is constant, the crushing degree increases with the increase of impact velocity, the crushing size decreases gradually, and the particles tend to be uniform.

(4) When the impact velocity is constant, with the increase of temperature, the changes of incident energy, transmission energy and absorption energy of the specimen are similar, and all increase first and then decrease with the increase of temperature. The relationship between the above energy and temperature is a quadratic function of opening upward. The transmitted energy decreases first and then increases with the increase of temperature, and there is a quadratic function relationship between them.

**Author Contributions:** Conceptualization, methodology, software, validation, formal analysis, writing—original draft, writing—review and editing: Y.W.; investigation, data curation: X.Z.; supervision, software: L.H.; supervision, methodology: J.W.; funding acquisition, project administration: X.L. All authors have read and agreed to the published version of the manuscript.

**Funding:** This study was financially supported by the National Natural Science Foundation of China (No. 52164010, No. 52064025), the General Project of Basic Research Program of Yunnan Province (No. 202201AT070178), and Yunnan major scientific and technological special project (202102AG050024). Their support is gratefully appreciated.

**Institutional Review Board Statement:** Not applicable.

**Informed Consent Statement:** Not applicable.

**Data Availability Statement:** Data sharing not applicable.

**Conflicts of Interest:** The authors declare no conflict of interest.

## References

1. He, M.C.; Xie, H.P.; Peng, S.P.; Jiang, Y.D. Study on rock mechanics in deep mining engineering. *Chin. J. Rock Mech. Eng.* **2005**, *24*, 2803–2813.
2. Xie, H.P.; Gao, F.; Ju, Y. Research and development of rock mechanics in deep ground engineering. *Chin. J. Rock Mech. Eng.* **2015**, *34*, 2161–2178.
3. Xie, H.P. Research review of the state key research development program of China: Deep rock mechanics and mining theory. *J. China Coal Soc.* **2019**, *44*, 1283–1305.
4. Wang, S.F.; Tang, Y.; Wang, S.Y. Influence of brittleness and confining stress on rock cuttability based on rock indentation tests. *J. Cent. South Univ.* **2021**, *28*, 2786–2800. [CrossRef]

5. Xie, H.P.; Gao, M.Z.; Zhang, R.; Peng, G.; Wang, W.; Li, A. Study on the mechanical properties and mechanical response of coal mining at 1000 m or deeper. *Rock Mech. Rock Eng.* **2019**, *52*, 1475–1490. [CrossRef]
6. Wang, S.F.; Tang, Y.; Li, X.B.; Kun, D.U. Analyses and predictions of rock cuttabilities under different confining stresses and rock properties based on rock indentation tests by conical pick. *Trans. Nonferr. Met. Soc. China* **2021**, *31*, 1766–1783. [CrossRef]
7. Wang, S.F.; Li, X.B.; Yao, J.R.; Gong, F.; Li, X.; Du, K.; Tao, M.; Huang, L.; Du, S. Experimental investigation of rock breakage by a conical pick and its application to non-explosive mechanized mining in deep hard rock. *Int. J. Rock Mech. Min. Sci.* **2019**, *21*, 104063. [CrossRef]
8. Wang, S.F.; Sun, L.C.; Li, X.B.; Wang, S.; Du, K.; Li, X.; Feng, F. Experimental investigation of cuttability improvement for hard rock fragmentation using conical cutter. *Int. J. Geomech.* **2021**, *21*, 06020039. [CrossRef]
9. Sun, B.; Zhang, Z.Y.; Meng, J.L.; Huang, Y.; Li, H.; Wang, J. Research on Deep-Hole Cutting Blasting Efficiency in Blind Shafting with High In-Situ Stress Environment Using the Method of SPH. *Mathematics* **2021**, *9*, 3242. [CrossRef]
10. Somani, A.; Nandi, T.K.; Pal, S.K.; Majumder, A.K. Pre-treatment of rocks prior to comminution—A critical review of present practices. *Int. J. Min. Sci. Technol.* **2017**, *27*, 339–348. [CrossRef]
11. Chen, G.F.; Yang, S.Q. Study on failure mechanical behavior of marble after high temperature. *Eng. Mech.* **2014**, *31*, 189–196. [CrossRef]
12. Zhao, H.B.; Yin, G.Z.; Chen, L.J. Experimental study on effect of temperature on sandstone damage. *Chin. J. Rock Mech. Eng.* **2009**, *28*, 2784–2788.
13. Zhai, S.T.; Wu, G.; Sun, H.; Pan, J.H. Acoustic emission characteristics of thermal cracking of marble under uniaxial compression. *Chin. J. Rock Mech. Eng.* **2012**, *31*, 1237–1244.
14. Ni, X.H.; Li, X.J.; Huang, D.W. Uniaxial compression tests on mechanical properties of marble after undergoing different numbers of temperature cycling. *J. Hydroelectr. Eng.* **2016**, *35*, 95–100.
15. Huang, Z.P.; Zhang, Y.; Wu, W.D. Analysis of mechanics and fluctuation characteristics of high temperature marble cooled by water. *Rock Soil Mech.* **2016**, *37*, 367–375.
16. Zeng, Y.J.; Rong, G.; Peng, J.; Sha, S. Experimental study of crack propagation of marble after high temperature cycling. *Rock Soil Mech.* **2018**, *39*, 220–226.
17. Li, Q.S.; Yang, S.Q.; Chen, G.F. Strength and deformation properties of post-high-temperature joint sandstone. *J. China Coal Soc.* **2014**, *39*, 1283–1305.
18. Zhang, Z.Z.; Gao, F.; Liu, Z.J. Research on rockburst proneness and its microcosmic mechanism of granite considering temperature effect. *Chin. J. Rock Mech. Eng.* **2010**, *29*, 1591–1602.
19. Xu, J.Y.; Liu, S. Effect of impact velocity on dynamic mechanical behaviors of marble after high temperatures. *Chin. J. Geotech. Eng.* **2013**, *35*, 879–883.
20. Yin, T.B.; Li, X.B.; Yin, Z.Q.; Zhou, Z.L.; Liu, X.L. Study and comparison of mechanical properties of sandstone under static and dynamic loadings after high temperature. *J. Rock Mech. Eng.* **2012**, *31*, 273–279.
21. Ping, Q.; Su, H.P.; Ma, D.D.; Zhang, H.; Ma, C.L. Experimental study on physical and dynamic mechanical properties of limestone after different high temperature treatments. *Rock Soil Mech.* **2021**, *42*, 932–942.
22. Yin, T.B.; Li, X.B.; Ye, Z.Y.; Gong, F.Q.; Zhou, Z.L. Energy dissipation of rock fracture under thermo-mechanical coupling and dynamic disturbances. *J. Rock Mech. Eng.* **2013**, *32*, 1197–1202.
23. Liu, L.; Li, R.; Qin, H.; Liu, Y. Dynamic mechanical properties and microscopic damage characteristics of deep skarn after high-temperature treatment. *Chin. J. Geotech. Eng.* **2022**, *44*, 1166–1174.
24. Li, M.; Mao, X.B.; Cao, L.L.; Mao, R.R.; Tao, J. Experimental study of mechanical properties on strain rate effect of sandstones after high temperature. *Rock Soil Mech.* **2014**, *35*, 3479–3488.
25. Zhang, R.R.; Jing, L.W. The relationship between the fracture degree of deep sandstone and energy dissipation after high and low temperature in the SHPB test. *J. China Coal Soc.* **2018**, *43*, 1884–1892.
26. Li, X.B.; Yin, T.B.; Zhou, Z.L.; Hong, L.; Gao, K. Study of dynamic properties of siltstone under coupling effects of temperature and pressure. *Chin. J. Rock Mech. Eng.* **2010**, *29*, 2377–2384.
27. Kraut, E.A. Advances in the theory of anisotropic elastic wave propagation. *Rev. Geophys.* **1962**, *1*, 401–448. [CrossRef]
28. Wang, Y.B.; Wen, Z.J.; Liu, G.Q.; Wang, J.; Bao, Z.; Lu, K.; Wang, D.; Wang, B. Explosion propagation and characteristics of rock damage in decoupled charge blasting based on computed tomography scanning. *Int. J. Rock Mech. Min. Sci.* **2020**, *136*, 104540. [CrossRef]
29. Zhao, Y.; Zhou, H.G.; Zhong, J.C.; Liu, D. Study on the relation between damage and permeability of sandstone at depth under cyclic loading. *Int. J. Coal Sci. Technol.* **2019**, *6*, 479–492. [CrossRef]
30. Wang, Y.B.; Yang, R.S. Study of the dynamic fracture characteristics of coal with a bedding structure based on the NSCB impact test. *Eng. Fract. Mech.* **2017**, *184*, 319–338. [CrossRef]
31. Liu, L.; Dong, L.Z.; An, H.M.; Fan, Y.; Wang, Y. Experimental Study of the Thermal and Dynamic Behaviors of Polypropylene Fiber-Reinforced Concrete. *Appl. Sci.* **2021**, *11*, 10757. [CrossRef]
32. Liu, S.; Xu, J.J.; Bai, E.L.; Zhi, L.P.; Chen, T.F. Experimental study of dynamic tensile behaviors of marble after high temperature. *Rock Soil Mech.* **2013**, *34*, 3500–3504.
33. Liu, L.; Li, R.; Qin, H.; Sun, W. Experimental SHPB Study of Limestone Damage under Confining Pressures after Exposure to Elevated Temperatures. *Metals* **2021**, *11*, 1663. [CrossRef]

34. Xia, X.H.; Lu, Y.P.; Huang, X.H.; Shen, W.P. Experimental research on ultrasonic characteristics of marble under the action of high temperature. *J. Shanghai Jiaotong Univ.* **2004**, *38*, 1225–1228.
35. Yang, R.S.; Wang, Y.B.; Ding, C.X. Laboratory study of wave propagation due to explosion in a jointed medium. *Int. J. Rock Mech. Min. Sci.* **2016**, *81*, 70–78. [CrossRef]
36. Gao, T.; Sun, W.; Liu, Z.; Cheng, H.Y. Cheng, Investigation on fracture characteristics and failure pattern of inclined layered cemented tailings backfill. *Constr. Build. Mater.* **2022**, *343*, 128110. [CrossRef]
37. Zuo, J.P.; Zhou, H.W.; Xie, H.P. Fracture characteristics of sandstone under thermal effects. *Eng. Mech.* **2008**, *25*, 124–130.
38. Zhang, R.R.; Jing, L.W. Analysis on the fragment and energy dissipation of deep sandstone after high/low temperature treatment in SHPB tests. *J. China Coal Soc.* **2018**, *43*, 1884–1892.

*Article*

# Development of Predictive Models for Determination of the Extent of Damage in Granite Caused by Thermal Treatment and Cooling Conditions Using Artificial Intelligence

Naseer Muhammad Khan [1,2,3], Kewang Cao [1,4,*], Muhammad Zaka Emad [5,*], Sajjad Hussain [6], Hafeezur Rehman [3,7], Kausar Sultan Shah [7], Faheem Ur Rehman [8] and Aamir Muhammad [9]

1 School of Art, Anhui University of Finance & Economics, Bengbu 233030, China
2 Department of Sustainable Advanced Geomechanical Engineering, Military College of Engineering, National University of Sciences and Technology, Risalpur 23200, Pakistan
3 Department of Mining Engineering, Balochistan University of Information Technology Engineering and Management Sciences, Quetta 87300, Pakistan
4 State Key Laboratory for Geomechanics & Deep Underground Engineering, China University of Mining and Technology, Xuzhou 221116, China
5 Department of Mining Engineering, University of Engineering and Technology, Lahore 54890, Pakistan
6 Department of Mining Engineering, University of Engineering & Technology, Peshawar 25000, Pakistan
7 School of Materials and Minerals Resources Engineering, University Sains Malaysia, Nibong Tebal 14300, Penang, Malaysia
8 Graduate School of Economics and Management, Ural Federal University, Mira 19, 620002 Ekaterinburg, Russia
9 Mineral Development Department Government of KP, Peshawar 25000, Pakistan
* Correspondence: tb18220001b0@cumt.edu.cn (K.C.); muhammad.emad@mail.mcgill.ca (M.Z.E.); Tel.: +92-333-463-4361 (M.Z.E.)

**Abstract:** Thermal treatment followed by subsequent cooling conditions (slow and rapid) can induce damage to the rock surface and internal structure, which may lead to the instability and failure of the rock. The extent of the damage is measured by the damage factor ($D_T$), which can be quantified in a laboratory by evaluating the changes in porosity, elastic modulus, ultrasonic velocities, acoustic emission signals, etc. However, the execution process for quantifying the damage factor necessitates laborious procedures and sophisticated equipment, which are time-consuming, costly, and may require technical expertise. Therefore, it is essential to quantify the extent of damage to the rock via alternate computer simulations. In this research, a new predictive model is proposed to quantify the damage factor. Three predictive models for quantifying the damage factors were developed based on multilinear regression (MLR), artificial neural networks (ANNs), and the adoptive neural-fuzzy inference system (ANFIS). The temperature ($T$), porosity ($\rho$), density ($D$), and P-waves were used as input variables in the development of predictive models for the damage factor. The performance of each predictive model was evaluated by the coefficient of determination ($R^2$), the A20 index, the mean absolute percentage error (MAPE), the root mean square error (RMSE), and the variance accounted for (VAF). The comparative analysis of predictive models revealed that ANN models used for predicting the rock damage factor based on porosity in slow conditions give an $R^2$ of 0.99, A20 index of 0.99, RMSE of 0.01, MAPE of 0.14, and a VAF of 100%, while rapid cooling gives an $R^2$ of 0.99, A20 index of 0.99, RMSE of 0.02, MAPE of 0.36%, and a VAF of 99.99%. It has been proposed that an ANN-based predictive model is the most efficient model for quantifying the rock damage factor based on porosity compared to other models. The findings of this study will facilitate the rapid quantification of damage factors induced by thermal treatment and cooling conditions for effective and successful engineering project execution in high-temperature rock mechanics environments.

**Keywords:** predictive models; damage factor; thermal treatment; computer simulations; ANNs; ANFIS

**MSC:** 68T07

**Citation:** Khan, N.M.; Cao, K.; Emad, M.Z.; Hussain, S.; Rehman, H.; Shah, K.S.; Rehman, F.U.; Muhammad, A. Development of Predictive Models for Determination of the Extent of Damage in Granite Caused by Thermal Treatment and Cooling Conditions Using Artificial Intelligence. *Mathematics* 2022, 10, 2883. https://doi.org/10.3390/math10162883

Academic Editor: Elena Benvenuti

Received: 22 February 2022
Accepted: 6 August 2022
Published: 11 August 2022

**Publisher's Note:** MDPI stays neutral with regard to jurisdictional claims in published maps and institutional affiliations.

**Copyright:** © 2022 by the authors. Licensee MDPI, Basel, Switzerland. This article is an open access article distributed under the terms and conditions of the Creative Commons Attribution (CC BY) license (https://creativecommons.org/licenses/by/4.0/).

## 1. Introduction

Temperature is an essential consideration that has a significant impact on a rock's chemical, physical, and mechanical properties. Underground coal gasification, geothermal resources, nuclear waste disposal, coal mine gas explosions, underground engineering, fire reconstruction, and improved oil recovery are examples of rocks being exposed to high-temperature conditions [1–4]. The interactions of rocks in these projects take place for a long time and they are continuously exposed to high-temperature ranges, from 500 to 1500 °C [5–16]. The long-term exposure to high temperatures yields voids, pores, and microcracks. It also propagates the lengths of existing microcracks, causing damage to the integrity and stability of rocks. Moreover, it further impacts the physical, chemical, and mechanical characteristics of rocks [4,17–23]. Therefore, it is imperative to evaluate the damages thoroughly induced in rocks from high temperatures or thermal treatments for the safe execution of engineering projects. Comprehensive investigations in research studies have been carried out on different rocks subjected to thermal treatments (for various time exposures and under different cooling conditions) to evaluate rock damage mechanisms, thermal cracking, deformation mechanisms, thermal-induced stresses, strength reductions, and changes in the physical properties under high temperatures [1,3,24–38]. However, long time exposures of rocks and vast contrasts in thermal interactions make it essential to evaluate and quantify the extent of thermal damage for the safe execution of engineering projects.

Numerous researchers have investigated the degree of damage using various approaches. Placido [39] studied concrete samples that were thermally treated up to 500 °C by thermoluminescence ($T_L$) to measure the degree of damage. Similarly, Chew [40] performed a number of experiments, such as visual observations, a rock sound test, the Schmidt hammer test, and ultrasonic pulse velocity, by thermally treating (up to 500 °C) and non-treating concrete samples, and quantifying the extent of damage by $T_L$. These findings are instrumental in determining the degree of damage to concrete and rock in civil and mining engineering structures, such as tunnels, highways, buildings, etc. [26,41].

The degree of damage was measured by investigating the development and propagation of microcracks using acoustic emission signals, ultrasonic wave velocities, and strain measurements [42–44]. The degree of damage was quantified using a thin section analysis, scanning electron microscope (SEM), and micro-CT scanning [45,46]. However, the aforementioned techniques for quantifying the extent of thermal damage require dedicated equipment for measuring and observing changes in strain, ultrasonic wave velocities, acoustic emission signals, and the internal morphology of a rock specimen. The rock specimens needed for these tests could be prepared according to ISRM Ulusay [47–52] using sophisticated equipment, which could cause a delay in the quantification process.

Based on the required testing time and economics, researchers generally prefer to use empirical, statistical, and other machine learning techniques to predict or estimate the required outputs. These techniques have been developed based on the concept of mathematics. These techniques, due to their versatile nature, have been successfully applied in various engineering fields. Nowadays, these techniques have gained more attention in solving complex rock engineering problems. In this regard, various researchers use statistical techniques, including simple regression (SR), multiple linear regression (MLR), and artificial intelligence (AI) techniques comprising artificial neural networks (ANNs) and the adaptive neuro-fuzzy inference system (ANFIS) to predict the strength and deformational properties of rocks using physical properties. These properties include density, porosity, and ultrasonic wave velocities as input variables [53–65]. These studies suggest that artificial intelligence technique prediction performances are superior to statistical techniques. Moreover, the above-mentioned literature studies show that statistical approaches, such as simple regression analysis (SRA) and multivariate regression analysis (MVRA), have been used to demonstrate a link between physical and mechanical parameters. Additionally, research studies have utilized soft computing methods, such as fuzzy inference system(s) (FIS), artificial neural network (ANNs), their combination, and the adaptive neuro-fuzzy inference system (ANFIS) to forecast the output parameters (mechanical characteristics) based on the input parameters (physical properties). The findings of these investigations indicate that, when compared to statistical methodologies, soft-computing tools are more accurate for predicting mechanical characteristics. Additionally, Sirdesai, et al. [66] concluded that an ANFIS model was shown to have a higher prediction efficiency than ANNs. Statistical and soft computing techniques, on the other hand, have been utilized to forecast the strength and elastic characteristics of untreated specimens. Sirdesai, et al. [66] predicted the degree of thermal damage from the elasticity modulus using MLR, ANN, and ANFIS techniques on thermally-treated and slow cooling fine-grained Indian sandstone, up to 1000 °C, using porosity ($\phi$), density ($\rho$), coefficients of linear and volumetric thermal expansion (EL and EV), and wave velocities ($V_P$ and $V_S$). After a comparative analysis of models, they proposed that the ANFIS model is the most suitable for the mentioned purpose because of its better performance over MLR and ANN.

After a detailed study of the literature, it was noticed that there is a lack of research on the prediction of the extent of damage/damage factors from porosity under slow and rapid cooling, the selection of the optimized neuron for the best results, comparative analysis of different algorithm functions in AI, and impoverished performances of ANNs. Thus, it was imperative to address the mentioned gaps by conducting innovative research on rocks other than sandstones using statistical and artificial intelligence to predict the extent of thermal damage.

In this research, the degree of thermal damage $D_T$ of granitic rocks was predicted under the slow and rapid cooling of thermally-treated granite. The physical properties, such as porosity ($\Phi$), density ($\rho$), temperature, and P-wave velocity ($P_V$) were used as input variables for multilinear regression (MLR) and artificial intelligence (ANN and ANFIS) techniques. The adequacy of each model was evaluated based on the mean absolute percentage error (MAPE), coefficient of determination ($R^2$), A20 index, the variance accounted for (VAF), and root mean square error (RMSE). The most effective model was proposed to predict the extent of thermal damage for granitic rocks. The novelty of research includes the prediction of damage extent based on porosity under cooling conditions, neuron optimization, comparative analysis of different algorithm functions, and monitoring the impoverished performances of ANNs as compared to ANFIS.

## 2. Design of the Experimentation Process

### 2.1. Sample Preparation

In this study, granite rock samples were used, which were collected from a quarry located in the Baba G Kandaw district Buner, Khyber Pakhtunkhwa, Pakistan, as shown in Figure 1. The cores were extracted from the bulk rock samples and waxed to preserve their initial mechanical properties and avoid mineralogical and size deterioration. The cylindrical core specimens (with dimensions of 54 × 108 mm) were prepared with high geometric integrity. The ends of each core were polished carefully with a grinding machine until the deviation in the flattening of the core end became less than 0.5–0.05 mm [67]. The cores were then heated to the selected temperatures (25 °C, 300 °C, 600 °C, and 900 °C) at a constant rate of 5 °C/min [68], followed by cooling to room temperature. Cooling was performed in two different ways: exposed to the air for slow cooling and placed in water for rapid cooling. Based on the cooling conditions, the rock samples were categorized into seven groups, namely, An, Bn, Cn, Dn, En, Fn, and Gn. The samples were kept as reference samples; the temperature was assumed as 25 °C; Bn, Cn, and Dn samples were used for slow cooling, and En, Fn, and Gn were used for rapid cooling. According to detailed petrographic investigations of the granite samples, they were mostly composed of perthite feldspar, plagioclase, and quartz, with little biotite, muscovite, and opaque oxides and sulfides. The average rock composition included: K-feldspar (47.29%), quartz (25.18%), plagioclase (24.38%), muscovite (0.15%), biotite (32.03%), and other (0.97%).

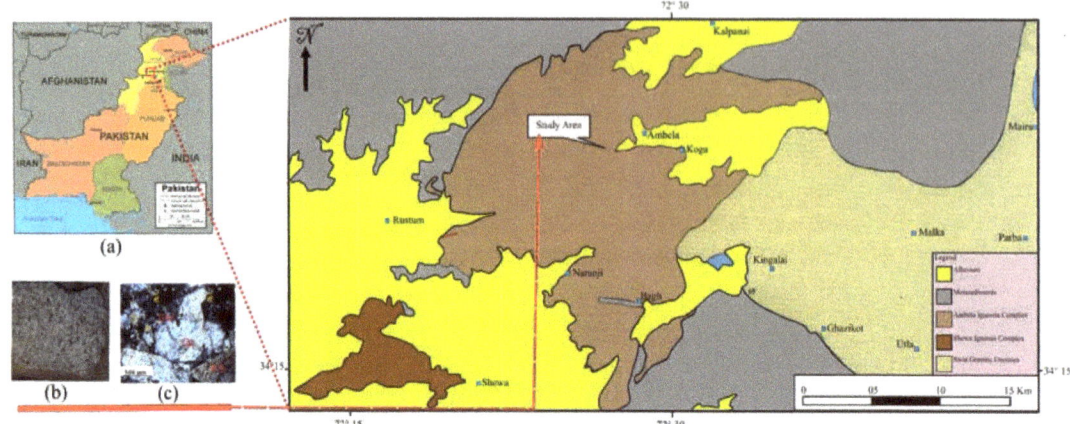

**Figure 1.** (a) Pakistan map and regional geological map showing the distribution of the Cambrian to Ordovician Swat Granite Gneisses, metasedimentary rocks, ranging in age from Late Proterozoic to Late-to-Middle Mesozoic and Late Carboniferous to Permian Ambela and the Shewa Igneous complex; (b) granite boulder; (c) micrographs of the thin sections (cross-polarized light).

## 2.2. Experimental Procedure and Instrument

A portable ultrasonic nondestructive digital indicating tester (PUNDIT) was used to compute the ultrasonic parameter, such as the ultrasonic P-wave velocity, ultrasonic S-wave velocity, and the transit time for each velocity. It is worth mentioning that the test procedure in this part tested the P-wave velocity of the unheated and post-thermal treatments under different cooling conditions of rock samples. The density and porosity of rock specimens were determined before and after heating. The samples were prepared and tested according to the International Society for Rock Mechanics (ISRM). Ten experimental runs for each physical property (density, porosity, P-waves, and elastic modulus) were conducted before and after the thermal treatment and subsequent cooling conditions. The study steps are shown in Figure 2. The average results obtained from testing the thermally-treated granite rock samples and subsequent cooling conditions (slow and rapid cooling) for density, porosity, and P-waves, are presented in Table 1.

**Table 1.** Thermal damage factors under slow cooling and rapid cooling.

| Sample No. | Cooling Condition | Temperature (°C) | Porosity (%) | Density (Kg/m³) | P-Wave (m/s) | Elasticity (GPa) | $D_{T\rho}$ | $D_{TE}$ |
|---|---|---|---|---|---|---|---|---|
| $A_n$ |  | 25 | 1.33 | 2681.67 | 4098.67 | 20.70 | 0.00 | 0.00 |
| $B_n$ | Slow | 300 | 3.43 | 2674.56 | 4047.56 | 16.50 | 0.41 | 0.19 |
| $C_n$ | cooling | 600 | 6.83 | 2673.17 | 3916.20 | 9.10 | 0.75 | 0.55 |
| $D_n$ |  | 900 | 10.83 | 2671.27 | 3700.27 | 3.62 | 0.86 | 0.82 |
| $A_n$ |  | 25 | 1.33 | 2681.67 | 4098.67 | 20.70 | 0.00 | 0.00 |
| $E_n$ | Rapid | 300 | 4.53 | 2673.09 | 3747.56 | 12.73 | 0.70 | 0.37 |
| $F_n$ | Cooling | 600 | 7.63 | 2672.16 | 3560.65 | 7.80 | 0.82 | 0.62 |
| $G_n$ |  | 900 | 13.53 | 2670.07 | 3210.27 | 2.62 | 0.90 | 0.87 |

**Figure 2.** Flowchart of the methodology for the prediction of thermal damage.

### 2.3. Thermal Damage Factor

The thermal damage factor ($D_T$) was used to evaluate the degree of damage induced by the thermal treatment and subsequent cooling conditions. It is a key parameter and can induce rock instability and failure when the severity of the damage is maximum. The thermal damage factor was calculated based on porosity and elasticity using Equation (1) and Equation (2), respectively. The calculated values are given in Table 1.

$$D_{TP} = \left(1 - \frac{1 - n_T}{1 - n_{T_0}}\right) \times 100\% \tag{1}$$

where $n_T$ is the porosity after temperature and $n_{T_0}$ represents the porosity before temperature.

$$D_{TE} = \left(1 - \frac{E_T}{E_0}\right) \tag{2}$$

where $E_T$ is the elasticity at high temperature and $E_0$ is the elasticity at room temperature.

## 3. Prediction Model

### 3.1. MLR Model

MLR is commonly used to predict the relevant parameters. MLR is an extended version of the simple linear regression used in the multiple predictive variables. It can model the input without variables considering their relationship and form a generalized equation, as shown in Equation (3) [69,70].

$$W = C + b_1 z_1 + b_2 z_2 + b_3 z_3 + \ldots\ldots + b_n z_n \tag{3}$$

where the partial regression coefficients are $b_1$ to $b_n$, $W$ is the dependent variable, $C$ is constant, and $z_1$ to $z_n$ are the independent variables.

## 3.2. ANN Model

Numerous AI techniques are used globally for prediction; ANN is one of them. It mimics the behavior of the human brain. It is generally a useful tool in pattern recognition, clustering data, and fitting a function. Because of its learning capacity, memory simulation, and excellent performance owing to features such as categorizing and filtering noisy data, ANN is a particularly significant sector in geotechnical and mining engineering [64,66,71–79]. Furthermore, it is a promising approach used for solving complicated engineering issues involving enormous amounts of data or several input parameters, making manual solutions more difficult. In general, an ANN is made up of components, such as inputs, outputs, weights, activation, training, and numerous neurons. Experiment-collected test data are multiplied by weights and applied to the existing activation functions. [77,79].

Mathematically, the basic ANN is expressed as

$$N = f(Kx + C) \tag{4}$$

where

$$K = K_1, K_2, K_3, K_4, \ldots\ldots, K_n$$

$$M = m_1, m_2, m_3, m_4, \ldots\ldots, m_n$$

where $K$, $m$, and $C$ refer to weights, input, and bias, respectively. The net ($L$) predicted values are calculated using Equation (5)

$$L = \sum_{i=1}^{n}(K_i M_i + C) \tag{5}$$

In this study, tangent sigmoid was used as the transferred function, which was calculated using Equation (6)

$$y = \tanh(L) \tag{6}$$

$$output = y = \tanh(L) = \tanh\left(\sum_{i=1}^{n}(K_i M_i + C)\right) \tag{7}$$

Generally, the error of the network expresses the difference between the actual and predicted values. This error, affected by the number of neuron weights in the hidden layers (and its value), either increased or decreased. The error of number points ($E_n$) can be calculated by using Equation (8)

$$E_n = Actual_{value} - Predicted_{value} \tag{8}$$

The total error ($E_T$) can be calculated by using Equation (9)

$$E_T = \frac{1}{2}\sum_{n} E_n^2 \tag{9}$$

The efficiencies of the ANN networks were assessed using various learning algorithms. The terms "learning algorithm" and "training algorithm" are used interchangeably. In this research, regarding the five learning functions, each function had its advantages and disadvantages. These functions were Levenberg–Marquardt (LM), BFGS quasi-Newton (BFG), resilient backpropagation (RP), scaled conjugate gradient (SCG), and conjugate gradient with Powell/Beale restarts (CBG); they were used as training functions. Additionally, the performance of ANN was greatly affected by hidden-layer neurons. The performance of the ANN network was evaluated by using feed-forward backpropagation type of neural networks, the tangent sigmoid activation function, and numerous neurons. To achieve optimum performance of the models, the normalization technique was used by applying Equation (10).

$$X_{norm} = \frac{(X_{actual} - X_{min})}{(X_{max} - X_{min})} \quad (10)$$

where $X_{norm}$ refers to the normalized value, $X_{actual}$ refers to the measured value, $X_{min}$ and $X_{max}$ refer to the corresponding minimum and maximum values of the dataset. The different numbers of neurons were used for different training functions followed by comparing the models; the best model was recommended in terms of the training function.

### 3.3. Adaptive Neural Fuzzy Interface System (ANFIS) Models

The fuzzy logic system was proposed by Zadeh [80] for the first time, which can be used to predict the solution mechanism for complex engineering problems. Owing to the shortcoming, it could not define a standardized procedure for designing such a system. After the advent of the neural network, Jang [81] introduced a new technique known as an adaptive neuro-fuzzy inference system (ANFIS). This technique mapped the output and input by exploiting the fuzzy systems and neural network learning and reasoning proficiencies. Using a combination of fuzzy logic and neural networks, the ANFIS can effectively solve various complex and non-linear problems in any engineering field. ANFIS uses fuzzy rules to predict the output from inputs; these fuzzy rules are developed during the training process. The ANFIS construct and its FIS membership are derived from training data. Two FISs commonly used Mamdani and Sugeno. The key distinction between the two is that the Sugeno output membership is linear or constant, while the Mamdani output membership is triangular, Gaussian, etc. In the present study, Sugeno FIS was used because it is computationally more efficient than Mamdani. The procedure of ANFIS can be described in the form of FIS, with two inputs (S) and (T) and one output (Z). Subsequently, if–then rules of the two-fuzzy were developed, which are given below:

Rule 1: If S is $J_1$ and $y$ is $P_1$, then $Z_1 = D_1 x + F_1 y + Q_1$

Rule 2: If $x$ is $J_2$ and $y$ is $P_2$, then $z_2 = D_2 x + F_2 y + Q_2$

where $J_1$, $P_1$, $J_2$, and $J_2$ refer to the input membership functions for 'S' and 'T'; whereas $D_1$, $F_1$, $Q_2$, $D_2$, $F_1$, and $Q_2$ refer to the output function parameters.

Numerous scholars have detailed the ANFIS model, consisting of five layers [66,82–84]. Moreover, the ANFIS model uses two learning algorithms, backpropagation and hybrid, to optimize the result with the minimal value of error between the predicted and estimated values [79–84]. A hybrid optimization method was used in the present study due to its high prediction results [61,77]. This model shows excellent performance, but the convergence of the model was slow due to the high if–and–or relationship.

## 4. Results and Discussion

### 4.1. MLR Models

The estimated thermal damage factor based on elasticity and porosity under both cooling conditions are given in Equations (11)–(14).

$$D_{TER} = 50.6946 + 0.0005T - 0.0032\,\rho - 0.0185\,\phi - 0.0002 P_V \quad (11)$$

$$D_{TPR} = 211.0464 + 0.00048T - 0.0265\,\rho - 0.0789\,\phi + 0.0001 P_V \quad (12)$$

$$D_{TES} = -61.34 + 0.00094T + 0.06195\,\rho + 0.0214\,\phi + 0.00093 P_V \quad (13)$$

$$D_{TPS} = 162.9 + 0.00094T - 0.04117\,\rho - 0.06099\,\phi + 0.00016 P_V \quad (14)$$

Graphically, the experimental and predicted thermal damage factors under each cooling condition are given in Figure 3. Figure 3a,b illustrate that the experimental and predicted thermal damage factors based on porosity and elasticity under slow cooling conditions yielded $R^2$ values of 0.97 and 0.94, respectively. Similarly, the RMSEs for porosity and elasticity were 0.061 and 0.083, respectively. On the other hand, Figure 3c,d show the experimental and predicted thermal damage factors based on porosity under rapid cooling resulting in $R^2$ and RMSE as 0.97 and 0.056, respectively. In the elasticity case, the $R^2$ and RMSE were 0.94 and 0.076, respectively.

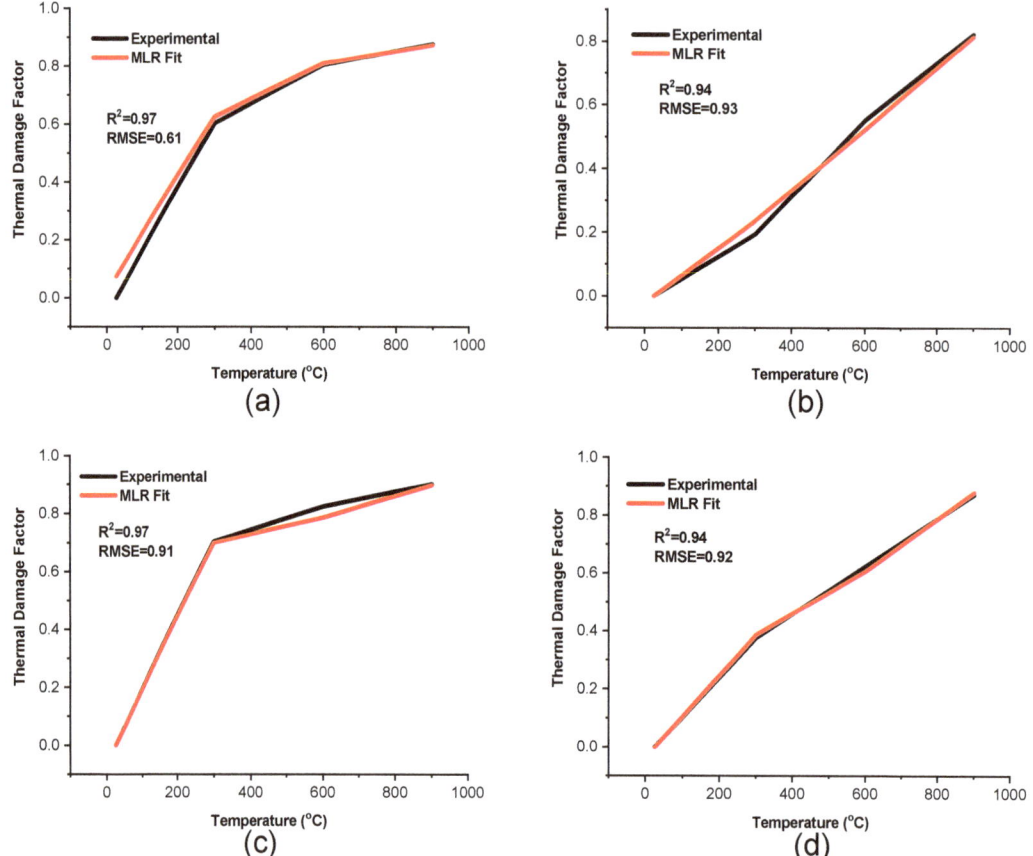

**Figure 3.** Experimental and MLR models; (**a**) porosity-based $D_T$ under slow cooling; (**b**) elasticity-based $D_T$ under slow cooling; (**c**) porosity-based $D_T$ under rapid cooling; and (**d**) elasticity-based $D_T$ under rapid cooling.

## 4.2. ANN Models

### 4.2.1. Model Design

A total of 2000 networks were generated for various training algorithms, each case comprising 500 networks. In the presence of a tangent sigmoid function as an activation function, the feed-forward backpropagation network with 5 training functions (and up to 100 neurons) was tested in the design for each learning algorithm. The model performance and comparative analysis of the different models were evaluated based on $R^2$, the a20 index, RMSE, MAPE, and VAF.

### 4.2.2. ANN Code Compilation in MATLAB

This study compiled self-generated code for ANN for n numbers of networks, keeping the same training and activation functions for a single loop as shown in Figure 4. A loop function was introduced in this code, which can run for the desired number of networks. The activation function overall in this code was fixed, which can be changed according to the data nature. In the present case, the code was executed for a hundred networks in a single execution. The number of neurons increased in each successor for each network in a loop; i.e., for network$_1$, there was one neuron, for network$_2$, there were two neurons, and so on. In both the hidden and output layers, the same activation function was used.

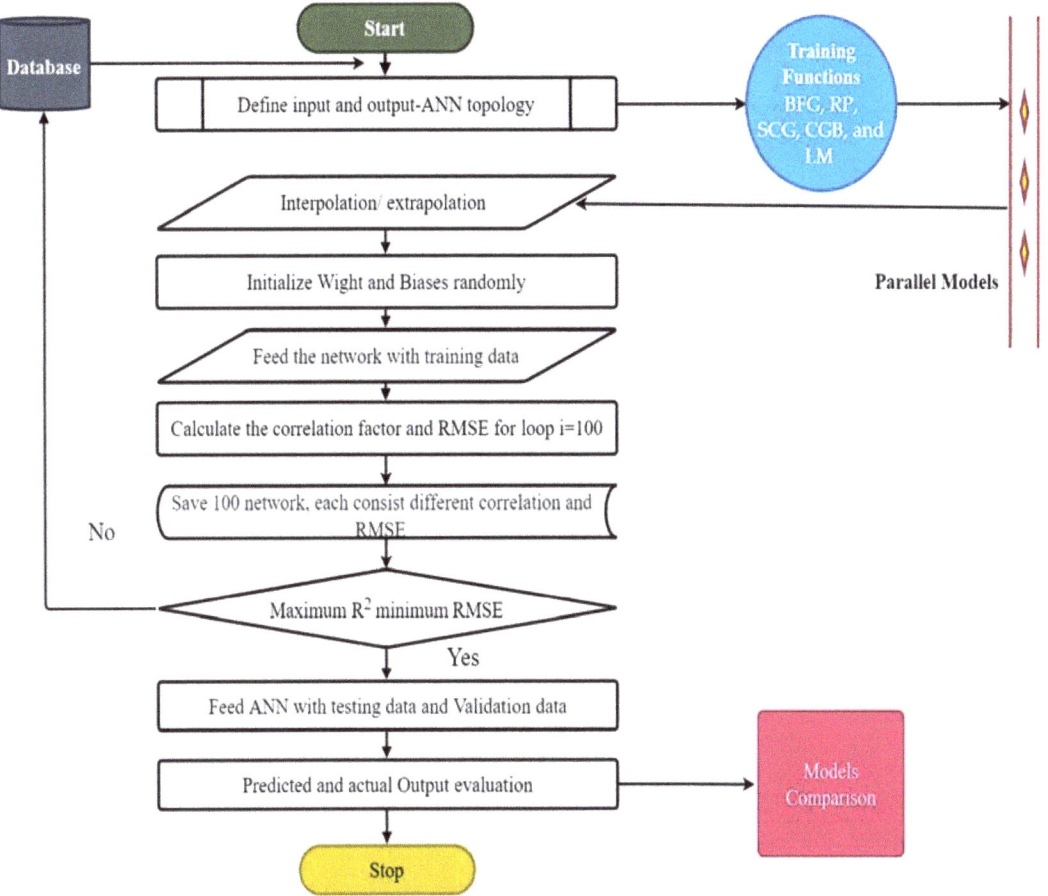

**Figure 4.** Flowchart of ANN for thermal damage model prediction.

### 4.2.3. Network Phases and Regression Models

In this research, the basic structure consisted of four inputs (temperature, porosity, density, and P-waves) and one output (thermal damage factor) in both cooling conditions, as was based on porosity and elasticity, as shown in Figure 5. A total of forty data points were taken as a dataset. The dataset was divided into three parts: training (75%), testing (15%), and validation (15%). Figure 6a,b show the training, validation, and testing for the slow cooling thermal damage factor based on porosity and elasticity. Similarly, Figure 6c,d show a rapid cooling thermal damage factor based on porosity and elasticity. Furthermore, prior to comparing various ANN models of thermal damage in both cooling conditions, it was desired to choose the best optimum training function at the first stage for the studied data. Therefore, five different training functions, namely BFG, RP, SCG, CGB, and LM, were evaluated to select the best performance training function for the optimum ANN prediction model.

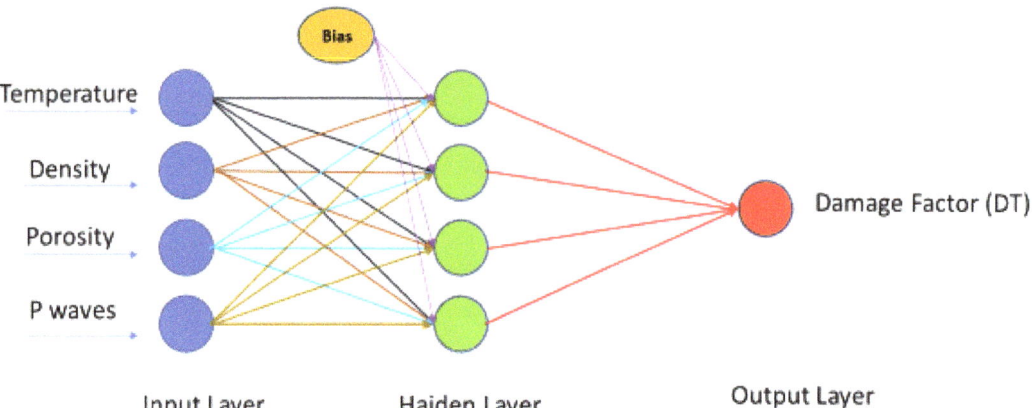

**Figure 5.** ANN-developed structure for the thermal damage factor.

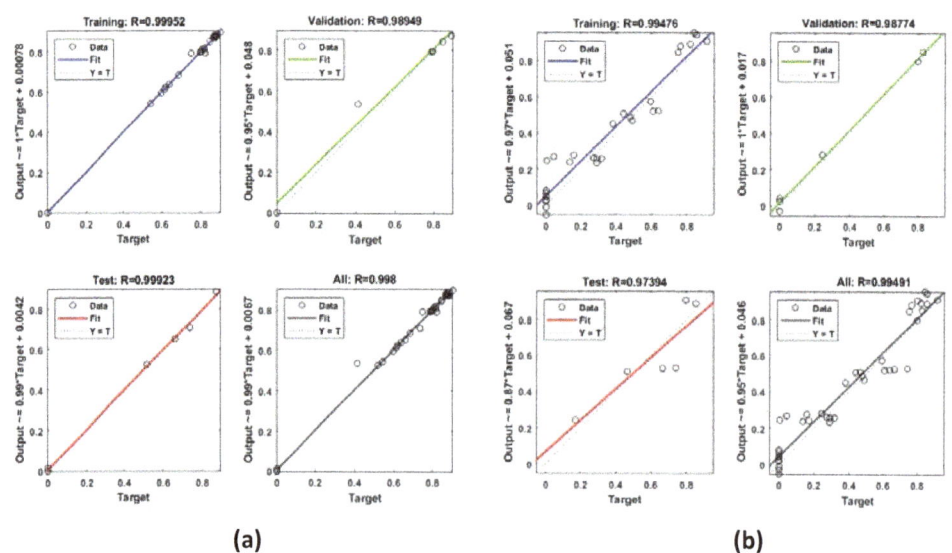

**Figure 6.** *Cont.*

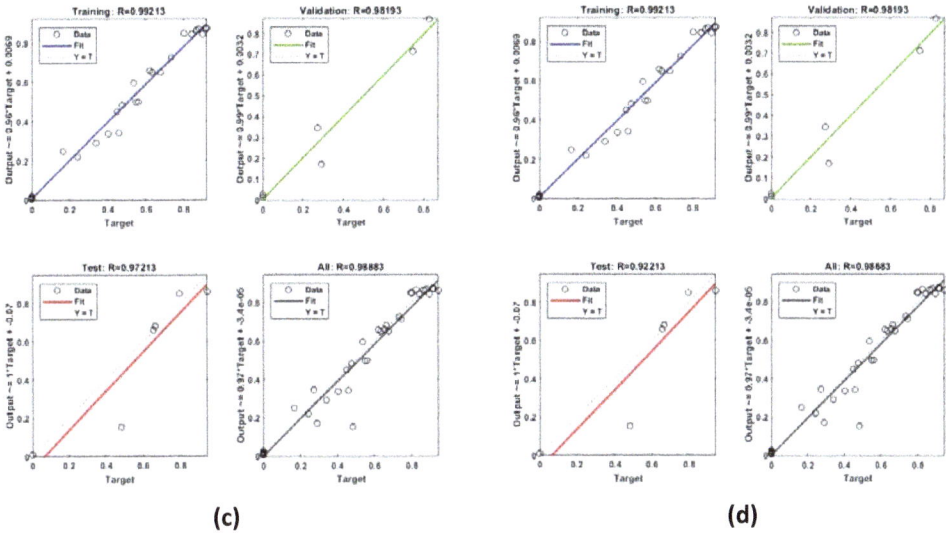

**Figure 6.** Regression model $D_T$, (**a**) porosity-based $D_T$ under slow cooling, (**b**) elasticity-based $D_T$ under slow cooling, (**c**) porosity-based $D_T$ under rapid cooling, and (**d**) elasticity-based $D_T$ under rapid cooling.

4.2.4. Model Performance

Table 2 shows the optimum results of each algorithm. In comparison to other functions, the overall efficiency of the LM function was very high in terms of $R^2$, RMSE, the number of neurons, and execution timing. As compared to other algorithms, LM converged data faster. Furthermore, the efficiency of LM for DT based on porosity under slow and fast cooling was better than the elasticity-based (in terms of RMSE).

**Table 2.** Performance evaluation of different training algorithms for $D_T$ under both cooling conditions.

| Cooling Conditions | Thermal Damage Based on | Training Function | $R^2$ | RMSE | Neuron | Time (s) |
|---|---|---|---|---|---|---|
| Slow cooling | Porosity | BFG | 0.99 | 0.03 | 61 | 307 |
| | | RP | 0.99 | 0.24 | 35 | 256 |
| | | SCG | 0.99 | 0.35 | 32 | 308 |
| | | CGB | 0.99 | 0.03 | 71 | 289 |
| | | LM | 0.999 | 0.01 | 80 | 65 |
| | Elasticity | BFG | 0.99 | 0.03 | 68 | 308 |
| | | RP | 0.99 | 0.25 | 53 | 256 |
| | | SCG | 0.99 | 0.35 | 93 | 310 |
| | | CGB | 0.99 | 0.04 | 34 | 291 |
| | | LM | 0.999 | 0.07 | 52 | 43 |
| Rapid cooling | Porosity | BFG | 0.99 | 0.02 | 72 | 307 |
| | | RP | 0.99 | 0.23 | 64 | 256 |
| | | SCG | 0.99 | 0.35 | 54 | 308 |
| | | CGB | 0.99 | 0.03 | 25 | 289 |
| | | LM | 0.999 | 0.02 | 18 | 34 |
| | Elasticity | BFG | 0.99 | 0.02 | 14 | 308 |
| | | RP | 0.99 | 0.22 | 4 | 254 |
| | | SCG | 0.99 | 0.32 | 32 | 310 |
| | | CGB | 0.99 | 0.03 | 12 | 291 |
| | | LM | 0.999 | 0.012 | 74 | 58 |

Further, the LM performance was better in slow cooling than in rapid cooling. Figure 7 shows the performance of LM with variations in the number of neurons for the thermal damage factors in both slow and rapid cooling based on porosity and elasticity. The optimum neurons for LM with high $R^2$ and low RSME with the least convergent time details are presented in Table 2, revealing that the optimum neuron numbers in slow cooling based on porosity and elasticity were 80 and 52, respectively. Similarly, for rapid cooling based on porosity and elasticity, the optimal neuron numbers were 18 and 72, respectively.

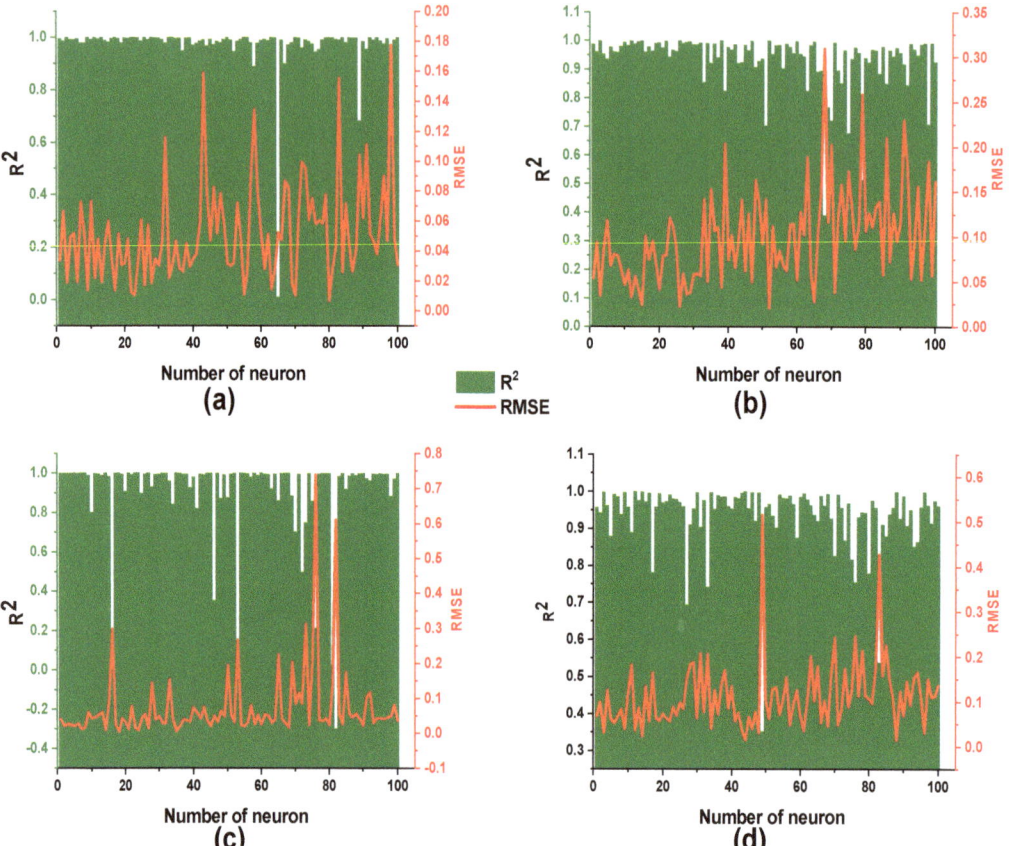

**Figure 7.** LM optimum number of neurons for (**a**) porosity-based $D_T$ under slow cooling, (**b**) elasticity-based $D_T$ under slow cooling, (**c**) porosity-based $D_T$ under rapid cooling, and (**d**) elasticity-based $D_T$ under rapid cooling.

Figure 6a shows that the thermal damage factor based on porosity under slow cooling conditions revealed correlation coefficients of 0.99, 0.98, 0.99, and 0.99 for training, validation, testing, and overall, respectively. Similarly, Figure 6b shows the thermal damage factor based on elasticity under slow cooling conditions revealed correlation coefficients of 0.99, 0.98, 0.97, and 0.99 for training, validation, testing, and overall, respectively. In contrast, for rapid cooling conditions, the thermal damage factors based on porosity and elasticity are shown in Figure 6c,d. These figures also revealed correlation coefficients of 0.99, 0.98, 0.97, 0.98 and 0.99, 0.98, 0.92, 0.97, and 0.98 for training, validation, testing, and overall, respectively.

4.2.5. ANN Predicted Models

The effectiveness of the developed ANN models was assessed by comparing the predicted and actual values, as shown in Figure 8. The porosity and elasticity-based damage factors in slow cooling conditions are shown in Figure 8a,b, with the corresponding correlation coefficient value as 0.99; likewise, the RMSE value was recorded as 0.01 and 0.07 for porosity and elasticity-based damage factor, respectively. It indicates that the porosity-based prediction model outperformed the elasticity-based thermal damage factor in slow cooling conditions. In addition, the thermal damage factor based on porosity in rapid cooling (Figure 8c) showed the correlation coefficient and RMSE value as 0.99 and 0.02, respectively.

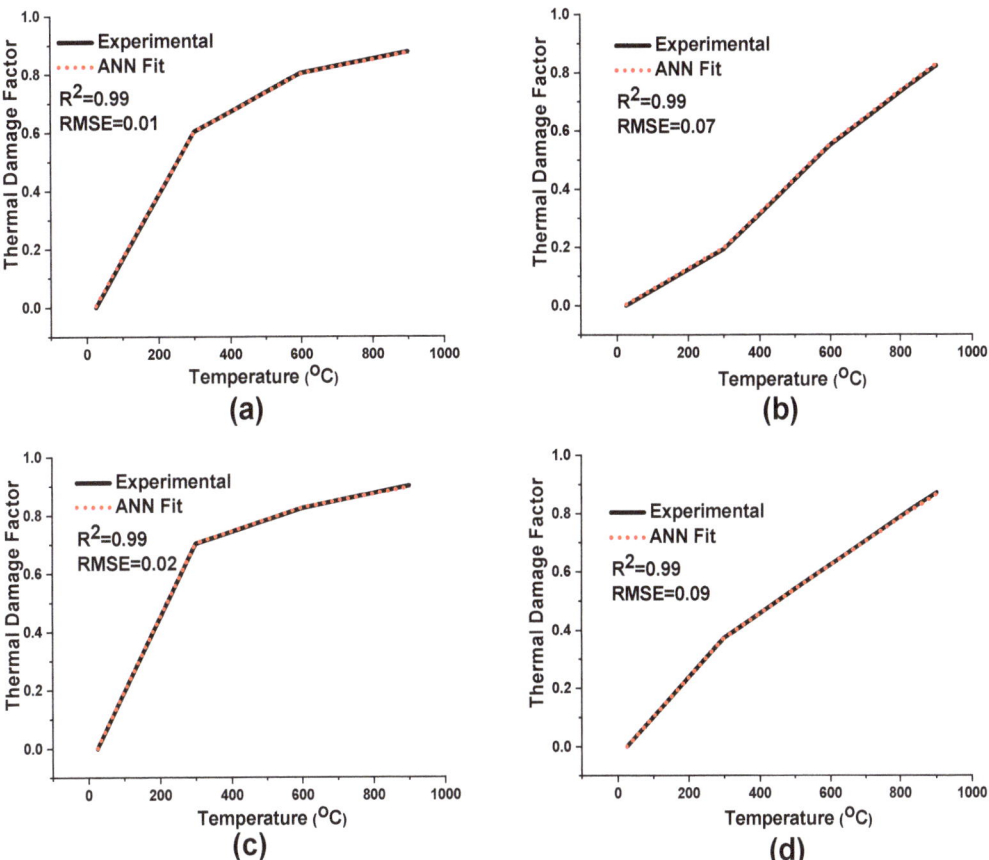

Figure 8. Experimental ANN model; (a) porosity-based $D_T$ under slow cooling, (b) elasticity-based $D_T$ under slow cooling, (c) porosity-based $D_T$ under rapid cooling, and (d) elasticity-based $D_T$ under rapid cooling.

Similarly, Figure 8d shows the elasticity-based damage factor in rapid cooling conditions that resulted in the correlation coefficient and RMSE values of 0.99 and 0.09, respectively. It is worth mentioning that the damage factor dependent on porosity and elasticity in both cooling conditions had almost the same high coefficient of determination and less RMSE than the elasticity-based value, as shown in Figure 8. Furthermore, the porosity-based prediction model is more accurate in terms of $R^2$, RMSE, the number of neurons, and convergent time.

## 4.3. ANFIS Models

Similar to ANN, the dataset was divided into three parts, training (75%), testing (15%), and validation (15%). The flowchart of the ANFIS for thermal damage is shown in Figure 9. The data division pattern was used in both cooling conditions to measure the thermal damage factors (porosity, elasticity). The ANFIS models were trained for up to 50 epochs. The fuzzy interface system (FIS) was generated for models using a sub-clustering algorithm and a hybrid training algorithm for FIS optimum methods. The linear Gaussian function was used to predict the thermal damage factor from input under both cooling conditions. Figure 10 shows the structure of the developed ANFIS model. Table 3 describes the details of each parameter used during the model's development.

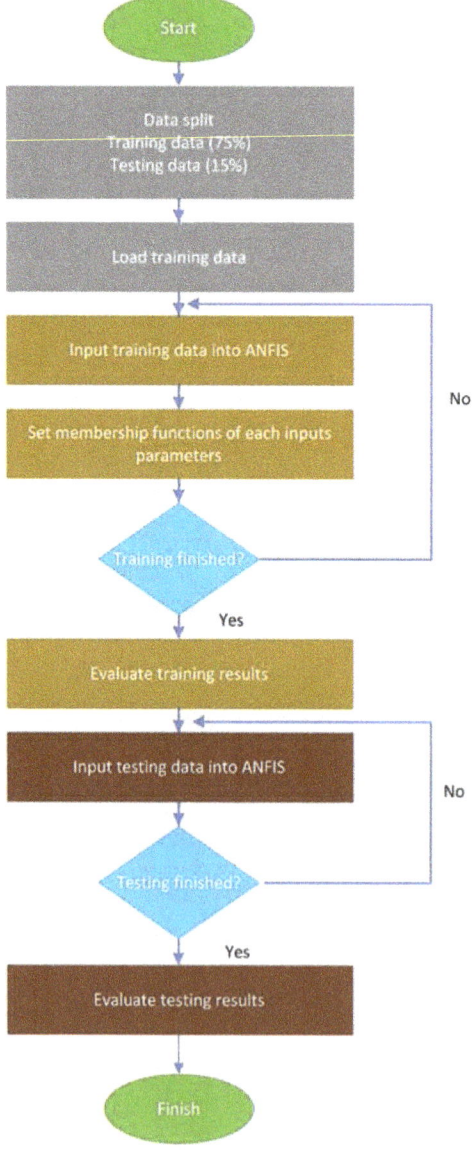

**Figure 9.** ANFIS flowchart for thermal damage prediction.

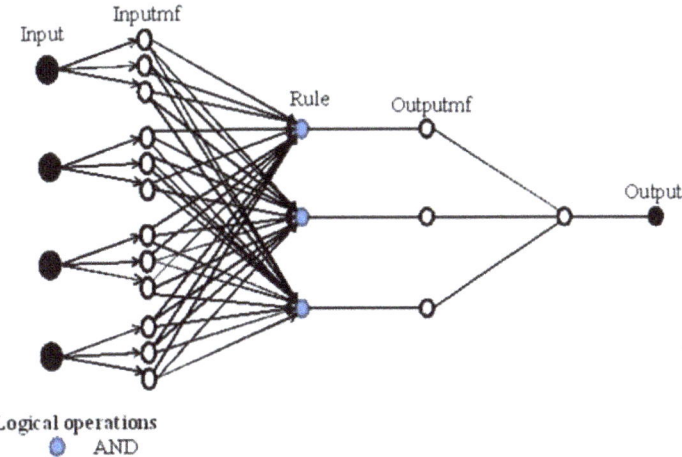

**Figure 10.** Proposed ANFIS model for thermal damage factor.

**Table 3.** The properties of the proposed ANFIS model under both cooling conditions.

| ANFIS Parameters | Value (Thermal Damage Factor on Porosity and Elasticity) | | | |
|---|---|---|---|---|
| | Slow Cooling | | Rapid Cooling | |
| | Porosity | Elasticity | Porosity | Elasticity |
| FIS generator types | Sub clustering | ✓ | ✓ | ✓ |
| Membership function types for each input | Gaussian | ✓ | ✓ | ✓ |
| Type Membership function types for each input | Linear | ✓ | ✓ | ✓ |
| Range of influence | 0.5 | ✓ | ✓ | ✓ |
| Squash Factor | 1.25 | ✓ | ✓ | ✓ |
| Accept Ratio | 0.5 | ✓ | ✓ | ✓ |
| Reject Ratio | 0.15 | ✓ | ✓ | ✓ |
| Number of fuzzy rules | 256 | ✓ | ✓ | ✓ |
| Number of epochs | 50 | ✓ | ✓ | ✓ |
| Number of data point | 40 | ✓ | ✓ | ✓ |
| Number training points | 28 | ✓ | ✓ | ✓ |
| Number of testing points | 6 | ✓ | ✓ | ✓ |
| Number of valid points | 6 | ✓ | ✓ | ✓ |

Note: ✓ mean valid.

The efficiencies of the developed ANFIS models were analyzed by comparing the predicted value to the actual value, as shown in Figure 11. Figure 11a shows the porosity-based $D_T$ in slow cooling, which reveals $R^2$ and RMSE values of 0.98 and 0.07, respectively. Similarly, Figure 11b shows the elasticity-based $D_T$ in slow cooling, revealing $R^2$ and RMSE values of 0.97 and 0.44, respectively. In contrast, Figure 11c shows the porosity-based $D_T$ in rapid cooling, which reveals $R^2$ and RMSE values of 0.98 and 0.88, respectively, while Figure 11d shows the porosity-based $D_T$ in rapid cooling, which shows $R^2$ and RMSE values of 0.94 and 0.88, respectively. Furthermore, the prediction damage based on porosity showed higher $R^2$ and lower RMSE values than the elasticity-based. Hence, porosity-based $D_T$ in both cooling conditions gives more reliable results than elasticity-based $D_T$ in terms of high ($R^2$, a20 index) and low RMSE values.

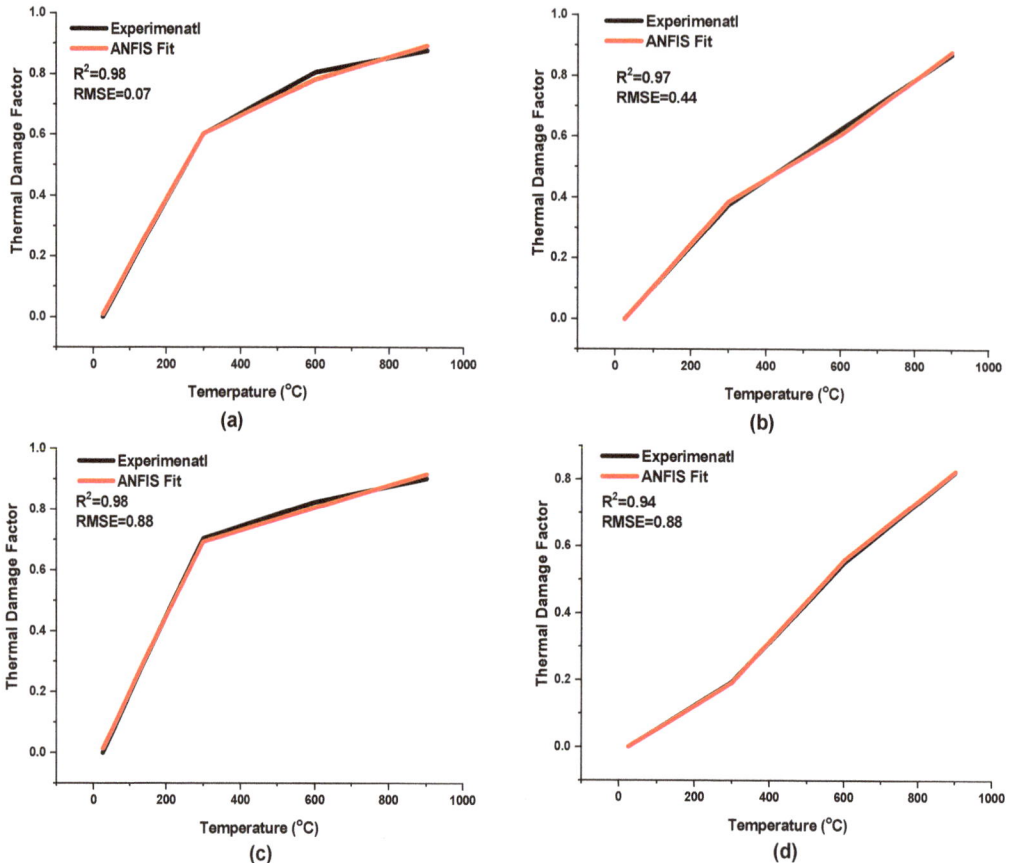

**Figure 11.** Experimental and ANFIS models; (**a**) porosity-based $D_T$ under slow cooling, (**b**) elasticity-based $D_T$ under slow cooling, (**c**) porosity-based $D_T$ under rapid cooling, and (**d**) elasticity-based $D_T$ under rapid cooling.

## 5. A Comparative Appraisal of Statistics and Intelligent Technique

The comparison of correlation efficiencies of various developed models was used in this study to improve the performances of the predicted models. The subsequent performance indices, such as $R^2$, MAPE, RMSE, and VAF, were evaluated. An excellent model can be represented by the following performance indices: $R^2 = 1$, a20 index, MAPE = RMSE = 0, and VAF = 100%. The performance indices were calculated using Equations (15)–(19).

$$R^2 = \frac{\sum_{i=1}^{n}(y_i)^2 - \sum_{i=1}^{n}(y_i - k'_i)^2}{\sum_{i=1}^{n}(y_i)^2} \tag{15}$$

$$\text{MAPE} = \frac{1}{2}\sum_{i=1}^{n}\left|\frac{y_i - k'_i}{y_i}\right| \times 100 \tag{16}$$

$$\text{RMSE} = \sqrt{\frac{\sum_{i=1}^{n}(y_i - k'_i)}{n}} \tag{17}$$

$$\text{VAF} = \left[1 - \frac{\text{var}(y - k')}{\text{var}(y)}\right] \times 100 \tag{18}$$

$$\text{a20} - \text{index} = \frac{k^{20}}{M} \tag{19}$$

where $y$ is the actual value, $k'$ is the predicted value, $k^{20}$ is the ratio of the original and predicted values in the range of 0.80–1.20, and $M$ is the total datasets.

As a result, the LM-based ANN model was selected compared to LMR and ANFIS. Table 4 illustrates the performance indices. The performance index values demonstrate that the ANN model performed better than the MLR and ANFIS approaches in the current study. The adequacy of ANN is higher than ANFIS and MRL. The most significant limitation of ANFIS over ANN observed in the present study was that the FIS generator training took a long time, particularly as the number of inputs and epochs increased, while ANN executed too fast. Additionally, Figure 12 depicts the predicted and experimental thermal damage factor dependent on porosity and elasticity under both cooling conditions. In both cases, the ANN showed a better prediction comparatively than ANFIS and MLR. Furthermore, all models gave high accuracies at low and high temperatures (below 200 °C and greater than 600 °C). This fluctuation in prediction and measure value was due to a nonlinear increase in thermal damage. The ANN model is better than other models and overlaps with the experimental curve, as shown in Figure 12.

Table 4. Performance indices of the developed models.

| Cooling Conditions | Thermal Damage Based on | Models | R² | A20 Index | RMSE | MAPE (%) | VAF (%) |
|---|---|---|---|---|---|---|---|
| Slow cooling | Porosity | MLR | 0.97 | 0.94 | 0.061 | 31.55 | 91.51 |
| | | ANFIS | 0.98 | 0.96 | 0.07 | 7.4 | 92.33 |
| | | ANN | 0.99 | 0.98 | 0.01 | 0.14 | 100 |
| | Elasticity | MLR | 0.94 | 0.91 | 0.93 | 31.53 | 91.51 |
| | | ANFIS | 0.97 | 0.96 | 0.44 | 8.96 | 78.52 |
| | | ANN | 0.99 | 0.98 | 0.07 | 1.18 | 99.19 |
| Rapid cooling | Porosity | MLR | 0.97 | 0.94 | 0.91 | 11.96 | 94.73 |
| | | ANFIS | 0.98 | 0.96 | 0.88 | 11.56 | 84.29 |
| | | ANN | 0.99 | 0.98 | 0.02 | 0.36 | 99.99 |
| | Elasticity | MLR | 0.94 | 0.91 | 0.92 | 29.53 | 94.51 |
| | | ANFIS | 0.97 | 0.96 | 0.88 | 15.03 | 80.68 |
| | | ANN | 0.99 | 0.98 | 0.09 | 1.53 | 99.75 |

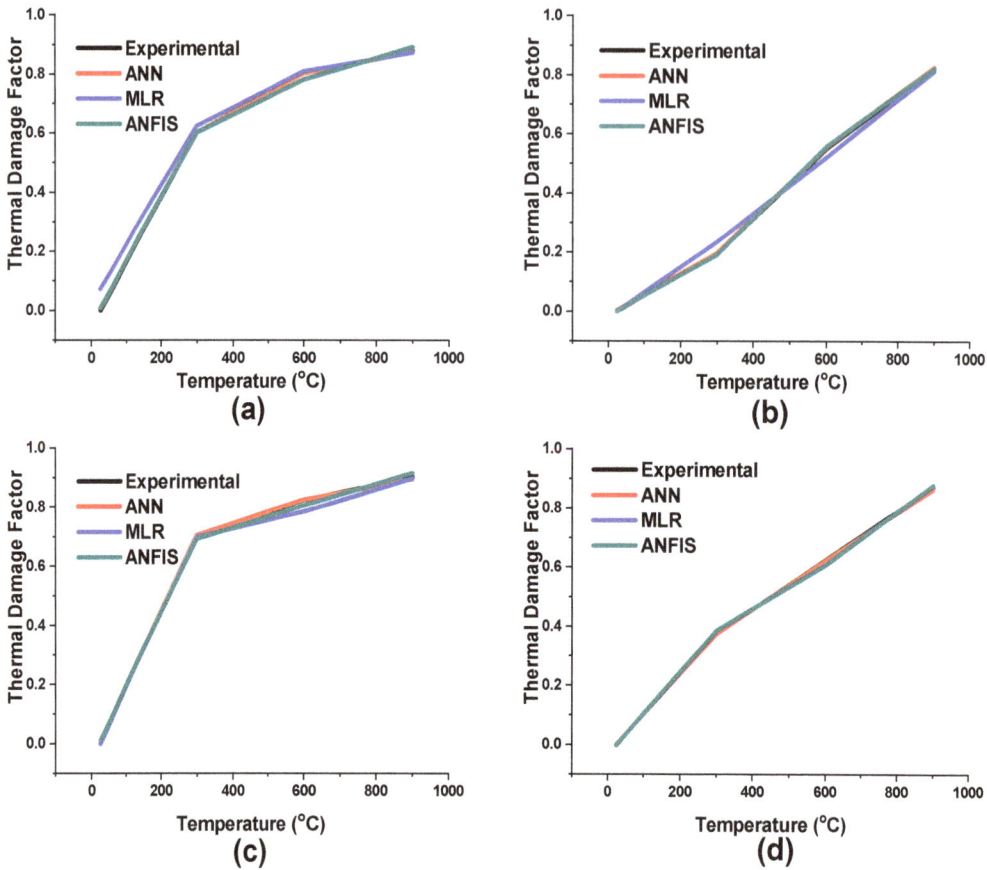

**Figure 12.** Experimental ANN, MLR, and ANFIS models; (**a**) porosity-based $D_T$ under slow cooling, (**b**) elasticity-based $D_T$ under slow cooling, (**c**) porosity-based $D_T$ under rapid cooling, and (**d**) elasticity-based $D_T$ under rapid cooling.

## 6. Limitations and Future Works

Khan et al. [77,78] claim that rock behavior varies depending on the region. In this study, the granite rock of a specific area was used for thermal damage. The study can be generalized by considering multiple rocks in different areas. However, in future research, care should be taken regarding thermal damage prediction as the rock behaviors are very sensitive and depend on multiple parameters, including mineralogy, physical, and mechanical properties. The proposed model of this study can also predict DT when rock input parameters, such as temperature, density, porosity, and P-waves, are available in the same range. To increase forecasting accuracy, future models should be trained with more datasets. This research focuses on traditional linear regression model(s) (MLR) and two artificial intelligence approaches (AI) (ANN and ANFIS). Using other approaches, such as decision tree, random forest (RF), K-nearest neighbor (KNN), ANN, and the ANFIS model to anticipate DT values may be investigated in the future. We may also present a greater database of non-destructive rock index tests to provide a more sophisticated intelligence approach since generalization is a crucial feature of predictive models.

## 7. Conclusions

The study investigated the damage factors from the porosity and elastic modulus under slow and rapid cooling. It was observed that the extent of damage to granite increased with the increase in temperature. However, the predominant damages to granite rock were observed in rapid cooling compared to slow cooling. Three predictive models were developed to quantify the extent of damages induced by thermal treatment and, subsequently, cooling conditions based on MLR, ANN, and ANFIS. In order to predict thermal damage, physical properties, such as temperature, density, porosity, and P-waves, were used as input variables. The efficiencies of the models were evaluated based on $R^2$, the A20 index, RMSE, MAPE, and VAF. The optimum training function was determined based on five different training functions, namely BFG, RP, SCG, CGB, and LM, for porosity and elasticity under different cooling conditions, to achieve the best ANN prediction model. It was revealed that the optimum result of the LM algorithm performance is better in terms of $R^2$, RMSE, the number of neurons, and execution timing. After a comparative analysis of predictive models, it has been suggested that the ANN-based predictive model is more efficient in the prediction of damage factors as compared to MLR and ANFIS. It has also been concluded that the efficacy of the prediction for the damage factor based on porosity is more predominant than the prediction of the damage factor based on elasticity. Therefore, it is recommended that damage factor prediction based on porosity should be used in the future. The findings of this study will facilitate the rapid quantification of damage factors induced by thermal treatment and cooling conditions for effective and successful engineering project execution in high-temperature rock mechanics environments. In the future, we will evaluate thermal damage in the presence of infrared radiation characteristics, acoustic emissions, and AI applications. These techniques will be adopted to obtain the real-time damage factor, crack intensity, propagation, and direction due to thermal heat.

**Author Contributions:** N.M.K. and S.H. contributed to the research, designed the experiments, and wrote the paper. K.C. and M.Z.E. conceived/were responsible for the research. A.M., H.R., F.U.R. and K.S.S. reviewed and revised the paper. All authors have read and agreed to the published version of the manuscript.

**Funding:** This research received no external funding.

**Institutional Review Board Statement:** Not applicable.

**Informed Consent Statement:** Not applicable.

**Data Availability Statement:** All the data and models employed and/or generated during the study appear in the submitted article.

**Acknowledgments:** The authors wish to acknowledge Qiupeng Yuan for his moral support and help.

**Conflicts of Interest:** The authors declare no conflict of interest.

## References

1. Wei, S.; Yang, Y.; Su, C.; Cardosh, S.R.; Wang, H. Experimental Study of the Effect of High Temperature on the Mechanical Properties of Coarse Sandstone. *Appl. Sci.* **2019**, *9*, 2424. [CrossRef]
2. Lian, X.; Hu, H.; Li, T.; Hu, D. Main geological and mining factors affecting ground cracks induced by underground coal mining in Shanxi Province, China. *Int. J. Coal Sci. Technol.* **2020**, *7*, 362–370. [CrossRef]
3. Chang, J.; He, K.; Pang, D.; Li, D.; Li, C.; Sun, B. Influence of anchorage length and pretension on the working resistance of rock bolt based on its tensile characteristics. *Int. J. Coal Sci. Technol.* **2021**, *8*, 1384–1399. [CrossRef]
4. Ju, Y.; Zhu, Y.; Xie, H.; Nie, X.; Zhang, Y.; Lu, C.; Gao, F. Technology. Fluidized mining and in-situ transformation of deep underground coal resources: A novel approach to ensuring safe, environmentally friendly, low-carbon, and clean utilisation. *Int. J. Coal Sci. Technol.* **2019**, *6*, 184–196. [CrossRef]
5. Burton, E.; Friedmann, S.; Upadhye, R. *Best Practices in Underground Coal Gasification*; Report: W-7405-Eng-48; Lawrence Livermore National Laboratory: Livermore, CA, USA, 2007.
6. Sirdesai, N.; Singh, R.; Singh, T.; Ranjith, P. Numerical and experimental study of strata behavior and land subsidence in an underground coal gasification project. *Proc. Int. Assoc. Hydrol. Sci.* **2015**, *372*, 455. [CrossRef]

7. Batugin, A.; Wang, Z.; Su, Z.; Sidikovna, S.S. Combined support mechanism of rock bolts and anchor cables for adjacent roadways in the external staggered split-level panel layout. *Int. J. Coal Sci. Technol.* **2021**, *8*, 659–673. [CrossRef]
8. Gao, R.; Kuang, T.; Zhang, Y.; Zhang, W.; Quan, C. Controlling mine pressure by subjecting high-level hard rock strata to ground fracturing. *Int. J. Coal Sci. Technol.* **2021**, *8*, 1336–1350. [CrossRef]
9. Jangara, H.; Ozturk, C.A. Longwall top coal caving design for thick coal seam in very poor strength surrounding strata. *Int. J. Coal Sci. Technol.* **2021**, *8*, 641–658. [CrossRef]
10. Li, C.; Guo, D.; Zhang, Y.; An, C. Compound-mode crack propagation law of PMMA semicircular-arch roadway specimens under impact loading. *Int. J. Coal Sci. Technol.* **2021**, *8*, 1302–1315. [CrossRef]
11. Liu, B.; Zhao, Y.; Zhang, C.; Zhou, J.; Li, Y.; Sun, Z. Characteristic strength and acoustic emission properties of weakly cemented sandstone at different depths under uniaxial compression. *Int. J. Coal Sci. Technol.* **2021**, *8*, 1288–1301. [CrossRef]
12. Zuo, J.; Wang, J.; Jiang, Y. Macro/meso failure behavior of surrounding rock in deep roadway and its control technology. *Int. J. Coal Sci. Technol.* **2019**, *6*, 301–319. [CrossRef]
13. Chen, B. Stress-induced trend: The clustering feature of coal mine disasters and earthquakes in China. *Int. J. Coal Sci. Technol.* **2020**, *7*, 676–692. [CrossRef]
14. Chen, Y.; Zuo, J.; Liu, D.; Li, Y.; Wang, Z. Experimental and numerical study of coal-rock bimaterial composite bodies under triaxial compression. *Int. J. Coal Sci. Technol.* **2021**, *8*, 908–924. [CrossRef]
15. Zhang, S.; Lu, L.; Wang, Z.; Wang, S. A physical model study of surrounding rock failure near a fault under the influence of footwall coal mining. *Int. J. Coal Sci. Technol.* **2021**, *8*, 626–640. [CrossRef]
16. Chi, X.; Yang, K.; Wei, Z. Breaking and mining-induced stress evolution of overlying strata in the working face of a steeply dipping coal seam. *Int. J. Coal Sci. Technol.* **2021**, *8*, 614–625. [CrossRef]
17. Feng, G.; Kang, Y.; Wang, X.-C. Fracture failure of granite after varied durations of thermal treatment: An experimental study. *R. Soc. Open Sci.* **2019**, *6*, 190144. [CrossRef] [PubMed]
18. Kim, B.-H.; Walton, G.; Larson, M.K.; Berry, S. Investigation of the anisotropic confinement-dependent brittleness of a Utah coal. *Int. J. Coal Sci. Technol.* **2021**, *8*, 274–290. [CrossRef]
19. Yang, D.; Ning, Z.; Li, Y.; Lv, Z.; Qiao, Y. In situ stress measurement and analysis of the stress accumulation levels in coal mines in the northern Ordos Basin, China. *Int. J. Coal Sci. Technol.* **2021**, *8*, 1316–1335. [CrossRef]
20. Lou, J.; Gao, F.; Yang, J.; Ren, Y.; Li, J.; Wang, X.; Yang, L. Characteristics of evolution of mining-induced stress field in the longwall panel: Insights from physical modeling. *Int. J. Coal Sci. Technol.* **2021**, *8*, 938–955. [CrossRef]
21. Ding, X.; Xiao, X.-C.; Wu, D.; Lv, X.-F. Mechanical properties and charge signal characteristics in coal material failure under different loading paths. *Int. J. Coal Sci. Technol.* **2019**, *6*, 138–149. [CrossRef]
22. Lin, K.; Huang, W.; Finkelman, R.B.; Chen, J.; Yi, S.; Cui, X.; Wang, Y. Distribution, modes of occurrence, and main factors influencing lead enrichment in Chinese coals. *Int. J. Coal Sci. Technol.* **2020**, *7*, 1–18. [CrossRef]
23. Liu, S.; Tan, F.; Huo, T.; Tang, S.; Zhao, W.; Chao, H. Origin of the hydrate bound gases in the Juhugeng Sag, Muli Basin, Tibetan Plateau. *Int. J. Coal Sci. Technol.* **2020**, *7*, 43–57. [CrossRef]
24. Chen, Y.-L.; Wang, S.-R.; Ni, J.; Azzam, R.; Fernandez-Steeger, T.M. An experimental study of the mechanical properties of granite after high temperature exposure based on mineral characteristics. *Eng. Geol.* **2017**, *220*, 234–242. [CrossRef]
25. Chen, Y.; Watanabe, K.; Kusuda, H.; Kusaka, E.; Mabuchi, M. Crack growth in Westerly granite during a cyclic loading test. *Eng. Geol.* **2011**, *117*, 189–197. [CrossRef]
26. Xue, D.; Lu, L.; Zhou, J.; Lu, L.; Liu, Y. Cluster modeling of the short-range correlation of acoustically emitted scattering signals. *Int. J. Coal Sci. Technol.* **2021**, *8*, 575–589. [CrossRef]
27. Kumari, W.; Ranjith, P.; Perera, M.; Chen, B.; Abdulagatov, I. Temperature-dependent mechanical behaviour of Australian Strathbogie granite with different cooling treatments. *Eng. Geol.* **2017**, *229*, 31–44. [CrossRef]
28. Kumari, W.; Ranjith, P.; Perera, M.; Shao, S.; Chen, B.; Lashin, A.; Al Arifi, N.; Rathnaweera, T. Mechanical behaviour of Australian Strathbogie granite under in-situ stress and temperature conditions: An application to geothermal energy extraction. *Geothermics* **2017**, *65*, 44–59. [CrossRef]
29. Liu, H.; Zhang, K.; Shao, S.; Ranjith, P.G. Numerical Investigation on the Mechanical Properties of Australian Strathbogie Granite under Different Temperatures Using Discrete Element Method. *Rock Mech. Rock Eng.* **2019**, *52*, 3719–3735. [CrossRef]
30. Liu, H.; Zhang, K.; Shao, S.; Ranjith, P.G. Numerical investigation on the cooling-related mechanical properties of heated Australian Strathbogie granite using Discrete Element Method. *Eng. Geol.* **2020**, *264*, 105371. [CrossRef]
31. Zhang, F.; Zhang, Y.; Yu, Y.; Hu, D.; Shao, J. Influence of cooling rate on thermal degradation of physical and mechanical properties of granite. *Int. J. Rock Mech. Min. Sci.* **2020**, *129*, 104285. [CrossRef]
32. Zhao, Z. Thermal influence on mechanical properties of granite: A microcracking perspective. *Rock Mech. Rock Eng.* **2016**, *49*, 747–762. [CrossRef]
33. Su, G.; Chen, Z.; Ju, J.W.; Jiang, J. Influence of temperature on the strainburst characteristics of granite under true triaxial loading conditions. *Eng. Geol.* **2017**, *222*, 38–52. [CrossRef]
34. Tian, Z.; Tang, C.a.; Liu, Y.; Tang, Y. Zonal disintegration test of deep tunnel under plane strain conditions. *Int. J. Coal Sci. Technol.* **2020**, *7*, 337–349. [CrossRef]
35. Zhou, A.; Zhang, M.; Wang, K.; Elsworth, D. Near-source characteristics of two-phase gas–solid outbursts in roadways. *Int. J. Coal Sci. Technol.* **2021**, *8*, 685–696. [CrossRef]

36. Song, Z.; Ji, H.; Liu, Z.; Sun, L. Study on the critical stress threshold of weakly cemented sandstone damage based on the renormalization group method. *Int. J. Coal Sci. Technol.* **2020**, *7*, 693–703. [CrossRef]
37. Dou, L.; Yang, K.; Chi, X. Fracture behavior and acoustic emission characteristics of sandstone samples with inclined precracks. *Int. J. Coal Sci. Technol.* **2021**, *8*, 77–87. [CrossRef]
38. Cheng, X. Damage and failure characteristics of rock similar materials with pre-existing cracks. *Int. J. Coal Sci. Technol.* **2019**, *6*, 505–517. [CrossRef]
39. Placido, F. Thermoluminescence test for fire-damaged concrete. *Mag. Concr. Res.* **1980**, *32*, 112–116. [CrossRef]
40. Chew, M.Y. The assessment of fire damaged concrete. *Build. Environ.* **1993**, *28*, 97–102. [CrossRef]
41. Sharma, L.; Sirdesai, N.; Sharma, K.; Singh, T. Experimental study to examine the independent roles of lime and cement on the stabilization of a mountain soil: A comparative study. *Appl. Clay Sci.* **2018**, *152*, 183–195. [CrossRef]
42. Chaki, S.; Takarli, M.; Agbodjan, W. Influence of thermal damage on physical properties of a granite rock: Porosity, permeability and ultrasonic wave evolutions. *Constr. Build. Mater.* **2008**, *22*, 1456–1461. [CrossRef]
43. Wang, M.; Tan, C.; Meng, J.; Yang, B.; Li, Y. Crack classification and evolution in anisotropic shale during cyclic loading tests by acoustic emission. *J. Geophys. Eng.* **2017**, *14*, 930–938. [CrossRef]
44. Inserra, C.; Biwa, S.; Chen, Y. Influence of thermal damage on linear and nonlinear acoustic properties of granite. *Int. J. Rock Mech. Min. Sci.* **2013**, *62*, 96–104. [CrossRef]
45. Yang, S.-Q.; Ranjith, P.; Huang, Y.-H.; Yin, P.-F.; Jing, H.-W.; Gui, Y.-L.; Yu, Q.-L. Experimental investigation on mechanical damage characteristics of sandstone under triaxial cyclic loading. *Geophys. J. Int.* **2015**, *201*, 662–682. [CrossRef]
46. Yang, S.-Q.; Ranjith, P.; Jing, H.-W.; Tian, W.-L.; Ju, Y. An experimental investigation on thermal damage and failure mechanical behavior of granite after exposure to different high temperature treatments. *Geothermics* **2017**, *65*, 180–197. [CrossRef]
47. Ulusay, R. *The ISRM Suggested Methods for Rock Characterization, Testing and Monitoring: 2007–2014*; Springer: Cham, Switzerland, 2014.
48. Zhou, J.; Lin, H.; Jin, H.; Li, S.; Yan, Z.; Huang, S. Cooperative prediction method of gas emission from mining face based on feature selection and machine learning. *Int. J. Coal Sci. Technol.* **2022**, *9*, 51. [CrossRef]
49. Gorai, A.K.; Raval, S.; Patel, A.K.; Chatterjee, S.; Gautam, T. Design and development of a machine vision system using artificial neural network-based algorithm for automated coal characterization. *Int. J. Coal Sci. Technol.* **2021**, *8*, 737–755. [CrossRef]
50. Xie, J.; Ge, F.; Cui, T.; Wang, X. A virtual test and evaluation method for fully mechanized mining production system with different smart levels. *Int. J. Coal Sci. Technol.* **2022**, *9*, 41. [CrossRef]
51. Bai, Q.; Zhang, C.; Paul Young, R. Using true-triaxial stress path to simulate excavation-induced rock damage: A case study. *Int. J. Coal Sci. Technol.* **2022**, *9*, 49. [CrossRef]
52. He, S.; Qin, M.; Qiu, L.; Song, D.; Zhang, X. Early warning of coal dynamic disaster by precursor of AE and EMR "quiet period". *Int. J. Coal Sci. Technol.* **2022**, *9*, 46. [CrossRef]
53. Tarawneh, A.S.; Chetverikov, D.; Verma, C.; Hassanat, A.B. Stability and reduction of statistical features for image classification and retrieval: Preliminary results. In Proceedings of the 2018 9th International Conference on Information and Communication Systems (ICICS), Irbid, Jordan, 3–5 April 2018; pp. 117–121.
54. Tarawneh, A.S.; Hassanat, A.B.; Almohammadi, K.; Chetverikov, D.; Bellinger, C. Smotefuna: Synthetic minority over-sampling technique based on furthest neighbour algorithm. *IEEE Access* **2020**, *8*, 59069–59082. [CrossRef]
55. Armaghani, D.J.; Amin, M.F.M.; Yagiz, S.; Faradonbeh, R.S.; Abdullah, R.A. Prediction of the uniaxial compressive strength of sandstone using various modeling techniques. *Int. J. Rock Mech. Min. Sci.* **2016**, *85*, 174–186. [CrossRef]
56. Momeni, E.; Armaghani, D.J.; Hajihassani, M.; Amin, M.F.M. Prediction of uniaxial compressive strength of rock samples using hybrid particle swarm optimization-based artificial neural networks. *Measurement* **2015**, *60*, 50–63. [CrossRef]
57. Parsajoo, M.; Armaghani, D.J.; Mohammed, A.S.; Khari, M.; Jahandari, S. Tensile strength prediction of rock material using non-destructive tests: A comparative intelligent study. *Transp. Geotech.* **2021**, *31*, 100652. [CrossRef]
58. Cabalar, A.F.; Cevik, A.; Gokceoglu, C. Some applications of adaptive neuro-fuzzy inference system (ANFIS) in geotechnical engineering. *Comput. Geotech.* **2012**, *40*, 14–33. [CrossRef]
59. Armaghani, D.J.; Mohamad, E.T.; Hajihassani, M.; Yagiz, S.; Motaghedi, H. Application of several non-linear prediction tools for estimating uniaxial compressive strength of granitic rocks and comparison of their performances. *Eng. Comput.* **2016**, *32*, 189–206. [CrossRef]
60. Barzegar, R.; Sattarpour, M.; Nikudel, M.R.; Moghaddam, A.A. Comparative evaluation of artificial intelligence models for prediction of uniaxial compressive strength of travertine rocks, case study: Azarshahr area, NW Iran. *Model. Earth Syst. Environ.* **2016**, *2*, 76. [CrossRef]
61. Majdi, A.; Rezaei, M. Prediction of unconfined compressive strength of rock surrounding a roadway using artificial neural network. *Neural Comput. Appl.* **2013**, *23*, 381–389. [CrossRef]
62. Minaeian, B.; Ahangari, K. Prediction of the uniaxial compressive strength and Brazilian tensile strength of weak conglomerate. *Int. J. Geo-Eng.* **2017**, *8*, 19. [CrossRef]
63. Yesiloglu-Gultekin, N.; Gokceoglu, C.; Sezer, E.A. Prediction of uniaxial compressive strength of granitic rocks by various nonlinear tools and comparison of their performances. *Int. J. Rock Mech. Min. Sci.* **2013**, *62*, 113–122. [CrossRef]
64. Singh, R.; Kainthola, A.; Singh, T. Estimation of elastic constant of rocks using an ANFIS approach. *Appl. Soft Comput.* **2012**, *12*, 40–45. [CrossRef]

65. Singh, T.N.; Verma, A.K. Comparative analysis of intelligent algorithms to correlate strength and petrographic properties of some schistose rocks. *Eng. Comput.* **2012**, *28*, 1–12. [CrossRef]
66. Sirdesai, N.N.; Singh, A.; Sharma, L.K.; Singh, R.; Singh, T. Determination of thermal damage in rock specimen using intelligent techniques. *Eng. Geol.* **2018**, *239*, 179–194. [CrossRef]
67. Shen, Y.-J.; Zhang, Y.-L.; Gao, F.; Yang, G.-S.; Lai, X.-P. Influence of temperature on the microstructure deterioration of sandstone. *Energies* **2018**, *11*, 1753. [CrossRef]
68. Sun, Q.; Geng, J.; Zhang, W.; Lü, C. Variation of wave velocity and thermal conductivity of concrete after high-temperature treatment. *Environ. Earth Sci.* **2017**, *76*, 88. [CrossRef]
69. Garson, G.D. *Multiple Regression*; Statistical Associates Publishers: Fargo, ND, USA, 2014.
70. Cohen, P.; West, S.G.; Aiken, L.S. *Applied Multiple Regression/Correlation Analysis for the Behavioral Sciences*; Lawrence Erlbaum Associates Publishers: Mahwah, NJ, USA, 2002.
71. Sharma, L.; Singh, R.; Umrao, R.; Sharma, K.; Singh, T. Evaluating the modulus of elasticity of soil using soft computing system. *Eng. Comput.* **2017**, *33*, 497–507. [CrossRef]
72. Sharma, L.; Singh, T. Regression-based models for the prediction of unconfined compressive strength of artificially structured soil. *Eng. Comput.* **2018**, *34*, 175–186. [CrossRef]
73. Zhang, Y.; Zhou, L.; Hu, Z.; Yu, Z.; Hao, S.; Lei, Z.; Xie, Y. Prediction of layered thermal conductivity using artificial neural network in order to have better design of ground source heat pump system. *Energies* **2018**, *11*, 1896. [CrossRef]
74. Arcaklioğlu, E.; Erişen, A.; Yilmaz, R. Artificial neural network analysis of heat pumps using refrigerant mixtures. *Energy Convers. Manag.* **2004**, *45*, 1917–1929. [CrossRef]
75. Kumar, R.; Aggarwal, R.; Sharma, J. Energy analysis of a building using artificial neural network: A review. *Energy Build.* **2013**, *65*, 352–358. [CrossRef]
76. Ma, L.; Khan, N.M.; Cao, K.; Rehman, H.; Salman, S.; Rehman, F.U. Prediction of Sandstone Dilatancy Point in Different Water Contents Using Infrared Radiation Characteristic: Experimental and Machine Learning Approaches. *Lithosphere* **2022**, *2021*, 3243070. [CrossRef]
77. Khan, N.M.; Ma, L.; Cao, K.; Hussain, S.; Liu, W.; Xu, Y.; Yuan, Q.; Gu, J. Prediction of an early failure point using infrared radiation characteristics and energy evolution for sandstone with different water contents. *Bull. Eng. Geol. Environ.* **2021**, *80*, 6913–6936. [CrossRef]
78. Khan, N.M.; Cao, K.; Yuan, Q.; Hashim, M.H.B.M.; Rehman, H.; Hussain, S.; Emad, M.Z.; Ullah, B.; Shah, K.S.; Khan, S. Application of Machine Learning and Multivariate Statistics to Predict Uniaxial Compressive Strength and Static Young's Modulus Using Physical Properties under Different Thermal Conditions. *Sustainability* **2022**, *14*, 9901.
79. Fidan, S.; Oktay, H.; Polat, S.; Ozturk, S. An Artificial Neural Network Model to Predict the Thermal Properties of Concrete Using Different Neurons and Activation Functions. *Adv. Mater. Sci. Eng.* **2019**, *2019*, 3831813. [CrossRef]
80. Zadeh, L.A. Fuzzy sets. *Inf. Control* **1965**, *8*, 338–353. [CrossRef]
81. Jang, J.-S. ANFIS: Adaptive-network-based fuzzy inference system. *IEEE Trans. Syst. Man Cybern.* **1993**, *23*, 665–685. [CrossRef]
82. Zhang, L.; Liu, J.; Lai, J.; Xiong, Z. Performance analysis of adaptive neuro fuzzy inference system control for MEMS navigation system. *Math. Probl. Eng.* **2014**, *2014*, 961067. [CrossRef]
83. Şahin, M.; Erol, R. Prediction of attendance demand in European football games: Comparison of ANFIS, fuzzy logic, and ANN. *Comput. Intell. Neurosci.* **2018**, *2018*, 5714872. [CrossRef] [PubMed]
84. Lawal, A.I.; Aladejare, A.E.; Onifade, M.; Bada, S.; Idris, M.A. Predictions of elemental composition of coal and biomass from their proximate analyses using ANFIS, ANN and MLR. *Int. J. Coal Sci. Technol.* **2021**, *8*, 124–140. [CrossRef]

Article

# Research on $b$ Value Estimation Based on Apparent Amplitude-Frequency Distribution in Rock Acoustic Emission Tests

Daolong Chen [1,2], Changgen Xia [1], Huini Liu [1], Xiling Liu [1,2,*] and Kun Du [1]

1 School of Resources and Safety Engineering, Central South University, Changsha 410083, China
2 State Key Laboratory of Coal Resources and Safe Mining, China University of Mining and Technology, Xuzhou 221116, China
* Correspondence: lxlenglish@csu.edu.cn

**Abstract:** The rock acoustic emission (AE) technique has often been used to study rock destruction properties and has also been considered an important measure for simulating earthquake foreshock sequences. Among them, the AE $b$ value is an essential parameter for the size distribution characteristics and probabilistic hazard analysis of rock fractures. Variations in $b$ values obtained in rock AE tests and earthquakes are often compared to establish analogies in the damage process and precursor analysis. Nevertheless, because the amplitudes measured on the sample boundary by an acoustic sensor (apparent amplitude) are often used to estimate the $b$ value, which cannot descript the source size distribution, it is necessary to develop a method to obtain the size distribution characteristics of the real source from the apparent amplitude in doubly truncated distribution. In this study, we obtain AE apparent amplitudes by applying an attenuation operator to source amplitudes generated by a computer with an underlying exponential distribution and then use these simulated apparent amplitudes to perform a comparative analysis of various $b$ value estimation methods that are used in earthquakes and propose an optimal $b$ value estimation procedure for rock AE tests through apparent amplitudes. To further verify the reliability of the newly proposed procedure, a $b$ value characteristics analysis was carried out on a non-explosive expansion agent rock AE test and transparent refractive index experiment with red sandstone, marble, granite, and limestone. The results indicate that mineral grains of different sizes and compositions and different types of discontinuities of rock specimens determine the rock fracture characteristics, as well as the $b$ value. The dynamic $b$ values decreased linearly during the loading process, which confirms that variations in the $b$ value also depend on the stress. These results indicate that the newly proposed procedure for estimating the $b$ value in rock AE tests based on apparent amplitudes has high reliability.

**Keywords:** rock acoustic emission; apparent amplitude distribution; $b$ value; completeness amplitude; bootstrap

**MSC:** 74-05; 86-05

Citation: Chen, D.; Xia, C.; Liu, H.; Liu, X.; Du, K. Research on $b$ Value Estimation Based on Apparent Amplitude-Frequency Distribution in Rock Acoustic Emission Tests. Mathematics 2022, 10, 3202. https://doi.org/10.3390/math10173202

Academic Editor: James M. Buick

Received: 29 June 2022
Accepted: 25 July 2022
Published: 5 September 2022

**Publisher's Note:** MDPI stays neutral with regard to jurisdictional claims in published maps and institutional affiliations.

**Copyright:** © 2022 by the authors. Licensee MDPI, Basel, Switzerland. This article is an open access article distributed under the terms and conditions of the Creative Commons Attribution (CC BY) license (https://creativecommons.org/licenses/by/4.0/).

## 1. Introduction

The power law size distribution relationship of source energy $E$ or seismic moment $M_0$ is an intrinsic characteristic of the frequency-size distribution in statistical seismology; it can well record the spatial and temporal distribution of rock fractures from a large number of small-scale ruptures to fewer large-scale ruptures, and it has been widely used in seismic research. Since there is a logarithmic relationship between the local magnitude $M$ and the source energy $E$ or seismic moment $M_0$, we can conclude that the local magnitude-frequency distribution obeys the exponential Gutenberg–Richter (G–R) law [1], which has also been widely used for probabilistic seismic hazard analysis [2–7]. The G–R law is expressed on a logarithmic scale given by

$$\log_{10}(N) = a - bM \tag{1}$$

where $a$ and $b$ are constants and $N$ is the number of earthquakes that occur in a specific time window with magnitude $\geq M$. More importantly, parameter $a$ reflects the size of the time window of observation; slope $b$ is an essential tool in seismotectonic studies and seismic-risk analysis within the same time window in a certain area [5,8], which is often referred to as the $b$ value. More recently, the $b$ value in the G–R law has also been interpreted as an indicator of the applied shear stress and material heterogeneity [9–14]. Thus, its correct computation represents an important challenge in seismology and rock mechanics [15–18].

The selected discontinuities and missing earthquake events in the magnitude-frequency distribution are the main effects on stable $b$ value estimation, which is why the two ends of the magnitude-frequency distribution deviate from the G–R law. For some authors, the right and left end points deviating from the G–R law correspond to the magnitude of completeness $M_c$ (which is defined as the lowest magnitude at which 100% of the events in a space–time volume are detected [8,19] and the auxiliary magnitude $M_0$, respectively. Many different procedures for correctly estimating $M_c$ and $M_0$ have been proposed [8,19–25]. Figure 1 shows that with the value of the assumed $M_c$ starting from the minimum magnitude in the catalog and increasing gradually, the corresponding $b$ value and goodness-of-fit change significantly as $M_c \leq 2$ and tend to be stable as $M_c \geq 2$. In view of this phenomenon, some researchers hope to select a sufficiently large $M_c$ to estimate the $b$ value, but for the statistical value of $M_c$ and $b$, which will reduce a large number of low-magnitude events and further lead to a decrease in the space–time resolution of variations in $M_c$ and reliability and robustness of the $b$ value estimation [26,27]. Therefore, accurately determining $M_c$ has become the key to stably estimating the $b$ values.

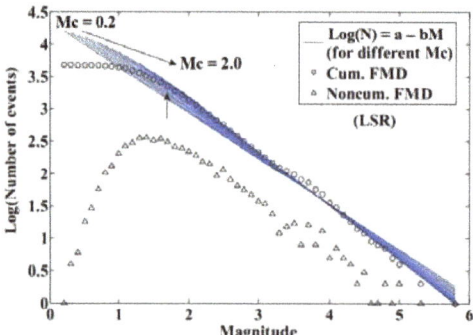

**Figure 1.** The effects of variations of assumed $M_c$ on $b$ value estimation [26]. The FMD and LSR are abbreviations of frequency-magnitude distribution and least-squares regression, respectively.

In rock mechanics, the acoustic emission (AE) technique is often used to study the destruction properties of rocks by recording elastic wave information radiated by crack initiation, propagation, and penetration during rock deformation [28–31]. Additionally, the AE test method is also an important means to simulate earthquake foreshock sequences and study focal mechanisms [14,32–42]. Therefore, the space–time variation characteristics of the $b$ value obtained in rock AE deformation tests have been used to simulate earthquake precursor characteristics [43–47]. However, unlike the magnitude used in Equation (1) for $b$ value estimation in seismology, AE equipment records the high-frequency elastic wave signal of the small-scale rupture, and the AE amplitude is the apparent amplitude measured by sensors at the sample boundary after attenuation from the seismic source [25]. The corresponding apparent amplitude-frequency distribution does not represent the source size distribution. Thus, the frequency-size distribution law of the source signals collected by the sensors in the rock AE test will be changed owing to the elastic wave attenuation, and the same deviation will appear at both ends of the amplitude-frequency as the magnitude-frequency distribution [33,37], which would affect the size of the real $b$ value. (Here, the analogy with the earthquake is used to define the left and right deviation points of the amplitude-frequency distribution of the rock AE test as the completeness amplitude point $A_c$ and auxiliary discontinuous amplitude point $A_0$, respectively.) Although some researchers have long been concerned about the influence of attenuation on the amplitude-frequency distribution in rock AE tests and have also proposed some corresponding compensation methods to obtain the equivalent AE magnitude with the same significance as the magnitude of the earthquake to analyze rock $b$ value characteristics [44,48], the equivalent amplitude distribution still cannot fully represent the real frequency-size distribution of rock cracks. To solve this problem, Liu [25] used a statistical method to prove that the apparent amplitude-frequency distribution retains the source frequency-size distribution characteristics, wherein the key to estimating the real $b$ value is to properly truncate the apparent amplitude-frequency distribution. A new $b$ value estimation method called the Fisher optimal split and global search algorithm (FGS) was proposed to identify the log-linear segment from the apparent amplitude-frequency distribution of the rock AE test for $b$ value estimation. In addition, because AE acquisition equipment is very sensitive to the interference of test conditions, such as environmental noise and current signals, a high threshold value of the signal acquisition is generally set for laboratory rock AE tests. Thus, the completeness amplitude $A_c$ is usually ignored. Therefore, the completeness of the amplitude data should also be considered when considering how to obtain the source size distribution characteristic parameters using the apparent amplitude-frequency distribution in the estimation of the rock AE $b$ value.

Based on the discussion above, firstly, we carried out a synthetic AE simulation test to compare and analyze the applicability of the completeness magnitude estimation methods commonly used in earthquakes for the estimation of rock AE completeness amplitude and proposed an optimal procedure for rock AE $b$ value estimation by combining Bootstrap [8] and the FGS method which is used for estimating the characteristic parameters of the source size distribution from the apparent amplitude-frequency distribution. Then, we designed a static dilation rock rupturing AE test to further verify the reliability of the newly proposed optimal procedure of $b$ value estimation based on the relationship between the $b$ value and rock microscopic composition and stress to provide a reliable and accurate $b$ value estimation procedure for laboratory rock AE tests. As a result, this research can provide new insights and methods in the analysis of the precursory characteristics in laboratory rock AE tests and rock mass engineering.

## 2. Optimal $b$ Value Estimation Procedure Based on Apparent Amplitude-Frequency Distribution

In rock AE tests, a high threshold is generally set to remove noise interference, and AE equipment will also define the upper limit amplitude, which will result in a doubly truncated distribution of apparent amplitude frequency, so the completeness amplitude $A_c$ in the $b$ value estimation is usually ignored. In this section, generate AE synthetic data with apparent amplitude and select the estimation method of completeness magnitude $M_c$ commonly used in seismic research to obtain an optimal algorithm for determining completeness magnitude $A_c$, which is a key step for $b$ value estimation. Then, combined with the nonparametric statistical Bootstrap method, we compared the obtained optimal algorithm of $A_c$ with the FGS method and determined an optimal procedure of the $b$ value estimated for the apparent amplitude data.

### 2.1. Synthetic Catalogues of Rock AE Apparent Amplitude

Because the true underlying completeness amplitude $A_c$ and $b$ values are not known in a laboratory rock AE test, we designed a specific simulation scheme to randomly generate synthetic AE data that can be used to clearly compare five $A_c$ estimation methods [8,23–25]. According to the previous statistical proof and synthetic data generation method [25,49], we designed to generate data arrays with the same length of source amplitude and amount of attenuation, which are all in decibels with a round-off interval of 1 dB. The apparent amplitude after attenuation can be obtained by the subtraction of two randomly arranged arrays of source amplitude and the amount of attenuation. The specific simulation schemes are as follows: firstly, as the $b$ value of most papers is equal to about 1 [50], we generated a source synthetic catalog of $i = 1, 2, \ldots, N$ events with amplitudes $A_i$ in decibels by randomly sampling an underlying Gutenberg–Richter distribution with $b = 1.0666$ and std = 8 (standard deviation) which varies between limits $A_i{}^{min} \leq A_i \leq A_i{}^{max}$ and has a probability density function $p(A_i)$. Then, we generated an attenuation amount catalog $\delta A_i$ also in decibels with the same length of $A_i$, which varies between limits $\delta A_i{}^{min} \leq \delta A_i \leq \delta A_i{}^{max}$ and has a probability density function $p(\delta A_i)$ that obeys the Poisson distribution (or other forms including normal, exponential, Gamma, and random uniform distributions). Finally, the catalog obtained by the subtraction of randomly arranged $A_i$ and $\delta A_i$ was used to model the amplitude observed at the sample boundary $A_i{}^{obs} = A_i - \delta A_i$. In other words, the interval of the apparent amplitude that still follows the exponential distribution was $[A_i{}^{min} - \delta A_i{}^{min}, A_i{}^{max} - \delta A_i{}^{max}]$. In this paper, we set $A_i{}^{min} = 50$ dB, $A_i{}^{max} = 109$ dB, $\delta A_i{}^{min} = 1$ dB, and $A_i{}^{max} = 10$ dB to make the apparent amplitude range of synthetic data close to that in normal rock AE experiment. As a matter of fact, the selection of the ranges for source amplitude and attenuation generation has no effect on the results [49]. In addition, to minimize the effect of data volume on deviation discussion, a data volume of 100,000 was generated. Figure 2A shows the apparent amplitude-frequency distribution of generated data.

### 2.2. Determination of Optimal Estimation Method for $A_c$ and $A_0$

In studies on the earthquake sequence, determining the completeness magnitude $M_c$ is the priority of the seismic sequence analysis. In fact, the core of various seismic $b$ value estimation methods is the algorithm for searching for $M_c$. As some theories in seismic research are often used in rock AE tests, these $M_c$ estimation methods can also be applied to estimate the completeness amplitude $A_c$ of the rock AE apparent amplitude-frequency distribution. Common $M_c$ estimation methods are as follows:

(1) Maximum curvature method (MAXC) [23]
(2) Goodness-of-fit test (GFT) [23]
(3) $M_c$ by $b$ value stability (MBS) [24]
(4) Median-based analysis of segment slope (MBASS) [8]
(5) Fisher optimal split and Global Search algorithm (FGS) [25]

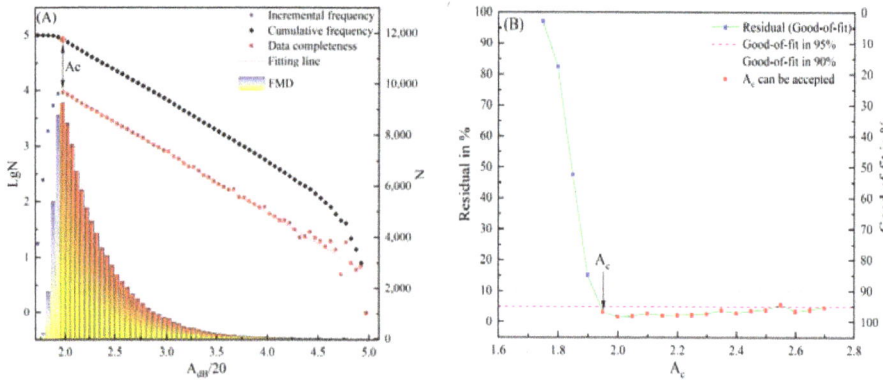

Figure 2. Cont.

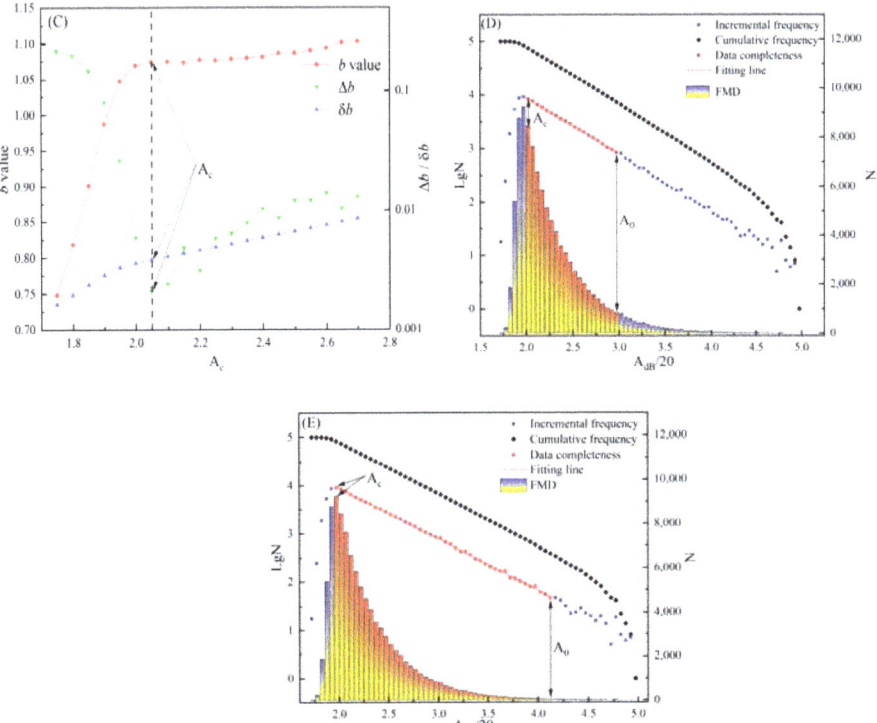

**Figure 2.** Schematic of five methods for determining the completeness amplitude. The amplitude data are the synthetic AE catalog generated by Section 2.1. (**A**) MAXC. (**B**) GFT, the figure shows the variations of residuals and goodness-of-fit with $A_c$, and the horizontal dashed lines indicate 90% and 95% confidence. (**C**) MBS, $b$ value, $\Delta b$, and $\delta b$ variations trend with cut-off amplitude, the vertical dashed line is $A_c$ determined by MBS method. $\Delta M = 0.05$, $dM = 0.25$. (**D**) MBASS. (**E**) FGS.

These methods have different algorithms for determining the completeness magnitude $M_c$. As shown in Figure 2A, the MAXC approach identifies the magnitude corresponding to the maximum curvature of the cumulative magnitude-frequency distribution as $M_c$. In fact, this point is also the magnitude corresponding to the maximum frequency of the incremental magnitude-frequency distribution. The GFT method in Figure 2B determines $M_c$ by comparing the goodness-of-fit $R$ of the fitted frequency-magnitude distribution with that of the actual magnitude-frequency distribution, and the $M_c$ corresponding to $R \geq 95\%$ confidence is taken as the completeness magnitude ($R \geq 90\%$ confidence can also be accepted as a completeness magnitude in the actual complex earthquake catalog). The MBS method selects the starting point of magnitude where the change in the $b$ value tends to be stable as $M_c$ (Figure 2C), that is:

$$\Delta b = |b_{ave} - b| \leq \delta b \tag{2}$$

where $b_{ave}$ is the average estimated $b$ value from each magnitude within the magnitude interval $[M_{co}, M_{co} + dM]$ and $\delta b$ is the uncertainty of the $b$ value proposed by Shi [51]. $b_{ave}$ and $\delta b$ can be obtained from Equations (3) and (4):

$$b_{ave} = \sum_{M_{co}}^{M_{co}+dM} b(M_{co}) \cdot \frac{\Delta M}{dM} \tag{3}$$

$$\delta b = 2.3 b^2 \sqrt{\frac{\sum_{i=1}^{N}(M_i - \langle M \rangle)^2}{N(N-1)}} \qquad (4)$$

where $b$ is the $b$ value of the current magnitude $M_{co}$, $N$ is the number of events, $M_i$ is the magnitude corresponding to event $N_i$, $\Delta M$ is the bin width, and <$M$> is the average magnitude of all events greater than $M_{co}$. The FGS method integrates the Fisher optimal split and global search algorithms to determine the log-linear segment of the incremental amplitude-frequency distribution. As shown in Figure 2E, the FGS fully considers the influence of data volume and goodness-of-fit on the estimation results.

Because the $b$ value is a statistical parameter, the $b$ value estimation will be more stable and accurate with the increase in data volume, and this conclusion has already been discussed by many researchers [8,50,52]. Here, we compared the accuracy of $b$ value estimation using synthetic AE amplitude data generated in Section 2.1 to explore the differences in the above five completeness amplitude estimation methods under different data volumes. We randomly generated a source amplitude that obeyed an exponential distribution with a theoretical $b$ value of 1.0666 and a data volume of 100,000 as [50, 109] dB and assumed that the attenuation obeyed the Poisson distribution with the interval of [1, 10] dB. According to the theoretical proof of Liu [25], the amplitude interval that still obeys the exponential distribution after attenuation is [49, 99] dB. Therefore, the theoretical completeness amplitude $A_c$ of the synthetic apparent amplitude data is 2.45. Then, Bootstrap was used to extract 1000 samples from apparent amplitude data with data volumes of 100, 200, 300, 500, 800, 1000, 2000, 3000, 5000, 8000, 10,000, 30,000, 50,000, and 100,000. Figure 3 shows the variation in average $A_c$ and average $b$ value of 1000 Bootstrap samples with different data volumes; the error bar in the figure is the Bootstrap 95% confidence limit.

As shown in Figure 3, the accuracy of $A_c$ estimated by the five methods was positively correlated with the accuracy of the $b$ value, which indicates that selecting an appropriate $A_c$ is very important for the correct $b$ value estimation. This also proves the availability of generated synthetic data to simulate real AE data to a certain degree. It can be seen from the stability of the estimation results that the goodness-of-fit of all methods exceeded 0.9 when the data volume was 3000. Because GFT-90% uses the cumulative amplitude-frequency distribution to estimate $A_c$, the goodness-of-fit can reach 0.9 just for a data volume of 100. An interesting phenomenon is that the accuracy of the $A_c$ and $b$ values decreased with an increase in the data volume, and only when the data volume was greater than 300, the results of 1000 Bootstrap samples could be successfully searched. MBASS is more dependent on the amount of data and requires at least 5000 data volumes to successfully search the results of 1000 Bootstrap samples. Therefore, these two methods are not suitable for estimating the $A_c$ and $b$ values. The confidence limits and uncertainty of MAXC and MBS were consistent when the data volume was less than 3000. However, when the data volume was greater than 3000, the confidence limits of the MAXC and FGS methods began to gradually decrease to 0, while the mean $A_c$ and $b$ value estimation of MBS exceeded the theoretical value, and the uncertainty of $A_c$ was evident. In addition, because both $A_c$ and $b$ are statistical values, the stability of the statistical results largely depends on the amount of data. To better search the log-linear segment, the doubly truncated amplitude-frequency distribution was accepted by FGS, which fully considers the amplitude distribution characteristics. Therefore, the uncertainty of the Bootstrap confidence limit was higher than that of other methods when the data volume was small. However, it can also be seen that the mean $A_c$ and $b$ values of the Bootstrap samples obtained by FGS were still accurate.

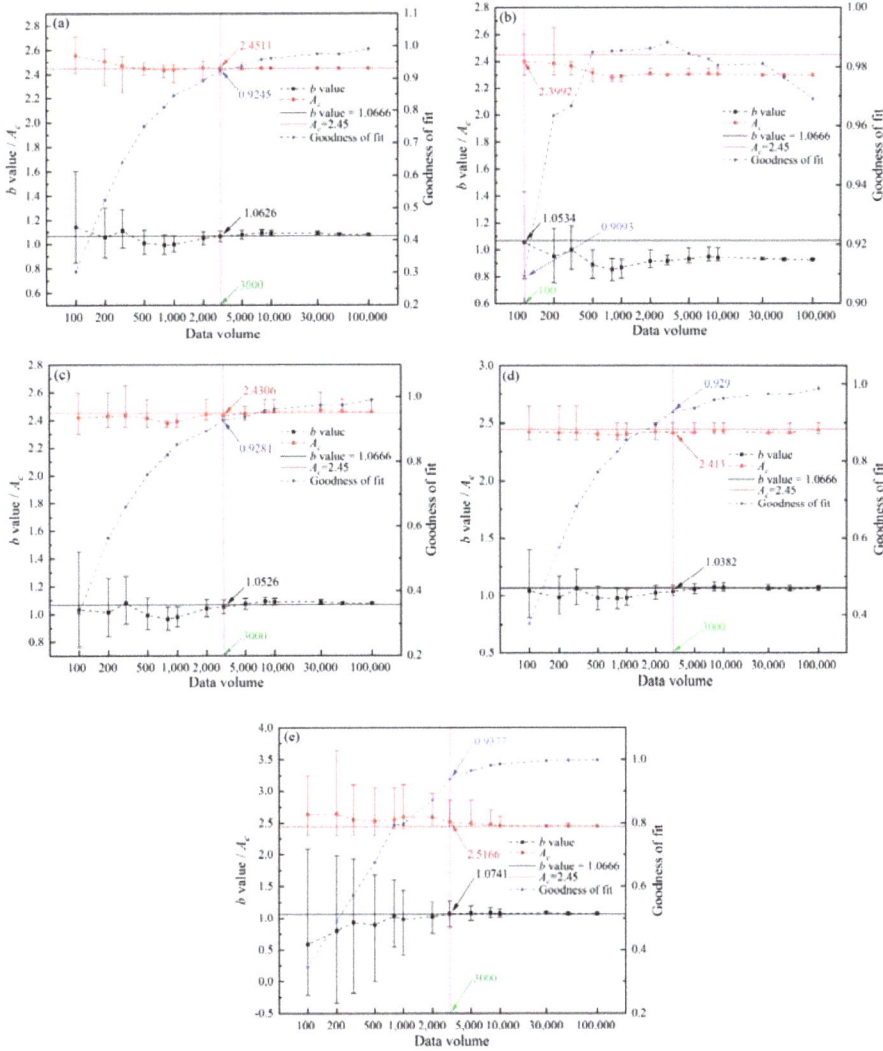

**Figure 3.** The variation of $A_c$ and $b$ values estimated by the five methods with different synthetic data volumes. The theoretical $A_c$ value is 2.45, theoretical $b$ value is 1.0666, and the data volume is 100,000. Estimated $A_c$ and $b$ values are the mean value of 1000 Bootstrap samples. The error bar is the 95% Bootstrap confidence limit. (**a**–**e**) MAXC, GFT-90%, MBS, MBASS, and FGS, respectively.

The column distribution of $A_c$ obtained by 1000 Bootstrap samples of various completeness amplitude estimation methods is shown in Figure 4. This shows that MAXC was the most stable and reliable, followed by the FGS method. Although the estimation result of the GFT method also seemed very stable, it clearly underestimated the theoretical $A_c$, which is inconsistent with the actual situation. Similarly, MBASS not only had unstable results but also overestimated $A_c$ by more than 15% of the samples. The MBS also overestimated $A_c$ and reached more than 10% of the samples when the data volume was 10,000 and 50,000. From the above analysis, it can be seen that the estimation methods of completeness magnitude in seismology are also applicable for completeness amplitude $A_c$

in small-scale rock AE tests, despite some differences in searching ability, accuracy, and stability of estimation results among different methods.

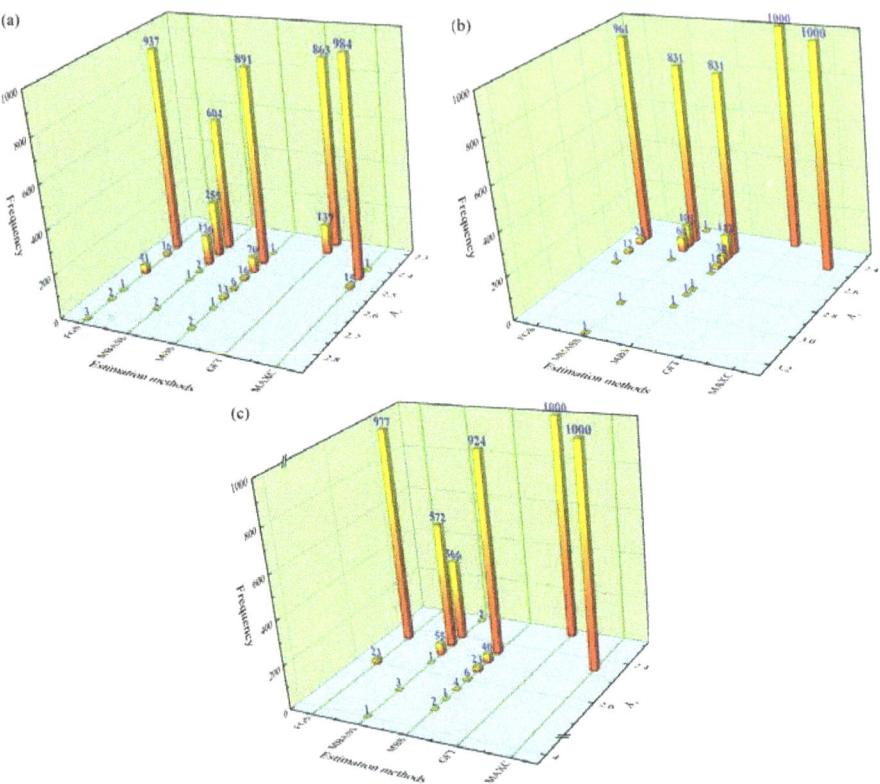

**Figure 4.** Estimation $A_c$ of 1000 Bootstrap samples of five methods with three data volume at (**a**) 10,000, (**b**) 50,000, and (**c**) 100,000.

As can be seen from the amplitude-frequency distribution in Figure 2, the rock AE data had an auxiliary discontinuous amplitude point $A_0$ at the end of the high amplitude segment, which was similar to $M_0$ in the earthquake sequence. Therefore, when estimating the $b$ value based on the G–R law, the high amplitude data greater than $A_0$ would inevitably affect the accuracy of the $b$ value estimation. As shown in Figure 2D,E, both the MBASS and FGS can estimate the auxiliary discontinuous point of the magnitude-frequency distribution; therefore, which one is more suitable for estimating the auxiliary discontinuous point is worth further discussing. Figure 5 clearly shows that $A_0$ estimated by MBASS was smaller than $A_c$. Therefore, we continued to estimate the third discontinuous point. However, only a few of the third discontinuous points met the requirements at the amplitude of 90 dB. By contrast, the FGS method was able to successfully find both end discontinuities, and the estimation $A_0$ was very close to the theoretical $A_0$ at the amplitude of 99 dB. Compared with Figure 5a,b, the log-linear segment of the apparent amplitude-frequency distribution between $A_c$ and $A_0$ identified by the FGS method was much more stable and reasonable than that of the MBASS method. Therefore, the FGS was more suitable for estimating the auxiliary discontinuous point $A_0$ at the right end of the apparent amplitude-frequency distribution in the rock AE.

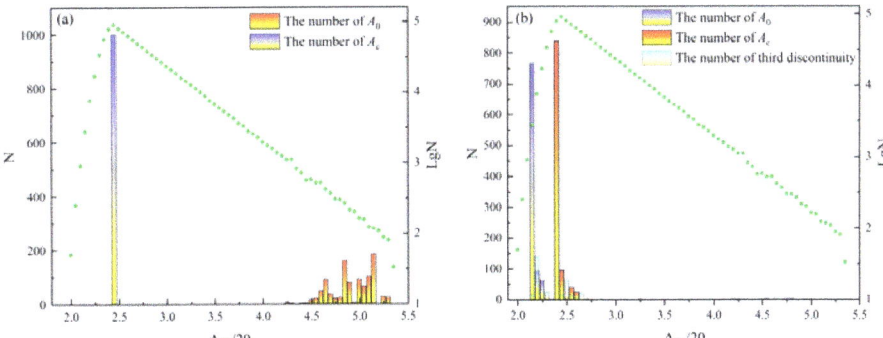

**Figure 5.** Search for $A_c$ and $A_0$ of apparent amplitude-frequency distribution by FGS and MBASS. In order for MBASS to estimate 1000 Bootstrap samples, we generated 100,000 data volumes. (**a**) FGS. (**b**) MBASS; we also counted the number of third discontinuities of 1000 Bootstrap samples.

*2.3. The Optimal b Value Estimation Procedure through Apparent Amplitude-Frequency Distribution for Rock AE Tests*

Because the Bootstrap approach can obtain a reliable estimation and avoid outliers, here, combined with the Bootstrap, we proposed to use MAXC to estimate the completeness amplitude $A_c$ and FGS to estimate the auxiliary discontinuous point $A_0$, respectively. However, after determining $A_c$ and $A_0$, another issue worth discussing was which regression method we needed to use to estimate the $b$ value of the apparent amplitude-frequency distribution between $A_c$ and $A_0$.

Most papers still use least-squares regression (LSR), which assumes that the frequency data errors are Gaussian, to estimate the $b$ value. However, frequencies based on count data have Poisson sampling uncertainties, which cause bias when using LSR for $b$ value estimation. Thus, a generalized linear model (GLM) subject to Poisson error can provide a more accurate fit of count data [45,49,53]. Here, we also used the data generation in Section 2.1 to compare LSR assuming a Gaussian error and GLM assuming a Poisson error with apparent amplitude data between $A_c$ and $A_0$ at a 95% confidence limit. As shown in Figure 6, the confidence intervals of LSR and GLM indicate significantly different changing trends. The confidence intervals of GLM gradually narrow as the amplitude decreases, and the whole amplitude show a "trumpet" shape. However, the confidence interval of LSR remains parallel from small to large amplitudes, which evidently does not conform to the characteristics of the amplitude-frequency distribution. Maximum likelihood estimation (MLE) is currently one of the most popular methods for estimating the $b$ value [54], and it can be seen from Table 1 that the standard deviation and bias of the $b$ value obtained by this method are also very small. Therefore, once the apparent amplitude-frequency distribution between $A_c$ and $A_0$ is determined, the MLE is also a good choice for regression [49]. However, it is worth noting that the MLE does not have an accurate confidence interval of the doubly truncated amplitude-frequency distribution and cannot further analyze the uncertainty of the estimation results. Thus, we chose GLM regression to fit log-linear amplitude of apparent amplitude-frequency between the left end point $A_c$ identified by MAXC and the right end point $A_0$ identified by FGS, and here we named this $b$ value estimation procedure as MFBG (MAXC-FGS-Bootstrap-GLM).

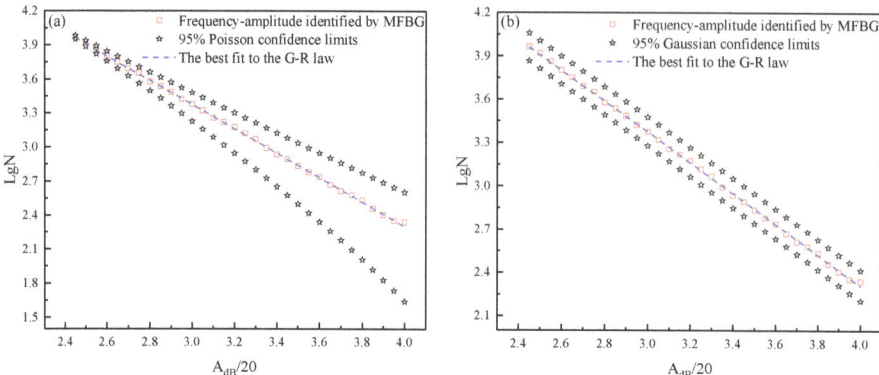

**Figure 6.** Ninety-five percent confidence limits of log-linear segment identified by MFBG from synthetic data with 100,000 data volumes. (**a**) GLM regression assuming Poisson error. (**b**) LSR regression assuming Gaussian error.

**Table 1.** Estimated $b$ values by MFBG when using GLM, LSR, and MLE regression.

| Theoretical $b$ Value | Estimating Method | Estimated $b$ Value | Standard Deviation | Bias |
| --- | --- | --- | --- | --- |
|  | GLM | 1.0705 | 0.0471 | 0.0039 |
| 1.0666 | LSR | 1.0714 | 0.0039 | 0.0048 |
|  | MLE | 1.0711 | 0.0233 | 0.0045 |

### 3. Application of MFBG in $b$ Value Estimation of Rock AE Test

To evaluate the performance of the new $b$ value estimation procedure MFBG, a non-explosive fracturing agent expansion was designed to conduct an AE test on red sandstone, marble, granite, and limestone. The rock broke and formed a specific failure surface because the non-explosive fracturing agent was injected into the three pre-drilled holes in the middle of the specimen (the mass ratio of expansion agent to water is 5:1.7). This experimental design ensured that the AE signals collected by the sensor were all generated by rock expansion fractures and did not rely on location technology to identify valid rupturing data, and a PCI-2 AE system used in this test with six sensors that were tightly attached to the two sides of rock specimen which parallel to the failure surface to collect the AE signals radiated during rock failure, and the parameter settings of AE equipment are shown in Table 2. The specific experimental process, rock sample size, and sensor distribution are shown in Figure 7.

Six sensors were used in the test: to completely remove the signals of non-rock fractures and ensure sufficient data volume, we set the AE signals arriving at the same time every four channels as the rock fracture signal. In this way, we obtained 15 channel combinations, each of which had 10 $b$ values, and used MFBG to estimate the mean value of the $b$ values for each channel. Table 3 shows the mean $b$ values of 1000 Bootstrap samples from the six sensors for red sandstone, marble, granite, and limestone. We can see that the $b$ values of the four types of rocks decrease successively because the four types of rocks have different scales of mineral particles, mineral composition, and discontinuity, which lead to different failure scales under the expansion force.

**Table 2.** Parameter settings of AE device.

| Sampling Rate/MSPS | Resonant Frequency of Sensor/KHz | Threshold/dB | PDT/μs | HLT/μs | HDT/μs |
| --- | --- | --- | --- | --- | --- |
| 10 | 140 | 40 | 50 | 300 | 200 |

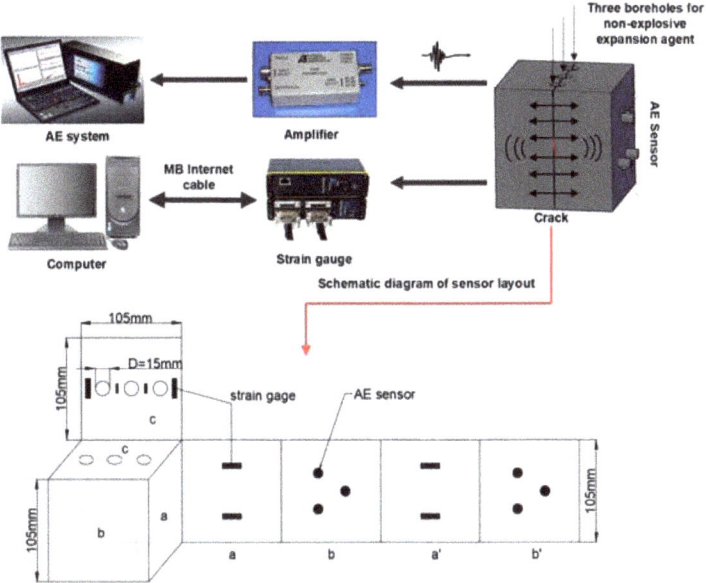

**Figure 7.** Schematic of non-explosive fracturing agent expansion rock AE test. Non-explosive fracture agent was injected into three boreholes of the specimen, and the fracture surface was formed in the center of the three boreholes. The label of specimen surface a' is parallel to a, and b' is parallel to b [25].

**Table 3.** $b$ values of 6 channels of red sandstone, marble, granite, and limestone.

| Channels | Mean $b$ Value | | | |
|---|---|---|---|---|
| | Red Sandstone | Marble | Granite | Limestone |
| 1 | 1.1009 | 0.8202 | 0.71992 | 0.40395 |
| 2 | 1.14325 | 1.0878 | 0.74096 | 0.55178 |
| 3 | 1.1957 | 1.10356 | 0.80763 | 0.59163 |
| 4 | 1.29028 | 1.15292 | 0.98828 | 0.63416 |
| 5 | 1.46777 | 1.2006 | 0.99417 | 0.75007 |
| 6 | 1.8879 | 1.2024 | 1.00422 | 0.82052 |

Generally, red sandstone with smaller mineral particles binding tightly is beneficial to the stress increase and the final large-scale fracture formed, but it also limits the initiation and propagation of rock cracks, resulting in a larger $b$ value, as the number of large-scale fractures is far less than that of small-scale fractures. In contrast, marble and granite with larger mineral particles and more defects will have more complex heterogeneity and internal structure characteristics, which is unbeneficial to the stress increase and the final large-scale fracture formation, but this also provides the opportunity for crack propagation and penetration, resulting in the generation of more large-scale fractures with smaller $b$ values during the rock failure. In particular, the mineral particles composition of limestone is also small and binds tightly, but unlike red sandstone, there is usually a large range of joints in limestone, which largely control the scale of rock failure, resulting in the smallest $b$ value than other rocks. Altogether, the estimated $b$ values of various types of rock samples are clearly different, which shows that the $b$ value depends on the material heterogeneity [55–57], which is also the basic idea for verifying the effectiveness of MFBG.

To explore in more detail the reasons why the $b$ values of different types of rocks showed an interval distribution, we use cross polar light technology to carry out a transparent refractive index experiment on rock slices with a thickness of 0.03 mm and the size of 1.7 mm × 1.3 mm to observe rock microstructure and further analyze the relationships between AE $b$ value characteristics and rock microscopic composition. As shown in Figure 8, red sandstone is mainly composed of fine-grained quartz, which is tighter than marble and composed of larger dolomite and calcite. Therefore, the $b$ value of red sandstone was slightly larger than that of marble. Granite has various mineral particles and defects or voids, which make it prone to large-scale fractures. Limestone is mainly composed of calcite and is even tighter than red sandstone. However, owing to the numerous joints created during deposition, more large-scale fractures are generated. Therefore, the $b$ value of red sandstone was the largest, followed by marble and granite, and the $b$ value of limestone was the smallest. The results of the four types of rock specimens with $b$ values from microstructural characteristics are the same as the estimated $b$ value using MFBG, which indicates that this method is accurate and stable for the estimation of the rock AE $b$ value.

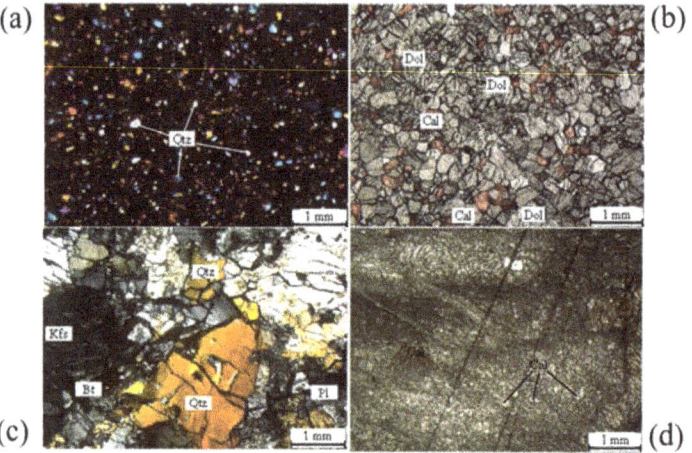

**Figure 8.** Microstructure of rocks obtained from transparent refractive index experiment. (**a**–**d**) Red sandstone, marble, granite, and limestone, respectively. Qt—quartz; Dol—dolomite; Cal—calcite; Kfs—potash feldspar; Bt—biotite; Pl—plagioclase [58].

The temporal variation characteristics of the $b$ value are often used for seismic hazard analysis, crack scale failure description, and damage accumulation assessment in rock; normally, the $b$ value is negatively correlated with the stress. As shown in Figure 9, we used the new $b$ value estimation procedure recommended in Section 2.3 to estimate the AE $b$ value with temporal variation and combined energy, amplitude, and strain to further verify the effectiveness of the MFBG through the internal relationship between the $b$ value and crack scale development during rock failure. Because the $b$ value is a statistical value, the accuracy of its estimation results is greatly affected by the data volume. Therefore, in order to improve the representativeness and the readability of the analysis results, here we only conduct a special analysis on the granite with the largest data volume collected. Figure 9c shows that the rock failure under expansion stress was manifested as a continuous increase in deformation macroscopically, which has experienced the entire process of compaction of existing defects and microcracks, initiation, propagation, and interpenetration of new cracks, and finally, the formation of the main fracture [59,60]. In this process, the appearance of energy and amplitude signals was usually triggered by a rupturing scale, which in turn led to a decrease or increase in the $b$ value under the constraints of statistical laws. Furthermore, Figure 9 shows that the temporal variation characteristics of $b$ values decreased continuously, and especially for the time before 16,550 s and after 16,600 s that $b$ value almost linearly decreased. This is consistent with Scholz's laboratory experiments [14], which also show that the $b$ value in the size distribution of AE events decreases linearly with differential stress. Therefore, the MFBG method estimated the $b$ value in the AE tests can accurately describe the size distribution characteristic of rock failure.

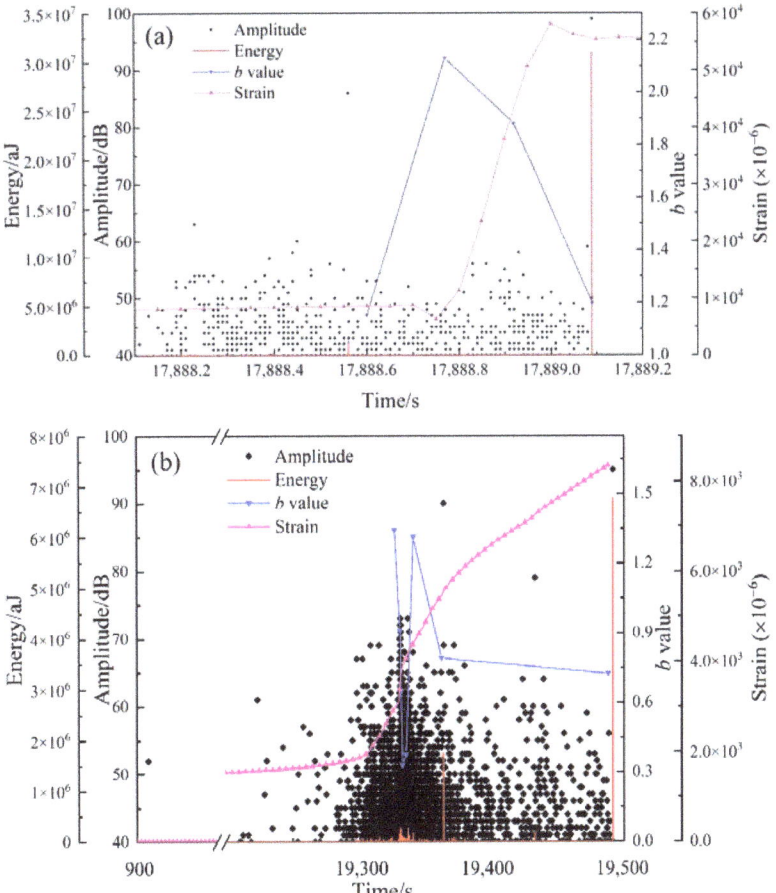

**Figure 9.** *Cont.*

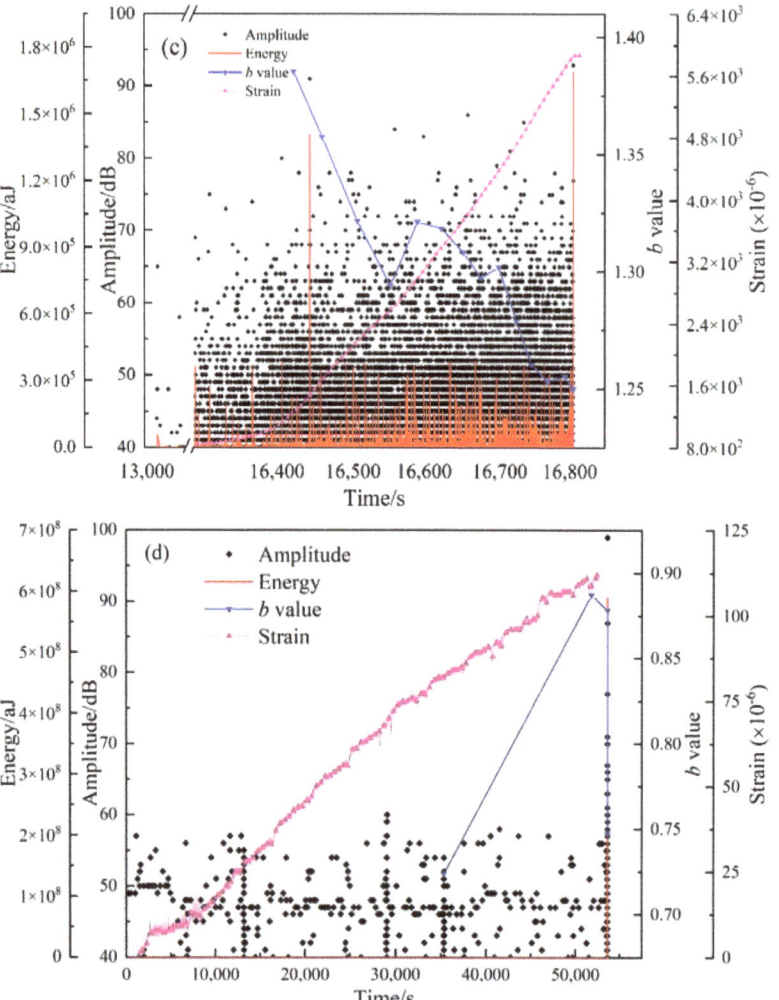

**Figure 9.** Temporal variation of AE $b$ value, energy, amplitude, and strain of (**a**) red sandstone, (**b**) marble, (**c**) granite, and (**d**) limestone. Since the development of non-explosive expansion agent was very slow and few signals were generated in the early stage of the tests, the starting time of the experimental analysis selected here was different.

## 4. Conclusions

To research the accurate $b$ value estimation procedure based on apparent amplitude distribution of rock AE, this paper performs a comparative analysis of various $b$ value estimation methods that are used in earthquakes by simulated apparent amplitudes. A new $b$ value estimation procedure was proposed, and its reliability is also further verified on rock AE testing and a transparent refractive index experiment. The following conclusions are drawn from this study:

Attenuation causes the two ends of the apparent amplitude-frequency distribution to deviate from the log-linear relationship. Of course, there also retains a finite amplitude interval that still obeys the G–R law, with the $b$ value being the same as the source. Therefore, we must search for the log-linear segment in the apparent amplitude-frequency distribution, which can represent the source size distribution characteristics. Furthermore, we generally set the acquisition threshold and maximum output amplitude of the AE equipment, resulting in a doubly truncated exponential distribution for the rock AE frequency-size distribution. We also define the left and right end amplitude points deviating from the G–R law as the completeness amplitude $A_c$ and auxiliary discontinuous amplitude $A_0$, which correspond to the completeness magnitude $M_c$ and auxiliary discontinuous magnitude $M_0$ in the earthquake catalog. Additionally, more attention must be paid to the completeness amplitude $A_c$ and auxiliary discontinuous amplitude $A_0$ to obtain the source size distribution through the $b$ value of the apparent amplitude frequency.

The estimation method of completeness magnitude commonly used in earthquakes was also suitable for identifying the completeness amplitude in rock AE. Especially, the MAXC can better estimate $A_c$, and the FGS can better estimate $A_0$. Moreover, we combined the Bootstrap approach to propose a new $b$ value estimation procedure named MFBG, which can better fit the apparent amplitude distribution without any attenuation compensation, and the effectiveness of the new method was verified by the relationships between rock crack size distribution and mineral grains and internal structure characteristics under laboratory rock AE tests and transparent refractive index experiments. This study can provide new insights and methods for studying the precursory characteristics of laboratory rock tests and rock mass engineering through the variation of rock AE $b$ value.

**Author Contributions:** Conceptualization: X.L. and C.X.; methodology: D.C.; investigation: D.C. and H.L.; software: C.X. and K.D.; writing—original draft: D.C. and X.L.; writing—review and editing: X.L. All authors have read and agreed to the published version of the manuscript.

**Funding:** This work was supported by the National Natural Science Foundation of China (Grant 42172316) and Natural Science Foundation of Hunan Province (2021JJ30810), and the Research Fund of The State Key Laboratory of Coal Resources and Safe Mining, CUMT (SKLCRSM21KF005). The authors are grateful for the financial support provided by the funds.

**Institutional Review Board Statement:** Not applicable.

**Informed Consent Statement:** Not applicable.

**Data Availability Statement:** Data associated with this research are available and can be obtained by contacting the corresponding author.

**Conflicts of Interest:** The authors declare no conflict of interest.

# References

1. Gutenberg, B.; Richter, C. Frequency of earthquakes in California. *Bull. Seism. Soc. Am.* **1944**, *34*, 185–188. [CrossRef]
2. Kagan, Y.Y. Seismic moment-frequency relation for shallow earthquakes: Regional comparison. *J. Geophys. Res. Earth Surf.* **1997**, *102*, 2835–2852. [CrossRef]
3. Triep, E.; Sykes, L.R. Frequency of occurrence of moderate to great earthquakes in intracontinental regions: Implications for changes in stress, earthquake prediction, and hazard assessment. *J. Geophys. Res. Earth Surf.* **1997**, *102*, 9923–9948. [CrossRef]
4. Main, I.G.; Li, L.; McCloskey, J.; Naylor, M. Effect of the Sumatran mega-earthquake on the global magnitude cut-off and event rate. *Nat. Geosci.* **2008**, *1*, 142. [CrossRef]
5. Jordan, T.H.; Chen, Y.-T.; Gasparini, P.; Madariaga, R.; Main, I.; Marzocchi, W.; Papadopoulos, G.; Sobolev, G.; Yamaoka, K.; Zschau, J. Operational earthquake forecasting: State of Knowledge and Guidelines for Utilization. *Ann. Geophys.* **2011**, *54*, 361–391.
6. Liu, X.; Liu, Z.; Li, X.; Gong, F.; Du, K. Experimental study on the effect of strain rate on rock acoustic emission characteristics. *Int. J. Rock Mech. Min. Sci.* **2020**, *133*, 104420. [CrossRef]
7. Liu, X.; Li, X.; Hong, L.; Yin, T.; Rao, M. Acoustic emission characteristics of rock under impact loading. *J. Cent. South Univ.* **2015**, *22*, 3571–3577. [CrossRef]
8. Amorese, D. Applying a change-point detection method on frequency-magnitude distributions. *Bull. Seism. Soc. Am.* **2007**, *97*, 1742–1749. [CrossRef]
9. Mogi, K. Study of the elastic shocks caused by the fracture of heterogeneous materials and its relations to earthquake phenomena. *Bull. Earthq. Res. Inst.* **1962**, *40*, 125–173.
10. Main, I.; Sammonds, P.; Meredith, P. Application of a modified Griffith criterion to the evolution of fractal damage during compressional rock failure. *Geophys. J. Int.* **1993**, *115*, 367–380. [CrossRef]

11. Mori, J.; Abercrombie, R. Depth dependence of earthquake frequency-magnitude distributions in California: Implications for rupture initiation. *J. Geophys. Res.* **1997**, *102*, 15081–15090. [CrossRef]
12. Wiemer, S.; Wyss, M. Mapping the frequency-magnitude distribution in asperities: An improved technique to calculate recurrence times? *J. Geophys. Res.* **1997**, *102*, 15115–15128. [CrossRef]
13. Schorlemmer, D.; Wiemer, S.; Wyss, M. Variations in earthquake size distribution across different stress regimes. *Nature* **2005**, *437*, 539–542. [CrossRef]
14. Scholz, C. On the stress dependence of the earthquake b value. *Geophys. Res. Lett.* **2015**, *42*, 1399–1402. [CrossRef]
15. Carpinteri, A.; Lacidogna, G.; Puzzi, S. From criticality to final collapse: Evolution of the "b-value" from 1.5 to 1.0. *Chaos Solitons Fractals* **2009**, *41*, 843–853. [CrossRef]
16. D'Angela, D.; Ercolino, M.; Bellini, C.; Cocco, V.D.; Iacoviello, F. Characterisation of the damaging micromechanisms in a pearlitic ductile cast iron and damage assessment by acoustic emission testing. *Fatigue Fract. Eng. Mater. Struct.* **2020**, *43*, 1038–1050. [CrossRef]
17. Xu, J.; Fu, Z.; Lacidogna, G.; Carpinteri, A. Micro-cracking monitoring and fracture evaluation for crumb rubber concrete based on acoustic emission techniques. *Struct. Health Monit.* **2018**, *17*, 946–958. [CrossRef]
18. Colombo, I.S.; Main, I.G.; Forde, M.C. Assessing Damage of Reinforced Concrete Beam Using "b-value" Analysis of Acoustic Emission Signals. *J. Mater. Civ. Eng.* **2003**, *15*, 280–286. [CrossRef]
19. Mignan, A.; Woessner, J. Estimating the magnitude of completeness for earthquake catalogs. *Community Online Resour. Stat. Seism. Anal.* **2012**, 1–45. [CrossRef]
20. Kijko, A.; Smit, A. Estimation of the frequency-magnitude Gutenberg-Richter b-value without level of completeness. *Seismol. Res. Lett.* **2017**, *88*, 311–318. [CrossRef]
21. Ross, Z.; Trugman, D.; Hauksson, E.; Shearer, P. Searching for hidden earthquakes in Southern California. *Science* **2019**, *364*, 767–771. [CrossRef]
22. Rydelek, P.; Sacks, I. Testing the completeness of earthquake catalogs and the hypothesis of self-similarity. *Nature* **1989**, *337*, 251–253. [CrossRef]
23. Wiemer, S.; Wyss, M. Minimum magnitude of completeness in earthquake catalogs: Examples from Alaska, the western United States, and Japan. *Bull. Seism. Soc. Am.* **2000**, *90*, 859–869. [CrossRef]
24. Cao, A.; Gao, S. Temporal variation of seismic b-values beneath northeastern Japan island arc. *Geophys. Res. Lett.* **2002**, *29*, 1334. [CrossRef]
25. Liu, X.; Han, M.; He, W.; Li, X.; Chen, D. A new b value estimation method in rock acoustic emission testing. *J. Geophys. Res.* **2020**, *125*, e2020JB019658. [CrossRef]
26. Han, Q.; Wang, L.; Xu, J.; Carpinteri, A.; Lacidogna, G. A robust method to estimate the b-value of the magnitude-frequency distribution of earthquakes. *Chaos Solit. Fractals* **2015**, *81*, 103–110. [CrossRef]
27. Marzocchi, W.; Spassiani, I.; Stallone, A.; Taroni, M. Erratum to: How to be fooled searching for significant variations of the b-value. *Geophys. J. Int.* **2020**, *221*, 351. [CrossRef]
28. Dong, L.; Chen, Y.; Sun, D.; Zhang, Y. Implications for rock instability precursors and principal stress direction from rock acoustic experiments. *Int. J. Min. Sci. Technol.* **2021**, *31*, 789–798. [CrossRef]
29. Lei, X.; Kusunose, K.; Nishizawa, O.; Cho, A.; Satoh, T. On the spatio-temporal distribution of acoustic emissions in two granitic rocks under triaxial compression: The role of pre-existing cracks. *J. Geophys. Res.* **2000**, *27*, 1997–2000. [CrossRef]
30. Lei, X.; Kusunose, K.; Rao, M.; Nishizawa, O.; Satoh, T. Quasi-static fault growth and cracking in homogeneous brittle rock under triaxial compression using acoustic emission monitoring. *J. Geophys. Res. Solid Earth* **2000**, *105*, 6127–6139. [CrossRef]
31. Thompson, B.; Young, R.; Lockner, D. Fracture in Westerly granite under AE feedback and constant strain rate loading: Nucleation, quasi-static propagation, and the transition to unstable fracture propagation. *Pure Appl. Geophys.* **2006**, *163*, 995–1019. [CrossRef]
32. Mogi, K. Magnitude-frequency relationship for elastic shocks accompanying fractures of various materials and some related problems in earthquakes. *Bull. Earthq. Res. Inst.* **1962**, *40*, 831–853.
33. Scholz, C. The frequency-magnitude relation of microfracturing in rock and its relation to earthquakes. *Bull. Seismol. Soc. Am.* **1968**, *58*, 399–415. [CrossRef]
34. Lockner, D. The role of acoustic emission in the study of rock fracture. *Int. J. Rock Mech. Min. Sci. Geomech. Abstr.* **1993**, *30*, 883–899. [CrossRef]
35. Lei, X. How do asperities fracture? An experimental study of unbroken asperities. *Earth Planet Sci. Lett.* **2003**, *213*, 347–359. [CrossRef]
36. Goebel, T.; Candela, T.; Sammis, C.; Becker, T.; Dresen, G.; Schorlemmer, D. Seismic event distributions and off-fault damage during frictional sliding of saw-cut surfaces with pre-defined roughness. *Geophys. J. Int.* **2014**, *196*, 612–625. [CrossRef]
37. Vorobieva, I.; Shebalin, P.; Narteau, C. Break of slope in earthquake-size distribution and creep rate along the San Andreas fault system. *Geophys. Res. Lett.* **2016**, *43*, 6869–6875. [CrossRef]
38. Dong, L.; Hu, Q.; Tong, X.; Liu, Y. Velocity-Free MS/AE Source Location Method for Three-Dimensional Hole-Containing Structures. *Engineering* **2020**, *6*, 827–834. [CrossRef]
39. Dong, L.; Tong, X.; Ma, J. Quantitative Investigation of Tomographic Effects in Abnormal Regions of Complex Structures. *Engineering* **2021**, *7*, 1011–1022. [CrossRef]

40. Dong, L.; Tong, X.; Hu, Q.; Tao, Q. Empty region identification method and experimental verification for the two-dimensional complex structure. *Int. J. Rock Mech. Min. Sci.* **2021**, *147*, 104885. [CrossRef]
41. Dong, L.; Zhang, L.; Liu, H.; Du, K.; Liu, X. Acoustic Emission $b$ Value Characteristics of Granite under True Triaxial Stress. *Mathematics* **2022**, *10*, 451. [CrossRef]
42. Dong, L.; Luo, Q. Investigations and new insights on earthquake mechanics from fault slip experiments. *Earth Sci. Rev.* **2022**, *228*, 104019. [CrossRef]
43. Main, I.; Meredith, P.; Jones, C. A reinterpretation of the precursory seismic $b$-value anomaly from fracture mechanics. *J. Geophys. Res.* **1989**, *96*, 131–138. [CrossRef]
44. Lockner, D.; Byerlee, J.; Kuksenko, V.; Ponomarev, A.; Sidorin, A. Quasi-static fault growth and shear fracture energy in granite. *Nature* **1991**, *350*, 39–42. [CrossRef]
45. Sammonds, P.; Meredith, P.; Main, I. Role of pore fluids in the generation of seismic precursors to shear fracture. *Nature* **1992**, *359*, 228–230. [CrossRef]
46. Goebel, T.; Schorlemmer, D.; Becker, T.; Dresen, G.; Sammis, C. Acoustic emissions document stress changes over many seismic cycles in stick-slip experiments. *Geophys. Res. Lett.* **2013**, *40*, 2049–2054. [CrossRef]
47. Lennartz-Sassinek, S.; Main, I.; Zaiser, M.; Graham, C. Acceleration and localization of subcritical crack growth in a natural composite material. *Phys. Rev. E* **2014**, *90*, 052401. [CrossRef]
48. Kwiatek, G.; Goebel, T.; Dresen, G. Seismic moment tensor and $b$ value variations over successive seismic cycles in laboratory stick-slip experiments. *Geophys. Res. Lett.* **2014**, *41*, 5838–5846. [CrossRef]
49. Chen, D.; Liu, X.; He, W.; Xia, C.; Gong, F.; Li, X.; Cao, X. Effect of attenuation on amplitude distribution and $b$ value in rock acoustic emission tests. *Geophys. J. Int.* **2021**, *229*, 933–947. [CrossRef]
50. Amorese, D.; Grasso, J.; Rydelek, P. On varying $b$ values with depth: Results from computer-intensive tests for Southern California. *Geophys. J. Int.* **2010**, *180*, 347–360. [CrossRef]
51. Shi, Y.; Blot, B. The standard error of the magnitude-frequency $b$ value. *Bull. Seismol. Soc. Am.* **1982**, *72*, 1677–1687. [CrossRef]
52. Clauset, A.; Shalizi, C.; Newman, M. Power-law distributions in empirical data. *Siam. Rev.* **2007**, *51*, 661–703. [CrossRef]
53. Greenhough, J.; Main, I. A Poisson model for earthquake frequency uncertainties in seismic hazard analysis. *Geophys. Res. Lett.* **2008**, *35*, L19313. [CrossRef]
54. Aki, K. Maximum likelihood estimate of b in the formula $\log N = a - bM$ and its confidence limits. *Bull. Earthq. Res. Inst.* **1965**, *43*, 237–239.
55. Wang, K.; Bilek, S. Do subducting seamounts generate or stop large earthquakes? *Geology* **2011**, *39*, 819–822. [CrossRef]
56. Yang, H.; Liu, Y.; Lin, J. Geometrical effects of a subducted seamount on stopping megathrust ruptures. *Geophys. Res. Lett.* **2013**, *40*, 2011–2016. [CrossRef]
57. Nishikawa, T.; Ide, S. Earthquake size distribution in subduction zones linked to slab buoyancy. *Nat. Geosci.* **2014**, *7*, 904–908. [CrossRef]
58. Liu, X.; Cui, J.; Li, X.; Liu, Z. Study on attenuation characteristics of elastic wave in different types of rocks. *Chin. J. Rock Mech. Eng.* **2018**, *37*, 3223–3230.
59. Xie, Q.; Li, S.; Liu, X.; Gong, F.; Li, X. Effect of loading rate on fracture behaviors of shale under mode I loading. *J. Cent. South Univ.* **2020**, *27*, 3118–3132. [CrossRef]
60. Wang, S.; Li, X.; Yao, J.; Gong, F.; Li, X.; Du, K.; Tao, M.; Huang, L.; Du, S. Experimental investigation of rock breakage by a conical pick and its application to non-explosive mechanized mining in deep hard rock. *Int. J. Rock Mech. Min. Sci.* **2019**, *21*, 104063. [CrossRef]

*Article*

# Pollutant Migration Pattern during Open-Pit Rock Blasting Based on Digital Image Analysis Technology

Jiangjiang Yin [1], Jianyou Lu [1,*], Fuchao Tian [2] and Shaofeng Wang [1,*]

1. School of Resources and Safety Engineering, Central South University, Changsha 410083, China
2. State Key Laboratory of Coal Mine Safety Technology, China Coal Technology & Engineering Group Shenyang Research Institute, Shenfu Demonstration Zone, Shenyang 113122, China
* Correspondence: jianyou.lu@csu.edu.cn (J.L.); sf.wang@csu.edu.cn (S.W.)

**Abstract:** Previous studies have revealed that toxic gases and dust (smoke dust) are the most common pollutants generated by the blasting operations in open-pit mines, which might lead to a threat to the environment's condition, health and safety, and properties protection around the blasting site. In order to deal with the problems, a pollution evaluation system was established based on the fractal dimension theory ($D_{box}(P)$) and grayscale average algorithm ($G_a$) in digital image-processing technology to recognize and analyze the distributions of the smoke-dust cloud, and subsequently determine the pollution degrees. The computation processes of $D_{box}(P)$ and $G_a$ indicate three fitted correlations between the parameters and diffusion time of smoke dust. Then, a pollution index ($Pi$) is put forward to integrate the global and local features of $D_{box}(P)$ and $G_a$, and develop a hazard classification mechanism for the blasting pollutants. Results obviously denote three diffusion stages of the pollutants, mainly including generation stage, cloud-formation stage, and diffusion stage. In addition, it has been validated that the proposed system can also be utilized in single-point areas within a whole digital image. Besides, there are variation trends of the thresholds $T_1$ and $T_2$ in binarization with the diffusion of pollutants. With this identification and evaluation system, the pollution condition of smoke dust can be obviously determined and analyzed.

**Keywords:** rock-blasting; smoke-dust pollution; digital image processing; fractal dimension; grayscale average; hazards classification

**MSC:** 54H30

## 1. Introduction

With the evolution in industrial fields, the mining industry is confronted with a huge energy demand, and is gradually emerging as the critical support for technological development and progress [1–3]. To adapt to community challenges, ore-deposit extractions are constantly expanding, especially for open-pit mines [4,5]. Blasting is a conventional excavation measure for the ores crushing on the ground, and also an option for constructing roads, tunnels and other constructions in mine projects [6]. However, during blasting operations, there are undesirable consequences engendered, such as seismic waves, explosive flying scatter (fly rocks), air shockwave, noise, toxic gases, blasting dust, etc. [6,7].

Within these hazards, blasting dust, the PM2.5 and PM10, and some toxic gases, including CO, $NO_x$, $SO_2$, $H_2S$, and so on, become prominent components of environmental pollutants in blasting sites [8]. Most of these toxic gases are released in a range of concentrations due to environmental and technical factors [9]. Inhaling a certain amount of these toxic gases during their diffusion period can be fatal [10]. Furthermore, prior studies have denoted that it can reach thousands of milligrams per cubic meter for the local blasting dust concentration in surface mining [11]. The combination of blasting dust with toxic gases, which is collectively referred to as smoke dust, has attracted extensive attention owing to its salient hazardousness on air quality in mining sites and detrimental effects on human

health [12,13]. It has been demonstrated that a fairly high percentage of miners suffer from respiratory diseases or reduction in respiratory-system immunity due to long-term exposures to high-concentration dust environments, especially pneumoconiosis [14,15]. In addition, the accumulation of dust reduces the humidity of the atmosphere, which then increases the ambient temperature [16]. Meanwhile, it is noteworthy that smoke dust reduces visibility in the mining site, resulting in high working risks and a significant reduction in production efficiency [17]. Large amounts of dust pollution can depose on the ground, causing vegetation degradation and animal habitat destruction [18]. With the characteristic of high concentration and wide range of diffusion it might spread into the water area for dust clusters, thereby contaminating the downstream areas [8]. Studies over the past decades have provided important information on the generation and diffusion mechanisms of smoke dust in open-pit mines. Numerical simulations, for instance, Fluent software, LS-DYNA etc., were conducted to figure out the smoke dust movement, diffusion rate, and the time consuming to float out of the pit, validating the effects of vortex action and the vertical height in the pit on coal-mine dust, and optimizing blasting parameters at the same time [19,20]. Inspired by the approaches, Tang et al. [21] established a circulating accumulation emission model to analyze dust diffusion, including dust emission, retention, and diffusion, respectively. Besides, pertinent artificial intelligence systems, such as particle swarm optimization (PSO) and the long short-term memory (LSTM), were employed to predict and control dust concentration [22–24]. In terms of the evaluation system of efficiency of dust reduction with multiple techniques, there are also studies [25,26] in virtue of some tools (e.g., computational fluid dynamics model (CFD): ANSYS/Fluent 10.0 software, ANSYS, Inc., Pittsburgh, Pennsylvania, USA) mainly aiming at monitoring the dust diffusion, and then guaranteeing the mitigation of the smoke-dust pollution.

Furthermore, there are increasing concerns that, exposed to high-concentration smoke dust in open-pit mines, measurement equipment has been a crucial factor for immediately monitoring the pollution condition. Attalla et al. [9] adopted non-dispersion infrared (NDIR) and differential optical absorption spectroscopy (DOAS) to examine the diffusion of fugitive $NO_x$ and other pollutant gases. In addition, dust sample sensors, which are commonly based on ultrasound, optical, and electrochemical sensing elements, have also emerged as conventional methods for assessing contaminant gases and particulate fractions of dust emission [2]. With the widespread application of unmanned aerial vehicles (UAVs), researches were performed to load a series of sensors in the rotary-winged platforms, such as $CO_2$, $NO_2$, $SO_2$, PM10, etc. [27]. When in the application process, it is essential for the sampling collection location and source scales to be considered owing to the differences in fixed-wing and multi-rotor UAVs, and thus the long response time, limited measurement distance, and the accuracy of sensing elements hindered further use of UAVs.

Recent developments in the field of machine vision have led to a renewed interest in various industries due to their merits in non-contact measurements, full-visualization monitoring, and affordable cost [28–31]. In spite of the fact that the related studies on these vision-based models are currently at an early stage, digital image technology, mainly based on grayscale features and morphological features, has been widely applied in pollution analysis and control [32–35]. Dust-pollution measurement models established on the basis of grayscale features attempted to develop a relationship between the dust concentration and grayscale features extracted from dust images. Yue et al. [30] presented a photo-based method for analyzing air pollution using grayscale data. Thereafter, a logarithmic relation was acquired between the grayscale values and the powder volume by Grasa et al. [34], providing a calibration curve without any fitting constants. On the other hand, morphological feature models are inherently associated with the connections between the morphological features (such as the particle shape, size distribution, and surface structure) and dust concentration. R. Davies [36] and M. Taylor [37] were convinced that parameters of concentration and morphology were important in particle detection, and the latter presented mathematical models to characterize the particles. M. Paphael et al. [38] estimated the mean particle size utilizing optical parameters, on-line turbidity, and solid concentrations. It is also notable for the fractal dimension, another aspect of morphological features, to describe the space occupancy and the irregularities of granulated materials [39–42]. To figure out the effects of fractal dimension on the porous texture of coal dust images, Mahamud et al. [41] conducted experiments to measure particles exposed to different temperatures. Zhang et al. [42] apply fractal dimension to record the particle size of crushed specimens and obtain a legible regularity of size distribution in different stress conditions. Nevertheless, traditional grayscale or morphological models only consider the local features of pollutants but ignore the global features of their distributions, resulting in a one-sided evaluation of the pollution environment.

To further present the main advantages and limitations of the technology and equipment of previous studies on the pollutant migration that happened during rock-blasting operations, an overall comparation between them is summarized as the Table 1:

Table 1. Comparison of previous studies on analysis of smoke dust.

| Methods | Main Advantages | Main Limitations |
|---|---|---|
| Numerical simulation methods [19–21] | Short research cycle, safety and low investment | Lack of authenticity |
| Machine learning methods [22–24] | Prediction effectiveness | High demand for dataset |
| Measurement equipment for smoke dust [9,28] | Visual and clear data with a reference of existing standard | limited measurement distance |
| Grayscale feature models [32,35] Morphological feature models [36–43] | High flexibility; non-contact measurements | Few field applications for smoke dust |

Overall, all the evidence reviewed here seems to require a comprehensive evaluation system and distribution analysis for smoke dust pollution caused by blasting operations in open-pit mines.

In this paper, a vision-based model was established based on the fractal dimension theory ($D_{box}(P)$) and a grayscale average algorithm ($G_a$) for smoke dust evaluation in open-pit mines. Framed pictures were first collected from the video recorded by a UAV, and then, through a series of image processing operations, $D_{box}(P)$ and $G_a$ were separately calculated, the results of which were fitted by logarithmic and linear functions, respectively. For the sake of considering both global and local characteristics of pollutants, and fully adopting simplified expressions to characterize the various generation stages of smoke dust in blasting sites, a pollution index ($Pi$) was proposed to integrate the $D_{box}(P)$ and $G_a$, developing a hazard classification mechanism corresponding to four-level regions. With this evaluation system, the pollution condition of smoke dust can be obviously developed and analyzed, and eventually adequate preparations in response time and emergency preparedness are capable of eliminating detrimental effects on health protection and property safety, as well as improving the environmental quality around the blasting sites.

## 2. Image Processing Method Based on Grayscale Average and Fractal Dimension

Digital image processing has been successfully applied in the engineering field depending on the difference in the morphological characteristics or the color features of the research object against the homologous background [44–46]. Based on the technical principles, and the available devices, it is possible to achieve the monitoring and evaluation of the smoke-dust. The specific procedures of the algorithm in this research can be illustrated as a flowchart in Figure 1:

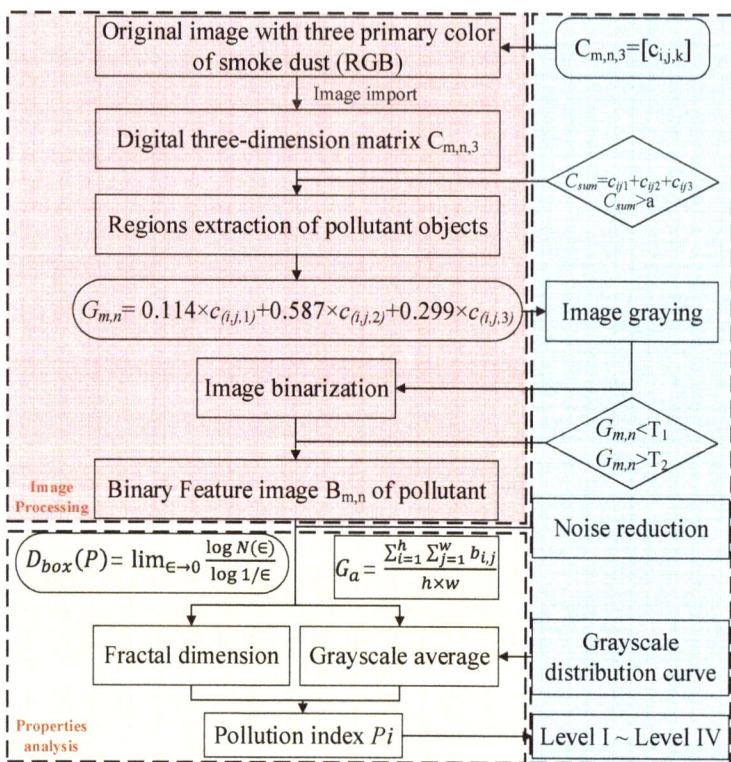

**Figure 1.** Flowchart of the image processing algorithms for extracting features of pollutants, and establishing an evaluation mechanism for hazards classification of smoke dust during blasting operations.

As shown in Figure 1, the proposed method can be divided into two parts, including the modules of image-processing operations and properties analysis, which primarily aim to acquire the feature image of the pollutants, and relevant calculation results about their distribution properties. According to the flowchart, pollution conditions in blasting sites can be analyzed and evaluated through a series of digital images. The specific application procedures are briefly presented below:

Step one: collect pollutants images of smoke dust at the blasting site, and then the software reads the images to form a three-dimensional digital matrix $C_{m \times n \times 3}$, which includes pixel values $c_{ijk}$ and homologous locations $(i, j)$; m, n represent the image size in height and width, and the third dimension of the matrix represents three color channels: R, G and B, respectively.

Step two: based on the image matrix $C_{m \times n \times 3}$, extract the main regions where pollutants distribute via Equations (1) and (2) below in accordance with the color characteristics of the smoke dust [47]. As is usual, the smoke dust pollutants in non-coal mines appear a brighter color, and thus, compared to several dark backgrounds, the pixel values of pollutants tend to be higher. Through the screening method, a series of pixels representing superfluous regions will be removed, whereby the images can be prepared for subsequent image processing operations.

$$C_{sum} = c_{ij1} + c_{ij2} + c_{ij3} \qquad (1)$$

$$C_{sum} > a \qquad (2)$$

Step three: fulfill further image-processing operations with pertinent programs. Image graying is enforced using the empirical formula shown in Figure 1, the matrix result of which is denoted as $G_{m \times n}$, and by virtue of image graying, the color dimensions are converted into two dimensions, viz., the image size. Then, binarization was served to recognize the regions of interest, in which a double-threshold method ($T_1$, $T_2$) was put forward to improve the performance of the feature extractions, and in this way, pixels within the gray image that are, respectively, lower or higher than $T_1$ and $T_2$ are assigned as 0 (black in color), while the intermediate areas between the thresholds are assigned as 1 (white in color). Noise reduction is then adopted to eliminate excrescent noise points caused by the forming transversion of pollutant images [48].

Step four: calculate the $D_{box}(P)$ and $G_a$ of the smoke-dust images to quantitively analyze the distribution changes of on-site pollutants. In the process, the two-dimensional box counting method was developed to acquire the fractal property of the pollutants [40]. Within the fractal calculation processes, the binary images are traversed by a slew of windows, the side lengths of which are decided by the original picture size, and are incremental pixel by pixel until the width and height reach half of the original length. Then, for each window, keep a track of the number of square boxes $N(\epsilon)$ intersecting the pollutant parts as well as the lengths of the boxes $\epsilon$. Afterwards, instead of the mathematical definition of fractal dimension theory as Equation (3), a regression method is used to analyze two groups of the box data through logarithmic processing, which can be expressed as Equation (4). Obviously, the slope of the regressed equation $D_{box}(P)$ is the fractal dimension of the smoke dust.

$$D_{box}(P) = \lim_{\epsilon \to 0} \frac{\log N(\epsilon)}{\log 1/\epsilon} \tag{3}$$

$$\log N(\epsilon) = D_{box}(P) * \log 1/\epsilon + C \ (C \text{ is a regressed constant}) \tag{4}$$

Meanwhile, $G_a$ of the binary images is calculated based on Equation (5), which can be defined as the division operation between the pixels denoting pollutants and site background, respectively. When in the calculation process, a grayscale distribution curve is plotted to develop the pollutants distribution along the directions of horizontal strike.

$$G_a = \frac{\sum_{i=1}^{h} \sum_{j=1}^{w} b_{i,j}}{h \times w} \tag{5}$$

where $h$ and $w$ represent the height and width of smoke-dust images.

Step five: through the computation of the $D_{box}(P)$ and $G_a$ of the pollutant, a pollution index $Pi$ is provided to achieve a comprehensive consideration of $D_{box}(P)$ and $G_a$, and the integration expression can be depicted as Equation (6):

$$Pi = D_{box}(P) + G_a \tag{6}$$

Then, according to the change tendency of $Pi$, it can be more accurate to evaluate the pollution condition from a quantitative aspect, and with a series of pollutant images collected from a whole blasting project, the index $Pi$ is capable of dividing into four regions of pollution levels, Level I~IV, viz. Therefore, the pollutant condition of smoke dust can be dramatically characterized no matter the period of monitoring or throughout the whole working process by this research.

## 3. Algorithm Application of $D_{box}(P)$ and $G_a$ with a Fugitive Dust Picture

For the sake of further demonstrating the proposed evaluation method of pollutant distribution in a blasting site, an image sample with fugitive dust shown as Figure 2 was applied to validate the effectiveness of the image-processing algorithm, and measurement of $D_{box}(P)$ with $G_a$. Firstly, the original color image of fugitive dust as Figure 2a was read, where in the image dust particles emerge distinctly with homologous pixels when compared to the black background. With the application of the image-processing method, the region of the floating dust was arguably extracted to produce a binary image, which can be visualized as Figure 2b. Based on the binary image, the calculation processes of $D_{box}(P)$, $G_a$ are also displayed in Figure 2c,d, respectively. As for the grayscale distribution, an ergodic window of 438 × 10 pixels in size was employed to cover the binary image along the direction of the horizontal, and with the traversal calculations, the grayscale distribution, cumulative distribution curve, and grayscale average were obtained, the results of which are displayed in Figure 2e. According to the grayscale parameters, $G_a$ of the whole image is 0.2490, and the dust objects primarily mainly distribute at 220~550 pixels of the horizontal strike. Similarly, the calculation procedures of $D_{box}(P)$ are devised as Figure 2d using the two-dimensional box counting method. With a series of measuring boxes covering the binary image, the computation procedures are revealed as the fitted equation in Figure 2f, and the $D_{box}(P)$ of the dust image is 1.977, the $R^2$ of which is 0.9998, embodying a precise fitting effect when applying it to research objects of fine grains.

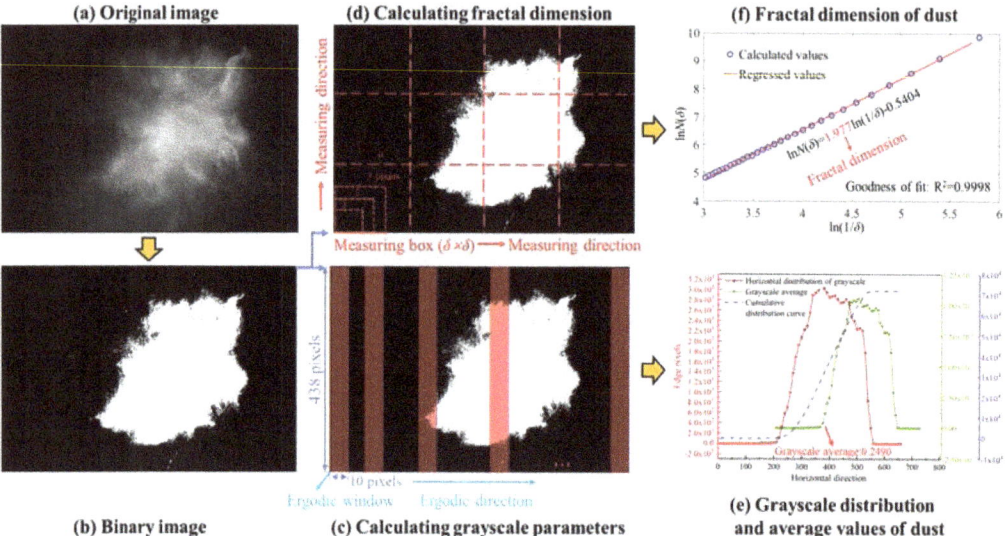

**Figure 2.** Description of the proposed method for the $D_{box}(P)$ and $G_a$ of the fugitive dust picture, including (**a**) original image of fugitive dust, (**b**) binary image through a series of image-processing operations, (**c**,**d**) calculation process of grayscale properties and $D_{box}(P)$ and (**e**,**f**) results of grayscale distribution, $D_{box}(P)$ and $G_a$ of the fugitive dust.

In order to verify the accuracy of calculation results in $D_{box}(P)$ and $G_a$ with the proposed binary dust image handled from the original image, the grayscale average distribution of the gray image, remaining quite complete image information with a 256-level grayscale form, was devised to analyze the change tendency of dust pixels as a comparison to the binary image, and quantitatively appraise the effectiveness on object segmentation within the application of image processing. The analysis results can be shown as Figure 3.

As is mentioned with the grayscale parameters, dust particles are primarily distributed at 220~550 pixels of the horizontal strike in accordance with the binary image. It can be perceived that the developed trend of the grayscale average from gray image tends to be consistent, performing a fairly smooth waveform shape. In addition, it is almost coincident with the high-distribution region of dust particles in any binary image or gray image. While there is a hysteresis effect for the grayscale parameter of gray image at the boundaries between research objects and background, producing two hysteresis intervals in the rising and falling stages of the grayscale average, the area of the hysteresis intervals accounts for about 5.58% of the total enclosed area by the grayscale distribution line of gray image. It is imperative to note the significance turning points, data turning point G1 (90, 25.16) of gray image embodying a hysteresis effect contrasting to B1 (210, 7.37 × 10$^{-5}$) of binary image for the first hysteresis interval, whereas G2 (560, 51.10) illustrates an almost the same horizontal position with B2 (560, 3.08 × 10$^{-5}$). A possible explanation for this might be the low pixel values of edge dust particles in the image (i.e., grayscale value). As a whole, in spite of the existence of hysteresis intervals, the application image of fugitive dust presents a validity in the object recognition of dust clouds and other fine-grained substances from a quantitative aspect.

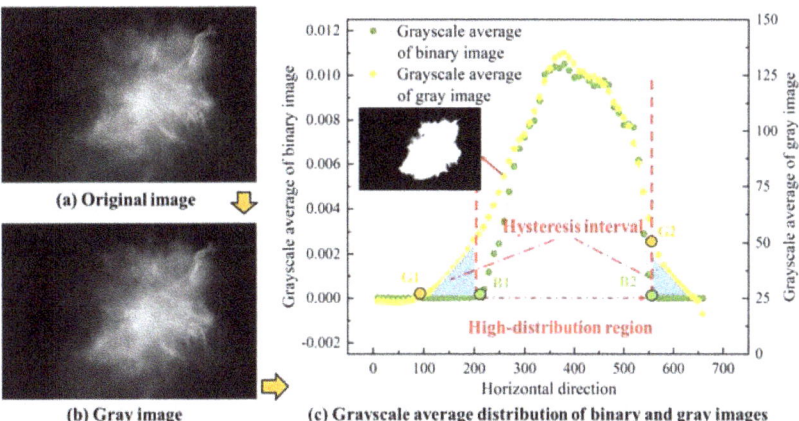

**Figure 3.** Result comparison on grayscale average between the binary image and grayscale image, including (**a**) original image of fugitive dust, (**b**) grayscale image, (**c**) grayscale average of binary and gray image for algorithm validation.

## 4. Results on the $D_{box}(P)$ with $G_a$ and the Pollution Evaluation System of Blasting Operations

A field experiment for analyzing smoke dust distribution, and evaluating the pollution condition based on the proposed method, was conducted in a deep open-pit mine with multi-step terrain production in Xinjiang, China. Shallow hole blasting was adopted for the ores crushing along the hillside wall, and the whole blasting operations with partial diffusion were recorded by a UAV platform flying directly above the blasting region with a fixed height. The platform can be predetermined in an autonomous direction, and illustrates high-temporal sampled pictures in real time.

A total of 95 images were extracted from the video recorded by the UAV with an interval of 1 s, which are 640 pixels in width and 368 pixels in height, integrally revealing the processes of blasting preparation, exploding and diffusion of smoke dust, respectively, which are shown in Figure 4.

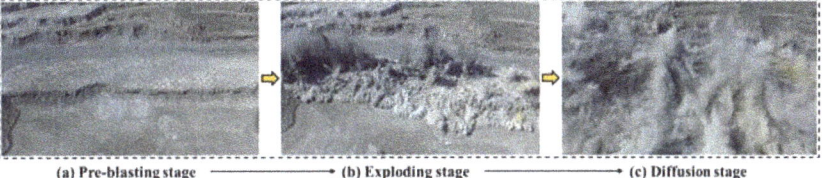

**Figure 4.** Frame pictures of pre-blasting, exploding stage and diffusion stages extracted from the UAV video data.

From the images in Figure 4, it can be found that there is an obvious contrast between smoke dust and the field background throughout the periods of blasting operation. At the initial stage, debris and dirt deposits on the ground were lifted up due to the shock wave of blasting, and with the gravity effect, the smoke dust was then dispersed suffering from the wind floating and other meteorological conditions. At this stage, most distribution regions of the pollutants perform as partially bright in color, while regions representing the ground surface and the bench tend to be dim. For a clearer description, a three-dimensional elevation grayscale image was put forward to show the grayscale distributions and the differences in elevation, as depicted in Figure 5. The elevation range in Figure 5e extracted from the region presents an exceedingly grayscale difference between the pollutants and ground surface. By this method, feature extraction of a complicated environment between the pollutants and background can be fulfilled through a series of image-processing algorithms proposed in this research.

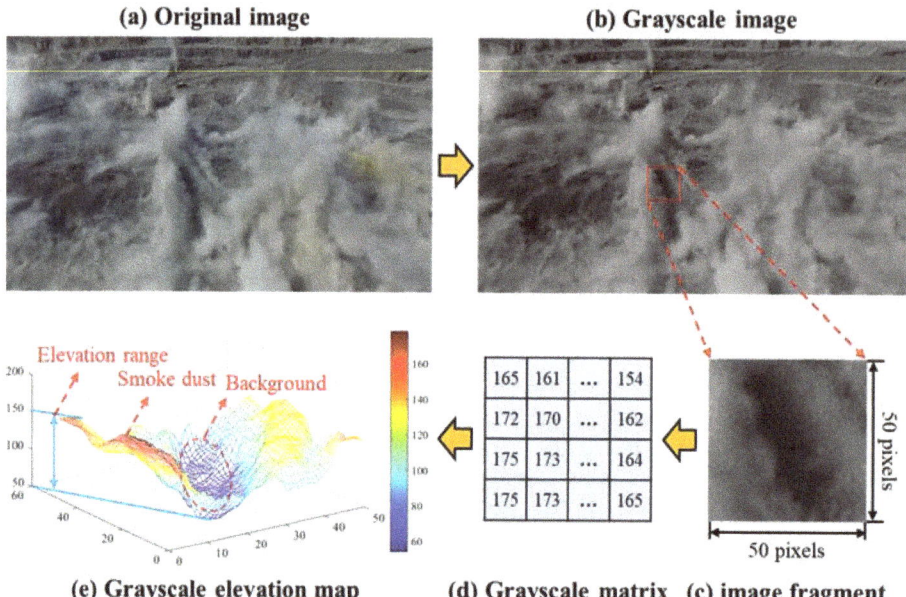

**Figure 5.** Grayscale elevation map of smoke dust with homologous calculation processes, including (a) original image of smoke dust, (b) gray image, (c) image fragment of gray image, (d) digital matrix of the image fragment, and (e) grayscale elevation map based on the image fragment.

To ulteriorly assess the effectiveness of the proposed method in blasting operations, the 95 images from the blasting work were processed by the image-processing algorithm, and then served to determine the $D_{box}(P)$ and $G_a$. Within the pollutant images, the computation processes begin from the 16th image because the 1st~15th images belong to the prior stage of blasting, and smoke dust is barely distributed in these images. Partial image-processing results of the 15th, 30th, 45th, 60th, 75th and 90th images are shown as Figure 6:

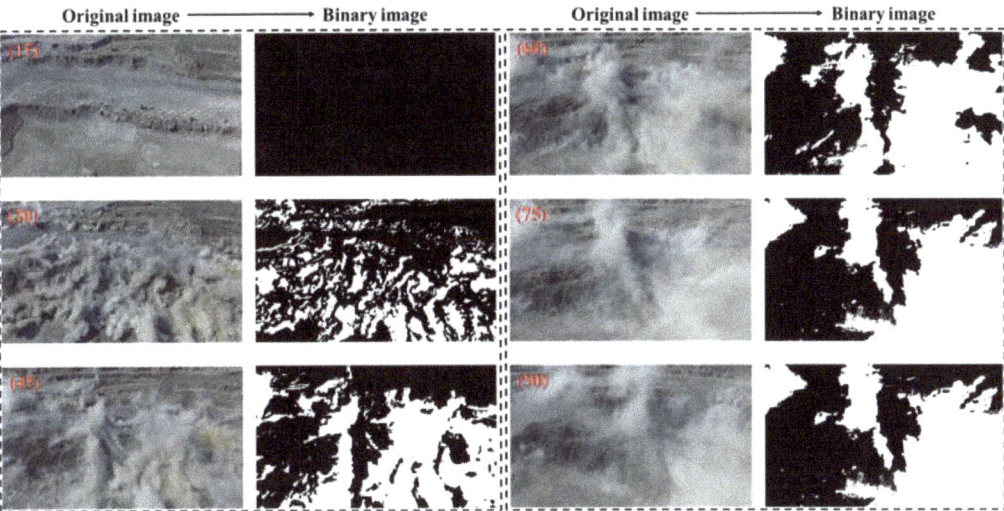

**Figure 6.** Partial visualization results of the image-processing operations, including original images and binary images, corresponding to the 15th, 30th, 45th, 60th, 75th and 90th images.

Following the image-processing results it can be discerned that at the first stage of blasting, a large amount of smoke and dust are engendered to form smoke-dust clouds, mainly due to the explosive at each charge point, such as the 30th picture. At this stage, dust particles start to float due to the shockwave caused by the explosion, which is much larger than the gravity of the dust particles, friction between dust particles and rock particles, and adhesion of dust against other items. Then, with the completion of the blasting operation, the smoke-dust clouds gradually develop, when in this process the smoke dust continues to move upward as a consequence of the inertia effect, and the motion track of a large amount of smoke dust is superimposed, subsequently generating a mushroom or mushroom-like cloud. In addition, from a qualitative perspective for the pollutant distribution, the amount of smoke dust appears to have an upward trend with the explosion process, and then enters into a volatility phase, (60)~(75), for instance. Eventually, as the smoke dust continues to spread, which mainly interfered with meteorological conditions in this period, especially for the disturbed wind flow, the distribution is confronted with a certain degree of reduction.

To further describe the amount of pollutant, $D_{box}(P)$ and $G_a$ for the 15th~95th smoke dust images were calculated, and the results with corresponding calculating time are demonstrated in Table 2.

**Table 2.** Calculation results of fractal dimension and grayscale average for partial pollutant images.

| Pollutant Image | Parameters | | Calculating Time of $G_a$ (s) | Calculating Time of $D_{box}(P)$ (s) |
| --- | --- | --- | --- | --- |
| | $G_a$ | $D_{box}(P)$ | | |
| 15th | 0 | 0 | 0.3491 | 1.5598 |
| 30th | 0.3317 | 1.7261 | 0.3511 | 1.1595 |
| 45th | 0.4655 | 1.7957 | 0.3521 | 1.1858 |
| 60th | 0.5023 | 1.8376 | 0.3502 | 1.1795 |
| 75th | 0.4777 | 1.8299 | 0.3671 | 1.1735 |
| 90th | 0.3685 | 1.7913 | 0.3541 | 1.205 |

According to the results of $G_a$ and $D_{box}(P)$, a relatively legible data trend is presented, which can be summarized as increasing to a peaking value, maintaining a stable fluctuation within a certain range, and then decreasing with time, respectively. Moreover, it is found that there is a discrepancy in calculating time between $G_a$ and $D_{box}(P)$, the reasons for which may be explained by the varying levels of program complexity.

For the sake of further analyzing the $D_{box}(P)$ and $G_a$ of the collected frame pictures from the video footage of field blasting, computations of all images by the proposed method were carried out and the specific results with related fitting curves can be denoted in Figure 7:

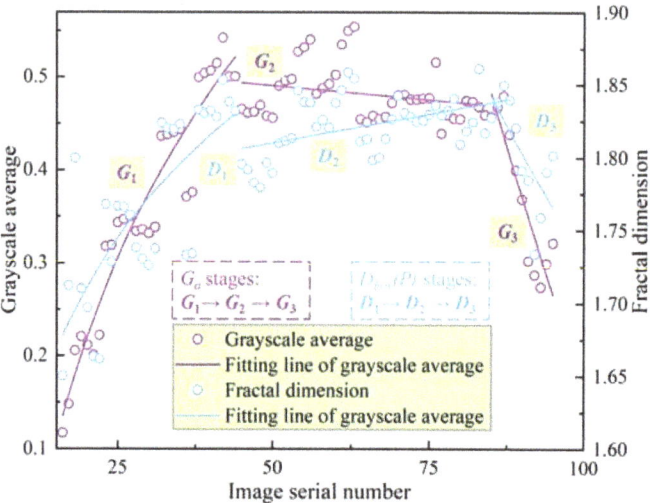

**Figure 7.** Calculating results of $G_a$ and $D_{box}(P)$ with corresponding fitting curves. $G_1$, $G_2$, $G_3$ and $D_1$, $D_2$, $D_3$ represent fitting curves of grayscale average and fractal dimension, respectively.

It can be easily discovered from Figure 7 that there are characteristic distributions for 80 image samples (16th~95th) on the basis of the results, which accord with a pattern consistent with the qualitative description, mainly including three stages: increasing, stable fluctuations, and decreasing. The fitted equations for the $G_a$ and $D_{box}(P)$ are listed in Table 3.

**Table 3.** Fitting results of $G_a$ and $D_{box}(P)$ with related $R^2$ for three stages.

| Group Number | Fitting Equation of $G_a$ and $D_{box}(P)$ | $R^2$ |
| --- | --- | --- |
| $G_1$ (Stage one) | $G_1 = 0.382 \ln(x) - 0.9239$ | 0.9165 |
| $G_2$ (Stage two) | $G_2 = -0.0006 x + 0.5212$ | 0.0583 |
| $G_3$ (Stage three) | $G_3 = -1.94 \ln(x) + 9.1007$ | 0.8188 |
| $D_1$ (Stage one) | $D_1 = 0.1508 \ln(x) + 1.2596$ | 0.5707 |
| $D_2$ (Stage two) | $D_2 = 0.0008 x + 1.771$ | 0.2101 |
| $D_3$ (Stage three) | $D_3 = -0.69 \ln(x) + 4.909$ | 0.4978 |

As illustrated in the fitted equations, for both of the $D_{box}(P)$ and $G_a$, stage one ($G_1$ and $D_1$) and stage three ($G_3$ and $D_3$) can be appropriately represented by logarithmic fits. Stage two ($G_2$ and $D_2$) in Figure 7 presents varying data fluctuation within a certain range, and therefore, a linear fit was employed to demonstrate the relationship between the pollutant parameters and dust images at different times.

In addition, from the fit coefficients $R^2$ of all fitted equations, it can be found that no matter $D_{box}(P)$ and $G_a$, there are differences in the logarithmic fit of stage one and stage three. For example, for the grayscale average, $R^2$ of stage one and three are 0.9165 and 0.8188, and as regards the fractal dimension, $R^2$ is 0.5707 and 0.4978, respectively. It is distinct that there is a numerical reduction from stage one to stage three, the possible reasons for which are mainly because of the different causes for the performances of the pollutants. Smoke dust in stage one is most likely caused by a dynamite explosion in the field, whereas smoke dust in stage three is more likely caused by a diffusion effect caused by meteorological conditions, particularly wind floating.

It is also important to denote that, with reference to the fit coefficient, the fitted equations of $G_a$ (the maximum is 0.9165) perform better when compared to the $D_{box}(P)$ (the maximum is 0.5707), and this phenomenon elucidates that smoke dust in images reflects more local features than global features because when in the process, $G_a$ is oriented to one calculation for a whole digital image, while $D_{box}(P)$ is confronted with multiple identical calculation procedures by a series of detecting boxes covering the image.

Based on the proposals of $D_{box}(P)$ and $G_a$, and while combining the benefits of local and global features, a pollution condition index ($Pi$) is developed to assess quantitative changes and spatial-temporal distributions in smoke-dust images. By this way, an integration of image parameters consisting of $D_{box}(P)$ and $G_a$ can be additionally completed, and in sites, the mathematical expression of $Pi$ is much more widely applied in engineering computation to guarantee acquisitions of pertinent information related to the engineering efficiency and practitioner safety. $Pi$ can be presented as Equation (6) above. On the basis of the equation, $Pi$ of the blasting images can be drawn as Figure 8:

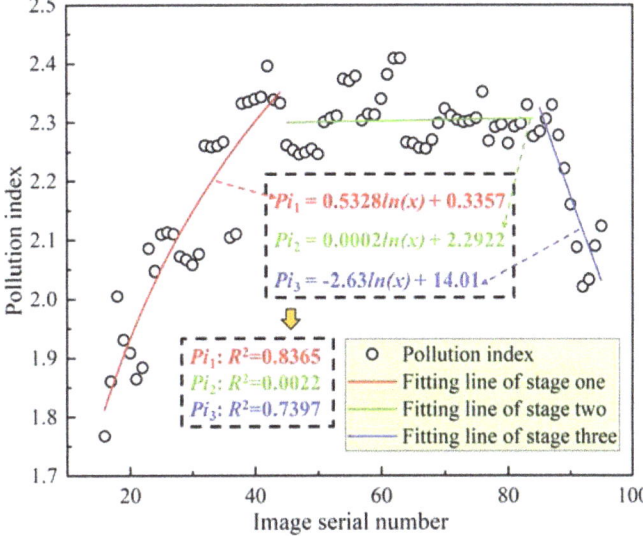

**Figure 8.** Calculating results of pollution index with fitting curves of pollutants distribution.

The results of the correlational analysis are presented in Figure 8, and the relevant fitted equations with homologous goodness of fits ($R^2$) are also shown. Compared to any of the parameters in Figure 7 and the calculated results of fitted equations in Table 3, data distributions of $Pi$ similarly illustrate the legible diffusion stages of smoke dust: generation stage, cloud-formation stage and diffusion stage. In the graph, the time intervals of stages one~three are 16~44 s, 45~84 s and 85~95 s, respectively. The single most striking observation to emerge from the data comparison is that the data distribution tendency of $Pi$ is similar to the results of $D_{box}(P)$ and $G_a$. Moreover, the $R^2$ of the fitted curves are 0.8365, 0.0022 and 0.7397, embodying a fair logarithmic relationship for stage one and stage three. At the same time, it also appears to have a more stable data fluctuation for stage two in contrast to the single parameter. In brief, the proposal of $Pi$ illustrates an ideal performance throughout blasting processes, and achieves one mathematical expression corresponding to three stages of pollution distribution. To observe the performance of the proposed method of smoke dust evaluation in this research, comparative results are summarized in Table 4.

Table 4. Comparison of calculation methods.

| Method | RMSE (PM2.5/PM10/NO$_2$) | R Squared (PM2.5/PM10/NO$_2$) |
| --- | --- | --- |
| $D_{box}(P) - G_a$ based method in this study ($Pi_{1/3}$) | $2.85 \times 10^{-3}/5.99 \times 10^{-4}$ | 0.8365/0.7397 |
| Liu et al. [32] | 38.28/62.51/25.88 | 0.70/0.462/0.328 |
| Zhang et al. [33] | 27.53/56.67/24.54 | 0.881/0.525/0.393 |
| Li et al. [35] | 50.67/65.19/29.88 | 0.563/0.349/0.070 |

Three previous studies on estimation of PM2.5, PM10 and NO$_2$ were presented based on the digital image processing, and RMSE along with R squared values are the metrics for evaluation models. From Table 4, although the three studies targeted three specific pollutants, the RMSE values of the proposed method (stage one and stage three) indicate a fair regression effectiveness when compared to the other these models. Similarly, the R squared values also reveal that the $D_{box}(P) - G_a$ based method is reliable for the analysis about pollutants migrations in blasting operations. Therefore, the RMSE and R squared values of the proposed method were confirmed by the comparisons.

Based on the comprehensive pollution index of blasting engineering, the proposed model can be further utilized in pollution hazard classifications. In this research, an attempt was made to provide a method to evaluate the pollution condition on site in accordance with the fitting curves shown in Figure 8, which were divided into four pollution levels, including the serious, the high, the middle, and the mild, as depicted in Figure 9. Detailed division procedures are also introduced.

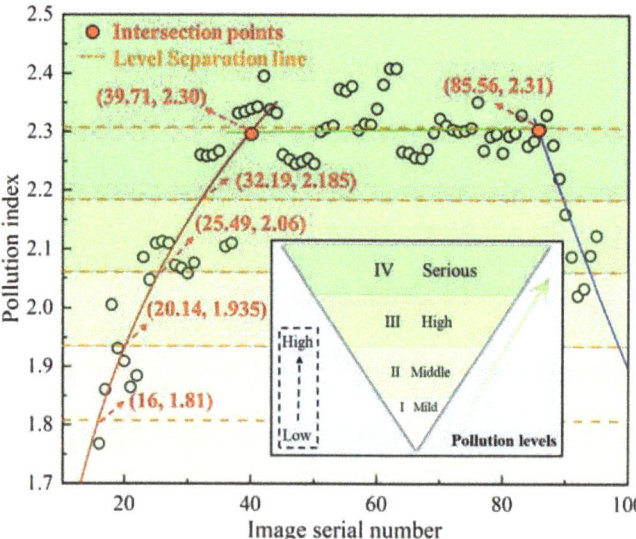

Figure 9. Four-level divisions of smoke dust pollution within the fitting plot, including a pollution level-pyramid graph representing the pollution condition.

(a) At the start of the blasting (from the 16th image), according to the fitting result of stage one, the *Pi* is 1.81, and at stage two of the fluctuation period, the logarithmic fitting results of stage one and three were extended to intersect with it to generate two intersection points, the coordinates of which are (39.71, 2.30) and (85.56, 2.31). Thus, the peak value of the model is dictated as the intersection point between stage two and three. In this way, the *Pi* interval is [1.81, 2.31].

(b) After determining the $Pi$ interval, four equal parts were then calculated and determined, and the $Pi$ values along with their corresponding occurrence times are $Pi_1$ (20.14 s, 1.935), $Pi_2$ (25.49 s, 2.06), $Pi_3$ (32.19 s, 2.185) and $Pi_4$ (85.56 s, 2.31), respectively.
(c) Based on the $Pi$ values, the distribution graph was divided into four regions. As a supplementary, the region below 1.81 of the $Pi$ value was also assigned to the first level, while that above 2.31 was assigned to the last level. Therefore, the whole graph of pollution distribution is divided into four levels, and a color pyramid is used to describe it. The detailed division criteria of level I~IV can be presented as Table 5.

**Table 5.** Divisions criteria of blasting pollution-levels with the homologous pollution regions.

| $Pi$ | <1.935 | 1.935~2.06 | 2.06~2.185 | >2.185 |
|---|---|---|---|---|
| Pollution-Level | Level I | Level II | Level III | Level IV |

By virtue of the critical factor of $Pi$, the pollution evaluation system can be established for analyzing the distribution conditions of smoke dust, and provide an approach to develop a comprehensive program in pollution prevention and control. Different from previous methods in monitoring smoke dust pollution, the proposed system in this research adopts a series of digital images, and then fulfills pollution classifications through computations of $Pi$ in the software. Subsequently, the final pollution levels at the target time point can be determined.

## 5. Discussion

### 5.1. Pollution Evaluation of Single-Point Area with Image Slices

The aforementioned research on $D_{box}(P)$, $G_a$ and $Pi$ were conducted by virtue of certain smoke dust images, in which the computation scope was oriented to the full range of one blasting image. However, sometimes it is necessary to monitor and evaluate the pollutants at a single point within a provided image to figure out whether the proposed method is capable of enforcing the task. Figure 10 demonstrates the application procedures for two single-point areas in the 30th image chosen from the same video.

As shown in Figure 10b, two pictures were extracted from the binary image, which are the bench and diffusion area, and the selected square regions are 50 × 50 and 70 × 70 in size, respectively. $D_{box}(P)$ and $G_a$ of the pictures were then calculated, and the fitted results of fractal dimension are illustrated in Figure 10c,d. Distinctly, $G_a$ of area one and two are 0.174 and 0.481, and $D_{box}(P)$ are 1.5454 and 1.8398. Thus, the pollution indexes ($Pi$ values) can be calculated, the results of which are 1.7194 and 2.3208. Depending on the proposed pollution-level evaluation system in the previous section, regions one and two are supposed to be classified as level I and level IV in smoke dust pollution. Consequently, in addition to the computation ability for the full range of an image, the proposed system can be also exceedingly applied in the calculation of a single-point pollution area, thereby satisfying relevant monitoring tasks. At the same time, the results of these two regions also demonstrate that it is feasible for the system to accomplish analysis on the pollution condition of smoke dust through digital images recorded at blasting sites.

### 5.2. Variation Trends on Binarization Thresholds within Image Processing Operations

In the conversion process from image graying to binarization, double threshold binarization was adopted to extract the pollutant features in an image, the thresholds of which are denoted as $T_1$ and $T_2$. Nonetheless, it is not always consistent for the threshold values with the blasting program in progress. Owing to the pollutants with variable quantities, and the complex background in blasting site, $T_1$ and $T_2$ are also required to adapt to the optimal image conversion in binarization operation. The thresholds used in this research are denoted in Table 6.

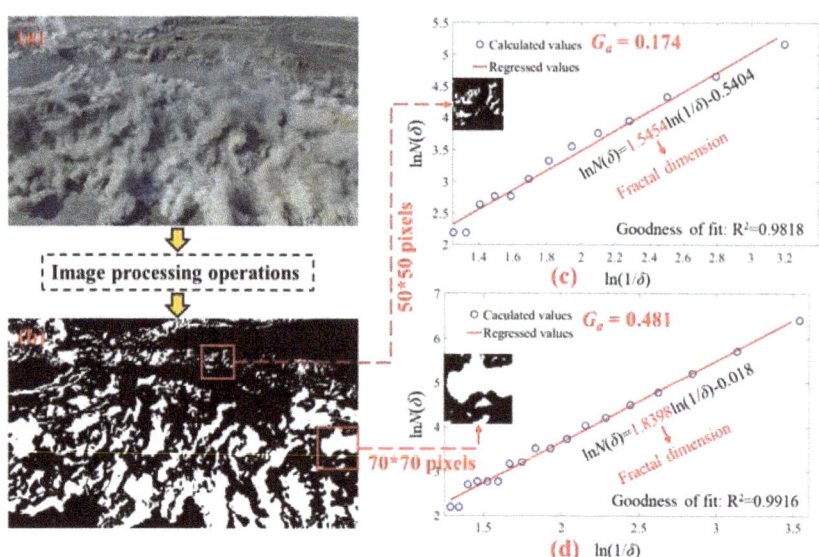

**Figure 10.** Calculation results of $D_{box}(P)$ and $G_a$ of two single-point pollution areas in the 30th image, including (**a**) original image selected at 30 s from the recorded video, (**b**) binary image through a series of image processing operations as described previously, and (**c**,**d**) $D_{box}(P)$ and $G_a$ of the pollutants in the selected areas.

**Table 6.** Threshold values of $T_1$ and $T_2$ with the time nodes of image acquiring.

| Thresholds | Threshold Values of $T_1$ and $T_2$ in Binarization | | | | | | | | |
|---|---|---|---|---|---|---|---|---|---|
| $T_1$ | 1–15 s | | 16–35 s | | 36–44 s | | 45–48 s | | 49–95 s |
| | <10 | | 100 | | 80 | | 60 | | <40 |
| $T_2$ | 1–16 s | 17–22 s | 23–31 s | 32–37 s | 38–56 s | 57–63 s | 64–76 s | | 77–95 s |
| | >240 | 180 | 160 | 150 | 140 | 150 | 160 | | >170 |

It is apparent from this table that there are different numbers of time nodes for $T_1$ and $T_2$ when choosing threshold values in the process of binarization, where $T_1$ consists of five nodes while $T_2$ possesses eight nodes. This result may be explained by the fact that there are more changes happening at the border of the highlight pixels, while the dark regions in the image mostly representing the background present fewer changes. In other words, the generation process of smoke dust is inherently more associated with the bright pixels in the pollutant images.

As for $T_1$, at the first time-interval of 1–15 s, the optimal threshold value tends to be chosen as less than 10, which is an important parameter for the segmentation between the pollutants and background. Thereafter, $T_1$ is preferably assigned as 100 in 16–35 s. Obviously, there is a pretty large increase from the first time-interval to the second, the reason for which might be the mixture of items produced in the initial stage, which mainly consist of mud blocks, gravel, dust particles, and so on, illustrated as grayish-black in morphology. For the sake of capturing the features of items while trying to remove the background part of the picture, it is essential for the threshold border $T_1$ to be moved up to 100.

After the first time-interval, the blasting operation began at 16 s, and then there is a steady decline for $T_1$ value until 49 s with a range of 20. A possible explanation for this might be that the generation process of pollutants has a relatively stable impact on image pixels in dark regions. The finding provides some supports for the conceptual premise of the generation stage aforementioned in the presentation of image parameters due to the three time nodes being from 16 s to 48 s, where the time interval defined before the generation stage is 16–44 s. Moreover, at the time interval of 49–95 s, it appears appropriate for the $T_1$ to be less than 40 so as to preserve dark-area features of pollutants, and the implication of this is the possibility that there is also a minor effect on $T_1$ for the pollutant distribution within the cloud-formation stage and diffusion stage. Potentially, this phenomenon indicates that in these two stages, there are few variations in the dark features of smoke dust.

Turning now to the $T_2$, it is obvious for it to have a data trend of decreasing and increasing in succession (>240–140–>170), the reasons for which could be attributed to the generation of a large amount of smoke dust, inducing the bright features to tend towards unified in a blasting image, and simultaneously masking the features of other bright areas in sites so that the grayscale values of bright pixels experience a decrease. Then, with the fading of time, the diffusion of smoke dust is confronted with a gradual reduction, and the grayscale distribution of the original image progressively reappears again.

At the pre-blast stage of 1–16 s, $T_2$ was decided as less than 240 to guarantee the removal of pixels not related to pollutants, which indicates that there are more distributions of bright pixels in the background part of the original image. On the other hand, different from the steady declines in $T_1$, $T_2$ emerges at decremental or incremental intervals throughout the whole time-node. Within the time nodes of 17–22 s, 23–31 s and 32–37 s, the decreasing of $T_2$ demonstrates that with the start of blasting, smoke dust gradually covers the bright areas in the background, contributing to a more centralized grayscale distribution. Additionally, the decremental intervals of $T_2$ depict that the generation of smoke dust slows down at a later stage. The finding further supports the logarithmic relationship discussed in the generation stage mentioned above. As for the time nodes from 38–76 s, the selections of $T_2$ also present stable fluctuations similar to the cloud-formation stage, and in this stage, the steady decline may be explained by the inertial motion of smoke dust, resulting in different development tracks. Then, at 77–95 s, $T_2$ are chosen at more than 170, which are in line with the previous description of the diffusion stage, when in this process the smoke dust is mainly subject to meteorological conditions, suffering from a sluggish spread.

## 6. Limitations and Future Studies

The insights gained from this study may be of assistance to evaluate the smoke-dust pollution caused by blasting operations in virtue of digital image technology, and has gone some way towards enhancing the understanding of the relationship between the $D_{box}(P)$ wtih $G_a$, and smoke-dust distribution in digital images. Nonetheless, there are limitations in this study which could have affected the parameters computation, such as the image quality, mine topography, illumination condition, shooting distance with angle and so on. Therefore, further research could also be conducted to determine the effectiveness of more possible factors existing in blasting sites on the application of the evaluation system.

## 7. Conclusions

A pollution evaluation system based on digital image-processing technology with the grayscale average algorithm and the fractal dimension theory was proposed to recognize the features of smoke dust, and determine the pollution conditions generated by blasting operations in open-pit mines. By using this method, the dust distribution, grayscale distribution, fitted curves of fractal dimension, grayscale average and pollution index can be characterized. These approaches can quantitatively analyze the smoke dust characteristics by means of a computer. Based on the present study, the following conclusions can be drawn:

(a) An image example of fugitive dust is employed to illustrate and validate the effectiveness of the algorithm in dust particles, and in spite of the existence of the hysteresis intervals, results of fractal dimension (0.9998 in $R^2$ of the fitted equation) and distributions with grayscale parameters show that the proposed approach successfully identifies the dust objects.

(b) A total of 95 pictures of pollutants were extracted for the parameter calculations. Within the image-processing operations, the grayscale difference between the smoke dust and background was revealed, which is the essential distinction for feature extraction of smoke dust. The $D_{box}(P)$ and $G_a$ results, as well as the related fitted curves, were then obtained, and it is clear that three development stages are required for dust diffusion to emerge. In addition, compared to $D_{box}(P)$, $G_a$ demonstrated a better fitted correlation for the distribution of pollutants, reflecting more local features.

(c) Based on the $D_{box}(P)$ and $G_a$, $Pi$ as well as the fitted results were proposed, simultaneously integrating the global and local features of pollutant images. The $Pi$ denoted three diffusion stages of smoke dust: generation stage, cloud-formation stage, and diffusion stage corresponding to 16~44 s, 45~84 s and 85~95 s, respectively. Then, an evaluation system associated with four levels of pollution conditions was also obtained, of which the $Pi$ values are <1.935, 1.935~2.06, 2.06~2.185 and >2.185. By this way, the final pollution levels of smoke dust can be determined through the provided images.

(d) The comparative results of RMSE and R squared values show that the proposed method (stage one and stage three) presents a fair performance when compared to the other models. Meanwhile, it also reveals that the vision-based method is reliable for the analysis about pollutants migrations in blasting operations. Therefore, the RMSE and R squared values of the proposed method were confirmed by the comparisons. Therefore, the above improvement significantly evaluates the on-site smoke-dust pollution with a high accuracy, and achieves a comprehensive bivariate index to avoid possible measurement errors due to univariate index.

**Author Contributions:** Conceptualization, S.W.; Methodology, J.Y. and J.L.; Supervision, S.W.; Data curation, J.Y.; Formal analysis, J.Y.; Funding acquisition, F.T. and S.W.; Validation, F.T. and S.W.; Writing—original draft, J.Y. All authors have read and agreed to the published version of the manuscript.

**Funding:** This research was supported by the National Natural Science Foundation of China (No. 52174099), the Natural Science Foundation of Hunan Province (No. 2021JJ30842), the Natural Science Foundation of Liaoning Province (No. 2021-KF-23-01), and the Fundamental Research Funds for the Central Universities of Central South University (No. 2022ZZTS0510).

**Institutional Review Board Statement:** Not applicable.

**Informed Consent Statement:** Not applicable.

**Data Availability Statement:** Not applicable.

**Acknowledgments:** We would like to acknowledge the editors and reviewers for their invaluable comments.

**Conflicts of Interest:** The authors declare no conflict of interest.

## References

1. Liu, T.; Liu, S. The impacts of coal dust on miners' health: A review. *Environ. Res.* **2020**, *190*, 109849. [CrossRef] [PubMed]
2. Miguel, A.; Felipe, G.; Andrew, F.; Ashray, D. Towards the development of a low cost airborne sensing system to monitor dust particles after blasting at open-pit mine sites. *Sensors* **2015**, *15*, 19667–19687.
3. Xie, C.; Nguyen, H.; Bui, X.; Nguyen, V.; Zhou, J. Predicting roof displacement of roadways in underground coal mines using adaptive neuro-fuzzy inference system optimized by various physics-based optimization algorithms. *J. Rock Mech. Geotech. Eng.* **2021**, *13*, 1452–1465. [CrossRef]
4. Yuan, M.; Ouyang, J.; Zheng, S. Research on ecological effect assessment method of ecological restoration of open-pit coal mines in alpine regions. *Int. J. Environ. Res. Public Health* **2022**, *19*, 7682. [CrossRef] [PubMed]
5. Blom, M.; Pearce, A.R.; Stuckey, P.J. Short-term planning for open pit mines: A review. *Int. J. Min. Reclam. Environ.* **2019**, *33*, 318–339. [CrossRef]

6. Vasović, D.; Kostić, S.; Ravilić, M.; Trajković, S. Environmental impact of blasting at Drenovac limestone quarry (Serbia). *Environ. Earth Sci.* **2014**, *72*, 3915–3928. [CrossRef]
7. Lu, W.; Luo, Y.; Chen, M.; Shu, D. An introduction to Chinese safety regulations for blasting vibration. *Environ. Earth Sci.* **2012**, *67*, 1951–1959. [CrossRef]
8. Abdollahisharif, J.; Bakhtavar, E.; Nourizadeh, H. Green biocompatible approach to reduce the toxic gases and dust caused by the blasting in surface mining. *Environ. Earth Sci.* **2016**, *75*, 191. [CrossRef]
9. Attalla, M.I.; Day, S.J.; Lange, T.; Lilley, W.; Morgan, S. NOx emissions from blasting operations in open-cut coal mining. *Atmos. Environ.* **2008**, *42*, 7874–7883. [CrossRef]
10. Zvyagintseva, A.V.; Sazonova, S.A.; Kulneva, V.V. Analysis of sources of dust and poisonal gases in the atmosphere formed as a result of explosions at quarries of the mining and integrated works. *IOP Conf. Ser. Mater. Sci. Eng.* **2020**, *962*, 42045. [CrossRef]
11. Sa, Z.; Li, F.; Qin, B.; Pan, X. Numerical simulation study of dust concentration distribution regularity in cavern stope. *Saf. Sci.* **2012**, *50*, 857–860. [CrossRef]
12. Chang, P.; Chen, Y.; Xu, G.; Huang, J.; Ghosh, A.; Liu, W.V. Numerical study of coal dust behaviors and experimental investigation on coal dust suppression efficiency of surfactant solution by using wind tunnel tests. *Energy Sources Part A Recovery Util. Environ. Eff.* **2021**, *43*, 2173–2188. [CrossRef]
13. Entwistle, J.A.; Hursthouse, A.S.; Reis, P.A.M.; Stewart, A.G. Metalliferous mine dust: Human health impacts and the potential determinants of disease in mining communities. *Curr. Pollut. Rep.* **2019**, *5*, 67–83. [CrossRef]
14. Cui, K.; Shen, F.; Han, B.; Yuan, J.; Suo, X.; Qin, T.; Liu, H.; Chen, J. Comparison of the cumulative incidence rates of coal workers' pneumoconiosis between 1970 and 2013 among four state-owned colliery groups in China. *Int. J. Environ. Res. Public Health* **2015**, *12*, 7444–7456. [CrossRef]
15. Cheng, W.; Yu, H.; Zhou, G.; Nie, W. The diffusion and pollution mechanisms of airborne dusts in fully-mechanized excavation face at mesoscopic scale based on CFD-DEM. *Process Saf. Environ.* **2016**, *104*, 240–253. [CrossRef]
16. Kayet, N.; Pathak, K.; Chakrabarty, A.; Kumar, S.; Chowdary, V.M.; Singh, C.P.; Sahoo, S.; Basumatary, S. Assessment of foliar dust using Hyperion and Landsat satellite imagery for mine environmental monitoring in an open cast iron ore mining areas. *J. Clean. Prod.* **2019**, *218*, 993–1006. [CrossRef]
17. Ajrash, M.J.; Zanganeh, J.; Moghtaderi, B. Impact of suspended coal dusts on methane deflagration properties in a large-scale straight duct. *J. Hazard. Mater.* **2017**, *338*, 334–342. [CrossRef]
18. Conesa, H.M.; Faz, Á.; Arnaldos, R. Heavy metal accumulation and tolerance in plants from mine tailings of the semiarid Cartagena–La Unión mining district (SE Spain). *Sci. Total Environ.* **2006**, *366*, 1–11. [CrossRef]
19. Wanjun, T.; Qingxiang, C. Dust distribution in open-pit mines based on monitoring data and fluent simulation. *Environ. Monit. Assess* **2018**, *190*, 11. [CrossRef]
20. Jia, Z.; Song, Z.; Fan, J.; Jiang, J.; Guo, S. Numerical simulation study on dust suppression mechanism of burning rock blasting in open-pit mine. *Front. Earth Sci.* **2022**, *10*. [CrossRef]
21. Tang, W.; Li, F. A new circulating accumulation emission model for assessing dust emission from open pit mine. *Sci. Rep.* **2021**, *11*, 24243. [CrossRef] [PubMed]
22. Bui, X.; Lee, C.W.; Nguyen, H.; Bui, H.; Long, N.Q.; Le, Q.; Nguyen, V.; Nguyen, N.; Moayedi, H. Estimating PM10 Concentration from Drilling Operations in Open-Pit Mines Using an Assembly of SVR and PSO. *Appl. Sci.* **2019**, *9*, 2806. [CrossRef]
23. Li, L.; Zhang, R.; Sun, J.; He, Q.; Kong, L.; Liu, X. Monitoring and prediction of dust concentration in an open-pit mine using a deep-learning algorithm. *J. Environ. Health Sci. Eng.* **2021**, *19*, 401–414. [CrossRef] [PubMed]
24. Qi, C.; Zhou, W.; Lu, X.; Luo, H.; Pham, B.T.; Yaseen, Z.M. Particulate matter concentration from open-cut coal mines: A hybrid machine learning estimation. *Environ. Pollut.* **2020**, *263*, 114517. [CrossRef] [PubMed]
25. Torno, S.; Toraño, J.; Menéndez, M.; Gent, M. CFD simulation of blasting dust for the design of physical barriers. *Environ. Earth Sci.* **2011**, *64*, 73–83. [CrossRef]
26. Wang, Z.; Zhou, W.; Jiskani, I.M.; Ding, X.; Liu, Z.; Qiao, Y.; Luan, B. Dust reduction method based on water infusion blasting in open-pit mines: A step toward green mining. *Energy Sources Part A Recovery Util. Environ. Eff.* **2021**, 1–15. [CrossRef]
27. Watai, T.; Machida, T.; Ishizaki, N.; Inoue, G. A lightweight observation system for atmospheric carbon dioxide concentration using a small unmanned aerial vehicle. *J. Atmos. Ocean. Technol.* **2006**, *23*, 700–710. [CrossRef]
28. Lu, G.; Yan, Y.; Riley, G.; Bheemul, H.C. Concurrent measurement of temperature and soot concentration of pulverized coal flames. *IEEE Trans. Instrum. Meas.* **2002**, *51*, 990–995.
29. Shirmohammadi, S.; Ferrero, A. Camera as the Instrument: The Rising Trend of Vision Based Measurement. *IEEE Trans. Instrum. Meas.* **2014**, *17*, 41–47. [CrossRef]
30. Yue, G.; Gu, K.; Qiao, J. Effective and Efficient Photo-Based PM2.5 Concentration Estimation. *IEEE Trans. Instrum. Meas.* **2019**, *68*, 3962–3971. [CrossRef]
31. Joshi, M.R.; Nkenyereye, L.; Joshi, G.P.; Islam, S.M.R.; Abdullah-Al-Wadud, M.; Shrestha, S. Auto-Colorization of Historical Images Using Deep Convolutional Neural Networks. *Mathematics* **2020**, *8*, 2258. [CrossRef]
32. Liu, C.; Tsow, F.; Zou, Y.; Tao, N. Particle pollution estimation based on image analysis. *PLoS ONE* **2016**, *11*, e145955.
33. Zhang, T.; Dick, R.P. Estimation of multiple atmospheric pollutants through image analysis. In Proceedings of the IEEE International Conference on Image Processing (ICIP), Taipei, Taiwan, 22–25 September 2019; pp. 2060–2064.

34. Grasa, G.; Abanades, J.C. A calibration procedure to obtain solid concentrations from digital images of bulk powders. *Powder Technol.* **2001**, *114*, 125–128. [CrossRef]
35. Li, Y.; Huang, J.; Luo, J. Using user generated online photos to estimate and monitor air pollution in major cities. In Proceedings of the ICIMCS '15: Proceedings of the 7th International Conference on Internet Multimedia Computing and Service, Zhangjiajie, China, 19–21 August 2015; pp. 1–5.
36. Davies, R. Summary of the particle characterization session. *Powder Technol.* **1996**, *88*, 191–196. [CrossRef]
37. Taylor, M.A. Quantitative measures for shape and size of particles. *Powder Technol.* **2002**, *124*, 94–100. [CrossRef]
38. Raphael, M.; Rohani, S. On-line estimation of solids concentrations and mean particle size using a turbidimetry method. *Powder Technol.* **1996**, *89*, 157–163. [CrossRef]
39. Mikula, W.I.F.R. Fractal dimensions of coal particles. *J. Colloid Interf. Sci.* **1987**, *120*, 263–271.
40. Pi, Z.; Zhou, Z.; Li, X.; Wang, S. Digital image processing method for characterization of fractures, fragments, and particles of soil/rock-like materials. *Mathematics* **2021**, *9*, 815. [CrossRef]
41. Mahamud, M.; López, Ó.; Pis, J.J.; Pajares, J.A. Textural characterization of coals using fractal analysis. *Fuel Process. Technol.* **2003**, *81*, 127–142. [CrossRef]
42. Zhang, B.; Liu, W.; Liu, X. Scale-dependent nature of the surface fractal dimension for bi-and multi-disperse porous solids by mercury porosimetry. *Appl. Surf. Sci.* **2006**, *253*, 1349–1355. [CrossRef]
43. Zhang, J.; Li, M.; Liu, Z.; Zhou, N. Fractal characteristics of crushed particles of coal gangue under compaction. *Powder Technol.* **2017**, *305*, 12–18. [CrossRef]
44. Albatayneh, O.; Forslöf, L.; Ksaibati, K. Developing and validating an image processing algorithm for evaluating gravel road dust. *Int. J. Pavement Res. Technol.* **2019**, *12*, 288–296. [CrossRef]
45. Fu, Y.; Wang, N. Measurement of dust concentration based on VBAI. *J. Phys. Conf. Ser.* **2013**, *418*, 12079. [CrossRef]
46. Li, G.; Wu, J.; Luo, Z.; Chen, X. Vision-based measurement of dust concentration by image transmission. *IEEE Trans. Instrum. Meas.* **2019**, *68*, 3942–3949. [CrossRef]
47. Wang, S.; Li, X.; Wang, S. Separation and fracturing in overlying strata disturbed by longwall mining in a mineral deposit seam. *Eng. Geol.* **2017**, *226*, 257–266. [CrossRef]
48. Gonzalez-Vidal, J.J.; Perez-Pueyo, R.; Soneira, M.J. Automatic morphology-based cubic p-spline fitting methodology for smoothing and baseline-removal of Raman spectra. *J. Raman Spectrosc.* **2017**, *48*, 878–883. [CrossRef]

Article

# Prediction of Uniaxial Compressive Strength in Rocks Based on Extreme Learning Machine Improved with Metaheuristic Algorithm

Junbo Qiu [1], Xin Yin [1,*], Yucong Pan [1], Xinyu Wang [2] and Min Zhang [3]

1 School of Civil Engineering, Wuhan University, Wuhan 430072, China
2 Yellow River Engineering Consulting Co., Ltd., Zhengzhou 450003, China
3 Beijing Aidi Geological Engineering Technology Co., Ltd., Beijing 100144, China
* Correspondence: yinxin_engineering@163.com

**Abstract:** Uniaxial compressive strength (UCS) is a critical parameter in the disaster prevention of engineering projects, requiring a large budget and a long time to estimate in different rocks or the early stage of a project. If predicted accurately, the UCS of rocks significantly affects geotechnical applications. This paper develops a dataset of 734 samples from previous studies on different countries' magmatic, sedimentary, and metamorphic rocks. Within the study context, three main factors, point load index, P-wave velocity, and Schmidt hammer rebound number, are utilized to estimate UCS. Moreover, it applies extreme learning machines (ELM) to map the nonlinear relationship between the UCS and the influential factors. Five metaheuristic algorithms, particle swarm optimization (PSO), grey wolf optimization (GWO), whale optimization algorithm (WOA), butterfly optimization algorithm (BOA), and sparrow search algorithm (SSA), are used to optimize the bias and weight of ELM and thus enhance its predictability. Indeed, several performance parameters are utilized to verify the proposed models' generalization capability and predictive performance. The minimum, maximum, and average relative errors of ELM achieved by the whale optimization algorithm (WOA-ELM) are smaller than the other models, with values of 0.22%, 72.05%, and 11.48%, respectively. In contrast, the minimum and mean residual error produced by WOA-ELM are less than the other models, with values of 0.02 and 2.64 MPa, respectively. The results show that the UCS values derived from WOA-ELM are superior to those from other models. The performance indices (coefficient of determination ($R^2$): 0.861, mean squared error (MSE): 17.61, root mean squared error (RMSE): 4.20, and value account for (VAF): 91% obtained using the WOA-ELM model indicates high accuracy and reliability, which means that it has broad application potential for estimating UCS of different rocks.

**Keywords:** uniaxial compressive strength; prediction model; extreme learning machine; metaheuristic algorithm

**MSC:** 68T99

Citation: Qiu, J.; Yin, X.; Pan, Y.; Wang, X.; Zhang, M. Prediction of Uniaxial Compressive Strength in Rocks Based on Extreme Learning Machine Improved with Metaheuristic Algorithm. *Mathematics* 2022, 10, 3490. https://doi.org/10.3390/math10193490

Academic Editors: Shaofeng Wang, Linqi Huang, Xin Cai and Zhengyang Song

Received: 26 August 2022
Accepted: 20 September 2022
Published: 24 September 2022

**Publisher's Note:** MDPI stays neutral with regard to jurisdictional claims in published maps and institutional affiliations.

**Copyright:** © 2022 by the authors. Licensee MDPI, Basel, Switzerland. This article is an open access article distributed under the terms and conditions of the Creative Commons Attribution (CC BY) license (https://creativecommons.org/licenses/by/4.0/).

## 1. Introduction

Uniaxial compressive strength (UCS) plays a vital role in rock engineering projects from design to construction and operation. In general, the UCS can be obtained by conducting laboratory tests using the approaches provided by the International Society of Rock Mechanics (ISRM2007) and the American Society for Testing Materials (ASTM2001a) [1]. However, the uniaxial compression test requires high quality and strict specimen size. Therefore, obtaining a core sample from soft, weak, highly weathered, or fragile rocks is almost impossible. In addition, direct estimation of UCS in the laboratory is costly, complicated, and time-consuming [2]. Therefore, the precise prediction of UCS is a challenge.

As a result, proposing a method for obtaining UCS conveniently and quickly to overcome associated problems and save time and cost is vital.

There are three methods to determine the UCS, including empirical formulation, multiple regression analysis, and soft computing modeling. Some empirical models with non-destructive test results to estimate UCS were proposed to overcome the difficulty in preparing core specimens. Several researchers investigated the relationship between UCS and other physical properties of rock mass, such as Brazilian tensile strength [3], point load strength index [4–6], slake durability index [7], Schmidt hammer rebound number [8,9], and P wave velocity [9–11]. The empirical formulas derived using these techniques are often applied to the sampling area or the same rock type. Empirical formulas include multiple fitting forms but usually consider a single factor, ignoring the effects of multiple factors. Other researchers proposed fuzzy and multiple regression analysis [12–15] to obtain UCS, hence controlling the aforementioned issues. However, these methods cannot solve the nonlinear relationship between UCS and other rock parameters; consequently, the soft computing method was presented to address this issue. Sarkar et al. [16] proposed an artificial neural network (ANN) model to estimate the UCS using slake durability index, dynamic wave velocity, density, and point load index. Yagiz et al. [17] predicted UCS using an ANN model and nonlinear technique. They discovered that ANN models are more accurate in determining UCS than regression techniques. In addition, Yesiloglu et al. [18] developed an adaptive neuro-fuzzy inference system (ANFIS) and an ANN to predict UCS, considering tensile strength, point load index, block punch index, and P-wave velocity as input parameters. They indicated that the performance evaluation of the ANFIS model was more precise than others. Gene expression programming (GEP) [19] and Multilayer Perceptron Neural Network (MLPNN) [20] were utilized to estimate UCS. Li and Tan [21] suggested a least squares vector machine for the UCS prediction model. Nevertheless, Mahmoodzadeh et al. [22] utilized machine learning methods to predict UCS, proving that Gaussian process regression (GPR) performed best. Gupta and Natarajan [23] assessed the ability of density-weighted least squares support vector machine, extreme learning machine (ELM), and random forest (RF) to estimate UCS of rocks and concluded that an improved unique machine learning model has a better predictive capability than other normal models. Recently, a comprehensive model has been combined with the ANN model and particle swarm algorithm (PSO) to predict UCS [24]. Fang et al. [25] also put effort into developing two comprehensive predictive models using hybrid ANN with a imperialism competitive algorithm (ICA) and artificial bee algorithm (ABC).

These methods are valuable for determining UCS with rock physical properties obtained by non-destructive tests. However, empirical formula measures performed unique effects with different factors. Multiple regression models cannot map the nonlinear relationship between UCS and influence factors. Machine learning models have a better predictive capability to estimate UCS than traditional models. Support vector machine (SVM) and Radial basic neural network (RBF) had good performance with small data [26,27]. However, the weight and bias of ANN and the hyper-parameters of the machine learning model demand optimization and have some constraints, such as falling into local minimum and including a low learning rate [28]. The ELM is a single hidden layer feedforward neural network introduced by Huang [29]. Some previous studies revealed that ELM is better than ANN and SVM in overcoming low learning rates and local minimum problems of regression analysis [30]. Therefore, the ELM is used to map the nonlinear relationship between UCS and the influential factors. Meanwhile, the ELM requires optimization algorithms to achieve improved performance. The metaheuristic algorithms inspired by the natural behavior of animals have good performance [31]. Additionally, the datasets for these associated measures for obtaining UCS come from the same area or rock type and are short datasets. The simple data mining methods normally do not provide the required efficiency for small data [32,33]. Hence, a bigger dataset must be established to estimate UCS. Accordingly, the present study aims to develop a new forecast model that estimates

UCS using a dataset of various rocks collected from previous research based on an ELM coupled metaheuristic algorithm.

The main contribution of this paper can be summarized as follows:

1. Collecting a dataset of 734 samples from previous studies of magmatic rocks, sedimentary rocks, and metamorphic rocks in different countries to overcome the problem of requiring a large budget and a long time to estimate UCS in different rocks or at the early stage of a project.
2. Optimizing the hidden neurons and activation function between ELM to map the nonlinear relationship between the UCS and the non-destructive test indices.
3. Utilizing five metaheuristic algorithms (PSO, GWO, WOA, BOA, and SSA) to estimate UCS.
4. Comparing the optimized model to other techniques to prove efficiency.

The remainder of this paper is organized as follows: Section 2 contains the characteristics and visualization of the dataset; Section 3 describes the mathematical relationships of the ELM and metaheuristic algorithm; Section 4 describes the optimization procedures of the ELM optimized by PSO, GWO, WOA, BOA, and SSA; Section 5 contains the statistical evaluation indices of the models; Section 6 summarizes the results of this work and compares the proposed models' effectiveness with other approaches; Section 7 contains the conclusions and recommendations for future research.

## 2. Dataset

One of the drawbacks of previous studies is that they mainly focused on datasets that are based on a single rock type. Accordingly, this study collects 734 magmatic, sedimentary, and metamorphic rock samples in a single dataset (see Supplementary Materials) to develop the prediction models. Some of these data points are rocks from quarries and natural outcrops in Turkey [14,34–38] and Iran [1,39], while others are natural outcrops and tunnels in India [15,40], Malaysia [24,41,42], and China [43]. Previously, the tensile strength, point load index ($I_s$), block punch index, density, porosity, and P-wave velocity were utilized as inputs to the numerical models for estimating the UCS. Some studies used the point load index, P-wave velocity ($V_p$), and Schmidt hammer rebound number ($SR_n$) to estimate UCS. Accordingly, this study collects these non-destructive test results when developing the UCS dataset. Considered ranges of UCS and influence factors are provided in the Table 1 and Figure 1. Table 1 shows brief descriptive statistics of the dataset used in this research. The $SR_n$ ranges from 10 to 72, the maximum value of $V_p$ is 4675 m/s, and its min value is 375 m/s. In addition, the $I_s$ value ranges from 0.53 MPa to 23.10 MPa. Moreover, the UCS ranges from 2.03 MPa to 239 MPa.

Table 1. Brief descriptive statistics of the dataset.

|  | $SR_n$ | $V_p$ (m/s) | $I_s$ (MPa) | UCS (MPa) |
| --- | --- | --- | --- | --- |
| Minimum | 10 | 375 | 0.53 | 2.03 |
| Maximum | 72 | 7943 | 23.10 | 239.00 |
| Average | 42 | 4675 | 4.33 | 75.05 |
| Standard deviation | 11.83 | 1383.14 | 3.01 | 44.70 |

Figure 1 shows a visualization of the collected dataset. There is a wide distribution of attributes and UCS in the dataset, which means that the collected data include a wide range of rock types. Meanwhile, it can be noticed that the Pearson's correlation coefficients between the UCS and $SR_n$, $V_p$ exceed 0.64, indicating strong correlations. The correlation between the UCS and $I_s$ is 0.42. Moreover, the correlations between the input parameters range between 0.22 and 0.51, showing slight interactions.

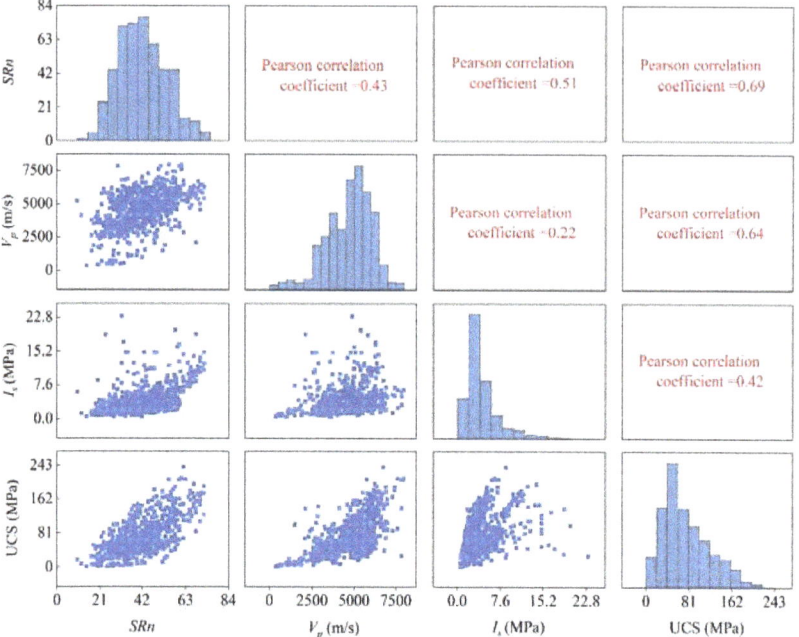

**Figure 1.** Visual illustration of the collected dataset.

## 3. Methods

UCS is a critical parameter for rock-mechanic-related investigations in civil, mining, and petroleum projects. However, experimentally evaluating this parameter is rather expensive, complicated, and time-consuming. As a result, previous investigations tended to develop soft-computing models for rapid UCS estimation. Indeed, this study aims to propose a generalized numerical model based on the wide-range dataset present to overcome the complexity of the test procedures. Within the study context, an ELM is used for mapping the nonlinear relationship between the UCS and the non-destructive test indices, and a metaheuristic algorithm is utilized to enhance the prediction ability of the ELM.

### 3.1. Extreme Learning Machine

The ELM is a single hidden layer feedforward neural network introduced by Huang [29]. The ELM was proposed to solve the time-consuming training problem in feedforward backpropagation neural networks. Similar to other feedforward neural networks, ELM has an input, a hidden, and an output layer, as depicted in Figure 2.

For a data set $R$ of $D$ arbitrary distinct training samples $R = \{(x_i, t_i) | i = 1, 2, 3, \ldots, D\}$, where $x_i = [x_{i1}, x_{i2}, \ldots x_{iD}]^T$ and $t_i = [t_{i1}, t_{i2}, \ldots t_{iD}]^T$ are the inputs and output, ELM mathematic model is defined by Equation (1).

$$o_i = \sum_{i=1}^{L} \beta_i g(x_i) = \sum_{i=1}^{L} \beta_i g(m_i x_i + n_i) \qquad (1)$$

where $o_i$ is the output vectors, $g(x)$ is the active function, typically defined as a sigmoid, sine, or hardlim function as shown in Figure 3, $m_i$ is the connection weights between the hidden layer and the input layer node, $n_i$ is the threshold between the hidden layer and the input layer node, $\beta_i$ is the weight vector between the hidden layer and output layer nodes, and $L$ is the hidden modes.

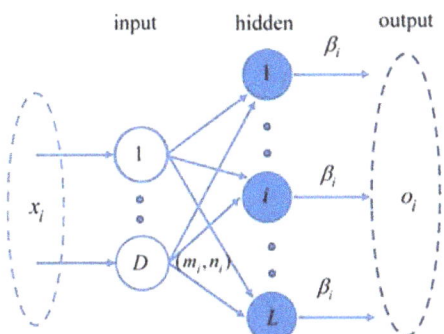

**Figure 2.** Flowchart of the ELM architecture.

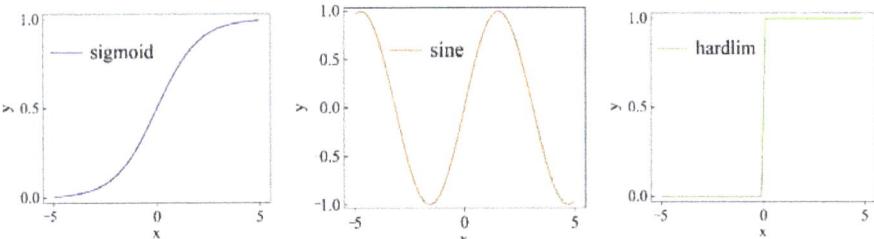

**Figure 3.** Various types of activation functions of ELM.

According to the two theorems proposed by Huang, when $g(x)$ is infinitely differentiable, the ELM with $L$ hidden nodes and activation function can be fit to achieve a zero-error approximation of any $D$ samples. Hence, Equation (2) is established.

$$\sum_{j=1}^{L}||o_i - t_i|| = 0 \tag{2}$$

According to Equation (2), there exists specific $m_i$, $n_i$, and $\beta_i$ to make the formula (3) hold.

$$\sum_{i=1}^{L}\beta_i g(m_i x_i + n_i) = t_i \tag{3}$$

The Equation (3) can be simplified in the form of $H\beta = T$, where $H$ is the output matrix of the hidden layer of ELM, $T$ is the target matrix. Unlike traditional gradient-based learning algorithms with fixed input weights and hidden layer bias, the ELM theories claim that the parameters $m_i$ and $n_i$ can be assigned randomly. Then, the issue for training the ELM is transformed into finding a least-square solution. The solution of Equation (3) in the matrix form is defined in Equation (4). According to the two theorems proposed by Huang, when the number of samples and hidden modes is the same, Equation (2) can be established. Therefore, the sample size of the dataset is normally much larger than the number of hidden neurons, and the pseudo-inverse of matrix $H$ is required.

$$\hat{\beta} = H^+ T = (H^T H)^{-1} H^T T \tag{4}$$

where $H^+$ is the Moore-Penrose generalized inverse of $H$.

Compared to the traditional intelligent algorithm, ELM can be rapidly trained by determining the number of hidden layers. Indeed, the ELM solves the shortcomings of the backpropagation gradient descent method represented by easily falling into local minima.

When solving the weights of the hidden and output layers, a mathematical method with uniqueness and global optimality is used. Therefore, the ELM has superior performance, yet shows some shortcomings. The selection of the number of hidden neurons and the activation function for an ELM model typically follows an iterative approach without a theoretical basis. For practical problems, the network topology and functions optimization require an experienced designer or lots of repeated trials, which increases its application difficulties. In the ELM calculation process, the weights and thresholds of the hidden layer and output layer are calculated using straightforward mathematical methods. However, the weights and biases of an ELM model's hidden and input layer are randomly initialized between 0 and 1. The random weights and thresholds restrict the mapping performance of the ELM. Therefore, the enhancement in the ELM is represented by improving the threshold of random weights generated through the original network, improving the stability of the network, and fully distilling the nonlinear relationship between input and output. In this study, various intelligent algorithms are proposed to improve the shortcomings of the ELM model.

### 3.2. Particle Swarm Algorithm (PSO)

The PSO algorithm is a bionic intelligent optimization algorithm proposed by Kennedy and Eberhart [44] in the 1990s. In this algorithm, each solution of the optimization problem is simplified to a particle, i.e., a bird swarm individual. The algorithm-solving process aims to find food for each bird swarm individual through group collaboration. The mathematical model of the PSO algorithm is as follows: based on the problem's type, the initial population is set in the D-dimensional search space, and the position and velocity of particles are determined by $pbest_{id}^t$ and $gbest_d^t$. The selection of $pbest_{id}^t$ and $gbest_d^t$ is intended to move each particle to a different point in the solution area. Finally, the optimal solution is obtained through a continuous change of velocity and position. Equations (5) and (6) are used to update the velocity and position, respectively.

$$v_{id}^{t+1} = v_{id}^t + c_1 r_1 (pbest_{id}^t - x_{id}^t) + c_2 r_2 (gbest_d^t - x_{id}^{t+1}) \quad (5)$$

$$x_{id}^{t+1} = x_{id}^t + v_{id}^t \quad (6)$$

where $v_{id}^{t+1}$ is the particle velocity in the $t+1$ generation, $c_1$ and $c_2$ are constants between (0, 2), $r_1$ and $r_2$ are constants between (0, 1), $t$ is the iteration time, and $x_{id}^{t+1}$ is the position of a particle in the $t+1$ generation.

### 3.3. Grey Wolf Optimization (GWO)

Grey wolf optimization is a meta-inspired algorithm that simulates the hunting behaviors of grey wolves. It was proposed by Mirjalili [45] in 2014. In this method, the wolves are divided into $\alpha$ wolf, $\beta$ wolf, $\gamma$ wolf, and $\omega$ wolf according to their fitness from high to low. The wolf of $\alpha$, $\beta$, and $\gamma$ leadership search and locate the prey. With the wolf group evolution, the distance of the prey is reduced, and the $\omega$ wolf is guided to track and capture the prey. The implementation of the grey wolf algorithm is shown in the following steps:

Step 1, surround the prey. Identify and surround the prey before preying. The following three equations show the distance and updating formulas between the wolf and prey in each grade of the grey wolf group.

$$D = |E \cdot X_p(t) - X(t)| \quad (7)$$

$$X(t+1) = X_p(t) - A \cdot E \quad (8)$$

$$\begin{aligned} A &= 2 \cdot a \cdot r_2 - a \\ E &= 2r_1 \end{aligned} \quad (9)$$

where $X_P$ and $X(t+1)$ are the location of prey when the number of iterations is $t$ and $t+1$, respectively, $X(t)$ is the position of a grey wolf when the number of iterations is $t$, $A$ and $E$

are the convergence vector and coefficient vector, respectively, *a* linearly decreases from 2 to 0, respectively, and $r_1$ and $r_2$ are constants between (0, 1).

Step 2, hunt for prey. Once the prey is surrounded, the wolves begin to hunt. The optimal, sub-optimal, and third-optimal solutions are $\alpha$, $\beta$, and $\gamma$ wolves according to the fitness ranking. Their positions are updated as shown in Equation (8). The first three grades of wolves guide the other wolves, and Equation (9) is the update mode.

$$\begin{aligned} D_\alpha &= |C \cdot X_\alpha(t) - X(t)|, X_1 = X_\alpha(t) - A_1 \cdot D_\alpha \\ D_\beta &= |C \cdot X_\beta(t) - X(t)|, X_2 = X_\beta(t) - A_2 \cdot D_\beta \\ D_\gamma &= |C \cdot X_\gamma(t) - X(t)|, X_3 = X_\gamma(t) - A_3 \cdot D_\gamma \end{aligned} \quad (10)$$

$$X(t+1) = \frac{X_1 + X_2 + X_3}{3} \quad (11)$$

where $X(t+1)$ is the position update of $\omega$ wolves, $D_\alpha$, $D_\beta$ and $D_\gamma$ are the distance update of $\alpha$, $\beta$, and $\gamma$ wolves and prey, respectively, and $X_1$, $X_2$ and $X_3$ are the position update of $\alpha$, $\beta$, and $\gamma$ wolves, respectively.

Step 3, attack prey. Similar to the last two steps, the wolf attacks when the prey is exhausted. The mathematical model can be expressed as follows (10) and (11), where *A* is a random number in the range of $[-2a, 2a]$. When *A* is outside $[-1, 1]$, it enhances ergodicity. In order to approach prey and reduce the value of *a*, *A* will decrease, and when *A* is within $[-1, 1]$, the grey wolf group attacks.

### 3.4. Whale Optimization Algorithm (WOA)

The whale optimization algorithm is a nature-inspired algorithm mimicking the motion of whales when hunting their prey. It was first developed by Mirjalili and Lewis [46] to solve optimization problems. The algorithm simulates the actions of the humpback whale in searching the prey and the bubble-net feeding method of encircling prey. The mathematical model of a whale's unique action is following:

#### 3.4.1. Encircling Prey

The humpback whale can recognize the location of prey when they enter the target area or perception space. WOA assumes that the best position (solution) is the target prey. Once the best search agent is proposed, the rest agents try to update their location toward the best position (solution) as described in (12)–(14).

$$DI = |C \cdot W_p(t) - W(t)| \quad (12)$$

$$W(t+1) = W_p(t) - K \cdot DI \quad (13)$$

$$\begin{aligned} K &= 2 \cdot k \cdot r_2 - k \\ C &= 2r_1 \end{aligned} \quad (14)$$

where *t* is the current iteration, $W(t)$ indicates the position of prey, *K* and *C* are coefficient vectors, $W_p$ is the position of the optimal solution, *k* is a variable linearly decreasing from 2 to 0, and $r_1$ and $r_2$ are constants between (0, 1).

#### 3.4.2. Bubble-Net Attack Method

This section mainly introduces the shrinking encircling mechanism and spiral update position. First, the value of *K* is changed with *k* decreases by Equation (14) to achieve the shrinking encircling mechanism, and the whales' positions are updated according to Equations (15) and (16). As the whales are close to the prey (best solution), the distance between the whales and the prey can be calculated. A spiral update equation is then created to mimic the helix-shaped movement of the whales as follows:

$$W(t+1) = DSe^{bt}\cos(2\pi t) + W_p(t) \quad (15)$$

$$DS = W_p(t) - W(t) \tag{16}$$

where $DS$ is the distance between the whale and the prey (current best solution), $b$ is a constant which defines the shape of the logarithmic spiral, and $t$ is a constant between $(0, 1)$.

According to the previous equation, the whale can have two strategies to move close to the prey. The mathematical equation is as follows:

$$W(t+1) = \begin{cases} W_p(t) - K \cdot DI & \text{if } p < 0.5 \\ DSe^{bt}\cos(2\pi t) + W_p(t) & \text{if } p > 0.5 \end{cases} \tag{17}$$

where $p$ is a random number in $(0, 1)$.

### 3.4.3. Exploration Phase

Humpback whales randomly search the prey based on the constant variation to obtain the best solution. This process is mathematically described as follows:

$$DI = |C \cdot W_{rand}(t) - W(t)| \tag{18}$$

$$W(t+1) = W_{rand}(t) - K \cdot DI \tag{19}$$

where $W_{rand}(t)$ represents the random whale in the current population.

### 3.5. Butterfly Optimization Algorithm (BOA)

Inspired by the living habits of butterflies in nature, a butterfly optimization algorithm [47] (BOA) was proposed to simulate butterflies' foraging and mating behaviors. Unlike other metaheuristic algorithms, this method's advantage is that each butterfly has its unique odor. The butterfly can perceive and analyze the odor in the air to determine the potential direction of food sources/mating partners. In BOA, the fragrance is formulated as a function of the stimulus's physical strength, as follows:

$$F = cI^a \tag{20}$$

where $F$ is the concentration of aroma emitted by butterflies, $c$ is the sensory mode, $I$ is the stimulus intensity, and $a$ is the power index dependent on the mode, indicating different absorption degrees of aroma among different butterflies.

In most cases, it is possible to define $a$ and $c$ within the range of $[0, 1]$. When $a$ is 1, the butterfly does not absorb the fragrance. That is, another butterfly perceives the amount of fragrance emitted by a specific butterfly at the same capacity.

The BOA algorithm is divided into three parts, and the detailed steps are as follows:

Initializes the butterfly population by randomly generating the butterfly position in the search space and calculating and storing each butterfly's fragrance and fitness value. The fitness values of randomly generated butterfly populations are sorted to store the butterfly in the best position. Butterflies move toward the best position. The position update equation is as follows:

$$X_i^{t+1} = X_i^t + (r^2 + p_{best}^t - X_i^t) \bullet F(X_i) \tag{21}$$

where $r$ is the random number in $(0, 1)$, indicating the best butterfly for current iterations $t$, and $F(X_i)$ represents the aroma fitness value of the first butterfly at the current iteration number.

The mathematical model of butterfly population local search stage is as follows

$$X_i^{t+1} = X_i^t + (r^2 + p_{r_1}^t - p_{r_2}^t) \bullet F(X_i) \tag{22}$$

where $p_{r_1}^t$ and $p_{r_2}^t$ represent random two butterfly locations for the $t$th iteration in the search space, and $r_1$ and $r_2$ are random numbers between $(0, 1)$.

## 3.6. Sparrow Search Algorithm (SSA)

Inspired by the group wisdom, foraging and anti-predation behaviors of the sparrow in nature, Xue [48] proposed the sparrow search algorithm to solve optimization problems. In the SSA, there are two types of sparrows: producer and scrounger. The producers with high levels of energy reserves can search for food sources and guide the movement of the entire population. The position update equation is as follows:

$$X_{i,j}^{t+1} = \begin{cases} X_{i,j}^t \cdot exp\left(\frac{-i}{\alpha \cdot iter_{max}}\right) & if\ R_2 < ST \\ X_{i,j}^t \cdot Q \cdot L & if\ R_2 \geq ST \end{cases} \quad (23)$$

where $t$ is the current iteration, $iter_{max}$ is the maximum number of iterations, $X_{i,j}^t$ and $X_{i,j}^{t+1}$ indicates the position of a sparrow, $i$ is the number of sparrows, $j$ is the dimension of the optimization problem, $\alpha$ is the random number in (0, 1), $R_2(R_2 \in [0,1])$ is the alarm value, represents the safety threshold, $Q$ is the random number which obeys normal distribution, and $L$ is a matrix in which each element inside is 1.

When producers expand the search range to find foods without predators threatening and enter the wide search mode, if $R_2 \geq ST$ the sparrows quickly move to safe areas when predators move close to them.

As for the scroungers, if they detect that the producer has found good food, they immediately move the objective position to get food. On the one hand, if scroungers defeat the producer, the update formula is as shown in Equation (23). In contrast, if the producer wins, the scrounger enforces Equation (24).

$$X_{i,j}^{t+1} = \begin{cases} Q \cdot exp\left(\frac{X_{worst}^t - X_{i,j}^t}{i^2}\right) & if\ i > n/2 \\ X_p^{t+1} + \left|X_{i,j}^t - X_p^{t+1}\right| \cdot A^+ \cdot L & otherwise \end{cases} \quad (24)$$

where $X_p^{t+1}$ is the optimal position of the producer, $X_{worst}^t$ is the current global worst position, $A^+ = A^T(AA^T)^{-1}$ and $A$ is a one-dimensional matrix with each element randomly assigned $-1$ or 1, when $i > n/2$, the scrounger with the worst fitness value cannot find the food.

In SSA, some sparrows, which account for 10% or 20% of the total population, are assumed to be aware of the danger. In such a case, sparrows at the edge of the group quickly move forward to the safety area to get a better position, and other sparrows in the middle group move to others. The mathematical model can be expressed by:

$$X_{i,j}^{t+1} = \begin{cases} X_{best}^t + \beta \cdot \left|X_{i,j}^t - X_{best}^t\right| & if\ f_i > f_g \\ X_{i,j}^t + \lambda \cdot \left(\frac{\left|X_{i,j}^t - X_{worst}^{t+1}\right|}{(f_i - f_w + \delta)}\right) & if\ f_i = f_g \end{cases} \quad (25)$$

where $X_{best}$ is the current global best position, $\beta$ is a step control parameter that obeys the normal distribution of random numbers with a mean value of 0 and a variance of 1, $\lambda$ is a random number in (0, 1), $f_i$, $f_g$ and $f_w$ are the fitness value of the current sparrow, current best fitness, and current worst values, respectively, and $\delta$ is the smallest constant to avoid zero-division-error.

## 4. ELM Optimized by PSO, GWO, WOA, BOA, and SSA

This study uses ELM to map the nonlinear relationship between influence factors and UCS. However, the weights and thresholds of the hidden and input layers of the ELM algorithm are random numbers between 0 and 1, which can cause problems. The random weights and thresholds restrict the mapping performance of ELM. To obtain a reliable prediction, it is essential to improve the predictability of ELM. Hence, as an optimizer of weights and thresholds between inputs and hidden layers, PSO, GWO, WOA, BOA, and

SSA are utilized in this study. The development of the optimized ELM to predict UCS has the following steps:

1. To considerably distill the information governing the relationship between the UCS and the input variables, a database including 734 samples was developed in this study and divided into 700 samples for the training and 34 for the testing.
2. Firstly, the training set is used to optimize the ELM model's hidden layer neurons and activation function. After that, the test set is input into the trained ELM, and the obtained results are used to compute the performance metrics, including the root mean squared error (RMSE). The optimized hidden neurons and activation function can be determined when the RMSE is minimized.
3. To enhance the ELM model predictability, the PSO, GWO, WOA, BOA, and SSA are utilized to optimize weights and thresholds between inputs and hidden layers. Figure 4 depicts a process for optimizing ELM using the multi-algorithm.
4. Compare the predicted results and calculate the statistical evaluation indices to select the most precise and reliable model.

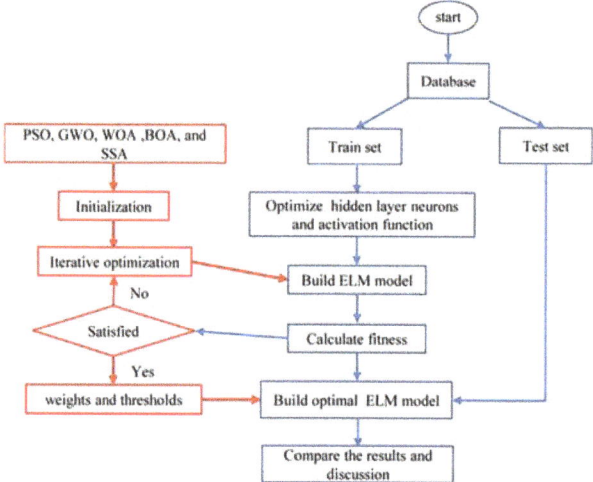

**Figure 4.** The process for optimizing the ELM using the PSO, GWO, WOA, BOA, and SSA.

## 5. Statistical Evaluation Indices

In order to evaluate the accuracy of the proposed prediction models, some statistical indices, including root mean squared error (RMSE), coefficient of determination ($R^2$), amount of value account for (VAF), and mean squared error (MSE), are calculated using Equations (26)–(29).

$$\text{RMSE} = \sqrt{(\frac{1}{n})\sum_{k=1}^{n}(y_i - y'_i)} \tag{26}$$

$$R^2 = 1 - \frac{\text{sum squared regression (SSR)}}{\text{sum of square total (SST)}} \tag{27}$$

$$\text{VAF} = \left[1 - \frac{var(y_i - y'_i)}{var(y_i)}\right] \times 100\% \tag{28}$$

$$\text{MSE} = (\frac{1}{n})\sum_{k=1}^{n}(y_i - y'_i) \tag{29}$$

where $y_i$ is the measured value, $y'_i$ is the predicted value, and $n$ is the number of observations.

## 6. Calculation Results and Discussion

### 6.1. ELM Parameters Optimization

As previously stated, the variables had distinct units and wide distribution. The data should be normalized to a value between 0 and 1 before training based on ELM to get good performance, as shown in Equation (30).

$$x_n = \frac{x_a - x_{min}}{x_{max} - x_{min}} \tag{30}$$

where $x_n$ is the normalized value, $x_a$ is the actual value, $x_{max}$ and $x_{min}$ are the maximum and minimum values of the dataset.

The hidden layer neurons and activation function must be optimized for the ELM. The RMSE of ELM was utilized to predict a model to tune them. Table 2 and Figure 5 indicate the effects of the number of hidden layer neurons and activation function.

Table 2. Effects of the number of hidden modes on the ELM performance.

| Number of Hidden Modes | RMSE | | |
|---|---|---|---|
| | Maximum | Average | Standard Deviation |
| 1 | 68.475 | 53.568 | 9.446 |
| 2 | 50.799 | 27.179 | 16.706 |
| 3 | 32.572 | 12.253 | 9.216 |
| 4 | 12.072 | 8.396 | 1.433 |
| 5 | 11.590 | 8.297 | 1.330 |
| 6 | 13.803 | 8.803 | 1.904 |
| 7 | 12.338 | 9.709 | 1.745 |
| 8 | 13.035 | 10.368 | 1.801 |
| 9 | 12.875 | 11.181 | 0.853 |
| 10 | 15.286 | 12.113 | 1.762 |

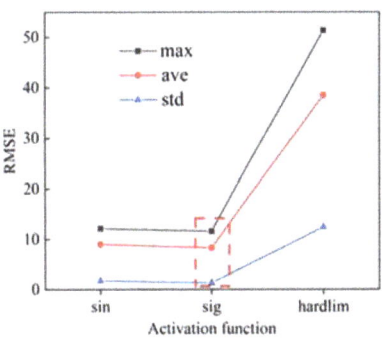

Figure 5. Effects of the activation function on the ELM performance.

Figure 5 depicts the impact of the number of hidden layer modes on the ELM performance. When the number of modes is 5, the standard deviation, maximum, and average error are the smallest. Therefore, there are five hidden modes in the present study. When the activation function for the ELM is a hardlim function, the maximum, average, and standard deviation of error are more significant than the other two functions. The predicted errors in the other two functions are relatively small when the activation function is the sigmoid function; hence, the activation function of the ELM model is the sigmoid function.

### 6.2. Calculation Results and Performance Comparison

A multi-algorithm is applied to enhance the ELM model predictability after optimizing the parameters of the activation function and the number of hidden neurons. Figure 6 depicts the predicted results using a single ELM model and ELM optimized by PSO, GWO, WOA, BOA, and SSA.

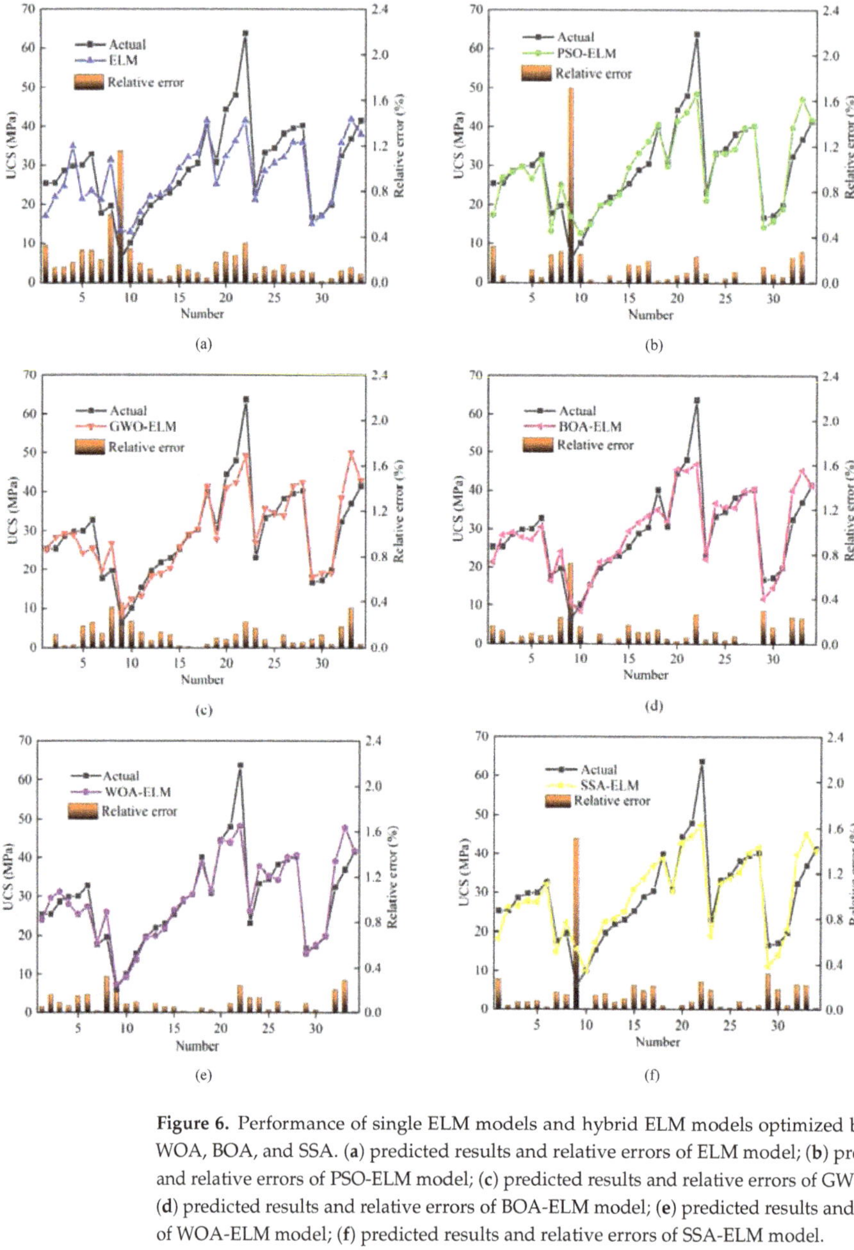

**Figure 6.** Performance of single ELM models and hybrid ELM models optimized by PSO, GWO, WOA, BOA, and SSA. (**a**) predicted results and relative errors of ELM model; (**b**) predicted results and relative errors of PSO-ELM model; (**c**) predicted results and relative errors of GWO-ELM model; (**d**) predicted results and relative errors of BOA-ELM model; (**e**) predicted results and relative errors of WOA-ELM model; (**f**) predicted results and relative errors of SSA-ELM model.

Figure 6a illustrates that only a few predicted values are close to the actual values; thus, a single ELM model mispredicted UCS. The random generation of the weights and thresholds of the input and hidden layers can limit the performance of ELM. Figure 6b,f show that the actual and predicted curves change together, indicating that the optimized ELM by PSO (PSO-ELM) and SSA (SSA-ELM) can estimate UCS using point load index,

P-wave velocity, and Schmidt hammer rebound. The predicted performance of an ELM optimized by the PSO and SSA model is better than a single ELM model. The minimum and average relative errors of PSO-ELM and SSA-ELM are 0.34% and 0.55%, respectively, which are smaller than the single ELM model. However, the maximum relative errors of PSO-ELM and SSA-ELM are 171.62% and 150.67%, respectively, relatively less than the single ELM model. It indicates that PSO and SSA can relatively enhance ELM predictability, and PSO-ELM and SSA-ELM models are unstable. Compared to the above two algorithms, BOA also improves the predictability of ELM. Figure 6d demonstrates that BOA-ELM predicts better performance than the single ELM, PSO-ELM, and SSA-ELM models. The minimum, maximum, and average relative errors of BOA-ELM are 0.22%, 72.05%, and 11.48%, respectively, smaller than single ELM, PSO-ELM, and SSA-ELM models. However, the maximum relative errors of single ELM, PSO-ELM, SSA-ELM, and BOA-ELM are nearly greater than 50%, indicating that at the lowest value of UCS, its predictive accuracy is almost awful. This can be utilized if data are lacking in ranges with low UCS values or if the ELM parameters require further optimization. As shown in Figure 6c,e, nearly all predicted values are close to actual values, demonstrating that GWO and WOA can further improve the predictability of the ELM model. At low values, the prediction accuracy of GWO-ELM and WOA-ELM models is superior to that of the other three algorithms. The minimum, maximum, and average relative errors of WOA-ELM are 0.22%, 72.05%, and 11.48%, respectively, smaller than the GWO-ELM model and significantly less than the single ELM, PSO-ELM, and SSA-ELM models.

Figure 7 depicts the residual error results using a single ELM model optimized by PSO, GWO, WOA, BOA, and SSA. The residual error histograms of six models exhibit normal distributions. The range of residual errors of the single ELM model is between 0.25 and 22.21 MPa, with a mean of 5.07 MPa. The mean value of residual errors using PSO-ELM is 3.2 MPa, varying widely from 0.10 to 15.28 MPa. The average residual errors of BOA-ELM and SSA-ELM are 2.91 MPa (0.06–16.78 MPa) and 3.34 MPa (0.06–16.16 MPa). The average value of GWO-ELM residual errors is 3.18, ranging from 0.05 to 14.51 MPa. The minimum, maximum, and average residual errors derived from optimized ELM models are less than the single ELM model. The maximum residual errors of PSO-ELM, GWO-ELM, BOA-ELM, WOA-ELM, and SSA-ELM models are less than 20 MPa, and the smallest of them is 14.51 MPa. The greatest residual error of the WOA-ELM model is 15.41 MPa, which is relatively bigger than the smallest maximum residual error. The minimum and mean values of residual errors (using WOA-ELM) are lower than others. It indicates that a multi-algorithm can improve the ELM model's predictability, and its best performance is WOA.

Figure 8 illustrates the $R^2$ results produced by a single ELM model and an ELM optimized by PSO, GWO, WOA, BOA, and SSA for UCS.

The ELM model produces an $R^2$ value for UCS of 0.682, as depicted in Figure 8a. The accuracy of optimized ELM models is more than 0.80 and higher than that of a single ELM model. It is understandable to see that a multi-algorithm can enhance the predictability of the ELM model. Figure 8b, f shows that the $R^2$ derived from PSO-ELM, SSA-ELM, and GWO-ELM models are 0.812, 0.827, and 0.835, respectively. The $R^2$ results generated by the above three models fall between 0.80 and 0.85. Accordingly, three algorithms enhance the prediction ability of ELM, but the accuracy must be improved. Figure 8d,e reveals that the $R^2$ of the BOA-ELM and WOA-ELM models is greater than 0.85, indicating their performance is superior to that of the above three algorithms. Meanwhile, the $R^2$ of the WOA-ELM model is 0.861, which is higher than the $R^2$ for the ELM and other optimized ELM models. Therefore, the WOA-ELM model, being a combinatorial approach to the modeling work, performed best compared to ELM and optimized models.

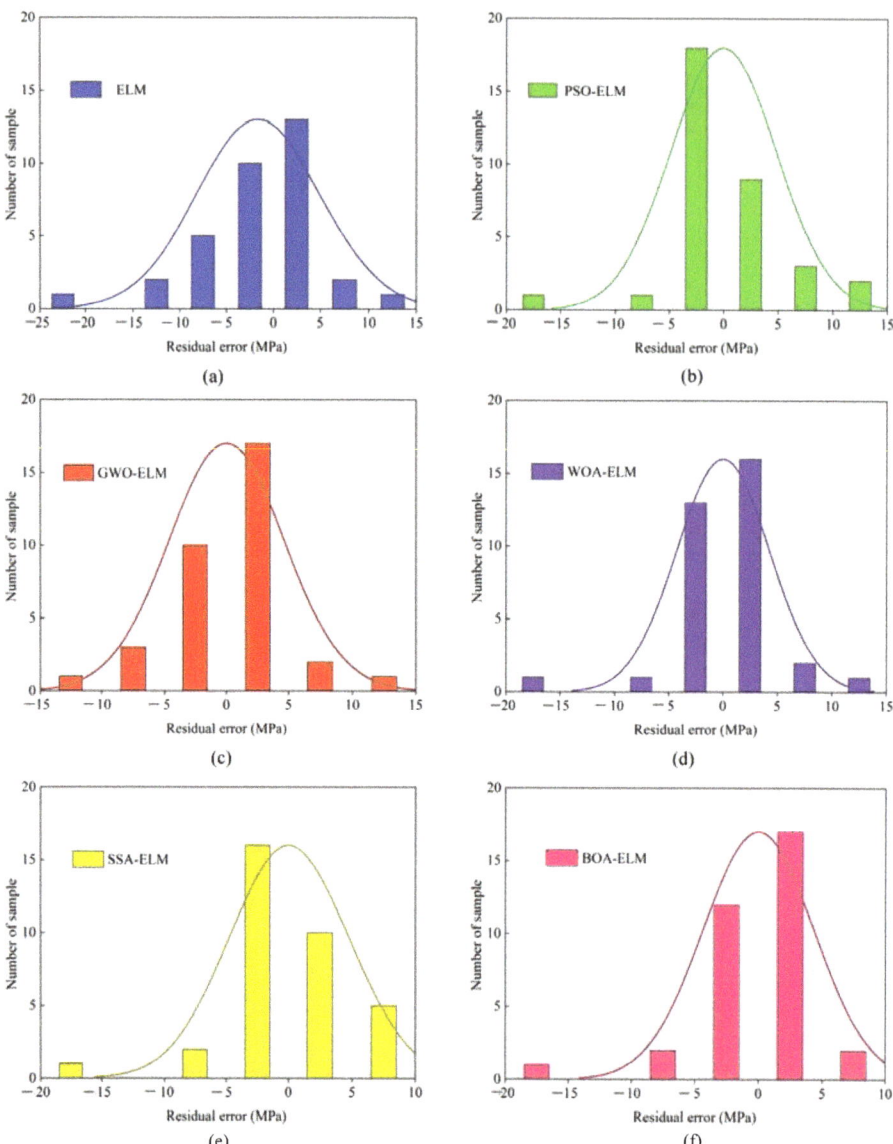

**Figure 7.** Frequency distributions of residual errors utilizing a single ELM model and hybrid ELM models optimized by PSO, GWO, WOA, BOA, and SSA. (**a**) residual errors based on ELM model; (**b**) residual errors based on PSO-ELM model; (**c**) residual errors based on GWO-ELM model; (**d**) residual errors based on BOA-ELM model; (**e**) residual errors based on WOA-ELM model; (**f**) residual errors based on SSA-ELM model.

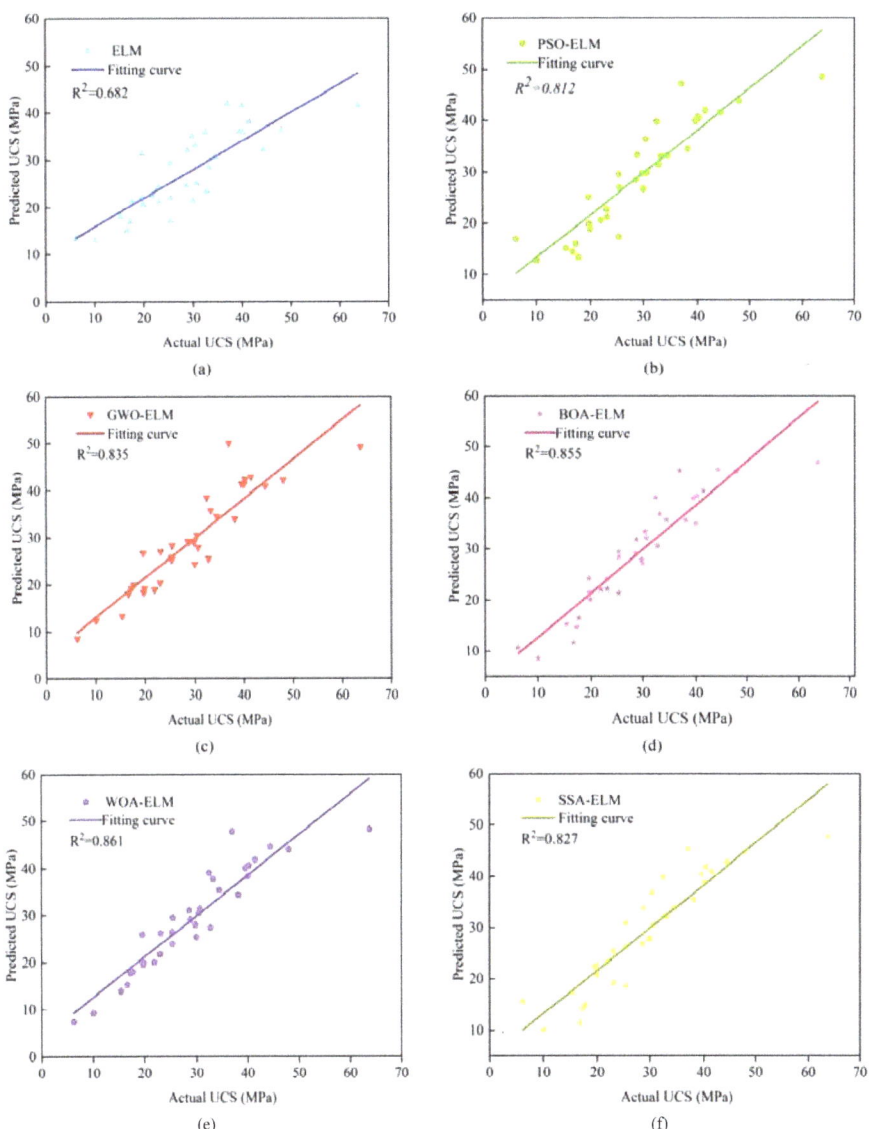

**Figure 8.** UCS results utilizing a single ELM and hybrid ELM models optimized by PSO, GWO, WOA, BOA, and SSA. (a) $R^2$ of measured and predicted values of UCS using ELM model; (b) $R^2$ of measured and predicted values of UCS using PSO-ELM model; (c) $R^2$ of measured and predicted values of UCS using GWO-ELM model; (d) $R^2$ of measured and predicted values of UCS using BOA-ELM model; (e) $R^2$ of measured and predicted values of UCS using WOA-ELM model; (f) $R^2$ of measured and predicted values of UCS using SSA-ELM model.

To further compare the proposed models, their performance indices, i.e., RMSE, VAF, and MSE, were calculated as presented in Table 3. Theoretically, a predictive model is better when the RMSE and MSE equal 0, and VAF is 100%. Table 3 indicates that the MSE and RMSE of the ELM model are more significant than those of optimized ELM models. The VAF value of the ELM model is 73% less than that of optimized ELM models.

It should be noted that the ELM model must be improved, and the multi-algorithm can increase the predictability of the ELM model. The RMSE and MSE of the WOA-ELM model are significantly lower than PSO-ELM, GWO-ELM, and SSA-ELM models, and the VAF produced by WOA-ELM is also larger than that of the above three models. Comparatively, the RMSE and MSE of WOA-ELM are smaller than those of the BOA-ELM model. As previously stated, the relative and residual errors of the WOA-ELM model are smaller than those of others, and the $R^2$ of the present model is closer to 1 than other models. In this study, the WOA-ELM model can predict UCS with a higher degree of accuracy than the ELM and combined ELM models.

Table 3. Performance indices of the proposed predictive models.

| Model | ELM | PSO-ELM | GWO-ELM | BOA-ELM | WOA-ELM | SSA-ELM |
|---|---|---|---|---|---|---|
| $R^2$ | 0.682 | 0.812 | 0.835 | 0.855 | 0.861 | 0.827 |
| MSE | 44.37 | 22.65 | 20.88 | 18.36 | 17.61 | 21.92 |
| RMSE | 6.66 | 4.76 | 4.57 | 4.28 | 4.20 | 4.68 |
| VAF (%) | 73 | 88 | 79 | 92 | 91 | 90 |

## 7. Conclusions

Predicting UCS is an interesting and challenging exercise. This study first collects 734 samples to conduct a new dataset that includes magmatic, sedimentary, and metamorphic rocks and rock-like materials from different countries. The ELM was proposed to map the relationship between UCS and point load index, P-wave velocity, and Schmidt hammer rebound number to estimate UCS. In order to further predict UCS, five algorithms (PSO, GWO, WOA, BOA, and SSA) were applied to improve the predictability of ELM. Based on the aforementioned statements, the following conclusions are drawn:

- The optimized ELM model consists of five hidden neurons and a sigmoid activation function.
- Compared to the models proposed above, it can be stated that the predicted performance of the six models for predicting UCS from high to low is as follows: WOA-ELM, BOA-ELM, GWO-ELM, SSA-ELM, PSO-ELM, and ELM. The predicted indices ($R^2$: 0.861; MSE: 17.61; RMSE: 4.20) produced by WOA-ELM illustrate that it is the more precise model.
- The minimum, maximum, and average relative errors produced by ELM optimized using the whale optimization algorithm (WOA-ELM) are 0.22%, 72.05%, and 11.48% smaller than the other models.
- The minimum and mean residual error produced by WOA-ELM are 0.02 and 2.64 MPa, respectively, smaller than other models.
- The results showed that the WOA-ELM model is the best among other techniques investigated in this study. Its performance indices reveal the high accuracy and reliability of the new model for predicting UCS.

In all, the hybrid models proposed in this study are suitable for different rocks. Thus, the proposed WOA-ELM model in this study has broad application potential in predicting the UCS of various rocks.

The main limitation of this paper is that only one dataset was utilized to evaluate the results of developed models. Meanwhile, this study did not consider that the proposed algorithms have some limitations, such as local minima trapping issues and the inability to exploit local space. To avoid this, additional research will be conducted in the future:

1. The developed model in this study will be applied to other datasets to demonstrate its generalization ability and robustness.
2. We will present strategies to avoid the problem of local minima trapping issues and the inability of metaheuristic algorithms to exploit local space and illustrate their impact on the current model.

**Supplementary Materials:** The following supporting information can be downloaded at: https://www.mdpi.com/article/10.3390/math10193490/s1. See [1,14,15,24,34–43].

**Author Contributions:** Conceptualization, J.Q.; Data curation, X.Y.; Formal analysis, J.Q.; Methodology, Y.P.; Resources, X.Y.; Software, J.Q. and X.W.; Supervision, X.Y.; Validation, M.Z.; Writing—review & editing, J.Q. and X.Y. All authors have read and agreed to the published version of the manuscript.

**Funding:** This research is supported by the National Natural Science Foundation of China under Grant Nos. 42177140 and 41807250. This support is gratefully acknowledged.

**Institutional Review Board Statement:** Not applicable.

**Informed Consent Statement:** Not applicable.

**Data Availability Statement:** The datasets generated during and/or analyzed during the current study are available from the corresponding author upon reasonable request.

**Conflicts of Interest:** The authors declare no conflict of interest.

## References

1. Heidari, M.; Mohseni, H.; Jalali, S.H. Prediction of uniaxial compressive strength of some sedimentary rocks by fuzzy and regression models. *Geotech. Geol. Eng.* **2017**, *36*, 401–412. [CrossRef]
2. Armaghani, D.J.; Mohamad, E.T.; Momeni, E.; Narayanasamy, M.S.; Amin, M. An adaptive neuro-fuzzy inference system for predicting unconfined compressive strength and Young's modulus: A study on Main Range granite. *Bull. Eng. Geol. Environ.* **2015**, *74*, 1301–1319. [CrossRef]
3. Mishra, D.A.; Basu, A. Use of the block punch test to predict the compressive and tensile strengths of rocks. *Int. J. Rock Mech. Min. Sci.* **2012**, *51*, 119–127. [CrossRef]
4. Şahin, M.; Ulusay, R.; Karakul, H. Point load strength index of half-cut core specimens and correlation with uniaxial compressive strength. *Rock Mech. Rock Eng.* **2020**, *53*, 3745–3760. [CrossRef]
5. Basu, A.; Kamran, M. Point load test on schistose rocks and its applicability in predicting uniaxial compressive strength. *Int. J. Rock Mech. Min. Sci.* **2010**, *47*, 823–828. [CrossRef]
6. Singh, T.N.; Kainthola, A.; Venkatesh, A. Correlation between point load index and uniaxial compressive strength for different rock types. *Rock Mech. Rock Eng.* **2012**, *45*, 259–264. [CrossRef]
7. Kahraman, S.; Fener, M.; Gunaydin, O. Estimating the uniaxial compressive strength of pyroclastic rocks from the slake durability index. *Bull. Eng. Geol. Environ.* **2017**, *76*, 1107–1115. [CrossRef]
8. Zhang, H.; Wu, S.; Zhang, Z. Prediction of uniaxial compressive strength of rock via genetic algorithm—Selective ensemble learning. *Nat. Resour. Res.* **2022**, *31*, 1721–1737. [CrossRef]
9. Yagiz, S. Correlation between slake durability and rock properties for some carbonate rocks. *Bull. Eng. Geol. Environ.* **2011**, *70*, 377–383. [CrossRef]
10. Khandelwal, M. Correlating P-wave velocity with the physico-mechanical properties of different rocks. *Pure Appl. Geophys.* **2013**, *170*, 507–514. [CrossRef]
11. Iyare, U.C.; Blake, O.O.; Ramsook, R. Estimating the uniaxial compressive strength of argillites using brazilian tensile strength, ultrasonic wave velocities, and elastic properties. *Rock Mech. Rock Eng.* **2021**, *54*, 2067–2078. [CrossRef]
12. Wang, S.; Li, X.; Yao, J.; Gong, F.; Du, S. Experimental investigation of rock breakage by a conical pick and its application to non-explosive mechanized mining in deep hard rock. *Int. J. Rock Mech. Min. Sci.* **2019**, *122*, 104063. [CrossRef]
13. Wang, S.; Sun, L.; Li, X.; Zhou, J.; Du, K.; Wang, S.; Khandelwal, M. Experimental investigation and theoretical analysis of indentations on cuboid hard rock using a conical pick under uniaxial lateral stress. *Geomech. Geophys. Geo-Energy Geo-Resour.* **2022**, *8*, 34. [CrossRef]
14. Karakus, M.; Tutmez, B. Fuzzy and multiple regression modelling for evaluation of intact rock strength based on point load, schmidt hammer and sonic velocity. *Rock Mech. Rock Eng.* **2006**, *39*, 45–57. [CrossRef]
15. Mishra, D.A.; Basu, A. Estimation of uniaxial compressive strength of rock materials by index tests using regression analysis and fuzzy inference system. *Eng. Geol.* **2013**, *160*, 54–68. [CrossRef]
16. Sarkar, K.; Singh, A. Estimation of strength parameters of rock using artificial neural networks. *Bull. Eng. Geol. Environ.* **2010**, *69*, 599–606. [CrossRef]
17. Yagiz, S.; Sezer, E.A.; Gokceoglu, C. Artificial neural networks and nonlinear regression techniques to assess the influence of slake durability cycles on the prediction of uniaxial compressive strength and modulus of elasticity for carbonate rocks. *Int. J. Numer. Anal. Methods Geomech.* **2012**, *36*, 1636–1650. [CrossRef]
18. Yesiloglu-Gultekin, N.U.; Gokceoglu, C.; Sezer, E.A. Prediction of uniaxial compressive strength of granitic rocks by various nonlinear tools and comparison of their performances. *Int. J. Rock Mech. Min. Sci.* **2013**, *62*, 113–122. [CrossRef]
19. Dindarloo, S.R.; Siami-Irdemoosa, E. Estimating the unconfined compressive strength of carbonate rocks using gene expression programming. *arXiv* **2016**, arXiv:1602.03854.

20. Gül, E.; Ozdemir, E.; Sarc, D.E. Modeling Uniaxial Compressive Strength of Some Rocks from Turkey Using Soft Computing Techniques. *Measurement* **2020**, *171*, 108781. [CrossRef]
21. Wen, L.; Tan, Z. Research on Rock Strength Prediction Based on Least Squares Support Vector Machine. *Geotech. Geol. Eng.* **2017**, *35*, 385–393.
22. Mahmoodzadeh, A.; Mohammadi, M.; Ibrahim, H.; Abdulhamid, S.N.; Ali, H. Artificial intelligence forecasting models of uniaxial compressive strength. *Transp. Geotech.* **2021**, *27*, 100499. [CrossRef]
23. Gupta, D.; Natarajan, N. Prediction of uniaxial compressive strength of rock samples using density weighted least squares twin support vector regression. *Neural Comput. Appl.* **2021**, *33*, 15843–15850. [CrossRef]
24. Momeni, E.; Armaghani, D.J.; Hajihassani, M.; Amin, M.M. Prediction of uniaxial compressive strength of rock samples using hybrid particle swarm optimization-based artificial neural networks. *Measurement* **2015**, *60*, 50–63. [CrossRef]
25. Fang, Q.; Bejarbaneh, B.Y.; Vatandoust, M.; Armaghani, D.J.; Mohamad, E.T. Strength evaluation of granite block samples with different predictive models. *Eng. Comput.* **2019**, *37*, 891–908. [CrossRef]
26. Izonin, I.; Tkachenko, R.; Shakhovska, N.; Lotoshynska, N. The additive input-doubling method based on the svr with nonlinear kernels: Small data approach. *Symmetry* **2021**, *13*, 612. [CrossRef]
27. Izonin, I.; Tkachenko, R.; Dronyuk, I.; Tkachenko, P.; Rashkevych, M. Predictive modeling based on small data in clinical medicine: Rbf-based additive input-doubling method. *Math. Biosci. Eng. MBE* **2021**, *18*, 2599–2613. [CrossRef]
28. Yin, X.; Liu, Q.; Pan, Y.; Huang, X.; Wang, X. Strength of stacking technique of ensemble learning in rockburst prediction with imbalanced data: Comparison of eight single and ensemble models. *Nat. Resour. Res.* **2021**, *30*, 1795–1815. [CrossRef]
29. Huang, G.B.; Chen, L.; Siew, C.K. Universal approximation using incremental constructive feedforward networks with random hidden nodes. *IEEE Trans. Neural Netw.* **2006**, *17*, 879–892. [CrossRef]
30. Kang, F.; Liu, J.; Li, J.; Li, S. Concrete dam deformation prediction model for health monitoring based on extreme learning machine. *Struct. Control. Health Monit.* **2017**, *24*, e1997. [CrossRef]
31. Li, E.; Yang, F.; Ren, M.; Zhang, X.; Zhou, J.; Khandelwal, M. Prediction of blasting mean fragment size using support vector regression combined with five optimization algorithms. *J. Rock Mech. Geotech. Eng.* **2021**, *13*, 18. [CrossRef]
32. Yin, X.; Liu, Q.; Huang, X.; Pan, Y. Perception model of surrounding rock geological conditions based on tbm operational big data and combined unsupervised-supervised learning. *Tunn. Undergr. Space Technol.* **2022**, *120*, 104285. [CrossRef]
33. Xin, Y.; Qla, B.; Xing, H.C.; Ypa, B. Real-time prediction of rockburst intensity using an integrated cnn-adam-bo algorithm based on microseismic data and its engineering application. *Tunn. Undergr. Space Technol.* **2021**, *117*, 104133.
34. Tuğrul, A.; Zarif, I.H. Correlation of mineralogical and textural characteristics with engineering properties of selected granitic rocks from Turkey. *Eng. Geol.* **1999**, *51*, 303–317. [CrossRef]
35. Kahraman, S. Evaluation of simple methods for assessing the uniaxial compressive strength of rock. *Int. J. Rock Mech. Min. Sci.* **2001**, *38*, 981–994. [CrossRef]
36. Dinner, I.; Acar, A.; Ural, S. Estimation of strength and deformation properties of Quaternary caliche deposits. *Bull. Eng. Geol. Environ.* **2008**, *67*, 353–366.
37. Kilic, A.; Teymen, A. Determination of mechanical properties of rocks using simple methods. *Bull. Eng. Geol. Environ.* **2008**, *67*, 237. [CrossRef]
38. Çobanoğlu, İ.; Çelik, S.B. Estimation of uniaxial compressive strength from point load strength, Schmidt hardness and P-wave velocity. *Bull. Eng. Geol. Environ.* **2008**, *67*, 491–498. [CrossRef]
39. Aliabadi, S. Prediction of uniaxial compressive strength and modulus of elasticity for Travertine samples using regression and artificial neural networks. *Min. Sci. Technol.* **2010**, *20*, 41–46.
40. Tandon, R.S.; Gupta, V. Estimation of strength characteristics of different Himalayan rocks from Schmidt hammer rebound, point load index, and compressional wave velocity. *Bull. Eng. Geol. Environ.* **2015**, *74*, 521–533. [CrossRef]
41. Jahed Armaghani, D.; Tonnizam Mohamad, E.; Hajihassani, M.; Yagiz, S.; Motaghedi, H. Application of several non-linear prediction tools for estimating uniaxial compressive strength of granitic rocks and comparison of their performances. *Eng. Comput.* **2016**, *31*, 189–206. [CrossRef]
42. Armaghani, D.J.; Mohamad, E.T.; Momeni, E.; Monjezi, M.; Narayanasamy, M.S. Prediction of the strength and elasticity modulus of granite through an expert artificial neural network. *Arab. J. Geosci.* **2016**, *9*, 48. [CrossRef]
43. Ng, I.T.; Yuen, K.V.; Lau, C.H. Predictive model for uniaxial compressive strength for Grade III granitic rocks from Macao. *Eng. Geol.* **2015**, *199*, 28–37. [CrossRef]
44. Kennedy, J. Particle swarm optimization. In Proceedings of the ICNN'95—International Conference on Neural Networks, Perth, Australia, 27 November–1 December 1995; Volume 4, pp. 1942–1948.
45. Mirjalili, S.; Mirjalili, S.M.; Lewis, A. Grey wolf optimizer. *Adv. Eng. Softw.* **2014**, *69*, 46–61. [CrossRef]
46. Mirjalili, S.; Lewis, A.D. The whale optimization algorithm. *Adv. Eng. Softw.* **2016**, *95*, 51–67. [CrossRef]
47. Arora, S.; Singh, S. Butterfly optimization algorithm: A novel approach for global optimization. *Soft Comput.* **2018**, *23*, 715–734. [CrossRef]
48. Xue, J.; Shen, B. A novel swarm intelligence optimization approach: Sparrow search algorithm. *Syst. Sci. Control. Eng. Open Access J.* **2020**, *8*, 22–34. [CrossRef]

Article

# Effect of Different Tunnel Distribution on Dynamic Behavior and Damage Characteristics of Non-Adjacent Tunnel Triggered by Blasting Disturbance

Jiadong Qiu [1,2,3,*] and Fan Feng [4]

1. School of Resources Environment and Safety Engineering, University of South China, Hengyang 421001, China
2. School of Resources and Safety Engineering, Central South University, Changsha 410083, China
3. Guangdong Provincial Key Laboratory of Deep Earth Sciences and Geothermal Energy Exploitation and Utilization, Institute of Deep Earth Sciences and Green Energy, College of Civil and Transportation Engineering, Shenzhen University, Shenzhen 518060, China
4. College of Energy and Mining Engineering, Shandong University of Science and Technology, Qingdao 266590, China
* Correspondence: 2022000058@usc.edu.cn

Citation: Qiu, J.; Feng, F. Effect of Different Tunnel Distribution on Dynamic Behavior and Damage Characteristics of Non-Adjacent Tunnel Triggered by Blasting Disturbance. *Mathematics* 2022, *10*, 3705. https://doi.org/10.3390/math10193705

Academic Editors: Shaofeng Wang, Linqi Huang, Xin Cai and Zhengyang Song

Received: 28 July 2022
Accepted: 6 October 2022
Published: 10 October 2022

**Publisher's Note:** MDPI stays neutral with regard to jurisdictional claims in published maps and institutional affiliations.

**Copyright:** © 2022 by the authors. Licensee MDPI, Basel, Switzerland. This article is an open access article distributed under the terms and conditions of the Creative Commons Attribution (CC BY) license (https://creativecommons.org/licenses/by/4.0/).

**Abstract:** When a blasting is executed near two tunnels, the blasting wave will trigger a dynamic response and damage to the tunnels. Depending on the tunnel distribution, the path of the blasting wave to the remote non-adjacent tunnels will change. The aim of this study is to analyze the effect of the tunnel distribution on the dynamic response characteristics of a remote non-adjacent tunnel. Numerical models of two tunnels were established by PFC2D and three different tunnel distributions were considered. The two tunnels were divided into the adjacent tunnel and the non-adjacent tunnel according to their relative distance to the blasting source. The dynamic stress evolution, damage characteristics and the evolution of strain energy of the non-adjacent tunnel were initially analyzed. The results show that the stress wave amplitude of the non-adjacent tunnel is closely related to the tunnel distribution, but only near the sidewalls of the non-adjacent tunnel is the stress wave waveform sensitive to the tunnel distribution. The larger the tunnel dip, the more severe the damage to the non-adjacent tunnel. In addition, as the tunnel dip increases, the maximum strain energy densities (SEDs) in the roof, floor and sidewalls of the non-adjacent tunnel exhibit different trends. The influence of the wavelength of the blasting wave is further discussed. It is shown that the dynamic stress amplification factor and damage degree around the non-adjacent tunnel is usually positively correlated with the wavelength of the blasting wave. Moreover, the release of strain energy around the non-adjacent tunnel has a positive correlation with the wavelength. The SED variations in different areas around the non-adjacent tunnel also exhibit different trends with the increase of tunnel dip.

**Keywords:** tunnel; dynamic disturbance; strain energy; damage; distribution; crack

**MSC:** 37M05

## 1. Introduction

In underground engineering excavation, a large number of tunnels are excavated in a limited area to reduce the workload and cost [1–3]. These tunnels are important structures to ensure the safety of underground engineering. However, with the increase of excavation depth and the number of engineering structures, the stress concentration around the engineering structures becomes more obvious and a large amount of strain energy is stored around them. These initial strain energies can induce a high risk of rock burst, collapse and fracture [4–6]. In addition, the dynamic disturbance in underground engineering is another major cause of engineering disasters [7–10]. In underground tunnels which suffer different distribution, the propagation of stress waves is also complex and diverse, which makes it very difficult to predict and prevent disasters. Therefore, it is necessary to understand the dynamic behavior and damage characteristics of underground tunnels with different distributions.

In recent decades, the static mechanical behavior of underground tunnels has attracted extensive attention. Some scholars have calculated the stress distribution around the tunnel by the elastic mechanics and complex function methods [11,12]. They generally believe that the lateral pressure coefficient and the tunnel cross-section shapes are important factors affecting stress distribution. For example, Kirsch first obtained the stress distribution function (Kirsch's solution) around the circular tunnel under different lateral pressure conditions based on elastic mechanic theory [12]. Subsequently, the stress distribution formula of the elliptical tunnel was obtained by using the conformal mapping method of complex function and the classical Kirsch's solution [12]. Recently, some scholars have also solved the stress distribution of specific shape tunnels (such as a rectangular and semi-circular tunnel) using numerical regression analysis, complex function theory and numerical simulation [13,14]. For example, Exadaktylos and Stavropoulou [13] adopted the complex function method to calculate the stress distribution of multiple shapes of underground tunnels with rounded corners and further verified the theoretical solution by the FLAC3D numerical simulation. Zhao et al. [14] also obtained the initial function for solving the stress distribution around the rectangular tunnel by defining a coefficient related to the height-width ratio. On the other hand, many scholars have studied the failure mechanism of underground tunnels [15–18]. For example, Zhu et al. [15] analyzed the influence of lateral pressure coefficient on the failure of a U-shaped tunnel based on RFPA numerical simulation. The results showed that, when the lateral pressure coefficient is 1, the roof and floor would suffer shear failure, while when the lateral pressure coefficient is 4, the sidewalls would suffer tensile failure. Gong et al. [16] also studied the rock burst mechanism of hard rock tunnels with a circular cross-section. They found that the rock burst process of deep hard rock tunnels has a typical time effect which can be divided into four stages and the spalling can further be developed into the rock burst. Si et al. [17] conducted a series of triaxial compression tests and investigated the spalling mechanism of sidewalls of D-shaped tunnels. The results show that the spalling will be inhibited and the depth of the V-notch will be reduced under higher lateral pressure.

Recently, some scholars have paid attention to the dynamic mechanical behavior and failure characteristics of underground tunnels [19–23]. In general, the dynamic disturbance or unloading disturbance can prompt the rapid deformation and energy conversion of surrounding rock in the form of stress waves. Li et al. [19] have indicated that the release of strain energy is closely related to the failure modes of underground tunnels. The result shows that, when roof spalling is induced, the release of strain energy will last for a long time, but when a violent strain rock burst occurs, massive strain energy will be released instantaneously. Si et al. [20] conducted the triaxial unloading compression test and investigated the strength-weakening effect of unloading and unloading rate on fine-grained granite. They found a lower unloading rate more conducive to the improvement of the bearing strength and the storage of elastic energy. In addition, some scholars have also analyzed the influence of disturbance location, in-situ stress, disturbance amplitude and disturbance duration on the dynamic stability of the underground tunnel [24–27]. For example, Qiu et al. [25] carried out a series of physical model tests on deep tunnels and they found that, even when the disturbance distance is the same but the disturbance dip is different, the dynamic stability of deep tunnels varies greatly. Li et al. [26] studied the effect of stress wave wavelength on the failure model of the deep tunnel and found that the short stress wave tends to cause spalling and the length stress wave tends to cause rock burst. Zhu et al. [27] analyzed the failure mechanism of the deep tunnel under different disturbance amplitudes. The results show that, the larger the disturbance amplitude, the more serious the dynamic failure. In addition, Kulynych et al. [28] studied the action process of gaseous products of explosive on rock fracturing behavior and found that the effect of rock mass disturbance would gradually decrease with increased relaxation of defect formation. Slashchov et al. [29] analyzed the relationship between the emanation activity of radon decay products in mining tunnels and the geological dislocations and believed that the hidden tectonic disturbances and high-stress concentrations can be determined by monitoring the gas-dynamic processes in mining tunnels. Arnau et al. [30] compared the dynamic behavior of a double-decker circular tunnel under train-induced loads with that of a simple tunnel and the results showed that the soil response would be significantly different across the frequency range studied. Behshad et al. [31] analyzed the influence of Dynamic Vibration Absorbers (DVA) on the vibration reduction of a double-deck circular railway tunnel and found that DVA can effectively reduce the total energy flow acting on the tunnel when trains pass by.

In underground engineering, numerous tunnels are usually excavated in a limited area, as shown in Figure 1. These tunnels are locally distributed horizontally, vertically and obliquely. During the excavation or internal blasting of these tunnels, existing tunnels will inevitably be affected by the adjacent working area, including the redistribution of static stress and the dynamic response. Usually, the impact of blasting disturbance in the adjacent working area is particularly significant. Numerous previous studies have confirmed the impact of blasting disturbance or dynamic disturbance on adjacent tunnels, which usually causes local stress surges, triggering rock bursts or surrounding rock spalling [19,24–26]. The object of these studies is usually a single tunnel or the tunnel near the disturbance source, but little attention has been paid to multiple tunnels, especially the remote non-adjacent tunnels. Limited studies have analyzed the dynamic behavior of multiple tunnels under dynamic or unloading disturbances [32,33]. For example, Feldgun et al. [33] analyzed the dynamic behavior of a rectangular existing tunnel induced by the internal blasting inside another horizontal parallel tunnel. The results show that the left sidewall of the existing tunnel will bend under the blasting disturbance. Li et al. [32] also analyzed the effect of unloading waves caused by neighboring tunnel excavation on the existing tunnel. The results show that the unloading wave can cause a strong dynamic response of the existing tunnel and the increase of the unloading rate can amplify the dynamic effect. However, due to the multiple transmission and reflection of stress waves among multiple tunnels, the dynamic stability and stress concentration of the non-adjacent tunnel will not only depend on the amplitude and wavelength of the initial incident wave, but also depend on the interaction with the adjacent tunnel. Therefore, the tunnel distribution is also an important factor, which can affect the dynamic response and fracturing behavior around the tunnels triggered by blasting disturbance [34,35]. For this reason, the main object of this study is to analyze the influence of tunnel distribution on the dynamic response and stability of the non-adjacent tunnel under blasting disturbance. Therefore, the numerical models with the two tunnels were established by the particle flow code (PFC2D) method and different tunnel distributions were also considered. In addition, the stress evolution, energy evolution and failure characteristics around the two tunnels caused by blasting disturbance were analyzed. The effect of stress wave wavelength on the dynamic behavior of a non-adjacent tunnel is further discussed.

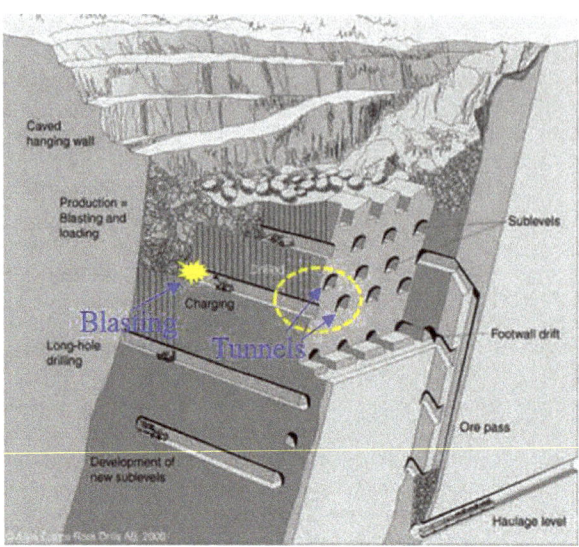

**Figure 1.** Mining methods in Kiruna Iron Mine in Sweden [36].

## 2. Description of Numerical Model

### 2.1. Description of PFC2D

The discrete element method PFC2D is widely used in rock engineering because it has the advantage of synchronous microcracks display and does not need to consider the convergence issue in calculations. PFC2D provides several typical modeling methods to simulate different mechanical properties of materials, such as the contact bond (CB) model, parallel bond (PB) model, smooth joint (SJ) model, flated joint (FJ) model, etc. Generally, the CB model is used to simulate the soil material or the bulk material, because it can only transfer the force and not moments through the contact between particles. The PB model is suitable for rock-like materials because it can effectively transmit forces and moments [37,38]. The SJ model is usually used to simulate structural planes such as joints, cracks and bedding-in materials. FJ mode is an increasingly popular new modeling method for rock-like materials because it provides a more realistic ratio between the tensile strength and compression strength of materials. However, because the FJ model will generate too many micro-cracks, it also has certain disadvantages in observing the failure mode of the rock mass. Therefore, the PB model was chosen to simulate the mechanical behavior of rock mass in this study. As shown in Figure 2a, a series of non-uniform-sized rigid particles can be seen as the basic constituent element of the PB model, the linear contact is arranged between the particles and a parallel bond can be conceived as a finite-size concrete cemented between particles. The mechanical behavior between particles can be assumed to be produced by a series of linear springs, viscous dashpots and two specific boned elements (with the normal and shear strengths $\bar{\sigma}_c$ and $\bar{\tau}_c$) [38], as shown in Figure 2b.

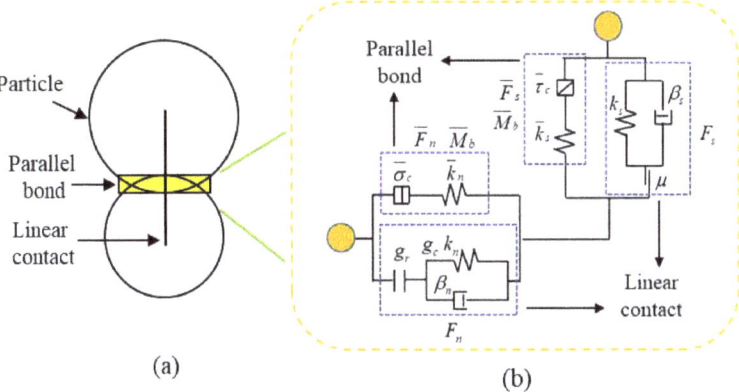

**Figure 2.** Schematic of parallel bond model: (a) composition; (b) mechanical behavior.

For the linear contact, the moment is zero and the contact force can be iterated by:

$$\begin{cases} F_n = F_n^l + F_n^d \\ F_s = F_s^l + F_s^d \end{cases} \quad (1)$$

where the subscripts $n$ and $s$ denote normal and shear direction, respectively. The subscripts $l$ and $d$ denote linear spring and dashpot contributions, respectively. It is worth noting that the contact activation state is determined by the comparison between the contact gap ($g_c$) and the reference gap ($g_r$). When $g_c > g_r$, the linear contact is inactivated and the calculations of force-displacement is ignored. When $g_c \leq g_r$, the linear contact is activated and the force components $F_n^l$, $F_s^l$, $F_n^d$, $F_s^d$ of linear contact can be upgraded by the following equations:

$$F_n^l = k_n(g_r - g_c) \quad (2)$$

$$F_s^l = \begin{cases} (F_s^{(l)})_0 - k_s \Delta U_s & \text{, if the contact is not sliding} \\ \mu F_n & \text{, if the contact is sliding} \end{cases} \quad (3)$$

$$F_n^d = -2\beta_n \sqrt{m_c k_n} v_n \quad (4)$$

$$F_s^d = \begin{cases} -2\beta_s \sqrt{m_c k_s} v_s & \text{, if the contact is not sliding} \\ 0 & \text{, if the contact is sliding} \end{cases} \quad (5)$$

where $(F_s^l)_0$ denotes the shear force of linear contact at the last step. $\Delta U_s$ represents the relative shear displacement increment. $\mu$ denotes the friction coefficient. $m_c$ denotes the effective mass of linear contact. $v_n$ and $v_s$ denote the relative normal velocity and shear velocity, respectively. $k_n$ and $k_s$ denote the normal and shear stiffness of linear contact, respectively.

For the parallel bond, there is a linear relationship between force and displacement. In addition, the bending moment $\overline{M}_b$ is also calculated. The force components $\overline{F}_n$, $\overline{F}_s$ and the bending moment $\overline{M}_b$ can be iterated by:

$$\overline{F}_n := \overline{F}_n - \overline{k}_n A \cdot \Delta U_n \quad (6)$$

$$\overline{F}_s := \overline{F}_s - \overline{k}_n A \cdot \Delta U_s \quad (7)$$

$$\overline{M}_b := \overline{M}_b - \overline{k}_n I \cdot \Delta \theta_b \quad (8)$$

where $A$ is the area of the parallel bond cross-section. $I$ is the moment of inertia of the parallel bond. $\Delta \theta_b$ is the relative rotation increment. $\overline{k}_n$ and $\overline{k}_s$ denote the normal and shear stiffness of parallel bond, respectively. The maximum normal and shear stresses acting on the parallel bond can be calculated:

$$\overline{\sigma}_{max} = \frac{\overline{F}_n}{A} + \frac{|\overline{M}_b|\overline{R}}{I} \qquad (9)$$

$$\overline{\tau}_{max} = \frac{|\overline{F}_s|}{A} \qquad (10)$$

where $\overline{R}$ is the radius of the bond cross-section. The failure state of the parallel bond can be determined by a comparison between these stresses and the tensile and shear strengths

$$\begin{cases} \overline{\sigma}_{max} > \overline{\sigma}_c, \text{ failed in tension} \\ \overline{\tau}_{max} > \overline{\tau}_c, \text{ failed in shear} \end{cases} \qquad (11)$$

where the tensile strength is preset manually and the shear strength can be updated by the Mohr-Coulomb criterion:

$$\overline{\tau}_c = \overline{c} - \overline{\sigma} \tan \phi \qquad (12)$$

where $\overline{c}$ is the cohesion and $\phi$ is the friction angle.

### 2.2. Modelling Procedure and Calibration of PB Model Parameters

Calibration of the numerical model should be performed to obtain appropriate microparameters of the PB model for matching macroscopic behaviors between the numerical model and experiment. In this work, the granite specimens from Linglong gold mine were tested by the uniaxial compression method and the corresponding numerical specimens were established to calibrate these results. A series of trial and error procedures are executed by adjusting the microscopic parameters of the numerical model so that the macroscopic mechanical characteristics of the numerical model, including UCS, elastic modulus and Poisson, have a good match with that of actual granite. The empirical uniaxial compression strength (UCS) is about 158.45 MPa, the elastic modulus is 32.3 GPa and the Poisson's ratio is 0.258. The corresponding numerical results are listed in Table 1. As shown in Table 1, the error between the numerical results and the real granite is less than 5%, indicating that the calibrated numerical model can well represent the real granite. The stress–strain curves and failure modes of the numerical model and granite are also compared in Figure 3 [24]. These results also show that the numerical model is in good agreement with the testing result The obtained calibrated micro-parameters of the PB model are listed in Table 2.

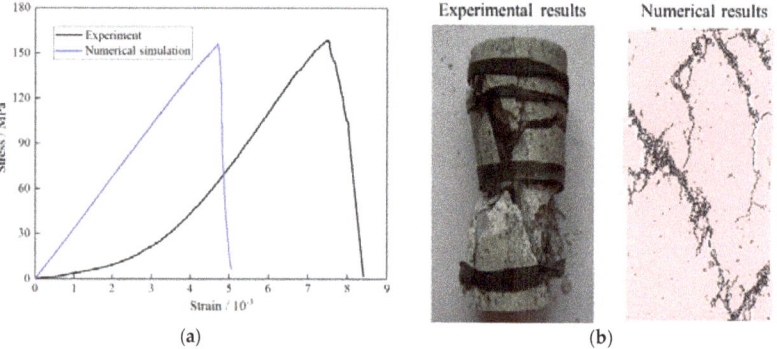

**Figure 3.** Experimental and numerical results of granite specimen under uniaxial compression: (**a**) stress-strain curve; (**b**) failure mode [24].

Table 1. Macro mechanical properties of materials.

| Mechanical Parameters | Granite | Numerical Sample | Error (± %) |
|---|---|---|---|
| Density (kg/m$^3$) | 2740 | 2740 | - |
| Uniaxial compressive strength (MPa) | 158.45 | 156.58 | 1.18 |
| Elastic modulus (GPa) | 32.3 | 31.54 | 2.35 |
| Poisson's ratio | 0.258 | 0.254 | 1.55 |

Table 2. Micro mechanical properties of PB model.

| Component | Parameters | Value |
|---|---|---|
| Particle | Density (kg/m$^3$) | 2740 |
| | Radius (m) | 0.06–0.096 |
| | Damping | 0.1 |
| Linear contact | Modulus $E_c$ (Gpa) | 15.7 |
| | Stiffness ratio ($k_n/k_s$) | 1.9 |
| | Friction coefficient $\mu$ | 0.7 |
| | Normal damping $\beta_n$ | 0 |
| | Shear damping $\beta_s$ | 0 |
| Parallel bond | Friction angle $\phi$ | 30° |
| | Modulus $\bar{E}_c$ (Gpa) | 15.7 |
| | Stiffness ratio ($\bar{k}_n/\bar{k}_s$) | 1.9 |
| | Tensile strength $\bar{\sigma}_c$ (MPa) | 94 ± 10 |
| | Cohesion $\bar{c}$ (MPa) | 94 ± 10 |

The in-situ stress of Linglong Gold Mine was considered in this work. The tunnels are assumed to be excavated along the direction of minimum horizontal principal stress. Thus, the linear functions of the maximum horizontal principal stress and vertical principal stress are presented as follows [39]

$$\sigma_{hmax} = 0.4612 + 0.0588h \tag{13}$$

$$\sigma_v = -0.4683 + 0.0316h \tag{14}$$

where $\sigma_{hmax}$ and $\sigma_v$ are the maximum horizontal principal stress and vertical principal stress, respectively. $h$ is the depth.

The numerical model with dimensions of 48 m × 24 m was established by the calibrated PB model, as shown in Figure 4. The radius of particles is in the range of 0.06 m–0.096 m. The viscous boundary condition is set to reduce the reflected wave at the boundary [40]. The depth of 1200 m was investigated. Correspondingly, the horizontal and vertical stresses applied to the model boundaries are 71.02 MPa and 37.45 MPa, respectively. Two tunnels excavated before these boundary stresses were loaded. The tunnel modelling process in this study involves the main factor: tunnel distribution. As shown in Figure 4, two circular tunnels with the same diameter (4 m) are considered. The distance between the two tunnel centers is set to 8 m. The tunnel dip $\beta$ is defined as the angle between the two tunnel centers and the horizontal direction. As shown in Figure 4a, the tunnel distribution can be obtained by changing the tunnel dip. In this study, three different tunnel dips were considered: 0°, 45,° and 90°.

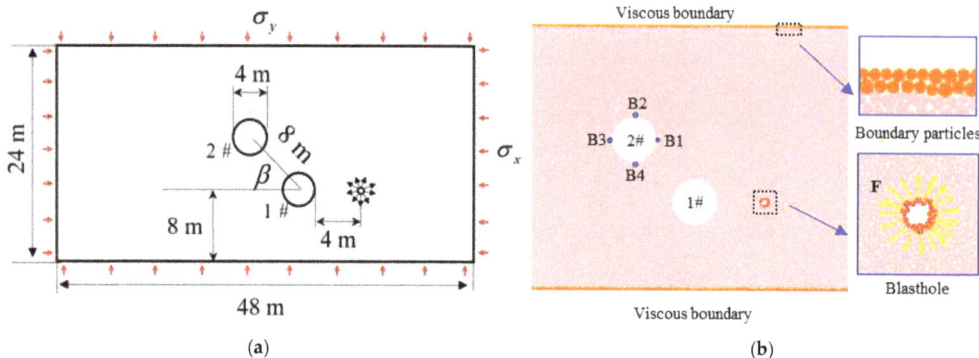

**Figure 4.** Schematic diagram of numerical models: (**a**) numerical model design scheme; (**b**) measuring circles setting and partial numerical model (1#—adjacent tunnel, 2#—non-adjacent tunnel).

The real blasting wave is extremely complex and it is almost impossible to completely reconstruct it through numerical simulation. For this reason, some scholars proposed the simplified triangular wave method to replace the real blasting wave [24,41,42]. Their results show that this simplified triangular wave can effectively reflect the effects of blasting. To this end, the triangular wave method was adopted in this study. Before the blasting, a borehole with a radius of 0.3 m was first excavated, then a triangle stress wave was applied to the borehole periphery, as shown in Figure 5. The tunnel close to the borehole can be regarded as the adjacent tunnel and the tunnel far away from the borehole is the non-adjacent tunnel. The distance between the borehole location and the adjacent tunnel is set as 4 m. The peak stress of the triangle stress wave is 3 GPa, the rising time $t_r$ is 250 μs and the total time $t_m$ is 1250 μs. The time ratio $k = t_m/t_r$, which is defined as the ratio of rising time to total time, is set to 5. Four measuring circles with a radius of 0.3 m are arranged around the non-adjacent tunnel. The measuring circles near the non-adjacent tunnel are named B1, B2, B3 and B4, as shown in Figure 4b.

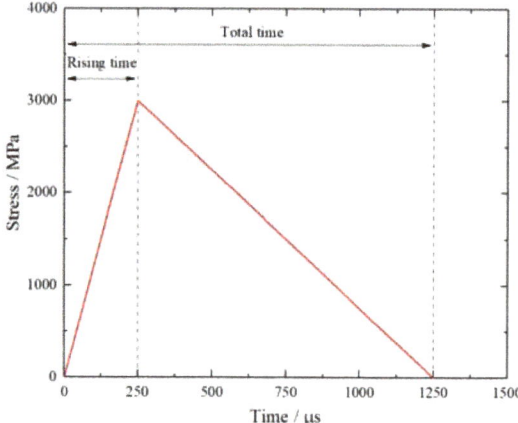

**Figure 5.** Blasting stress wave.

## 3. Modelling Results

### 3.1. Dynamic Stress Characteristics

When a blast is executed, the nearby surrounding rock will directly break into pieces and the far-field surrounding rock will accumulate or release deformation under the attenuated stress wave, causing unexpected damage. Generally, the stress evolution of surrounding rock induced by the blasting disturbance is mainly manifested in two aspects: dynamic stress and static stress. In PFC2D, the stress recorded by the measuring circle actually includes the static part and dynamic part. Figure 6 presents the typical stress–time curve recorded by measuring circles. It can be seen from Figure 6 that the static stress before blasting ($t < 0$ μs) is usually a stable value and the static stress after blasting will be stabilized again. For expedient analysis, the dynamic part is separated from the superimposed curve in the subsequent sections. Furthermore, it should be noted that the tensile stress is positive and the compressive stress is negative.

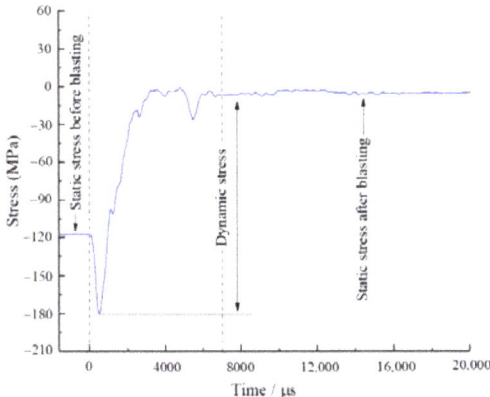

**Figure 6.** Typical stress–time curve recorded by measuring circle.

In the periphery of the tunnel, the radial stress is usually very small, so only the tangential stress is discussed in this study. In this section, the dynamic tangential stress was examined. Figure 7 presents the tangential stress waves around non-adjacent tunnels under different tunnel dips. As shown in Figure 7, these stress curves generally undergo one or multiple peaks, of which the compression peak is less than zero and the tensile peak is greater than zero. It can be found these peaks exhibit different variation trends at different locations, as follows:

(1) For zone B1, when $\beta = 0°$ and $45°$, the maximum tensile peaks are generally greater than the maximum compression peaks, so attention should be paid to the tensile failure of surrounding rock in the vicinity of this zone. When $\beta = 90°$, the tensile peak is not obvious and the maximum compression peak is 180.4 MPa, which is far greater than the maximum tensile stress. The result shows that, when $\beta = 90°$, the compression failure tends to occur near zone B1.

(2) For zone B2, the maximum tensile peak is generally greater than the maximum compression peak, which indicates that the tensile failure tends to be near this zone.

(3) For zone B3, the stress amplitudes of these curves are commonly smaller than those of other zones. When $\beta = 0°$ and $45°$, the maximum peak stress is tensile and when $\beta = 90°$, the maximum stress is compressive. The result is similar to that of zone B1.

(4) For zone B4, the result is similar to that of zone B2, in which the maximum stress is generally tensile. In addition, it should be noted that, when $\beta = 90°$, the tensile peak is also not obvious.

(5) Generally, the stress wave waveform will not change significantly in zones B2 and B4, but the stress amplitude will. In zones B1 and B3, both the waveform and amplitude of the stress wave will change. In addition, it can be observed that the first peaks of zones B1, B3 and B4 decrease first and then increase and the first peaks of zone B2 increase first and then decrease.

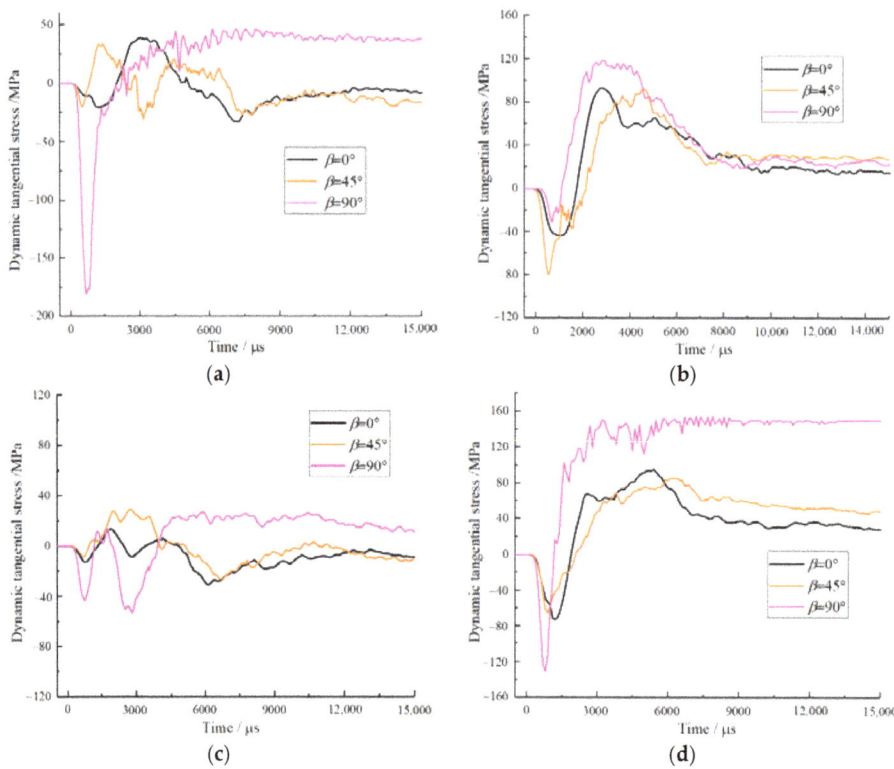

**Figure 7.** Tangential stress waves around non-adjacent tunnel under different tunnel dips: (a) B1; (b) B2; (c) B3; (d) B4.

### 3.2. Damage Characteristics

Figure 8 presents the microcrack distribution under different tunnel dips. As shown in Figure 8, when $\beta = 0°$, the microcracks were mainly distributed in the right sidewall of the adjacent tunnel and almost no microcracks were formed in the vicinity of the non-adjacent tunnel. When $\beta = 45°$, there are some microcracks distributed at the roof, right sidewall and floor of the non-adjacent tunnel and the vicinity of the adjacent tunnel, while almost no microcracks are generated between the adjacent and non-adjacent tunnels. Besides, it can be observed that the failure on the right sidewall of the non-adjacent tunnel is spalling. When $\beta = 90°$, there are a large number of microcracks generated at the roof, right sidewall and floor of the non-adjacent tunnel. Obviously, the larger the tunnel dip is, the more severe the damage to the non-adjacent tunnel caused by blasting disturbance. In addition, it can also be found that, when $\beta = 90°$, an obvious penetrating failure zone merges between adjacent and the non-adjacent tunnels. Based on these results, it can be inferred that, when the tunnel dip exceeds a critical value, the disaster hazard induced by blasting will be more severe, because the cascading failure tends to occur between multiple tunnels.

Figure 9 shows the development process of this microcrack. As shown in Figure 9, the microcrack development process can be generally divided into four stages: no crack generation stage ($t < 0.1$ ms), rapid microcrack growth stage ($t = 0.1$–$2.5$ ms), slow microcrack growth stage ($t = 2.5$–$5.6$ ms) and stable microcrack stage ($t < 5.6$ ms). In the no crack generation stage ($t < 0.1$ ms), there are almost no new microcracks formations in the models. In the rapid microcrack growth stage ($t = 0.1$–$2.5$ ms), the microcracks will increase rapidly and the damage caused by this stage is also the most serious. In this stage, the microcrack curves of different tunnel dip almost coincide, because the damage of surrounding rock is mainly concentrated around the borehole and the left sidewall of the adjacent tunnel. In the slow microcrack growth stage ($t > 2.5$ ms), the damage begins to occur around the non-adjacent tunnel as the stress wave propagation. Therefore, the three microcrack curves gradually separate. In this stage, the growth rate of the microcrack gradually slows down. In the stable microcrack stage ($t > 5.6$ ms), the total number of microcracks in the surrounding rock gradually tends to be stable and the damage of the surrounding rock is basically completed.

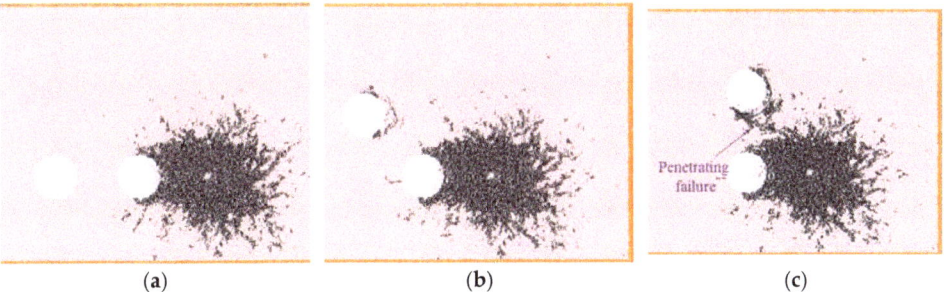

**Figure 8.** Microcrack distribution under different tunnel dip: (**a**) $\beta = 0°$; (**b**) $\beta = 45°$; (**c**) $\beta = 90°$.

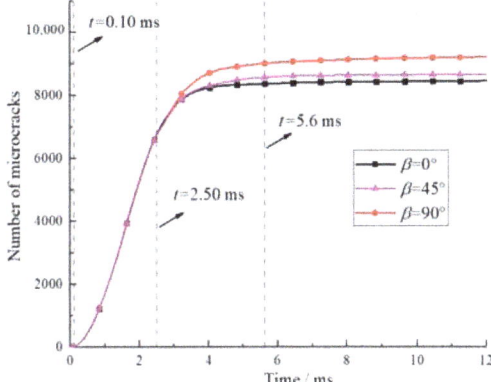

**Figure 9.** Development process of the microcrack.

### 3.3. Evolution Characteristics of Strain Energy

The blasting disturbance usually causes the accumulation, release and dissipation of the strain energy. Some studies believe that the evolution of strain energy is a major cause of disasters and an important feature reflecting the stability of surrounding rock. [4,43–45]. For example, Li et al. [4] assessed the rock burst characteristics around a tunnel based on an energy index, namely strain energy density (SED). The results show that as a large amount of strain energy is released, the strain rock burst will occur on the floor and corner. Luo and Gong [43] also assessed the established invariable feature of the ultimate internal elastic index based on the law of energy release and dissipation during rock failure. To accurately evaluate the evolution characteristics of strain energy, the strain energy density (SED) is applied in this work because it is not affected by the volume of the measuring area. According to PFC2D, the strain energy stored in linear contact and parallel bond can be obtained:

$$E_s = \frac{1}{2}(\frac{|F_n|^2}{k_n} + \frac{|F_s|^2}{k_s}) \qquad (15)$$

$$\overline{E}_s = \frac{1}{2}\left(\frac{|\overline{F}_n|^2}{A\overline{k}_n} + \frac{|\overline{F}_s|^2}{A\overline{k}_s} + \frac{|\overline{M}_b|^2}{I\overline{k}_n}\right) \qquad (16)$$

where $E_s$ and $\overline{E}_s$ denote the strain energies of linear contact and parallel bond, respectively. $F_n$ and $F_s$ denote the normal and shear force of linear contact, respectively. $\overline{F}_n$ and $\overline{F}_s$ denote the normal and shear force of parallel bond, respectively. Therefore, the SED can be given by:

$$SED = \frac{\sum_m (E_s)_i + (\overline{E}_s)_i}{A'} \qquad (17)$$

where $m$ is the total number of linear contacts in the measuring area. $A'$ is the area of the measuring area.

Figure 10 shows the SED-time curve of typical areas under different tunnel dips. As shown in Figure 10, before the blasting wave arrives ($t < 0$ μs), some strain energy is accumulated in the surrounding rock and can be regarded as the initial SED. During the blasting, the SED will increase sharply, then release rapidly and finally reach an approximately stable value (final SED). In addition, it can be found that, for zones B1 and B3, the maximum SEDs tend to decrease first and then increase with the tunnel dip. However, for zone B2, the maximum SEDs increase first and then decrease with the tunnel dip, which is contrary to the cases of zones B1 and B3. For zone B4, the maximum SEDs are positively correlated with tunnel dip. Furthermore, it can be found that, after the blasting wave path, the strain energy does not recover to the initial value, indicating that the blasting disturbance causes some irreversible deformation and even some severe damage.

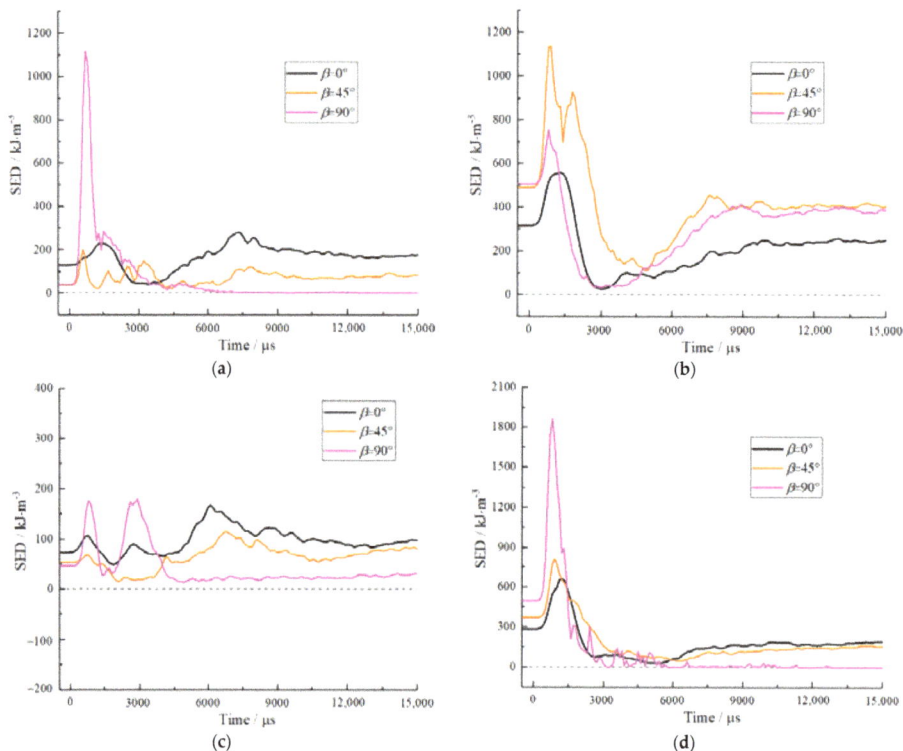

**Figure 10.** SED-time curve of typical zones under different tunnel dips: (**a**) B1; (**b**) B2; (**c**) B3; (**d**) B4.

## 4. Discussion

In the past decades, some scholars have realized that the stress wave wavelength is an important factor affecting and controlling the failure characteristics of surrounding rock [30,46,47]. For this reason, we will focus on the influence of stress wave wavelength on the dynamic response and damage characteristics of the non-adjacent tunnel. Generally, the different stress wave wavelengths can be obtained by adjusting the duration of the stress wave. Therefore, in this section, the blasting wave amplitude and rise time are kept the same as those in Section 2.2 and three time ratios $k = t_m/t_r$ (2.5, 5 and 10) are set.

Usually, the damage behavior of the surrounding rock is controlled by its total stress. However, the total stress of the surrounding rock is not only related to the dynamic stress but also closely related to the static stress. In order to accurately evaluate the dynamic effect caused by blasting disturbance, some scholars generally define a dynamic stress amplification factor (DSAF) [40,48]. For this reason, a dynamic stress amplification factor is applied to this work:

$$\varphi = \max\left(\frac{\sigma(t)}{\sigma_{s0}}\right) \tag{18}$$

where $\varphi$ is the dynamic stress amplification factor. $\sigma(t)$ is the total stress and $\sigma_{s0}$ is the static stress before blasting. Figure 11 presents the dynamic stress amplification factor around a non-adjacent tunnel. As shown in Figure 11, for zone B1, the DSAFs increase slightly at first and then increase sharply with the tunnel dip $\beta$. For zone B2, the DSAFs tend to increase first and then decrease with the tunnel dip. Especially, when the time ratio $k = 10$, the DSFA decreases slightly at first. For zones B3 and B4, the DSAFs tend to decrease initially and then increase with the tunnel dip, but for the case of $k = 2.5$, it can be found that the DSAFs monotonically increase with the tunnel dip. On the other hand, the DSAF generally increases with the time ratio $k$, which means that the longer the stress wave wavelength, the greater the total maximum stress in the surrounding rock.

Figure 12 presents the microcrack distribution in surrounding rock under different wavelengths. When $\beta = 0°$, there are almost no microcracks around the non-adjacent tunnel, but when the wavelength increases to a certain extent (e.g., $k = 10$), the microcracks will gradually extend from the adjacent tunnel to the non-adjacent tunnel, such as the microcrack C1. This phenomenon shows that, when the wavelength exceeds a certain critical value, the instability of adjacent tunnels may lead to instability in non-adjacent tunnels. When $\beta = 45°$ and $\beta = 90°$, it is clear that, with the increase of time ratio $k$, the damage around the non-adjacent tunnel becomes more and more serious. Besides, the interaction between the two tunnels seems to be more obvious under the higher wavelength. For example, when $\beta = 45°$, no penetrating failure zone forms between the two tunnels under the smaller time ratios (e.g., $k = 2.5$), but does do so under larger time ratios (e.g., $k = 10$). Certainly, when $\beta = 90°$, the penetrating failure zones were also formed between the two tunnels, but it is obvious that the penetrating failure zones increase with the wavelength. These results show that the long stress wave is more likely to cause damage to the non-adjacent tunnel than the short stress wave. Therefore, the designing and protecting strategy of underground engineering can be optimized. For example, for dynamic disturbance with a short wavelength, the roof and floor of a non-adjacent tunnel should be protected. However, for dynamic disturbance with a long wavelength, the areas between the adjacent tunnel and non-adjacent tunnel should also be monitored to determine whether there is a trend of penetrating failure.

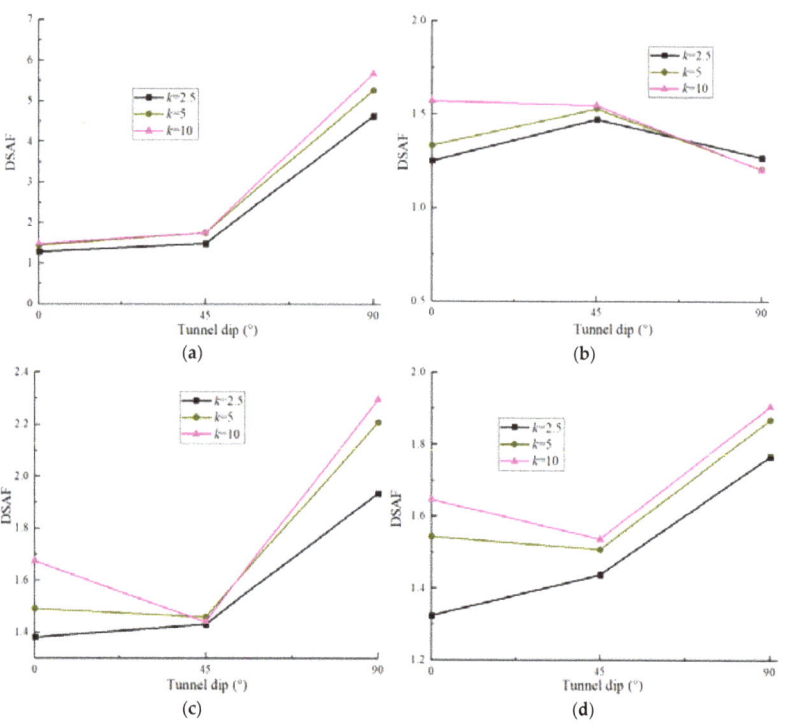

**Figure 11.** Dynamic stress amplification factor under various tunnel dips and wavelengths: (**a**) B1; (**b**) B2; (**c**) B3; (**d**) B4.

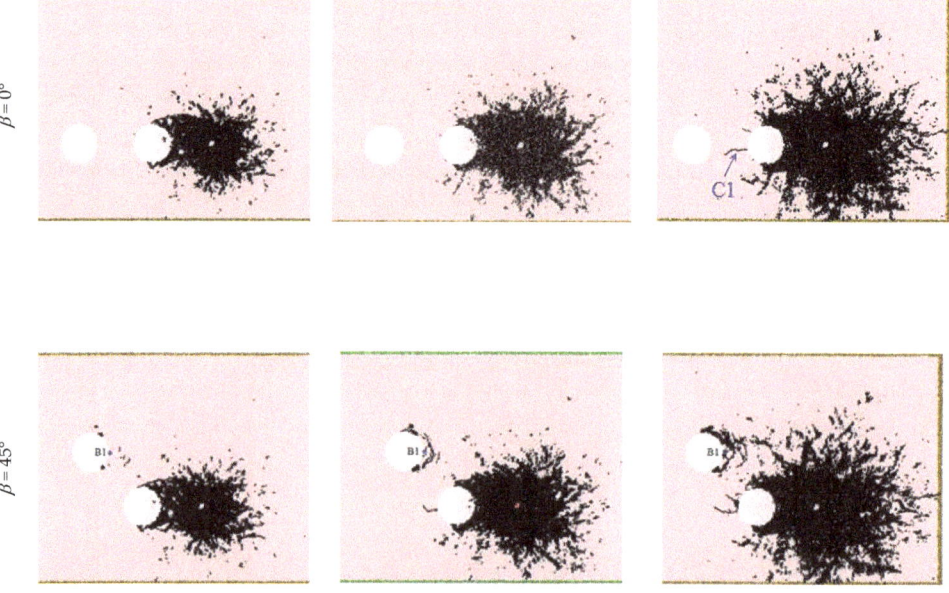

**Figure 12.** *Cont.*

$\beta = 90°$

$k = 2.5$

$k = 5$

$k = 10$

**Figure 12.** Microcrack distribution in surrounding rock under different wavelength.

The rapid release of strain energy is an important index of rock burst intensity. Generally, more release of strain energy will cause severe rock burst. To further evaluate the strain energy evolution law before and after blasting, the SED variation is defined, which is the difference between initial SED and final SED. The value of SED variation greater than zero represents the accumulation of strain energy and the value less than zero represents the release of strain energy.

Figure 13 presents the variation of strain energy density before and after blasting. For zone B1, the SED variations tend to initially increase and then decrease with the tunnel dip $\beta$. Especially, when $k = 10$, the SED variation directly decreases with the tunnel dip $\beta$. This is the reason that the accumulated deformation of zone B1 tends to increase with the tunnel dip $\beta$, but when the tunnel dip approaches a specific value, some damage will occur around the zone B1, which leads to the partial deformation recovery of the zone B1 and the decrease in SED variation. For example, when $\beta = 45°$ and $k = 2.5$ or 5, there is almost no damage in zone B1, so the corresponding SED variation is positive; but when $\beta = 45°$ and $k = 10$, there is obvious damage in zone B1 (as shown in Figure 12), so the corresponding SED variation is negative.

For zone B2, as the tunnel dip $\beta$ increases, the damage to surrounding rock will be more and more serious. Therefore, the SED variation tends to decrease with the tunnel dip $\beta$ (such as in the case of $k = 5$ and 10). Especially, when $k = 2.5$, the SED variation exhibits a trend of decreasing first and then increasing. This is because, when the tunnel dip is 90°, the total energy obtained by zone B2 is greater than those of the other dips. Another reason is that when $k = 2.5$, the stress wavelength is too short and there is not enough damage in zone B2. The combination of these two causes leads to the insufficient release of strain energy. Therefore, the SED variation in the case of $\beta = 90°$ and $k = 2.5$ is the largest.

For zones B3 and B4, the SED variations decrease with the tunnel dip $\beta$. In addition, it is worth noting that, for zones B2 and B4, the SED variation decreases with the time ratio $k$. The results suggest that the strain energy release of the roof and floor will increase with the wavelength. For zones B1 and B3, there is no simple positive or negative correlation between the SED variation and wavelength.

In summary, the stress evolution, energy evolution and damage characteristics of the surrounding rock are closely related to the tunnel dip and stress wave wavelength. In practical engineering, the effect of the nearby blasting disturbance can be predicted to a certain extent based on the existing wavelength information of the blasting wave and tunnel distribution information. For example, in two successive blasting activities with different charge lengths, the information of the second blasting, such as the damage and energy evolution characteristics of the roof and floor of the non-adjacent tunnel, can be effectively predicted based on the first blasting. Therefore, it is very necessary to evaluate the dynamic response and damage of non-adjacent tunnels with different tunnel distributions. It should be noted that the real rock stratum may contain a large number of random discontinuities (not considered in this study). According to previous studies [49,50], these discontinuities often affect the mechanical behavior of surrounding rock widely. Therefore, in our subsequent research, the properties of these discontinuities, including size, density, distribution and cohesiveness, will be further considered to reveal the dynamic behavior of the tunnels.

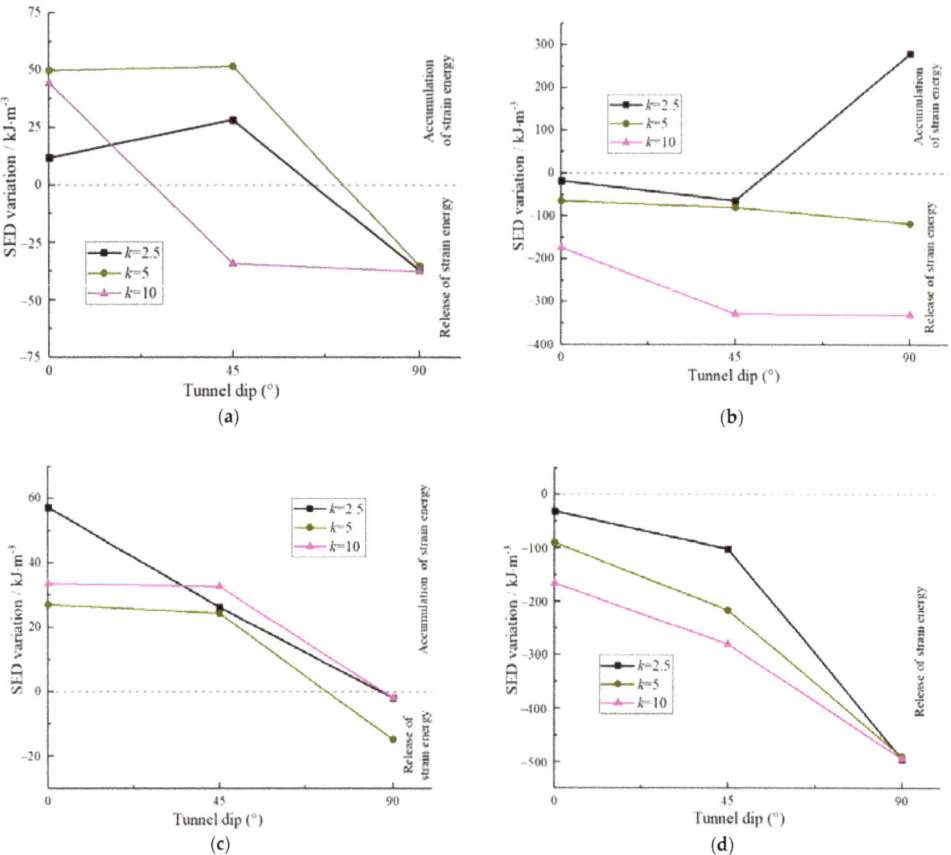

**Figure 13.** Variation of strain energy density before and after blasting: (**a**) B1; (**b**) B2; (**c**) B3; (**d**) B4.

## 5. Conclusions

This work extends the existing research on the mechanical problem of multiple tunnels under static load to the dynamic problem, because blasting disturbance often triggers a different mechanical response from that under static load. In addition, it is also different from previous studies in that the focus of this work has shifted from a single tunnel or the tunnel near the disturbance source to a remote non-adjacent tunnel. To study the dynamic behavior of the non-adjacent tunnel, the numerical models of two tunnels with different distributions were established by the particle flow code (PFC2D).

The dynamic stress evolution around the non-adjacent tunnel is initially examined. It can be found that the tunnel distribution can affect the dynamic stress response around the non-adjacent tunnel. In the roof and floor of the non-adjacent tunnel, the stress wave waveform is commonly unchanged, while the stress amplitude will change obviously. In the sidewalls of the non-adjacent tunnel, both the waveform and amplitude of the stress wave will change obviously. In addition, the damage of the surrounding rock is closely related to the tunnel distribution. Generally, the damage around the non-adjacent tunnel increases with the tunnel dips. When $\beta = 0°$, there is no damage around the non-adjacent tunnel, but when $\beta = 90°$, there is obvious damage around the non-adjacent tunnel and the penetrating failure forms between the two tunnels. On the other hand, the evolution of strain energy was examined. In general, the strain energy density (SED) will undergo a stage of rapid accumulation and release and the maximum strain energy density in different areas around the non-adjacent tunnel will show different trends with the increase in tunnel dip.

The dynamic response and damage characteristic of the non-adjacent tunnel caused by the blasting wave with different wavelengths was further examined. It can be found that the tunnel dip has an obvious influence on the dynamic stress amplification factor (DSAF) and the effect of tunnel dip changes with wavelength. Generally, the DSAF around the non-adjacent tunnel increases with the wavelength. By observing the distribution characteristics of microcracks around non-adjacent tunnel under different wavelength, it can be found that the long wavelength is more likely to induce rock mass damage than the short wavelength. Subsequently, the SED variation before and after blasting was further analyzed. In the right sidewall of the non-adjacent tunnel, the SED variations tend to increase first and then decrease with the tunnel dip. In the roof of the non-adjacent tunnel, the SED variations tend to decrease with the tunnel dip. In the left sidewall and floor, the SED variations tend to decrease with the tunnel dip. In addition, the longer the wavelength, the more conducive to the strain energy release of the roof and floor. Overall, this study provides some insight into the dynamic behavior of local twin tunnels. Some prediction and analysis, including stability analysis of surrounding rock, vibration assessment of surrounding rock and optimization and control of blasting method, can be preliminarily given.

**Author Contributions:** Methodology, J.Q.; investigation, J.Q. and F.F.; writing—original draft preparation, J.Q.; writing—review and editing F.F.; project administration, J.Q.; funding acquisition, F.F. All authors have read and agreed to the published version of the manuscript.

**Funding:** This research was funded by the National Natural Science Foundation of China (No. 52004143) and the China postdoctoral science foundation (2020M682881 and 2021T140473).

**Data Availability Statement:** The data used to support the findings of this study are available from the corresponding author upon request.

**Conflicts of Interest:** The authors declared that there are no conflict of interest to the work submitted.

## References

1. Xie, H.P.; Gao, F.; Ju, Y.; Zhang, R.; Gao, M.Z.; Deng, J.H. Novel idea and disruptive technologies for the exploration and research of deep earth. *Adv. Eng. Sci.* **2017**, *49*, 1–8. (In Chinese)
2. Wang, S.; Sun, L.; Li, X.; Zhou, J.; Du, K.; Wang, S.; Khandelwal, M. Experimental investigation and theoretical analysis of indentations on cuboid hard rock using a conical pick under uniaxial lateral stress. *Geomech. Geophys. Geo-Energ. Geo-Resour.* **2022**, *8*, 34. [CrossRef]
3. Feng, F.; Chen, S.J.; Li, D.Y.; Hu, S.T.; Huang, W.P.; Li, B. Analysis of fractures of a hard rock specimen via unloading of central hole with different sectional shapes. *Energy Sci. Eng.* **2019**, *7*, 2265–2286. [CrossRef]
4. Weng, L.; Huang, L.; Taheri, A.; Li, X.B. Rockburst characteristics and numerical simulation based on a strain energy density index: A case study of a roadway in Linglong gold mine, china. *Tunn. Undergr. Space Technol.* **2017**, *69*, 223–232. [CrossRef]
5. Chen, S.J.; Feng, F.; Wang, Y.J.; Li, D.Y.; Huang, W.P.; Zhao, X.D.; Jiang, N. Tunnel failure in hard rock with multiple weak planes due to excavation unloading of in-situ stress. *J. Cent. South. Un.* **2020**, *27*, 2864–2882. [CrossRef]
6. Lu, J.; Yin, G.Z.; Gao, H.; Li, X.; Zhang, D.M.; Deng, B.Z.; Wu, M.Y.; Li, M.H. True triaxial experimental study of disturbed compound dynamic disaster in deep underground coal mine. *Rock Mech. Rock Eng.* **2020**, *53*, 2347–2364. [CrossRef]
7. Xie, H.P.; Gao, F.; Ju, Y. Research and development of rock mechanics in deep ground engineering. *Chin. J. Rock Mech. Eng.* **2015**, *34*, 2161–2178. (In Chinese)
8. Li, X.B.; Qiu, J.D.; Zhao, Y.Z.; Chen, Z.H.; Li, D.Y. Instantaneous and long-term deformation characteristics of deep room-pillar system induced by pillar recovery. *Trans. Nonferrous Met. Soc. China* **2020**, *30*, 2775–2791. [CrossRef]
9. Li, D.Y.; Han, Z.Y.; Sun, X.L.; Zhou, T.; Li, X.B. Dynamic mechanical properties and fracturing behavior of marble specimens containing single and double flaws in SHPB tests. *Rock Mech. Rock Eng.* **2019**, *52*, 1623–1643. [CrossRef]

10. Lu, J.; Zhang, D.M.; Huang, G.; Li, X.; Gao, H.; Yin, G.Z. Effects of loading rate on the compound dynamic disaster in deep underground coal mine. *Int. J. Rock Mech. Min. Sci.* **2020**, *134*, 104453. [CrossRef]
11. Brady, B.H.G. *Rock Mechanics: For Underground Mining*; Springer: Berlin, Germany, 2004.
12. Timoshenko, S.; Goodier, J.N. *Theory of Elasticity*; McGrawHill Book Company: New York, NY, USA, 1951.
13. Exadaktylos, G.E.; Stavropoulou, M.C. A closed form elastic solution for stresses and displacements around tunnels. *Int. J. Rock Mech. Min. Sci.* **2002**, *39*, 905–916. [CrossRef]
14. Zhao, K.; Liu, C.W.; Zhang, G.L. Solution for perimeter stresses of rocks around a rectangular chamber using the complex function of elastic mechanics. *J. Min. Safety Eng.* **2007**, *24*, 361–365. (In Chinese)
15. Zhu, W.C.; Liu, J.; Tang, C.A.; Zhao, X.D.; Brady, B.H. Simulation of progressive fracturing processes around underground excavations under biaxial compression. *Tunn. Undergr. Space Technol.* **2005**, *20*, 231–247. [CrossRef]
16. Gong, F.Q.; Luo, Y.; Li, X.B.; Si, X.F.; Tao, M. Experimental simulation investigation on rockburst induced by spalling failure in deep circular tunnels. *Tunn. Undergr. Space Technol.* **2018**, *81*, 413–427. [CrossRef]
17. Si, X.F.; Huang, L.Q.; Li, X.B.; Ma, C.D.; Gong, F.Q. Experimental investigation of spalling failure of D-shaped tunnel under three-dimensional high-stress conditions in hard rock. *Rock Mech. Rock Eng.* **2021**, *54*, 3017–3038. [CrossRef]
18. Luo, Y. Influence of water on mechanical behavior of surrounding rock in hard-rock tunnels: An experimental simulation. *Eng. Geo.* **2020**, *277*, 105816. [CrossRef]
19. Li, X.B.; Weng, L. Numerical investigation on fracturing behaviors of deep-buried opening under dynamic disturbance. *Tunn. Undergr. Space Technol.* **2016**, *54*, 61–72. [CrossRef]
20. Si, X.F.; Gong, F.Q. Strength-weakening effect and shear-tension failure mode transformation mechanism of rockburst for fine-grained granite under triaxial unloading compression. *Int. J. Rock Mech. Min. Sci.* **2020**, *131*, 104347. [CrossRef]
21. Xia, X.; Li, H.B.; Li, J.C.; Liu, B.; Yu, C. A case study on rock damage prediction and control method for underground tunnels subjected to adjacent excavation blasting. *Tunn. Undergr. Space Technol.* **2013**, *35*, 1–7. [CrossRef]
22. Chen, Z.; Huang, L.Q.; Li, X.B.; Weng, L.; Wang, S. Influences of the height to diameter ratio on the failure characteristics of marble under unloading conditions. *Int. J. Geomech.* **2020**, *20*, 04020148. [CrossRef]
23. Feng, F.; Chen, S.J.; Wang, Y.J.; Huang, W.P.; Han, Z.Y. Cracking mechanism and strength criteria evaluation of granite affected by intermediate principal stresses subjected to unloading stress state. *Int. J. Rock Mech. Min. Sci.* **2021**, *143*, 104783. [CrossRef]
24. Qiu, J.D.; Li, D.Y.; Li, X.B.; Zhu, Q.Q. Numerical investigation on the stress evolution and failure behavior for deep roadway under blasting disturbance. *Soil. Dyn. Earthq. Eng.* **2020**, *137*, 106278. [CrossRef]
25. Qiu, J.D.; Li, X.B.; Li, D.Y.; Zhao, Y.Z.; Hu, C.W.; Liang, L.S. Physical model test on the deformation behavior of an underground tunnel under blasting disturbance. *Rock Mech. Rock Eng.* **2021**, *54*, 91–108. [CrossRef]
26. Li, C.J.; Li, X.B. Influence of wavelength-to-tunnel-diameter ratio on dynamic response of underground tunnels subjected to blasting loads. *Int. J. Rock Mech. Min. Sci.* **2018**, *112*, 323–338. [CrossRef]
27. Zhu, W.C.; Zuo, Y.J.; Shang, S.M.; Li, Z.H.; Tang, C.A. Numerical simulation of instable failure of deep rock tunnel triggered by dynamic disturbance. *Chin. J. Rock Mech. Eng.* **2007**, *26*, 915–921. (In Chinese)
28. Kulynych, V.; Chebenko, V.; Puzyr, R.; Pieieva, I. Modelling the influence of gaseous products of explosive detonation on the processes of crack treatment while rock blasting. *Min. Miner. Depos.* **2021**, *15*, 102–107. [CrossRef]
29. Slashchova, O.; Yalanskyi, O. Forecast of potentially dangerous rock pressure manifestations in the mine roadways by using information technology and radiometric control methods. *Min. Miner. Depos.* **2019**, *13*, 9–17. [CrossRef]
30. Arnau, C.; Robert, A.; Jordi, R.; Teresa, P. Dynamic response of a double-deck circular tunnel embedded in a full-space. *Tunn. Undergr. Space. Technol.* **2016**, *59*, 146–156.
31. Behshad, N.; Robert, A.; Arnau, C.; Jordi, R. Control of ground-borne underground railway-induced vibration from double-deck tunnel infrastructures by means of dynamic vibration absorbers. *J. Sound Vib.* **2019**, *461*, 114914.
32. Li, C.J.; Li, X.B.; Liang, L.S. Dynamic response of existing tunnel under cylindrical unloading wave. *Int. J. Rock Mech. Min. Sci.* **2020**, *131*, 104342. [CrossRef]
33. Feldgun, V.R.; Karinski, Y.S.; Yankelevsky, D.Z. The effect of an explosion in a tunnel on a neighboring buried structure. *Tunn. Undergr. Space Technol.* **2014**, *44*, 42–55. [CrossRef]
34. Chen, R.S.; Chen, W.S.; Hao, H.; Li, J.D. Effect of internal explosion on tunnel secondary and adjacent structures: A review. *Tunn. Undergr. Space Technol.* **2022**, *126*, 104536. [CrossRef]
35. Li, J.C.; Li, H.B.; Ma, G.W.; Zhou, Y.X. Assessment of underground tunnel stability to adjacent tunnel explosion. *Tunn. Undergr. Space Technol.* **2013**, *35*, 227–234. [CrossRef]
36. Wen, X. Investigation report on intelligent mining technology of Kiruna Iron Mine. *Min. Technol.* **2014**, *14*, 1343–1347. (In Chinese) [CrossRef]
37. Qiu, J.D.; Luo, L.; Li, X.B.; Li, D.Y.; Chen, Y.; Luo, Y. Numerical investigation on the tensile fracturing behavior of rock-shotcrete interface based on discrete element method. *Int. J. Min. Sci. Technol.* **2020**, *3*, 293–301. [CrossRef]
38. Itasca Consulting Group Inc. *Pfc2d User's Manual, Version 4.0*; Itasca Consulting Group Inc.: Minneapolis, MN, USA, 2008.
39. Cai, M.F.; Liu, W.D.; Li, Y. In-situ stress measurement at deep position of Linglong gold mine and distribution of in-situ stress field in mine area. *Chin. J. Rock Mech. Eng.* **2010**, *29*, 227–233. (In Chinese)
40. Li, X.B.; Li, C.J.; Cao, W.Z.; Tao, M. Dynamic stress concentration and energy evolution of deep buried tunnels under blasting loads. *Int. J. Min. Sci. Tech.* **2018**, *104*, 131–146. [CrossRef]

41. Gibson, R.L.; Toksöz, M.N.; Dong, W. Seismic radiation from explosively loaded cavities in isotropic and transversely isotropic media. *Bull. Seismol. Soc. Am.* **1996**, *86*, 1910–1924.
42. Krauthammer, T.; Astarlioglu, S.; Blasko, J.; Soh, T.B.; Ng, P.H. Pressure–impulse diagrams for the behavior assessment of structural components. *Int. J. Impact Eng.* **2008**, *35*, 771–783. [CrossRef]
43. Luo, S.; Gong, F. Linear energy storage and dissipation laws of rocks under preset angle shear conditions. *Rock Mech. Rock Eng.* **2020**, *53*, 3303–3323. [CrossRef]
44. Mansurov, V.A. Prediction of rockbursts by analysis of induced seismicity data. *Int. J. Rock Mech. Min. Sci.* **2001**, *38*, 893–901. [CrossRef]
45. Ma, D.; Wang, J.J.; Cai, X.; Ma, X.T.; Zhang, J.X.; Zhou, Z.L. Effects of height/diameter ratio on failure and damage properties of granite under coupled bending and splitting deformation. *Eng. Fract. Mech.* **2019**, *220*, 106640. [CrossRef]
46. Zhang, Y.; Liu, Y.X.; Tan, Y.Z.; Feng, J. Effect of underground stress waves with varied wavelengths on dynamic responses of tunnels. *Geotech. Geol. Eng.* **2017**, *35*, 2371–2380. [CrossRef]
47. Wang, X.; Cai, M. Influence of wavelength-to-excavation span ratio on ground motion around deep underground excavations. *Tunn. Undergr. Space Technol.* **2015**, *49*, 438–453. [CrossRef]
48. Pao, Y.H.; Mow, C.C. Diffraction of elastic waves and dynamic stress concentrations. *J. Appl. Mech.* **1973**, *40*, 213–219. [CrossRef]
49. Xia, C.C.; Sun, Z.Q. *Jointed Rock Mechanics of Engineering Rock*; Tongji University Press: Shanghai, China, 2002. (In Chinese)
50. Prudencio, M.; Jan, M.V.S. Strength and failure modes of rock mass models with non-persistent joints. *Int. J. Rock Mech. Min. Sci.* **2007**, *44*, 890–902. [CrossRef]

*Article*

# Mechanical Properties and Strength Evolution Model of Sandstone Subjected to Freeze–Thaw Weathering Process: Considering the Confining Pressure Effect

Xin Xiong [1,2], Feng Gao [1,2,*], Keping Zhou [1,2], Chun Yang [1,2] and Jielin Li [1,2]

1. School of Resources and Safety Engineering, Central South University, Changsha 410083, China
2. Research Center for Mining Engineering and Technology in Cold Regions, Central South University, Changsha 410083, China
* Correspondence: csugaofeng@csu.edu.cn

**Citation:** Xiong, X.; Gao, F.; Zhou, K.; Yang, C.; Li, J. Mechanical Properties and Strength Evolution Model of Sandstone Subjected to Freeze–Thaw Weathering Process: Considering the Confining Pressure Effect. *Mathematics* **2022**, *10*, 3841. https://doi.org/10.3390/math10203841

Academic Editor: Fernando Simoes

Received: 4 September 2022
Accepted: 13 October 2022
Published: 17 October 2022

**Publisher's Note:** MDPI stays neutral with regard to jurisdictional claims in published maps and institutional affiliations.

**Copyright:** © 2022 by the authors. Licensee MDPI, Basel, Switzerland. This article is an open access article distributed under the terms and conditions of the Creative Commons Attribution (CC BY) license (https://creativecommons.org/licenses/by/4.0/).

**Abstract:** Freeze-and-thaw (F&T) weathering cycles induced by day–night and seasonal temperature changes cause a large number of rock mass engineering disasters in cold areas. Investigating the impact of F&T weathering process on the strength and deformation characteristics of frozen–thawed rocks is therefore of critical scientific importance for evaluating the stability and optimizing the design of rock mass engineering in these areas. In this research, the evolution characteristics of F&T damage were analyzed based on $T_2$ spectrum distribution curves of sandstone specimens before and after F&T weathering cycles. The coupling impact of the quantity of F&T weathering cycles and confining pressure on pre-peak and post-peak deformation behaviors of sandstone specimens were analyzed in detail. By introducing the confining pressure increase factor (CPIF), the impact of confining pressure on the triaxial compressive strength (TCS) of sandstone specimens after undergoing different quantities of F&T weathering cycles was further investigated. A novel strength evolution model was proposed that could effectively describe the coupling impact of the quantity of F&T weathering cycles and confining pressure on TCS of rocks after undergoing the F&T weathering process. The proposed strength evolution model was cross-verified with experimental data from the published literature and all correlation coefficients were above 0.95, which proved that the strength evolution model proposed in this paper was reasonable; in addition, this model has strong applicability.

**Keywords:** freeze-and-thaw weathering cycles; confining pressure; confining pressure increase factor (CPIF); strength evolution model; nuclear magnetic resonance (NMR)

**MSC:** 74-XX; 74L10

## 1. Introduction

During the construction of rock mass engineering (such as mines, roads, and tunnels) in cold regions, the recurrence of F&T weathering processes induced by day–night and seasonal temperature changes causes rapid damage and the deterioration of rock masses and has initiated a large number of F&T disasters such as rock falls, landslides [1–3], and the cracking of rock surrounding tunnels [4,5], which has a major impact on the design, construction, and operation of rock mass engineering in cold areas. The strength and deformation behaviors of rocks are the theoretical basis for evaluating the stability and optimizing the engineering design in rock mass engineering [6]. Therefore, investigating the mechanical properties of rocks after undergoing F&T weathering cycles has great significance in evaluating the stability and optimizing the design in rock mass engineering in cold areas.

The impact of F&T weathering process on rock mechanical properties have been investigated by a considerable number of scholars. These investigation results indicated that after undergoing the F&T weathering process, the elastic modulus [7–11], uniaxial compressive strength (UCS) [7,8,10–14], Brazilian tensile strength (BTS) [15–18], point load strength (PLS) [15,16], dynamic uniaxial compressive strength ($UCS_d$) [7,8,10,19–22] and dynamic tensile strength ($BTS_d$) [19,23] of rocks such as sandstone, tuff, gneiss, granite and shale all decreased as the quantity of F&T weathering cycles increased, but to different extents. To reveal the change laws in these mechanical parameters with the quantity of F&T weathering cycles, a sequence of regression analysis models [24,25] and exponential decay models [15,16,26–28] were proposed based on the relationships between these mechanical parameters and the quantity of F&T weathering cycles. In addition, Liu et al. [29] regarded F&T weathering cycles as a kind of fatigue damage and thus established a fatigue damage model of rocks after undergoing F&T weathering cycles. A prediction model of UCS of rocks after undergoing F&T weathering cycles was obtained based on this fatigue damage model. Gao et al. [30] established a UCS evolution model of frozen–thawed rocks based on the energy evolution characteristics of rock failure. However, these research findings mainly focused on the uniaxial mechanical properties of rocks after undergoing F&T weathering cycles and did not consider the impact of the confining pressure on the mechanical properties of rocks after undergoing F&T weathering process. There is no doubt that actual rock mass engineering is always in a certain stress field [31,32]. To be closer to the actual engineering, it is necessary to study the triaxial mechanical properties of rocks after undergoing F&T weathering cycles.

Recently, scholars have increasingly studied the triaxial mechanical properties of rocks after undergoing F&T weathering cycles. Tan et al. [9] used granite as the research object to investigate the impact of the quantity of F&T weathering cycles on uniaxial and triaxial mechanical properties according to uniaxial compression tests (UCTs) and triaxial compression tests (TCTs) after granite specimens being underwent F&T weathering process. They found that both the UCS and TCS decreased exponentially as the quantity of F&T weathering cycles increased, as did the elastic modulus and cohesion. The relationships between these mechanical properties and the quantity of F&T weathering cycles were built according to an exponential function. Wang et al. [31] and Hosseini and Khodayari [33] also carried out similar studies but took sandstone as the research object; the research results for both were in accordance with those of Tan et al. [9]. In addition, Hosseini and Khodayari [33] also found that the rate of reduction in the TCS was less than that of the UCS at the equivalent quantity of F&T weathering cycles and that the higher the confining pressure was, the lower the rate of reduction. It was evident that the confining pressure had a significant impact on the TCS of rocks after undergoing F&T weathering cycles. To this end, Fu et al. [34] operated a sequences of TCTs after transversely isotropic rocks underwent an F&T weathering process and found that the quantity of F&T weathering cycles, bedding plane orientation, and confining pressure had a significant impact on the TCS of slate. A TCS prediction model for transversely isotropic rocks after undergoing an F&T weathering process was proposed based on the single discontinuity theory and the functional relationships between cohesion and internal friction angle and the quantity of F&T weathering cycles. Seyed Mousavi et al. [35] also carried out similar studies taking calc-schist rock specimens as the research objects. Finally, an empirical expression among the TCS, the quantity of F&T weathering cycles, and the confining pressure was obtained according to experimental results and the prediction model suggested by Fu et al. [34]. Although the prediction model proposed by Fu et al. [34] could effectively reflect the coupling impact of the quantity of F&T weathering cycles and confining pressure on TCS of rocks after undergoing an F&T weathering process, this prediction model was based on transversely isotropic rocks and its applicability was not strong. Therefore, it is necessary to establish a more applicable strength evolution model to reveal the coupling impact of the quantity of F&T weathering cycles and confining pressure on TCS of rocks after undergoing an F&T weathering process. In addition, the above-mentioned studies mainly focused on investigating the strength-deterioration characteristics of rocks after undergoing an F&T weathering process and did not deeply investigate the deformation behaviors of rocks, especially the coupling impact of the quantity of F&T weathering cycles and confining pressure on deformation behaviors of rocks during the entire loading procedure.

In this study, saturated sandstone specimens were first subjected to different quantities of F&T weathering cycles, then change laws in the $T_2$ spectrum distribution curves of sandstone specimens before and after the F&T weathering cycles were investigated. UCTs and TCTs of sandstone specimens after undergoing different quantities of F&T weathering cycles were conducted to obtain the UCS and TCS and the corresponding stress–strain curves. The coupling impact of the quantity of F&T weathering cycles and confining pressure on the deformation behaviors of rocks were investigated. A novel strength evolution model that considered the coupling impact of the quantity of F&T weathering cycles and confining pressure on the TCS of rocks after undergoing the F&T weathering process was established; the proposed strength evolution model was cross-verified with experimental data from the published literature.

## 2. Experimental Materials and Methods

### 2.1. Rock Specimen Preparation

In this paper, rock specimens of sandstone were taken from the Jiama open pit copper mine located in the Tibet Autonomous Region of China. The sampling site is shown in Figure 1a. Figure 1b shows the distribution map for the frozen soil of China. It can be seen in Figure 1b that the sampling site was on the boundary between the permafrost regions and seasonal frozen regions; therefore, the rock was subjected to repeated F&T weathering cycles. Table 1 shows the mineral composition of sandstone obtained via an X-ray diffraction (XRD) technique.

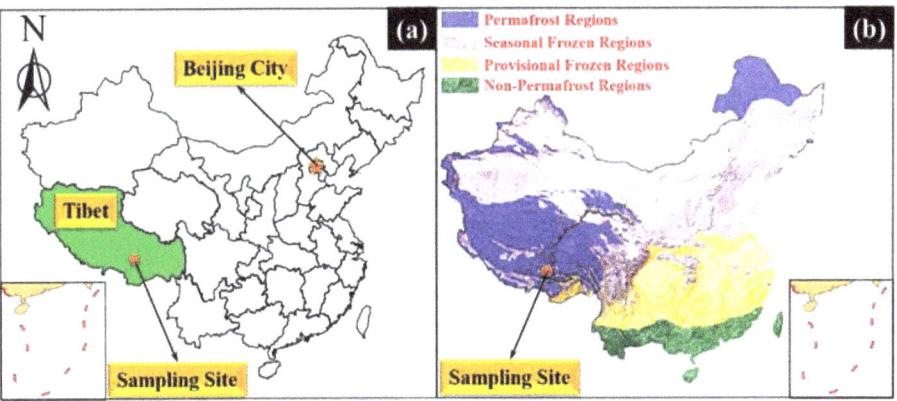

**Figure 1.** Location of the sampling site: (**a**) location of the Jiama open pit copper mine; (**b**) distribution map for frozen soil of China.

**Table 1.** Mineral composition of sandstone specimens.

| Rock Type | Mineral Composition | | | |
| --- | --- | --- | --- | --- |
| | Quartz (%) | Kaolinite (%) | Feldspar (%) | Mica (%) |
| Sandstone | 88.14 | 7.44 | 3.05 | 1.37 |

Based on the method suggested by the International Society for Rock Mechanics (ISRM), all rock specimens were processed into a cylinder with a diameter of 50 mm; we ensured that the flatness of the end surfaces was less than 0.05 mm [36]. Careful preparations ensured that the maximum deviations of the diameter and height were less than 0.30 mm and the vertical variance was less than 0.25° [36]. In this study, 15 and 60 rock specimens were used in UCTs and TCTs, respectively, and the length/diameter ratio of the rock specimens was 2.0 [36]. These specimens were divided into five groups (labeled A, B, C, D, and E); each group comprised 15 rock specimens (labeled 1, 2 ... 14, 15). The sandstone specimens from groups A, B, C, D, and E were treated in 0 cycles, 10 cycles, 20 cycles, 30 cycles, and 40 cycles, respectively. As shown in Figure 2a, the sandstone specimens labeled 1–3 in each group were used in the UCTs. The confining pressures were 3, 6, 9, and 12 MPa in the TCTs, corresponding to the sandstone specimens labeled 4–6, 7–9, 10–12, and 13–15 in each group, as shown in Figure 2b.

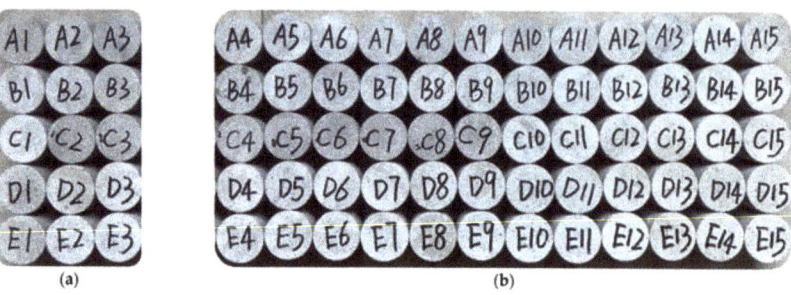

**Figure 2.** Rock Specimens: (**a**) specimens for uniaxial compression tests; (**b**) specimens for triaxial compression tests.

## 2.2. Test Procedures and Experimental Apparatus

All sandstone specimens were divided into five groups and dried in an oven for 48 h at 65 °C. The sandstone specimens that did not undergo F&T weathering cycles were used directly in the UCTs and TCTs. The other sandstone specimens were placed in a vacuum pump at a pressure of 0.1 MPa for 4 h and then soaked in distilled water for 24 h. The saturated specimens then went through the specified quantity of F&T weathering cycles in a TDS-300 automatic F&T testing machine (as shown in Figure 3a). When the quantity of F&T weathering cycles reached the specified quantities, the corresponding sandstone specimens were removed and UCTs and TCTs were conducted using an MTS815 electrohydraulic servo-controlled rock-testing machine (as shown in Figure 3c).

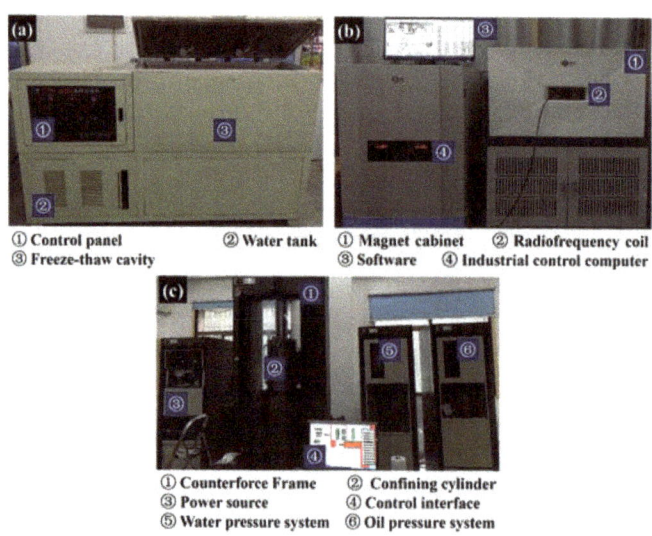

**Figure 3.** Experiment instrument: (**a**) TDS-300 automatic freeze–thaw test machine; (**b**) MesoMR23-060H-I NMR system; (**c**) MTS815 electrohydraulic servo-controlled rock-testing machine.

## 2.3. F&T Weathering Cycle Tests

Designed based on the local climate of the sampling site, one F&T weathering cycle in our tests included freezing the saturated rock specimens at −20 °C for four hours and then thawing in water at +20 °C for four hours. The temperature variation curve of the F&T weathering process is shown in Figure 4. In this study, four groups of sandstone specimens were subjected to F&T weathering tests corresponding to 10 cycles, 20 cycles, 30 cycles and 40 cycles. To reveal the evolution characteristics of the F&T damage, the MesoMR23-060H-I NMR system (as shown in Figure 3b) was used to conduct nuclear magnetic resonance (NMR) tests to obtain $T_2$ spectrum distribution curves before and after the F&T weathering cycles [37–43].

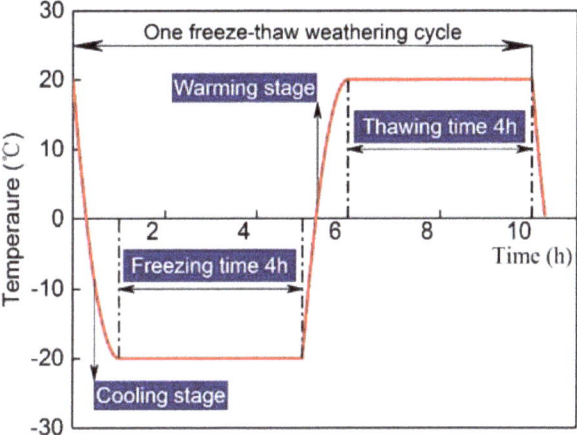

**Figure 4.** Temperature variation curves for one F&T weathering cycle.

Figure 5 displays $T_2$ spectrum distribution curves of the sandstone specimens before and after 20 (as shown in Figure 5a) and 40 (as shown in Figure 5b) F&T weathering cycles. In the $T_2$ spectrum distribution curves, the $T_2$ relaxation time (horizontal axis) is a measurement of the internal pore sizes and the porosity component (vertical axis) is the proportion of the corresponding pore sizes [20]. As can be seen in Figure 5a, after the sandstone specimens underwent 20 cycles, the peak values of the $T_2$ spectrum distribution curve increased, indicating that the sizes of the internal pores increased. As shown in Figure 5b, when the sandstone specimens underwent 40 cycles, the increases in the peak values were even more significant. In addition, the expansion of the curve to the left suggested that the sizes of some small pores increased. This demonstrated that in the early stage of the F&T weathering cycles, the original internal pores and microcracks were constantly developing. With the increase in the quantity of F&T weathering cycles, in the later stage of the cycles, in addition to the expansion of original internal pores and the constant extension of microcracks, new pores and microcracks were generated; i.e., with the increase in the quantity of the F&T weathering cycles, the accumulated damage to the inner sandstone specimens constantly increased.

## 2.4. Uniaxial and Triaxial Compression Tests

UCTs and TCTs were conducted on an MTS815 electrohydraulic servo-controlled rock-testing machine; axial and circumferential extensometers were used in our experiment to measure the axial and lateral strains. In our experiment, the displacement-control loading mode was used at a loading rate of 0.1 mm/min. The measured UCSs and TCSs of the sandstone specimens are listed in Table 2.

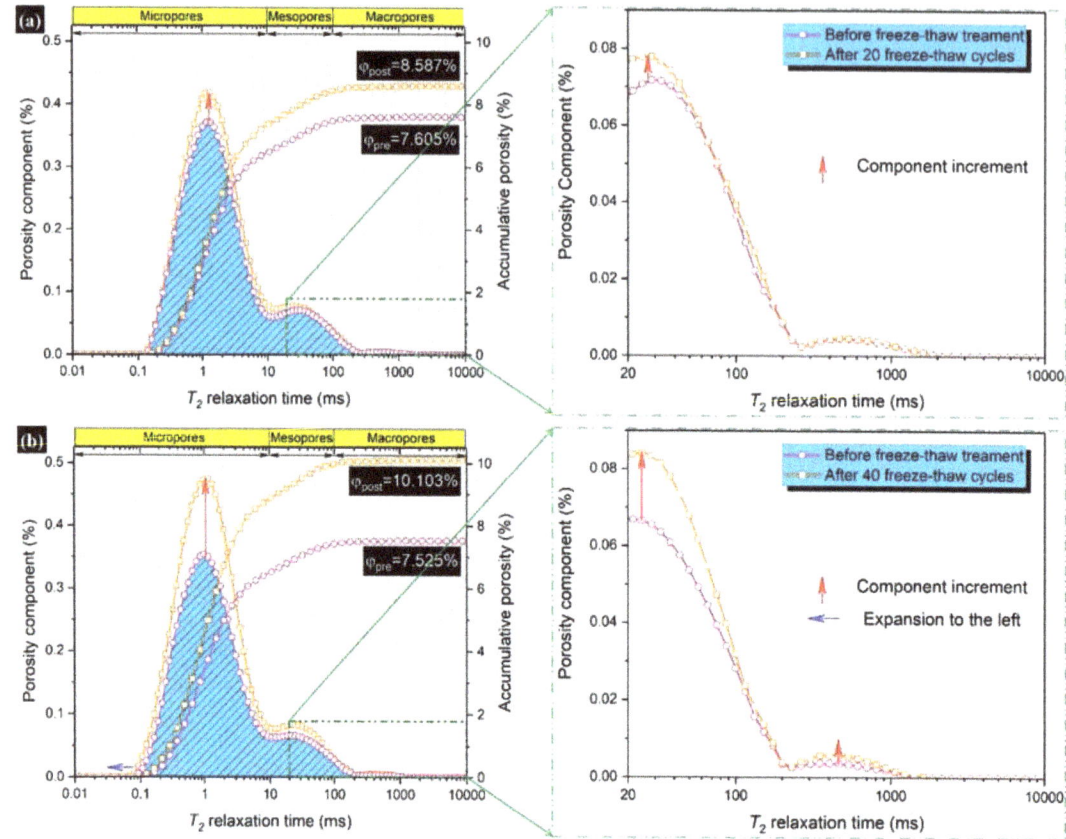

**Figure 5.** $T_2$ spectrum distribution curves for sandstone specimens at different quantities of F&T weathering cycles: (**a**) 20 F&T weathering cycles; (**b**) 40 F&T weathering cycles.

**Table 2.** Uniaxial and triaxial compression test results for sandstone specimens after undergoing different quantities of F&T weathering cycles.

| Quantity of F&T Weathering Cycles | Confining Pressure (MPa) | Specimen ID | Diameter (mm) | Height (mm) | Peak Compressive Strength (Mpa) | |
|---|---|---|---|---|---|---|
| | | | | | Tested Value | Average Value |
| 0 | 0 | A1 | 48.54 | 100.26 | 26.94 | |
| | | A2 | 49.12 | 100.28 | 27.51 | 27.50 |
| | | A3 | 48.96 | 99.88 | 28.05 | |
| | 3 | A4 | 49.06 | 100.02 | 48.78 | |
| | | A5 | 49.14 | 99.84 | 47.99 | 49.34 |
| | | A6 | 49.02 | 100.16 | 51.26 | |
| | 6 | A7 | 48.94 | 100.10 | 62.87 | |
| | | A8 | 49.06 | 100.14 | 64.75 | 63.28 |
| | | A9 | 49.00 | 100.28 | 62.23 | |
| | 9 | A10 | 48.74 | 100.22 | 72.12 | |
| | | A11 | 48.88 | 100.08 | 75.46 | 74.61 |
| | | A12 | 48.96 | 100.20 | 76.25 | |
| | 12 | A13 | 49.48 | 99.84 | 83.76 | |
| | | A14 | 48.94 | 99.88 | 85.24 | 85.08 |
| | | A15 | 48.04 | 100.16 | 86.25 | |

Table 2. Cont.

| Quantity of F&T Weathering Cycles | Confining Pressure (MPa) | Specimen ID | Diameter (mm) | Height (mm) | Peak Compressive Strength (Mpa) | |
|---|---|---|---|---|---|---|
| | | | | | Tested Value | Average Value |
| 10 | 0 | B1 | 49.12 | 100.02 | 25.60 | |
| | | B2 | 49.46 | 100.02 | 24.11 | 24.38 |
| | | B3 | 48.96 | 99.84 | 23.44 | |
| | 3 | B4 | 48.86 | 100.04 | 44.88 | |
| | | B5 | 48.74 | 100.28 | 45.58 | 44.58 |
| | | B6 | 48.56 | 100.06 | 43.28 | |
| | 6 | B7 | 48.52 | 100.12 | 56.86 | |
| | | B8 | 49.10 | 100.12 | 57.22 | 57.57 |
| | | B9 | 49.04 | 100.66 | 58.64 | |
| | 9 | B10 | 49.02 | 100.18 | 70.33 | |
| | | B11 | 48.98 | 99.94 | 67.40 | 68.99 |
| | | B12 | 48.96 | 100.24 | 69.24 | |
| | 12 | B13 | 49.14 | 99.94 | 81.88 | |
| | | B14 | 48.82 | 99.72 | 79.55 | 80.13 |
| | | B15 | 48.84 | 100.16 | 78.96 | |
| 20 | 0 | C1 | 49.04 | 100.02 | 19.68 | |
| | | C2 | 48.88 | 100.10 | 20.62 | 20.79 |
| | | C3 | 49.18 | 99.90 | 22.06 | |
| | 3 | C4 | 48.96 | 100.24 | 39.12 | |
| | | C5 | 49.04 | 100.10 | 42.89 | 40.11 |
| | | C6 | 49.04 | 100.12 | 38.33 | |
| | 6 | C7 | 49.08 | 100.18 | 52.11 | |
| | | C8 | 48.76 | 99.82 | 54.48 | 53.25 |
| | | C9 | 48.52 | 100.22 | 53.15 | |
| | 9 | C10 | 48.74 | 99.98 | 65.40 | |
| | | C11 | 48.70 | 99.86 | 64.06 | 64.24 |
| | | C12 | 49.12 | 100.14 | 63.25 | |
| | 12 | C13 | 49.20 | 100.20 | 74.59 | |
| | | C14 | 49.78 | 99.86 | 72.66 | 74.28 |
| | | C15 | 48.88 | 99.96 | 75.58 | |
| 30 | 0 | D1 | 49.52 | 100.16 | 19.04 | |
| | | D2 | 48.84 | 99.88 | 18.2 | 18.17 |
| | | D3 | 49.04 | 100.02 | 17.26 | |
| | 3 | D4 | 48.36 | 100.02 | 35.18 | |
| | | D5 | 49.12 | 99.78 | 38.97 | 36.47 |
| | | D6 | 48.76 | 100.06 | 35.26 | |
| | 6 | D7 | 48.82 | 100.16 | 48.80 | |
| | | D8 | 49.06 | 99.78 | 50.81 | 49.29 |
| | | D9 | 49.92 | 100.04 | 48.25 | |
| | 9 | D10 | 48.80 | 99.86 | 58.28 | |
| | | D11 | 49.06 | 100.02 | 60.16 | 59.41 |
| | | D12 | 49.82 | 99.90 | 59.78 | |
| | 12 | D13 | 49.02 | 100.22 | 66.62 | |
| | | D14 | 49.28 | 100.16 | 65.37 | 67.26 |
| | | D15 | 49.12 | 99.94 | 69.78 | |
| 40 | 0 | E1 | 48.84 | 99.84 | 15.88 | |
| | | E2 | 48.84 | 100.04 | 16.41 | 16.39 |
| | | E3 | 48.60 | 100.20 | 16.88 | |
| | 3 | E4 | 49.02 | 100.18 | 33.06 | |
| | | E5 | 48.86 | 99.88 | 31.78 | 32.84 |
| | | E6 | 48.68 | 100.30 | 33.68 | |
| | 6 | E7 | 48.76 | 99.84 | 45.82 | |
| | | E8 | 48.98 | 100.08 | 42.75 | 43.94 |
| | | E9 | 48.68 | 100.14 | 43.25 | |
| | 9 | E10 | 48.96 | 10.14 | 52.73 | |
| | | E11 | 48.88 | 100.02 | 49.9 | 52.29 |
| | | E12 | 49.08 | 100.14 | 54.25 | |
| | 12 | E13 | 48.92 | 100.18 | 61.77 | |
| | | E14 | 49.16 | 99.92 | 59.38 | 61.13 |
| | | E15 | 48.90 | 100.20 | 62.25 | |

## 3. Experimental Results and Analysis

### 3.1. Uniaxial Mechanical Properties Variation Characteristics for Sandstone after Undergoing F&T Weathering Cycles

#### 3.1.1. Stress–Strain Curve

Figure 6 displays the stress–strain curves for the sandstone specimens after undergoing different quantities of F&T weathering cycles under uniaxial compression conditions. All of the stress–strain curves had the same variation patterns and could be separated into five stages during the entire loading process; that is, the compaction stage, elastic deformation stage, yield stage, failure stage, and strain softening stage. As the quantity of F&T weathering cycles increased, the stress–strain curves showed three obvious features: (1) the compaction stage became longer; (2) the slope at the linear deformation stage decreased, as did the UCS; and (3) the stress-dropping rate of the post-peak decreased. The main reason was that the length of the compaction stage and the slope of the linear deformation stage were proportional to the number of microdefects inside the rock [44]. Under the F&T weathering process, water migration and transformation from water to ice caused microdefects to gradually develop; the number of microdefects increased with the increase in the quantity of F&T weathering cycles [45,46]. The main reason for the reduction in the stress-dropping rate of the post-peak was that the F&T weathering cycles caused the cohesion between the particles to gradually decrease, which caused the sandstone specimens to become soft and the plasticity to increase.

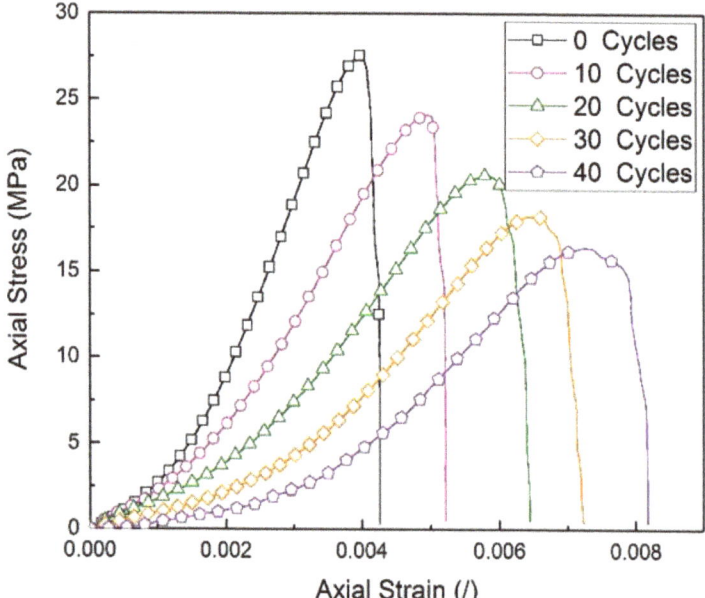

**Figure 6.** Stress–strain curves for sandstone specimens after undergoing different quantities of F&T weathering cycles in uniaxial compression tests.

#### 3.1.2. UCS

Figure 7 shows the changes in the UCS and its reduction ratio for different quantities of F&T weathering cycles. The reduction ratio for UCS is defined as follows:

$$\eta = \frac{\sigma_0 - \sigma_N}{\sigma_0} \times 100\% \tag{1}$$

where $\sigma_0$ is the UCS of sandstone specimens without any F&T weathering cycles, $\sigma_N$ is the UCS of sandstone specimens after undergoing N quantity of F&T weathering cycles, and $\eta$ is the reduction ratio of the UCS.

As shown in Figure 7, compared with the original average UCS (27.50 MPa), the reduction ratios were 11.33% (24.38 MPa), 24.41% (20.79 MPa), 33.94% (18.17 MPa), and 40.40% (16.39 MPa), corresponding to 10 cycles, 20 cycles, 30 cycles, and 40 cycles, respectively. The reason can be explained as follows: the water migration and transformation from water to ice under the F&T weathering process caused microdefects to gradually develop and the sandstone specimens to become more fragmented. It was noticeable that the UCS exponentially decayed as the quantity of F&T weathering cycles increased, similar to laws found in the literature [16,26,28]. The experimental data were fitted by the decay model suggested by Mutlutürk et al. [26]; this decay model is defined as follows:

$$I_N = I_0 e^{-\lambda N} \qquad (2)$$

where $I$ is the rock integrity, $\lambda$ is the decay coefficient, and N is the quantity of F&T weathering cycles.

In this paper, the UCS was regarded as the rock integrity; therefore, the decay model became as follows:

$$\sigma_N = \sigma_0 e^{-\lambda N} \qquad (3)$$

The fitting curves of our test are shown in Figure 7. The model fit well with the experimental data: the fitting coefficient of determination ($R^2$) was greater than 0.99.

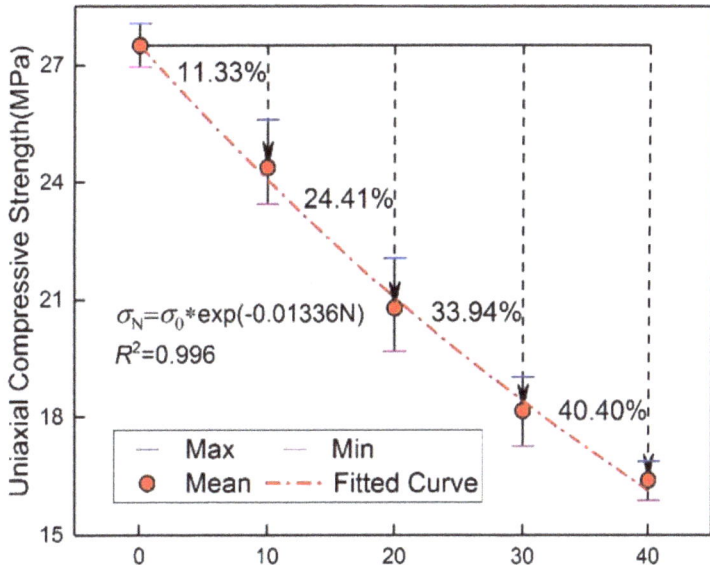

Figure 7. UCS and its reduction ratio for sandstone specimens after undergoing different quantities of F&T weathering cycles.

3.1.3. Failure Modes

Figure 8 shows the failure modes of the sandstone specimens after undergoing different quantities of F&T weathering cycles in uniaxial compression conditions. The failure mode was single inclined plane shear failure when the sandstone specimens did not undergo F&T weathering cycles. The failure modes became tension-shear comprehensive failure and splitting failure as the quantity of F&T weathering cycles increased. Tension-shear comprehensive failure occurred in the sandstone specimens after undergoing 10 cycles and 20 cycles and the sandstone specimens were fragmented. Splitting failure occurred in the sandstone specimens when the quantity of F&T weathering cycles was 30 and 40. The increase in the number of macroscopic cracks on the surfaces of sandstone specimens caused them to become more fragmented. The reason why the failure modes changed with the quantity of F&T weathering cycles was that the F&T weathering process causes microdefects to gradually develop inside the sandstone specimens, which caused cracks to be more likely to expand in the axial direction under uniaxial compression conditions.

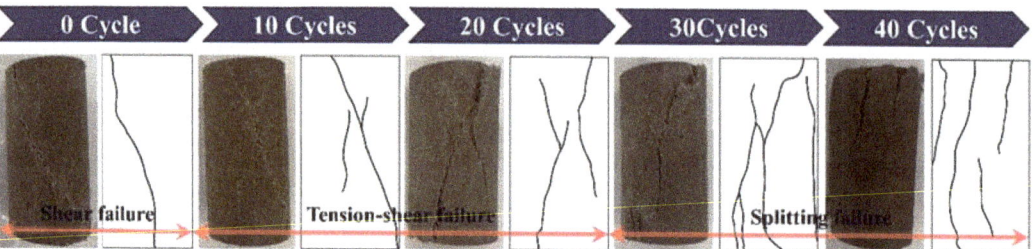

**Figure 8.** Failure modes of sandstone specimens after undergoing different quantities of F&T weathering cycles in uniaxial compression tests.

*3.2. Triaxial Mechanical Properties' Variation Characteristics for Sandstone after Undergoing F&T Weathering Cycles*

3.2.1. Stress–Strain Curve

Figure 9 displays the stress–strain curves for the sandstone specimens after undergoing different quantities of F&T weathering cycles under different confining pressures. Compared with the stress–strain curves of sandstone specimens after undergoing different quantities of F&T weathering cycles under uniaxial compression conditions, all of the stress–strain curves had obvious residual strength characteristics. In addition, the variation characteristics of the stress–strain curves were similar under different confining pressures as the quantity of F&T weathering cycles increased. All of the stress–strain curves could be separated into six stages: compaction stage, elastic deformation stage, yield stage, failure stage, strain softening stage, and residual strength stage. When the confining pressure was constant, with the increase in the quantity of the F&T weathering cycles, except for a gradual decrease in the residual strength, the other variation characteristics were similar to those in uniaxial compression conditions: (1) the compaction stage became longer; (2) the slope at the linear deformation stage decreased, as did the TCS; and (3) the stress-drop rate in the post-peak stress decreased. The main reason for these characteristics was the same as that under uniaxial compression conditions.

Figure 10 displays the stress–strain curves of the sandstone specimens after undergoing 20 F&T weathering cycles at different confining pressures. With the increase in confining pressure, the stress–strain curves showed four obvious features: (1) the compaction stage became shorter; (2) the slope at the linear deformation stage increased, as did the TCS; (3) the stress-dropping ratio of the post-peak decreased; and (4) the residual strength increased. The main reason was that the length of the compaction stage and the slope of the linear deformation stage are proportional to the number of microdefects in the rock. Under the confining pressure, microdefects inside the rock caused by the F&T weathering process were pre-compression, which caused a decrease in the number of microdefects; the higher the confining pressure was, the larger the number of microdefects that the pre-compression had. The main reason for the decrease in the stress-dropping ratio of the post-peak and the increase in residual strength was that the confining pressure could make the post-peak deformation behavior of the rocks transition from brittleness to plasticity [47–50].

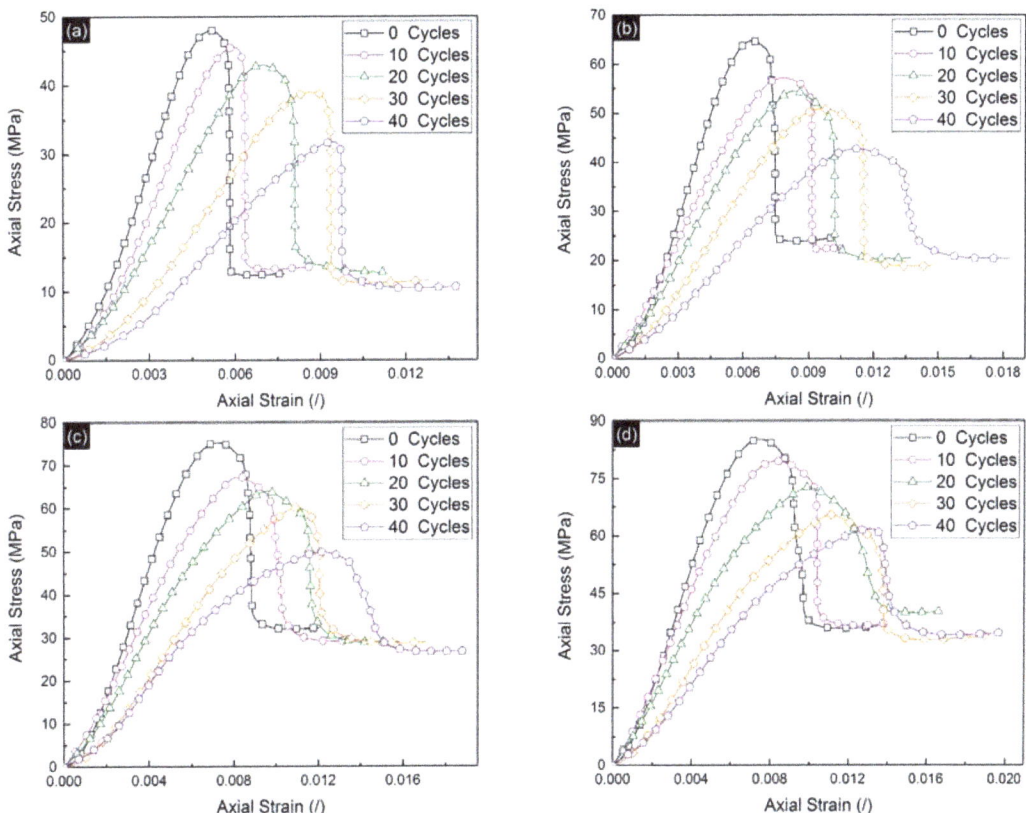

**Figure 9.** Stress–strain curves of sandstone specimens after undergoing different quantities of F&T weathering cycles under triaxial compression tests: (**a**) 3 MPa; (**b**) 6 MPa; (**c**) 9 MPa; (**d**) 12MPa.

These variation characteristics indicated that the impact of the quantity of F&T weathering cycles on the pre-peak deformation behavior and residual strength was the opposite of the confining pressure while the post-peak deformation behaviors were similar to the confining pressure.

3.2.2. TCS

Figure 11 displays the relationship between the TCS and its reduction ratio and the quantity of F&T weathering cycles at different confining pressures. It can be seen that the TCS decreased with an increase in the quantity of F&T weathering cycles when the confining pressure was constant, which was similar to laws in the uniaxial compression conditions. Compared with the original average TCS, the reduction ratios were: 9.55%, 18.71%, 26.09%, and 33.45% for 10 cycles, 20 cycles, 30 cycles, and 40 cycles, respectively, when the confining pressure was 3 MPa; 9.02%, 15.86%, 22.12%, and 30.57% for 10 cycles, 20 cycles, 30 cycles, and 40 cycles, respectively, when the confining pressure was 6 MPa; 7.53%, 13.90%, 20.38%, and 29.91% for 10 cycles, 20 cycles, 30 cycles, and 40 cycles, respectively, when the confining pressure was 9 MPa; and 5.82%, 12.70%, 20.95%, and 30.57% for 10 cycles, 20 cycles, 30 cycles, and 40 cycles, respectively, when the confining pressure was 12 MPa. At different confining pressures, the variation characteristics between the TCS of the sandstone specimens and the quantity of F&T cycles were similar to the UCS. Therefore, the experimental data could be used to fit the model suggested by Mutlutürk et al. [26]; the fitting results of our tests are shown in Figure 11. The model fit well with experimental data: the fitting coefficient of determination ($R^2$) was greater than 0.98. The decay coefficient was 0.01018, 0.00881, 0.00819, and 0.00778 for 3, 6, 9, and 12 MPa, respectively. The results indicated that the decay coefficient decreased as the confining pressure increased and that the higher the confining pressure was, the larger the reduction in the decay coefficient. Therefore, the TCS of the sandstone after undergoing F&T weathering process was impacted by the confining pressure. Further study of the impact of confining pressure on the TCS of sandstone after undergoing the F&T weathering process referred to the definition of the dynamic increase factor [51,52]. The confining pressure increase factor (CPIF) could be defined as TCS/UCS.

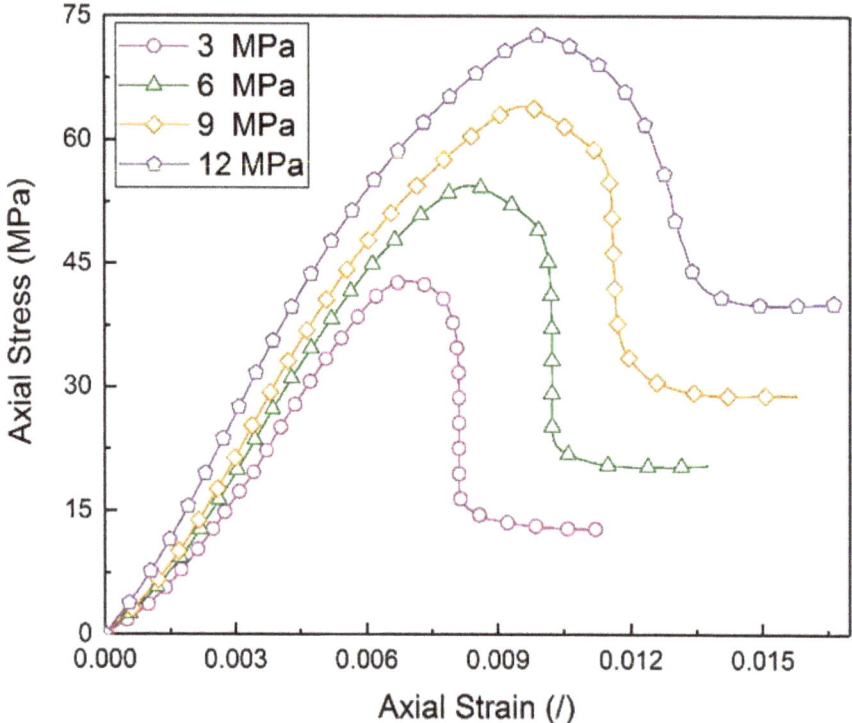

**Figure 10.** Stress–strain curves for sandstone specimens at different confining pressures (20 F&T weathering cycles).

Figure 12 displays the CPIF curves of the sandstone specimens after undergoing different quantities of F&T weathering cycles in different confining pressures. As shown in Figure 12, the variation characteristics of the CPIF curves were similar under different confining pressures as the quantity of F&T weathering cycles increased; that is, the CPIF increased as the quantity of F&T weathering cycles increased. However, the higher the confining pressure was, the larger the increased amplitude of the CPIF. For example, when the confining pressure was 3 MPa, the value of the CPIF was 1.79 without F&T weathering cycles; the CPIF is 2.31 after the sandstone underwent F&T weathering cycles, an increase ratio of 28.97%; when the confining pressure was 12 MPa, the value of the CPIF was 3.09 without F&T weathering cycles and the CPIF was 4.83 after the sandstone underwent F&T weathering cycles, an increase ratio of 56.27%. This indicated that sandstone specimens were more sensitive to the confining pressure after undergoing more F&T weathering cycles.

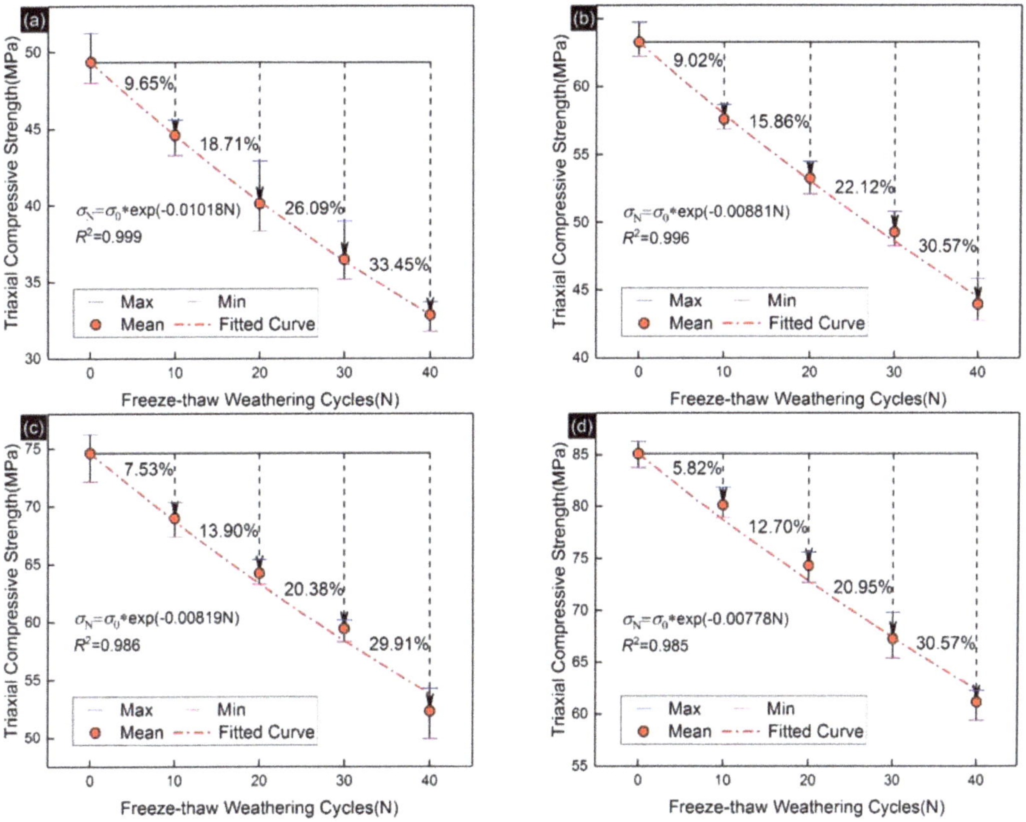

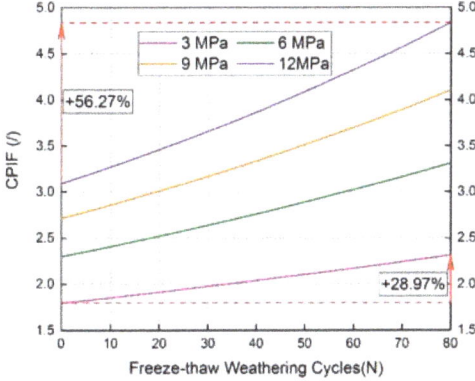

Figure 11. TCS and its reduction ratio for sandstone specimens after undergoing different quantities of F&T weathering cycles: (**a**) 3 MPa; (**b**) 6 MPa; (**c**) 9 MPa; (**d**) 12 MPa.

Figure 12. Confining pressure increase factor curves at different confining pressures.

These results demonstrated that the UCS of the sandstone after undergoing F&T weathering process was mainly controlled by the quantity of F&T weathering cycles under uniaxial compression conditions. The TCS of the sandstone after undergoing the F&T weathering process was impacted by the quantity of F&T weathering cycles and confining pressure under triaxial compression conditions; these two factors had opposite impacts. The main reason was that the water–ice phase and water migration under the F&T weathering cycles caused microdefects to gradually develop inside the sandstone specimens, which induced F&T damage. However, under confining pressure conditions, some microdefects inside the sandstone specimens were closed, which lessened the damage induced by the F&T weathering process. Therefore, for the slope engineering of open-pit mines in cold areas, the application of anchor reinforcement technology to provide pre-stress could lessen the damage induced by the F&T weathering process and improve the stability of the slope.

3.2.3. Failure Modes

Under different quantities of F&T weathering cycles, the failure modes of the sandstone specimens had the same evolution characteristics with the change in confining pressure. Therefore, Figure 13 only shows the failure modes under different confining pressures after the sandstone specimens underwent 20 F&T weathering cycles. As shown in Figure 13, under different confining pressures, the failure modes of the sandstone specimens all were single incline plane shear failure; however, the length of the shear failure plane became shorter with the increase in the confining pressure. The main reason was that the lateral deformation was limited under the confining pressure, so the sandstone specimens only exhibited single inclined plane shear failure. In addition, the higher the confining pressure was, the more severe the limiting effect, so the length of the shear failure plane became shorter with the increase in the confining pressure.

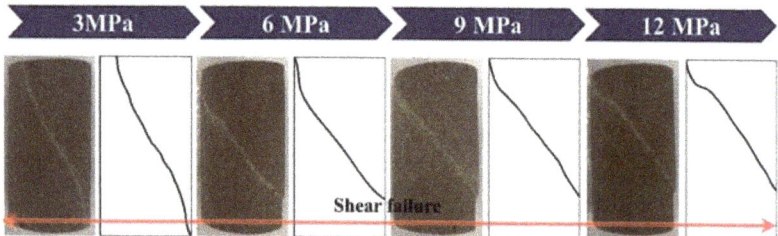

**Figure 13.** Failure modes of sandstone specimens at different confining pressures (20 F&T weathering cycles).

## 4. Strength Evolution Model of Rock Specimens Considering the Freeze–Thaw Weathering Process and Confining Pressure

The experimental results demonstrated that the TCS of rocks after undergoing the F&T weathering process was impacted by the quantity of F&T weathering cycles and the confining pressure under triaxial compression conditions. The model suggested by Mutlutürk et al. [26] could only describe the change in the peak compressive strength of rocks after undergoing the F&T weathering process at a specific confining pressure, which did not consider the coupling impact of the quantity of F&T weathering cycles and the confining pressure. Therefore, it was necessary to establish a novel model that could reflect the evolution laws of the TCS of rocks after undergoing the F&T weathering process. The impact of the confining pressure on the TCS could be described by the rock-strength criterion. The Hoek–Brown strength criterion proposed by Hoek–Brown could describe the failure of the broken rock mass. The expression of the Hoek–Brown strength criterion is as follows [53,54]:

$$\sigma_1 = \sigma_3 + \sqrt{m_i \sigma_{ci} \sigma_3 + \sigma_{ci}^2} \tag{4}$$

where $\sigma_{ci}$ is the UCS, $\sigma_1$ is the TCS, $m_i$ is the material constant, and $\sigma_3$ is the confining pressure.

Under the F&T weathering process, the water migration and transformation from water to ice caused microdefects to gradually develop, which caused the rock specimens to become more fragmented. Therefore, the Hoek–Brown strength criterion could be adopted to describe the impact of the confining pressure on the TCS of rocks after undergoing the F&T weathering process. According to the expression of the Hoek–Brown strength criterion, the relationship between the TCS $\sigma_1$ and the confining pressure $\sigma_3$ could be simplified into a quadratic function expression. Based on this simplified relationship and the model suggested by Mutlutürk et al. [26], this paper proposed a novel strength evolution model to describe the coupling impact of the quantity of F&T weathering cycles and the confining pressure on the TCS. The expression of the strength evolution model is as follows:

$$\sigma_1 = \left(a + b\sigma_3 + c\sigma_3^2\right) \exp\left[\left(d + e\sigma_3 + f\sigma_3^2\right)N\right] \tag{5}$$

where $a$, $b$, $c$, $d$, $e$, and $f$ are fitting parameters determined by the properties of rocks.

Using Equation (5), MATLAB was adopted to fit the experimental data of the TCS of the sandstone specimens after undergoing different quantities of F&T weathering cycles and different confining pressures; the fitting surface is shown in Figure 14 and the fitting parameters are shown in Table 3. As shown in Figure 14 and Table 3, the fitting surface agreed well with the experimental data: the correlation coefficient was up to 0.992, which indicated that the proposed model could effectively describe the coupling impact of the quantity of F&T weathering cycles and the confining pressure on the TCS of the sandstone after undergoing the F&T weathering process.

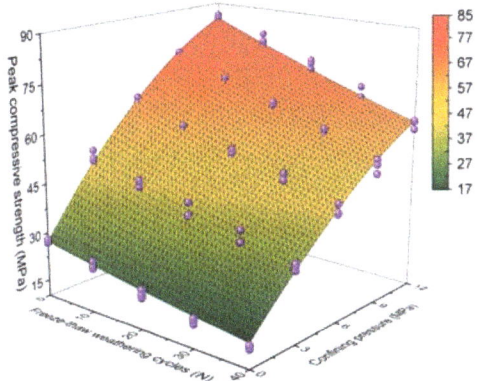

**Figure 14.** Fitting results of TCS of sandstone specimens for different quantities of F&T weathering cycles and different confining pressures.

**Table 3.** Fitting parameters of strength evolution model of sandstone specimens.

| Fitting Parameters | a | b | c | d | e | f | $R^2$ | RMSE |
| --- | --- | --- | --- | --- | --- | --- | --- | --- |
| Value | 27.358 | 7.412 | −0.216 | $1.101 \times 10^{-2}$ | $3.257 \times 10^{-4}$ | $-6.043 \times 10^{-6}$ | 0.992 | 1.731 |

To further validate the rationality of the proposed model in this paper, Equation (5) was adopted to fit the tested value from the published literature [32–35]. The fitting surfaces are shown in Figure 15 and the fitting parameters are shown in Table 4. As shown in Figure 15 and Table 4, the fitting surfaces agreed well with the tested value and all fitting correlation coefficients were above 0.95, which proved that the strength evolution model proposed in this paper was reasonable; in addition, this model has strong applicability.

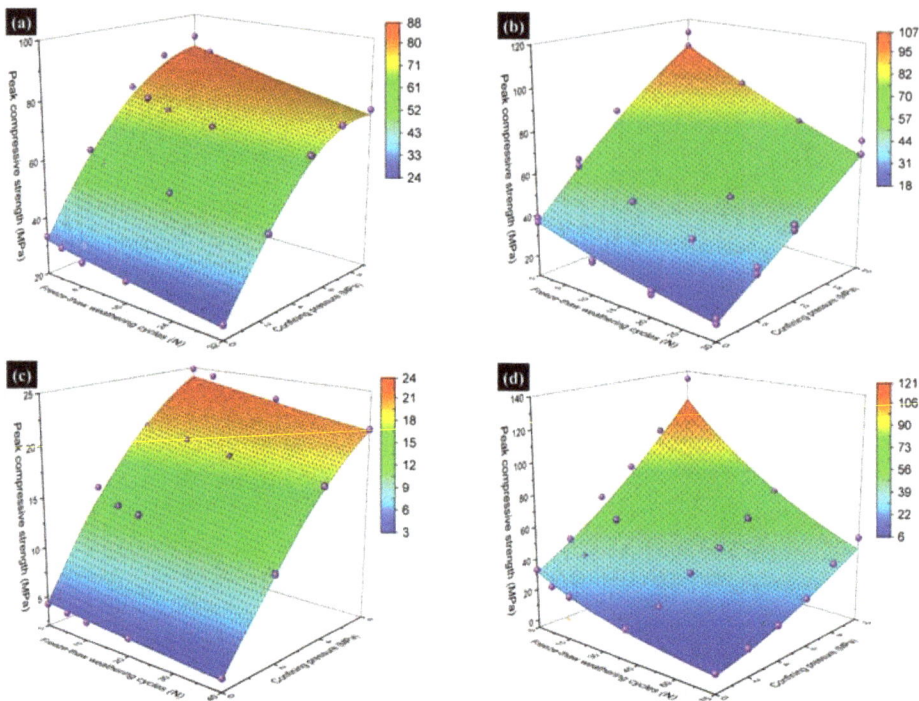

**Figure 15.** Fitting results of TCS of rocks for different quantities of F&T weathering cycles and different confining pressures: (**a**) from [33]; (**b**) from [34]; (**c**) from [32]; (**d**) from [35].

**Table 4.** Fitting parameters of the strength evolution model of rock specimens from the published literature.

| Data Source | Fitting Parameters | | | | | | | |
|---|---|---|---|---|---|---|---|---|
| | a | b | c | d | e | f | $R^2$ | RMSE |
| [33] | 32.242 | 11.493 | −0.580 | $9.190 \times 10^{-3}$ | $1.570 \times 10^{-3}$ | $-1.309 \times 10^{-4}$ | 0.988 | 2.249 |
| [34] | 34.444 | 4.333 | −0.042 | $2.314 \times 10^{-2}$ | $3.788 \times 10^{-4}$ | $-2.546 \times 10^{-7}$ | 0.977 | 4.341 |
| [32] | 4.387 | 5.155 | −0.313 | $8.880 \times 10^{-3}$ | $1.500 \times 10^{-3}$ | $-9.298 \times 10^{-5}$ | 0.992 | 0.688 |
| [35] | 31.680 | 5.907 | 0.299 | $-2.328 \times 10^{-2}$ | $1.810 \times 10^{-3}$ | $-8.714 \times 10^{-5}$ | 0.965 | 5.817 |

## 5. Conclusions

In this paper, the evolution characteristics of the F&T damage of sandstone were analyzed based on NMR techniques. Uniaxial and triaxial compression tests of sandstone after undergoing different quantities of F&T weathering cycles were conducted to investigate the coupling impact of the quantities of F&T weathering cycles and the confining pressure on the mechanical properties and failure modes. A novel strength evolution model was proposed to describe the coupling impact of the quantity of F&T weathering cycles and the confining pressure on the TCS of rocks after undergoing the F&T weathering process. The following main conclusions could be drawn from this research:

(a). In the early stage of the F&T weathering cycles, original internal pores and microcracks were constantly developing. As the quantity of F&T weathering cycles increased, in the later stage of the F&T weathering cycles, in addition to the expansion of the original internal pores and the constant extension of microcracks, new pores and microcracks were generated; i.e., the accumulated damage inside the sandstone specimens constantly increased as the quantity of F&T weathering cycles increased.

(b). The impact of the quantity of F&T weathering cycles on the pre-peak deformation behaviors, peak compressive strength, and residual strength was the opposite of the confining pressure while the post-peak deformation behaviors were similar to confining pressure. When the confining pressure was constant, with an increase in the quantity of F&T weathering cycles, the compaction stage became longer while the slope at the linear deformation stage, the peak compressive strength, the residual strength, and the stress-dropping rate of the post-peak all decreased. When the quantity of the F&T weathering cycles was constant, with an increase in the confining pressure, the compaction stage became shorter and the slope at the linear deformation stage, the peak compressive strength, and the residual strength all increased, but the stress-dropping rate of the post-peak decreased.

(c). In the uniaxial compression tests, the failure mode of the sandstone specimens changed as the quantity of F&T cycles increased. The failure mode was a single inclined plane shear failure when the sandstone specimens did not undergo F&T weathering cycles. In the early and later stages of the F&T weathering cycles, the failure modes became tension–shear comprehensive failure and splitting failure, respectively. In the triaxial compression tests, the failure mode of the sandstone specimens under different confining pressures was a single inclined plane shear failure regardless of the quantity of F&T weathering cycles experienced. However, the length of the shear failure plane became shorter as the confining pressure increased.

(d). The variation characteristics of the CPIF curves were similar under different confining pressures as the quantity of F&T weathering cycles increased; that is, the CPIF increased as the quantity of F&T weathering cycles increased. However, the higher the confining pressure was, the larger the increased amplitude of the CPIF. This indicated that the sandstone specimens were more sensitive to the confining pressure after undergoing more F&T weathering cycles.

(e). A novel strength evolution model that could describe the coupling impact of the quantity of F&T weathering cycles and the confining pressure on the TCS of rocks after undergoing the F&T weathering process was proposed. The proposed model was cross-verified with tested values from the published literature. Fitting surfaces agreed well with the tested value and all fitting correlation coefficients were above 0.95, which proved that the strength evolution model proposed in this paper was reasonable; in addition, this model has strong applicability.

**Author Contributions:** Conceptualization, K.Z. and C.Y.; Data curation, X.X. and F.G.; Funding acquisition, X.X., F.G., K.Z. and J.L.; Investigation, X.X. and C.Y.; Methodology, X.X.; Supervision, K.Z.; Writing—original draft, X.X.; Writing—review & editing, F.G. All authors have read and agreed to the published version of the manuscript.

**Funding:** This work was supported by the National Natural Science Foundation of China (Grant No. 51774323), the Hunan Provincial Natural Science Foundation of China (Grant Nos. 2020JJ4704 and 2020JJ4712), and the Fundamental Research Funds for the Central Universities of Central South University (Grant No. 2021zzts0279).

**Institutional Review Board Statement:** Not applicable.

**Informed Consent Statement:** Not applicable.

**Data Availability Statement:** Not applicable.

**Conflicts of Interest:** The authors declare no conflict of interest.

# References

1. Matsuoka, N. Direct observation of frost wedging in alpine bedrock. *Earth Surf. Process. Landf.* **2001**, *26*, 601–614. [CrossRef]
2. Nicholson, D.T.; Nicholson, F.H. Physical deterioration of sedimentary rocks subjected to experimental freeze-thaw weathering. *Earth Surf. Process. Landf.* **2000**, *25*, 1295–1307. [CrossRef]
3. Matsuoka, N. Frost weathering and rockwall erosion in the southeastern Swiss Alps: Long-term (1994–2006) observations. *Geomorphology* **2008**, *99*, 353–368. [CrossRef]

4. Lai, Y.; Wu, H.; Wu, Z.; Liu, S.; Den, X. Analytical viscoelastic solution for frost force in cold-region tunnels. *Cold Reg. Sci. Technol.* **2000**, *31*, 227–234. [CrossRef]
5. Zhang, S.; Lai, Y.; Zhang, X.; Pu, Y.; Yu, W. Study on the damage propagation of surrounding rock from a cold-region tunnel under freeze–thaw cycle condition. *Tunn. Undergr. Space Technol.* **2004**, *19*, 295–302. [CrossRef]
6. Kang, K.; Hu, N.; Sin, C.; Rim, S.; Han, E.; Kim, C. Determination of the mechanical parameters of rock mass based on a GSI system and displacement back analysis. *J. Geophys. Eng.* **2017**, *14*, 939–948. [CrossRef]
7. Zhang, J.; Deng, H.; Taheri, A.; Ke, B.; Liu, C. Deterioration and strain energy development of sandstones under quasi-static and dynamic loading after freeze-thaw cycles. *Cold Reg. Sci. Technol.* **2019**, *160*, 252–264. [CrossRef]
8. Wang, P.; Xu, J.; Liu, S.; Wang, H.; Liu, S. Static and dynamic mechanical properties of sedimentary rock after freeze-thaw or thermal shock weathering. *Eng. Geol.* **2016**, *210*, 148–157. [CrossRef]
9. Tan, X.; Chen, W.; Yang, J.; Cao, J. Laboratory investigations on the mechanical properties degradation of granite under freeze–thaw cycles. *Cold Reg. Sci. Technol.* **2011**, *68*, 130–138. [CrossRef]
10. Wang, P.; Xu, J.; Liu, S.; Liu, S.; Wang, H. A prediction model for the dynamic mechanical degradation of sedimentary rock after a long-term freeze-thaw weathering: Considering the strain-rate effect. *Cold Reg. Sci. Technol.* **2016**, *131*, 16–23. [CrossRef]
11. Fang, X.; Xu, J.; Wang, P. Compressive failure characteristics of yellow sandstone subjected to the coupling effects of chemical corrosion and repeated freezing and thawing. *Eng. Geol.* **2018**, *233*, 160–171. [CrossRef]
12. Khanlari, G.; Sahamieh, R.Z.; Abdilor, Y. The effect of freeze–thaw cycles on physical and mechanical properties of Upper Red Formation sandstones, central part of Iran. *Arab. J. Geosci.* **2014**, *8*, 5991–6001. [CrossRef]
13. Momeni, A.; Abdilor, Y.; Khanlari, G.R.; Heidari, M.; Sepahi, A.A. The effect of freeze–thaw cycles on physical and mechanical properties of granitoid hard rocks. *Bull. Eng. Geol. Environ.* **2016**, *75*, 1649–1656. [CrossRef]
14. Yavuz, H. Effect of freeze–thaw and thermal shock weathering on the physical and mechanical properties of an andesite stone. *Bull. Eng. Geol. Environ.* **2010**, *70*, 187–192. [CrossRef]
15. Altindag, R.; Alyildiz, I.S.; Onargan, T. Mechanical property degradation of ignimbrite subjected to recurrent freeze–thaw cycles. *Int. J. Rock Mech. Min. Sci.* **2004**, *41*, 1023–1028. [CrossRef]
16. Jamshidi, A.; Nikudel, M.R.; Khamehchiyan, M. Predicting the long-term durability of building stones against freeze–thaw using a decay function model. *Cold Reg. Sci. Technol.* **2013**, *92*, 29–36. [CrossRef]
17. Jia, H.; Xiang, W.; Krautblatter, M. Quantifying Rock Fatigue and Decreasing Compressive and Tensile Strength after Repeated Freeze-Thaw Cycles. *Permafr. Periglac. Process.* **2015**, *26*, 368–377. [CrossRef]
18. Zhang, J.; Fu, H.; Huang, Z.; Wu, Y.; Chen, W.; Shi, Y. Experimental study on the tensile strength and failure characteristics of transversely isotropic rocks after freeze-thaw cycles. *Cold Reg. Sci. Technol.* **2019**, *163*, 68–77. [CrossRef]
19. Weng, L.; Wu, Z.; Taheri, A.; Liu, Q.; Lu, H. Deterioration of dynamic mechanical properties of granite due to freeze-thaw weathering Considering the effects of moisture conditions. *Cold Reg. Sci. Technol.* **2020**, *176*, 103092. [CrossRef]
20. Li, J.; Kaunda, R.B.; Zhou, K. Experimental investigations on the effects of ambient freeze-thaw cycling on dynamic properties and rock pore structure deterioration of sandstone. *Cold Reg. Sci. Technol.* **2018**, *154*, 133–141. [CrossRef]
21. Ke, B.; Zhou, K.; Xu, C.; Deng, H.; Li, J.; Bin, F. Dynamic Mechanical Property Deterioration Model of Sandstone Caused by Freeze—Thaw Weathering. *Rock Mech. Rock Eng.* **2018**, *51*, 2791–2804. [CrossRef]
22. Ma, Q.; Ma, D.; Yao, Z. Influence of freeze-thaw cycles on dynamic compressive strength and energy distribution of soft rock specimen. *Cold Reg. Sci. Technol.* **2018**, *153*, 10–17. [CrossRef]
23. Liu, C.; Deng, H.; Zhao, H.; Zhang, J. Effects of freeze-thaw treatment on the dynamic tensile strength of granite using the Brazilian test. *Cold Reg. Sci. Technol.* **2018**, *155*, 327–332. [CrossRef]
24. Bayram, F. Predicting mechanical strength loss of natural stones after freeze–thaw in cold regions. *Cold Reg. Sci. Technol.* **2012**, *83–84*, 98–102. [CrossRef]
25. İnce, İ.; Fener, M. A prediction model for uniaxial compressive strength of deteriorated pyroclastic rocks due to freeze–thaw cycle. *J. Afr. Earth Sci.* **2016**, *120*, 134–140. [CrossRef]
26. Mutluürk, M.; Altindag, R.; Türk, G. A decay function model for the integrity loss of rock when subjected to recurrent cycles of freezing–thawing and heating–cooling. *Int. J. Rock Mech. Min. Sci.* **2004**, *41*, 237–244. [CrossRef]
27. Gao, F.; Xiong, X.; Zhou, K.; LI, J.; SHI, W. Strength deterioration model of saturated sandstone under freeze-thaw cycles. *Rock Soil Mech.* **2019**, *40*, 926–932. [CrossRef]
28. Ghobadi, M.H.; Taleb Beydokhti, A.R.; Nikudel, M.R.; Asiabanha, A.; Karakus, M. The effect of freeze–thaw process on the physical and mechanical properties of tuff. *Environ. Earth Sci.* **2016**, *75*, 846. [CrossRef]
29. Liu, Q.; Huang, S.; Kang, Y.; Liu, X. A prediction model for uniaxial compressive strength of deteriorated rocks due to freeze–thaw. *Cold Reg. Sci. Technol.* **2015**, *120*, 96–107. [CrossRef]
30. Gao, F.; Cao, S.; Zhou, K.; Lin, Y.; Zhu, L. Damage characteristics and energy-dissipation mechanism of frozen–thawed sandstone subjected to loading. *Cold Reg. Sci. Technol.* **2020**, *169*, 102920. [CrossRef]
31. Wang, L.; Li, N.; Qi, J.; Tian, Y.; Xu, S. A study on the physical index change and triaxial compression test of intact hard rock subjected to freeze-thaw cycles. *Cold Reg. Sci. Technol.* **2019**, *160*, 39–47. [CrossRef]
32. Zhang, H.; Yuan, C.; Yang, G.; Wu, L.; Peng, C.; Ye, W.; Shen, Y.; Moayedi, H. A novel constitutive modelling approach measured under simulated freeze–thaw cycles for the rock failure. *Eng. Comput.* **2021**, *37*, 779–792. [CrossRef]

33. Hosseini, M.; Khodayari, A.R. Effect of freeze-thaw cycle on strength and rock strength parameters (A Lushan sandstone case study). *J. Min. Environ.* **2019**, *10*, 257–270. [CrossRef]
34. Fu, H.; Zhang, J.; Huang, Z.; Shi, Y.; Chen, W. A statistical model for predicting the triaxial compressive strength of transversely isotropic rocks subjected to freeze–thaw cycling. *Cold Reg. Sci. Technol.* **2018**, *145*, 237–248. [CrossRef]
35. Seyed Mousavi, S.Z.; Tavakoli, H.; Moarefvand, P.; Rezaei, M. Assessing the effect of freezing-thawing cycles on the results of the triaxial compressive strength test for calc-schist rock. *Int. J. Rock Mech. Min. Sci.* **2019**, *123*, 104090. [CrossRef]
36. Ulusay, R. *The ISRM Suggested Methods for Rock Characterization, Testing and Monitoring 2007–2014*; Springer International Publishing: Cham, Switzerland, 2015; p. 292.
37. Li, J.; Zhou, K.; Liu, W.; Deng, H. NMR research on deterioration characteristics of microscopic structure of sandstones in freeze–thaw cycles. *Trans. Nonferrous Met. Soc. China* **2016**, *26*, 2997–3003. [CrossRef]
38. Gao, F.; Wang, Q.; Deng, H.; Zhang, J.; Tian, W.; Ke, B. Coupled effects of chemical environments and freeze–thaw cycles on damage characteristics of red sandstone. *Bull. Eng. Geol. Environ.* **2016**, *76*, 1481–1490. [CrossRef]
39. Li, J.; Zhou, K.; Zhang, Y.; Xu, Y. Experimental study of rock porous structure damage characteristics under condition of freezing-thawing cycles based on nuclear magnetic resonance technique. *Chin. J. Rock Mech. Eng.* **2012**, *31*, 1208–1214.
40. Liu, C.; Deng, J.; Yu, S.; Li, P.; Lin, Y. Effect of Freezing and Thawing on Microstructure Damage and Dynamic Flexural Tension of Granite. *Rock Mech. Rock Eng.* **2020**, *53*, 3853–3858. [CrossRef]
41. Shen, Y.; Wang, Y.; Wei, X.; Jia, H.; Yan, R. Investigation on meso-debonding process of the sandstone–concrete interface induced by freeze–thaw cycles using NMR technology. *Constr. Build. Mater.* **2020**, *252*, 118962. [CrossRef]
42. Sun, Y.; Zhai, C.; Xu, J.; Cong, Y.; Qin, L.; Zhao, C. Characterisation and evolution of the full size range of pores and fractures in rocks under freeze-thaw conditions using nuclear magnetic resonance and three-dimensional X-ray microscopy. *Eng. Geol.* **2020**, *271*, 105616. [CrossRef]
43. Wang, F.; Cao, P.; Wang, Y.; Hao, R.; Meng, J.; Shang, J. Combined effects of cyclic load and temperature fluctuation on the mechanical behavior of porous sandstones. *Eng. Geol.* **2020**, *266*, 105466. [CrossRef]
44. Xie, S.; Han, Z.; Lin, H. A quantitative model considering crack closure effect of rock materials. *Int. J. Solids Struct.* **2022**, *251*, 111758. [CrossRef]
45. Pak, J.; Hyun, C.; Park, H. Changes in microstructure and physical properties of rocks caused by artificial freeze–thaw action. *Bull. Eng. Geol. Environ.* **2015**, *74*, 555–565. [CrossRef]
46. Li, B.; Zhu, Z.; Ning, J.; Li, T.; Zhou, Z. Viscoelastic–plastic constitutive model with damage of frozen soil under impact loading and freeze–thaw loading. *Int. J. Mech. Sci.* **2022**, *214*, 106890. [CrossRef]
47. Rummel, F.; Fairhurst, C. Determination of the post-failure behavior of brittle rock using a servo-controlled testing machine. *Rock Mech. Rock Eng.* **1970**, *2*, 189–204. [CrossRef]
48. Zhang, F.; Sheng, Q.; Zhu, Z.; Zhang, Y. Study on post-peak mechanical behaviour and strain-softening model of three gorges granite. *Chin. J. Rock Mech. Eng.* **2008**, *27*, 2651–2655.
49. Yao, M.; Rong, G.; Zhou, C.; Peng, J. Effects of Thermal Damage and Confining Pressure on the Mechanical Properties of Coarse Marble. *Rock Mech. Rock Eng.* **2016**, *49*, 2043–2054. [CrossRef]
50. Zhao, J.; Feng, X.-T.; Zhang, X.-W.; Zhang, Y.; Zhou, Y.-Y.; Yang, C.-X. Brittle-ductile transition and failure mechanism of Jinping marble under true triaxial compression. *Eng. Geol.* **2018**, *232*, 160–170. [CrossRef]
51. Wang, P.; Xu, J.; Liu, S.; Wang, H. Dynamic mechanical properties and deterioration of red-sandstone subjected to repeated thermal shocks. *Eng. Geol.* **2016**, *212*, 44–52. [CrossRef]
52. Cadoni, E. Dynamic Characterization of Orthogneiss Rock Subjected to Intermediate and High Strain Rates in Tension. *Rock Mech. Rock Eng.* **2010**, *43*, 667–676. [CrossRef]
53. Hoek, E.; Brown, E.T. Practical Estimates of Rock Mass Strength. *Int. J. Rock Mech. Min. Sci.* **1997**, *34*, 1165–1186. [CrossRef]
54. Hoek, E.; Carranza-Torres, C.; Corkum, B. Hoek-brown failure criterion—2002 edition. In Proceedings of the 5th North American Rock Mechanics Symposium and the 17th Tunnelling Association of Canada Conference—NARMS-TAC 2002, Toronto, ON, Canada, 7–10 July 2002; pp. 267–273.

Article

# Predicting Angle of Internal Friction and Cohesion of Rocks Based on Machine Learning Algorithms

Niaz Muhammad Shahani [1,2,*], Barkat Ullah [3,*], Kausar Sultan Shah [4], Fawad Ul Hassan [1,5], Rashid Ali [6], Mohamed Abdelghany Elkotb [7,8], Mohamed E. Ghoneim [9,10] and Elsayed M. Tag-Eldin [11]

[1] School of Mines, China University of Mining and Technology, Xuzhou 221116, China
[2] The State Key Laboratory for Geo Mechanics and Deep Underground Engineering, China University of Mining & Technology, Xuzhou 221116, China
[3] School of Resources and Safety Engineering, Central South University, Changsha 410083, China
[4] Department of Mining Engineering, Karakoram International University, Gilgit 15100, Pakistan
[5] Department of Mining Engineering, Baluchistan University of Information Technology, Engineering and Management Sciences, Quetta 87300, Pakistan
[6] School of Mathematics and Statistics, Central South University, Changsha 410083, China
[7] Mechanical Engineering Department, College of Engineering, King Khalid University, Abha 61421, Saudi Arabia
[8] Mechanical Engineering Department, College of Engineering, Kafrelsheikh University, Kafrelsheikh 33516, Egypt
[9] Department of Mathematical Sciences, Faculty of Applied Science, Umm Al-Qura University, Makkah 21955, Saudi Arabia
[10] Faculty of Computers and Artificial Intelligence, Damietta University, Damietta 34517, Egypt
[11] Center of Research and Faculty of Engineering and Technology, Future University in Egypt, New Cairo 11835, Egypt
* Correspondence: shahani.niaz@cumt.edu.cn (N.M.S.); barkat_ullah@csu.edu.cn (B.U.)

**Abstract:** The safe and sustainable design of rock slopes, open-pit mines, tunnels, foundations, and underground excavations requires appropriate and reliable estimation of rock strength and deformation characteristics. Cohesion ($c$) and angle of internal friction ($\varphi$) are the two key parameters widely used to characterize the shear strength of materials. Thus, the prediction of these parameters is essential to evaluate the deformation and stability of any rock formation. In this study, four advanced machine learning (ML)-based intelligent prediction models, namely Lasso regression (LR), ridge regression (RR), decision tree (DT), and support vector machine (SVM), were developed to predict $c$ in (MPa) and $\varphi$ in (°), with P-wave velocity in (m/s), density in (gm/cc), UCS in (MPa), and tensile strength in (MPa) as input parameters. The actual dataset having 199 data points with no missing data was allocated identically for each model with 70% for training and 30% for testing purposes. To enhance the performance of the developed models, an iterative 5-fold cross-validation method was used. The coefficient of determination ($R^2$), mean absolute error (MAE), mean square error (MSE), root mean square error (RMSE), and a10-index were used as performance metrics to evaluate the optimal prediction model. The results revealed the SVM to be a more efficient model in predicting $c$ ($R^2 = 0.977$) and $\varphi$ ($R^2 = 0.916$) than LR ($c$: $R^2 = 0.928$ and $\varphi$: $R^2 = 0.606$), RR ($c$: $R^2 = 0.961$ and $\varphi$: $R^2 = 0.822$), and DT ($c$: $R^2 = 0.934$ and $\varphi$: $R^2 = 0.607$) on the testing data. Furthermore, to check the level of accuracy of the SVM model, a sensitivity analysis was performed on the testing data. The results showed that UCS and tensile strength were the most influential parameters in predicting $c$ and $\varphi$. The findings of this study contribute to long-term stability and deformation evaluation of rock masses in surface and subsurface rock excavations.

**Keywords:** angle of internal friction; cohesion; geotechnical parameters; support vector machine; intelligent prediction

**MSC:** 86-10

Citation: Shahani, N.M.; Ullah, B.; Shah, K.S.; Hassan, F.U.; Ali, R.; Elkotb, M.A.; Ghoneim, M.E.; Tag-Eldin, E.M. Predicting Angle of Internal Friction and Cohesion of Rocks Based on Machine Learning Algorithms. *Mathematics* 2022, 10, 3875. https://doi.org/10.3390/math10203875

Academic Editor: Ripon Kumar Chakrabortty

Received: 13 August 2022
Accepted: 14 October 2022
Published: 19 October 2022

**Publisher's Note:** MDPI stays neutral with regard to jurisdictional claims in published maps and institutional affiliations.

**Copyright:** © 2022 by the authors. Licensee MDPI, Basel, Switzerland. This article is an open access article distributed under the terms and conditions of the Creative Commons Attribution (CC BY) license (https://creativecommons.org/licenses/by/4.0/).

## 1. Introduction

The safe and sustainable design of rock slopes, open-pit mines, tunnels, foundations, and underground excavations needs a proper and reliable estimation of rock strength and deformation characteristics. Cohesion ($c$) and angle of internal friction ($\varphi$) are two widely used key mechanical strength parameters to characterize a material's shear strength [1,2]. Thus, the prediction and estimation of these parameters are essential to evaluate the deformation and stability of any rock formation [3]. The strength parameters $c$ and $\varphi$ can be obtained directly from laboratory tests (triaxial tests), which are destructive, laborious, and expensive. In addition, samples of the required quality are difficult to collect, especially in highly jointed and fragile rocks [2,4]. In rock mechanics and geotechnical engineering, it is imperative to analyze rock's performance and estimate its related mechanical properties [5–7]. Therefore, it is worthwhile to adapt the intelligent approaches for determining $c$ and $\varphi$.

One of the earliest adopted failure criterion for determining $c$ and $\varphi$ was the Mohr–Coulomb (MC) failure criterion.

Due to its mathematical convenience, simplicity, and conventional use in the field of rock mechanics, the MC criterion is still widely used [1,8–10]. The MC criterion includes two parameters, $c$ and $\varphi$. The parameter $c$ is used to identify the bond between rock particles and the parameter $\varphi$ is related to the internal friction generated along the shear surface [11]. Before the practical application of the MC criterion, the parameters $c$ and $\varphi$ need to be estimated [12,13]. In order to evaluate the MC parameters of $c$ and $\varphi$, triaxial tests are performed at different confining pressures. However, considering the factors of time and high cost associated with triaxial tests, there is a dire need for alternative methods to obtain MC parameters, especially at the preliminary stages of any project, where triaxial tests results are limited [14–16]. For this reason, efforts have been devoted to the development of fast and inexpensive methods for indirect estimation. Tests such as point load test [17], the Schmidt hammer test [18], sound velocity [19], impact strength [20], or the Los Angeles abrasion test [21] have been used to estimate uniaxial compressive strength (UCS) indirectly. Some researchers have investigated the applicability of UCS and uniaxial tensile strength (UTS) for estimating the $c$ and $\varphi$ of rocks in the absence of triaxial test data [16,22–24]. Additionally, some indirect estimation models have been introduced for the prediction of $c$ and $\varphi$. Weingarten and Perkins found a correlation between $\varphi$ and porosity [25] of sandstone. Plumb [26] determined the correlation between $\varphi$ and neutron porosity, which was improved by Asquith et al. [27] and Jaeger et al. [28]. Moreover, Edlmann et al. [29] determined a linear relationship between $\varphi$ and lab-measured core porosity. Abbas et al. evaluated the correlation of $\varphi$ with compressional waves and gamma rays using wireline logging data [30,31]. In all cases, $c$ was found to be dependent on $\varphi$ and UCS, as revealed by Almalikee and Strength [32]. Though the results of these methods have significant application in estimating $c$ and $\varphi$, they are not enough for long-term stability and deformation evaluation of rocks. Therefore, there is still a need to investigate $c$ and $\varphi$ of rocks using indirect estimation methods (i.e., intelligent approaches).

Recently, intelligent approaches have been widely used in the field of geotechnical engineering and rock mechanics [24,33–43]. Numerous researchers have used intelligent techniques, i.e., machine learning (ML) methods, to extend their knowledge for predicting $c$ and $\varphi$. Shen et al. applied genetic programming (GP) to predict the $c$ and $\varphi$ of sandstone rocks. The proposed model provided adequate predictive performance in the absence of triaxial data [16]. Mahmoodzadeh et al. employed Gaussian process regression (GPR), support vector regression (SVR), decision trees (DT), and long short-term memory (LSTM) to predict $c$ and $\varphi$ of intact rocks using three input parameters, i.e., UCS, UTS, and confining stress ($\sigma_3$) [24]. Khandelwal et al. implemented different approaches, namely simple and multiple regression, artificial neural network (ANN), and genetic algorithm (GA)-ANN, to predict the cohesion of limestone. For this purpose, P-wave velocity, UCS, and Brazilian tensile strength (BTS) were chosen as inputs [43]. Hiba et al. aimed to construct a predictive model using actual well-logging data. The study was carried out using two ML techniques, namely DT and random forest (RF). Bulk density (ROHB), neutron porosity (NPHI), and compression time (DTC) were used as input parameters to predict $c$ and $\varphi$ [44]. Kainthola et al. used an adaptive neuro-fuzzy inference system (ANFIS) and simple linear regression (SLR) to develop correlations between some basic physico-mechanical properties, including UCS, UTS, $c$, $\varphi$, and P-wave velocity [45]. Based on the above literature, it can be inferred that some useful, but not fully sufficient, insights have been provided in predicting $c$ and $\varphi$. The use of a particular procedure can be appropriate in certain circumstances, but not in others. More precisely, it has been noted in the literature that only a small amount of work has been carried out to predict $c$ and $\varphi$, especially using various types of rocks. Therefore, there is a need for novel ML-based intelligent methods to provide an accurate predictive model for predicting rock $c$ and $\varphi$ in order to safely install underground engineering projects.

In this study, P-wave velocity, density, UCS, and tensile strength are used as input parameters to predict $c$ (MPa) and $\varphi$ (°). In addition, four advanced ML-based prediction models, namely Lasso regression (LR), ridge regression (RR), decision tree (DT), and support vector machine (SVM), are developed to achieve the desired goals. To enhance the performance of the developed models, an iterative 5-fold cross-validation method is used. At present, the use of ML-based intelligent methods in predicting the mechanical and physical properties of rocks is gaining attention and providing an important contribution to rock excavation in different geotechnical and mining engineering projects [46–53]. The performance of the developed models is checked by some analytical metrics such as coefficient of determination ($R^2$), mean absolute error (MAE), mean square error (MSE), root mean square error (RMSE), and a10-index. The findings of this study could be helpful for long-standing stability and deformation evaluation of rock masses in surface and subsurface rock excavations. Figure 1 depicts the flowchart of the ML-based intelligent approach in this study.

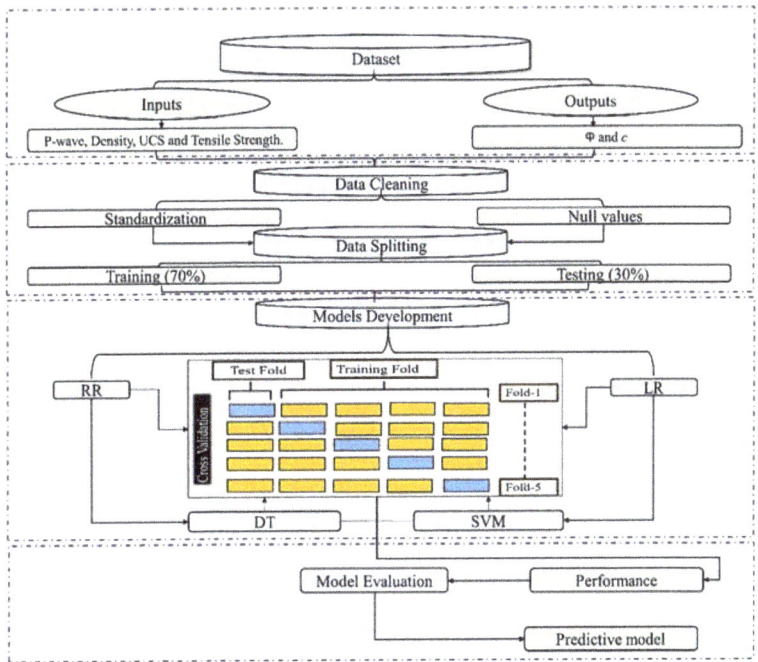

**Figure 1.** Flowchart of the ML-based intelligent approach in this study.

## 2. Data Curation

In this study, $c$ (MPa) and $\varphi$ (°), including P-wave velocity in m/s, density in gm/cc, UCS in MPa, and tensile strength in MPa as input parameters, were predicted by LR, RR, DT, and SVM from the reported literature [45] for various rocks, namely limestone, quartzite, slate, and quartz mica schist.

The actual dataset having 199 data points with no missing data was split into 70% for training purposes and 30% for testing purposes. To enhance the performance of the developed models, an iterative 5-fold cross-validation method is used. Figure 2 exhibits the test equipment for rock strength parameter measurement: (A) uniaxial testing machine, (B) tensile strength test, (C) P-wave velocity, and (D) triaxial test [45]. Figure 2 shows the histogram representation of the statistical distribution of the input parameters and output parameters of the actual dataset used in this study. Table 1 shows the lithology-based minimum and maximum, mean, and standard deviation (STD) values of the dataset.

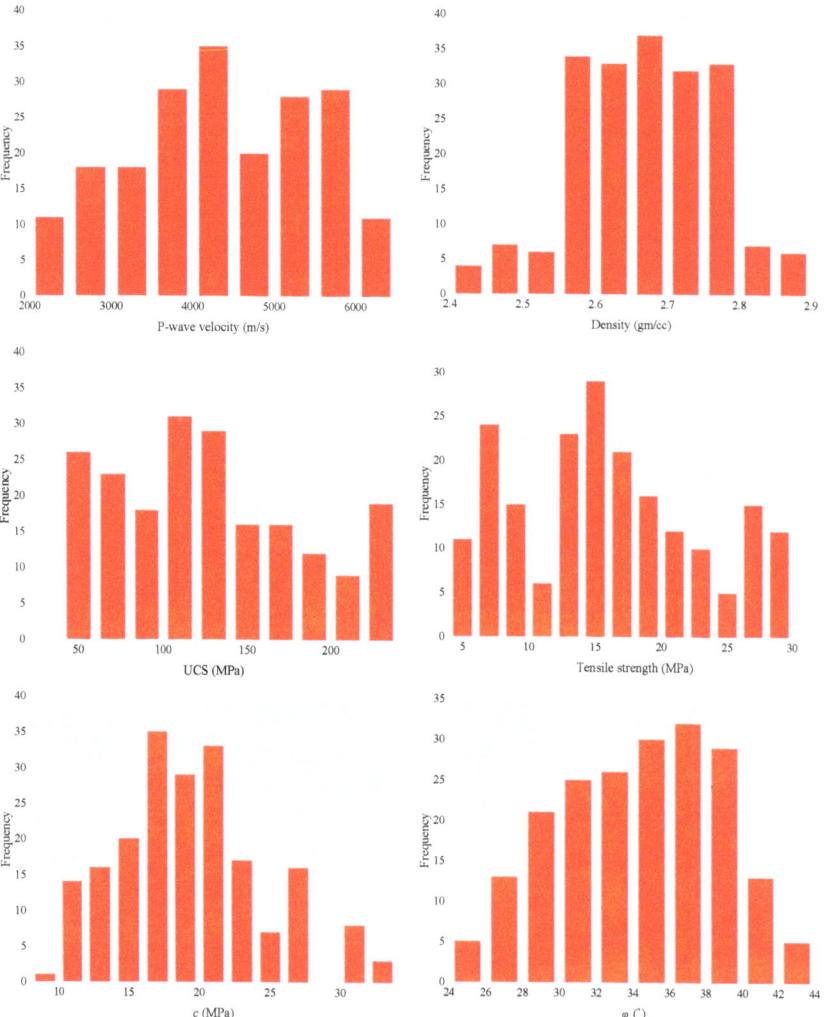

**Figure 2.** The statistical description of the inputs and output parameters of the actual dataset.

Table 1. Lithology-based minimum and maximum, mean, and standard deviation (STD) values of the dataset in this study.

| Items | P-Wave (m/s) | Density (gm/cc) | UCS (MPa) | Tensile Strength (MPa) | c (MPa) | $\varphi$ (°) |
|---|---|---|---|---|---|---|
| **Limestone** | | | | | | |
| No. of sample | 147 | 147 | 147 | 147 | 147 | 147 |
| Max | 4899.10 | 2.79 | 139 | 17.45 | 21.60 | 38.12 |
| Min | 3590.70 | 2.55 | 95.10 | 11.7 | 16.40 | 27.55 |
| Mean | 4092.73 | 2.65 | 111.26 | 13.88 | 18.99 | 33.47 |
| STD | 429.83 | 0.06 | 14.03 | 1.76 | 1.73 | 2.99 |
| **Quartzite** | | | | | | |
| No. of sample | 150 | 150 | 150 | 150 | 150 | 150 |
| Max | 6328.14 | 2.77 | 237.76 | 29.85 | 32.11 | 42.34 |
| Min | 5105.3 | 2.41 | 135.24 | 16.8 | 19 | 28.75 |
| Mean | 5675.90 | 2.58 | 198.52 | 24.89 | 25.80 | 35.95 |
| STD | 373.94 | 0.10 | 30.36 | 3.82 | 3.62 | 4.00 |
| **Slate** | | | | | | |
| No. of sample | 150 | 150 | 150 | 150 | 150 | 150 |
| Max | 5960.12 | 2.89 | 186.46 | 22.96 | 23.88 | 38.99 |
| Min | 4038.1 | 2.55 | 99.1 | 14.00 | 14.85 | 24.57 |
| Mean | 4690.12 | 2.68 | 141.53 | 17.85 | 19.12 | 31.53 |
| STD | 623.37 | 0.10 | 24.52 | 2.68 | 2.63 | 4.68 |
| **Quartz mica schist** | | | | | | |
| No. of sample | 150 | 150 | 1150 | 150 | 150 | 150 |
| Max | 4000.68 | 2.85 | 80.89 | 9.50 | 16.78 | 43.35 |
| Min | 2209.34 | 2.63 | 40.97 | 5.20 | 9.96 | 28.05 |
| Mean | 2938.11 | 2.72 | 58.14 | 7.18 | 13.13 | 35.88 |
| STD | 464.84 | 0.05 | 10.11 | 1.09 | 1.59 | 4.26 |

## 3. Developing ML-Based Intelligent Prediction Models

### 3.1. Lasso Regression

Lasso regression (LR) was proposed in 1986 and 1996 as a biased estimator in the field of geophysics [54]. Unlike ridge regression (RR), LR has the ability to perform both feature selection and penalty regularization to improve prediction accuracy. It combats multicollinearity by selecting the most important predictor from any set of highly correlated independent variables and removing all other variables. LR uses an L1-norm penalty term to shrink regression coefficients, some to zero, thus assuring the choice of the most important explanatory variables [52]. LR has an additional advantage that if a dataset of size n is fitted to a regression model with p parameters and p > n, the LR model can choose only n parameters [55]. To obtain estimates of the regression, the following loss function is minimized with Equation (1) [52]:

$$\tilde{\beta} = argmin_\beta \|y - X\beta\|_2^2 + \lambda |\beta|_1, \quad (|\beta|_1 = \sum_{j=1}^{p} |\beta|_1) \tag{1}$$

The parameter $\lambda$ can be selected using cross-validation. Though the LR and RR as given in Equations (1) and (2) bear a resemblance to each other, the results $\tilde{\beta}$ *ridge* and $\tilde{\beta}$ *lasso* show significant differences. In the process of shrinking the coefficients, the LR demonstrates the ability to set some of the coefficients to exactly zero. RR shrinks the coefficients, but never sets any of them to zero. LR performs variable selection by setting some coefficients to zero and retaining the coefficients that have a significant impact on output. Identifying these variables can improve the interpretability of the resulting model, especially when there is a large number of predictors [51].

## 3.2. Ridge Regression

Ridge regression (RR), also known as penalized least squares, provides a reduction in the variance of the estimated regression coefficients. RR shrinks the coefficients to zero and makes the estimates more stable than ordinary least squares (OLS) estimates [51]. RR was presented by Hoerl et al. [56] to enhance the prediction accuracy of the regression model by minimizing the following loss function Equation (2) [52]:

$$\tilde{\beta} = \mathrm{argmin}_\beta \|y - X\beta\|_2^2 + \lambda \|\beta\|_2^2, \quad (\|\beta\|_2^2 = \sum_{j=1}^p \beta_j^2) \quad (2)$$

If $\lambda$ is equal to 0, the obtained estimates are the OLS of multilinear regression (MLR). The parameter $\lambda$ can be selected by using cross-validation. In RR, the L2-norm penalty term is used to shrink the regression coefficient to a non-zero value to prevent overfitting, but it does not play the role of feature selection.

## 3.3. Decision Tree

The decision tree (DT) is a supervised learning hierarchical model in which local regions are recognized in fewer steps through a series of iterative splits. Internal decision nodes and terminal leaves form the decision tree. Both classification and regression can be performed with this method. The regression tree is built in a similar way to a classification tree, with the exception that the impurity measure used for classification is substituted with a measure used for regression. Let us state that $X_m$ is the subset of X that reaches node m, i.e., the set of all $x \in X$ that satisfy the conditions of all decision nodes on the path from the root to node m. We specify:

$$b_m(x) = \begin{cases} 1, & if \ x \in X_m : x \ reaches \ node \ m \\ 0, & otherwise \end{cases} \quad (3)$$

The mean square error from the estimated value determines a good tree split. In the regression, let $g_m$ be the anticipated value in node m.

$$E_m = \frac{1}{N_m} \sum_t (r^t - g_m)^2 b_m(x^t) \quad (4)$$

$$N_m = |X_m| \sum_t b_m(x^t)$$

The variance at m is associated to $E_m$. In a node, the mean of the desired outputs of the samples arriving at the node is employed.

$$g_m = \frac{\sum_t b_m(x^t) r^t}{\sum_t b_m(x^t)} \quad (5)$$

If a node's error is satisfactory ($E_m < \theta r$), a leaf node is generated, and the $g_m$ value is stored. Specifically, a piecewise constant approximation with discontinuities is generated at the boundary of the leaf. If the error is unacceptable, the data arriving at node m will be split again so that the sum of the errors in each branch is as small as possible [57,58].

## 3.4. Support Vector Machine

Support vector machine (SVM) is a supervised learning tool that was originally proposed by Vapnik [59]. SVM is widely used in classification and regression analysis using hyperplane classifiers. The optimal hyperplane maximizes the boundary between the two classes in which the support vector is located [50]. It uses a high-dimensional feature space to construct prediction functions by introducing kernel function and Vapnik's $\varepsilon$-insensitive loss function [46]. For a dataset P = {$(x_1, y_2), (x_2, y_2) \ldots (x_n, y_n)$}, where $x_i \in R^n$ is the input and $y_i \in R^n$ is the output, the SVM uses a kernel function to map the nonlinear input data in a high-dimensional feature space and tries to find the optimal hyperplane to separate them. This allows relating the original input to the output through a linear regression function [60,61], defined as follows:

$$f(x) = M_v \cdot \varphi(x) + l_b \qquad (6)$$

where $\varphi(x)$ is the kernel function, and $M_v$ and $l_b$ denote the weight vector and the bias term, respectively. To obtain $M_v$ and $l_b$, the cost function proposed by Cortes and Vapnik [62] needs to be minimized as follows:

$$\text{cost function} = \tfrac{1}{2} M_v^2 + C \sum_{i=1}^{k} \left( \xi_i^- + \xi_i^+ \right)$$

$$\text{Subject to}: \begin{cases} y_i - (M_v \cdot \varphi(x_1) + l_b) \leq \varepsilon_0 + \xi_i^+ \\ (M_v \cdot \varphi(x_1) + l_b) - y_i \leq \varepsilon_0 + \xi_i^- \\ \xi_i^-, \xi_i^+ \geq 0, \ i = 1, 2, \ldots, n \end{cases} \qquad (7)$$

Equation (4) can be minimized when transformed into dual space using the Lagrange multiplier method, giving the following solution:

$$f(x) = \sum_{i=1}^{n} (\infty_i - \infty_i') \varphi(x_i, x_j) + l_b \qquad (8)$$

where $\infty_i$ and $\infty_i'$ are Lagrange multipliers with $0 \leq \infty_i$ and $\infty_i' \leq C$, and $\varphi(x_i, x_j)$ is the kernel function. The choice of the latter is significant to the success of SVR. A large number of kernel functions was examined in SVM, such as linear, polynomial, sigmoid, Gaussian, radial basis, and exponential radial basis [63]. Figure 3 shows the basic structure of the SVM model.

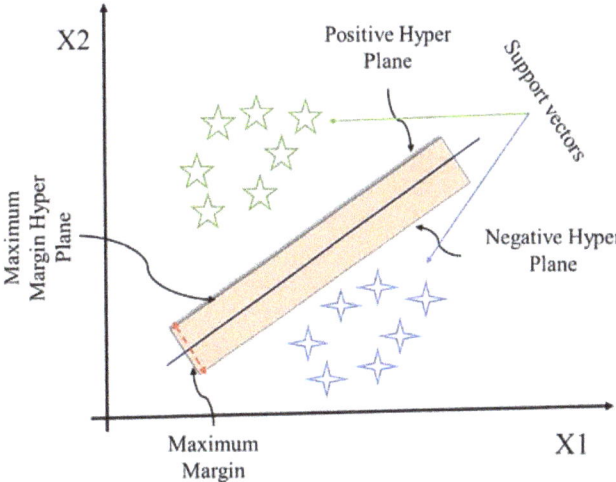

Figure 3. Basic structure of SVM model.

*3.5. Hyperparameters*

An ML algorithm needs to have optimized hyperparameters for better performance. These hyperparameters should be calibrated to the data as opposed to being defined manually. To minimalize the bias related to the random partition of the training and validation data, $k$-fold cross-validation was implemented in this paper, where $k$ represents the number of folds. By using cross-validation, the validity and accuracy of ML models can be evaluated by partitioning a dataset into different subsets and assessing the accuracy of the ML model on each subset [64]. The detail of optimized hyperparameters of RR, LR,

DT, and SVR models is presented Table 2. The λ values for the RR model were randomly selected in the range of 0.0–1.0, while the λ values for the LR model were kept at 1.0 and 0.01 for $c$ (MPa) and $\varphi$ (°), respectively. The random_state and capacity constant (C) for SVM were kept by default in the Python module for $c$ (MPa) and $\varphi$ (°). Moreover, three different functions, namely radial basis function (rbf), linear function, and polynomial function, were checked, and the performance of the rbf function was determined to be the best.

Table 2. Optimized hyperparameters.

| | Models | Parameters |
|---|---|---|
| $c$ (MPa) | Ridge | Alpha = 0.0–1.0, n_splits = 5, n_repeats = 3, random_states = 42 |
| | Lasso | Alpha = 1.0, n_splits = 5, n_repeats = 3, random_states = 42 |
| | DT | n_splits = 5, n_repeats = 5, random_states = 42, max_depth = 3 |
| | SVR | n_splits = 5, n_repeats = 5, random_states = 1, C = 1, function = SVR(kernel = 'rbf') |
| $\varphi$ (°) | Ridge | Alpha = 0.0–1.0, n_splits = 5, n_repeats = 3, random_states = 42 |
| | Lasso | Alpha = 0.01, n_splits = 5, n_repeats = 3, random_states = 42 |
| | DT | n_splits = 5, n_repeats = 5, random_states = 42, max_depth = 3 |
| | SVR | n_splits = 5, n_repeats = 5, random_states = 1, C = 1 function = SVR(kernel = 'rbf') |

## 4. Model Evaluation

The performance indices play a key role in the assessment of model evaluation. The most suitable model is one with the highest $R^2$ [65]; the smallest MAE, MSE [66], and RMSE [65]; and a suitable a10-index [66]. The model evaluation of each investigated model is evaluated by Equations (9)–(13), as follows.

$$R^2 = \frac{\sum_{i=1}^{n}(S_o - \overline{S_o})(S_p - \overline{S_p})}{\sqrt{\sum_{i=1}^{n}(S_o - \overline{S_o})^2((S_p - \overline{S_p})^2}} \quad (9)$$

$$MAE = \frac{1}{N}\sum_{i=1}^{n}|S_o - S_p| \quad (10)$$

$$MSE = \frac{\sum_{i=1}^{n}(S_o - S_p)^2}{N} \quad (11)$$

$$RMSE = \sqrt{\frac{\sum_{i=1}^{n}(S_o - S_p)^2}{N}} \quad (12)$$

$$a10 - index = \frac{m10}{N} \quad (13)$$

where $\overline{S_o}$ and $\overline{S_p}$ are the mean values of the actual and predicted values of the angle of internal friction and cohesion; $S_o$ and $S_p$ are the actual and predicted values of the angle of internal friction and cohesion, respectively; m10 signifies the datasets with a value of rate actual/predicted values between 0.90 and 1.10; and N is the number of datasets.

## 5. Results and Discussion

We aimed to investigate the ability of developed ML-based intelligent models such as LR, RR, DT, and SVM to predict rock shear strength parameters, namely $\varphi$ (°) and $c$ (MPa), using Python programming. In order to introduce the most suitable prediction model for predicting targeted output, the selection of appropriate input parameters can be considered as one of the most essential jobs. In this study, P-wave velocity (m/s), density (gm/cc), UCS (MPa), and tensile strength (MPa) were chosen as the input parameters for all developed models. Then, the actual and output values were arranged and plotted in such a way to examine the performance and correlations of each model. Based on the final prediction results, the performance and evaluation of the developed models were investigated employing different analytical indices such as $R^2$, MAE, MSE, RMSE, and a10-index. The actual dataset of 199 datapoints was split into 70% for training purposes and 30% for testing purposes.

Figure 4 shows a comparison of scatter plots and performance plots between the actual and predicted values of the $\varphi$ (°) at the test level for the LR, RR, DT, and SVM models. Based on the test prediction, the $R^2$ of each model is computed. The $R^2$ values of LR, RR, DT, and SVM models for the $\varphi$ (°) are 0.606, 0.607, 0.822, and 0.916, respectively.

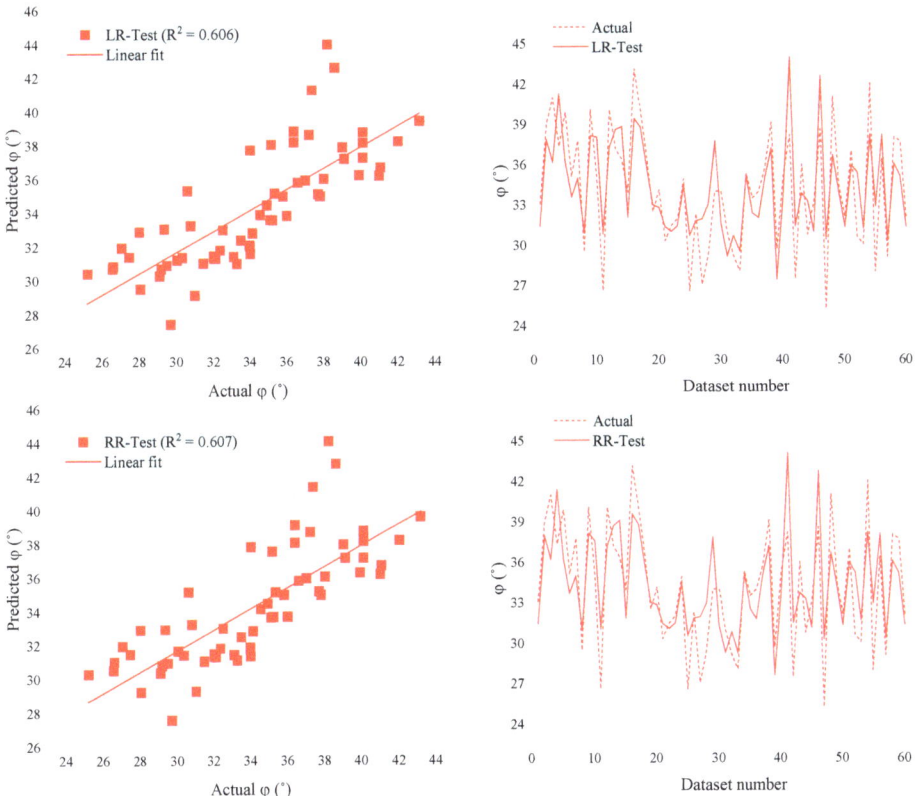

**Figure 4.** *Cont.*

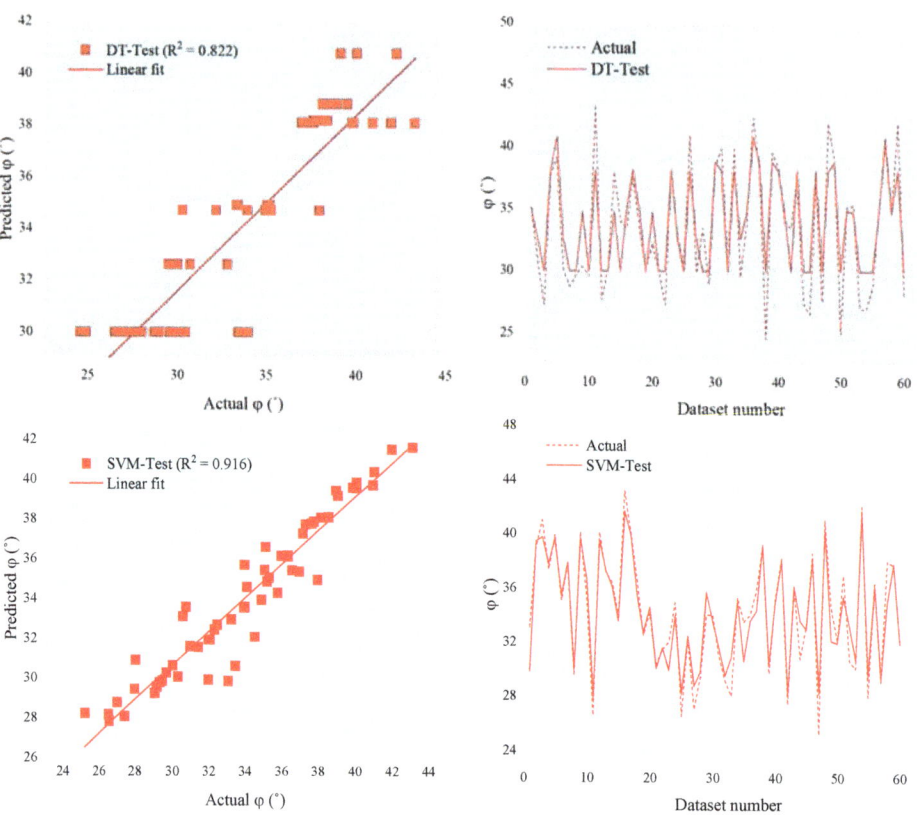

**Figure 4.** Performance plots of LR, RR, DT, and SVM models for the $\varphi$ (°) at the testing level.

In the same manner, Figure 5 shows a comparison of scatter plots and performance plots between the actual and predicted values of the $c$ (MPa) at the test level for the LR, RR, DT, and SVM models. Based on the test prediction, the $R^2$ of each model is computed. The $R^2$ values of LR, RR, DT, and SVM models for the $c$ (MPa) are 0.928, 0.934, 0.961, and 0.977, respectively.

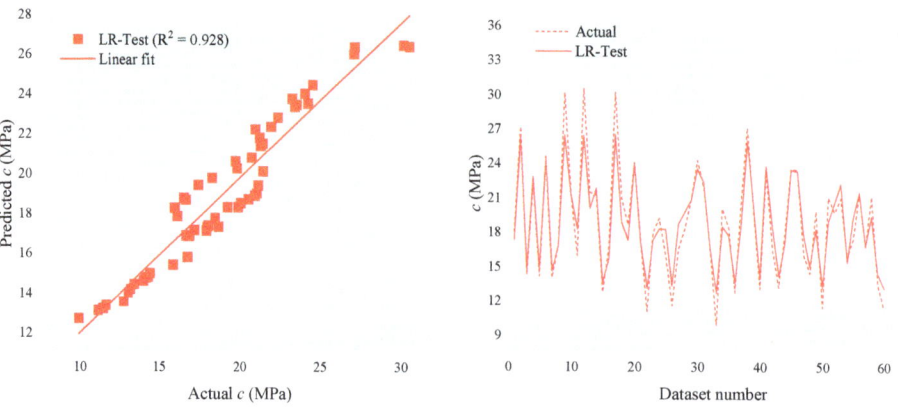

**Figure 5.** Cont.

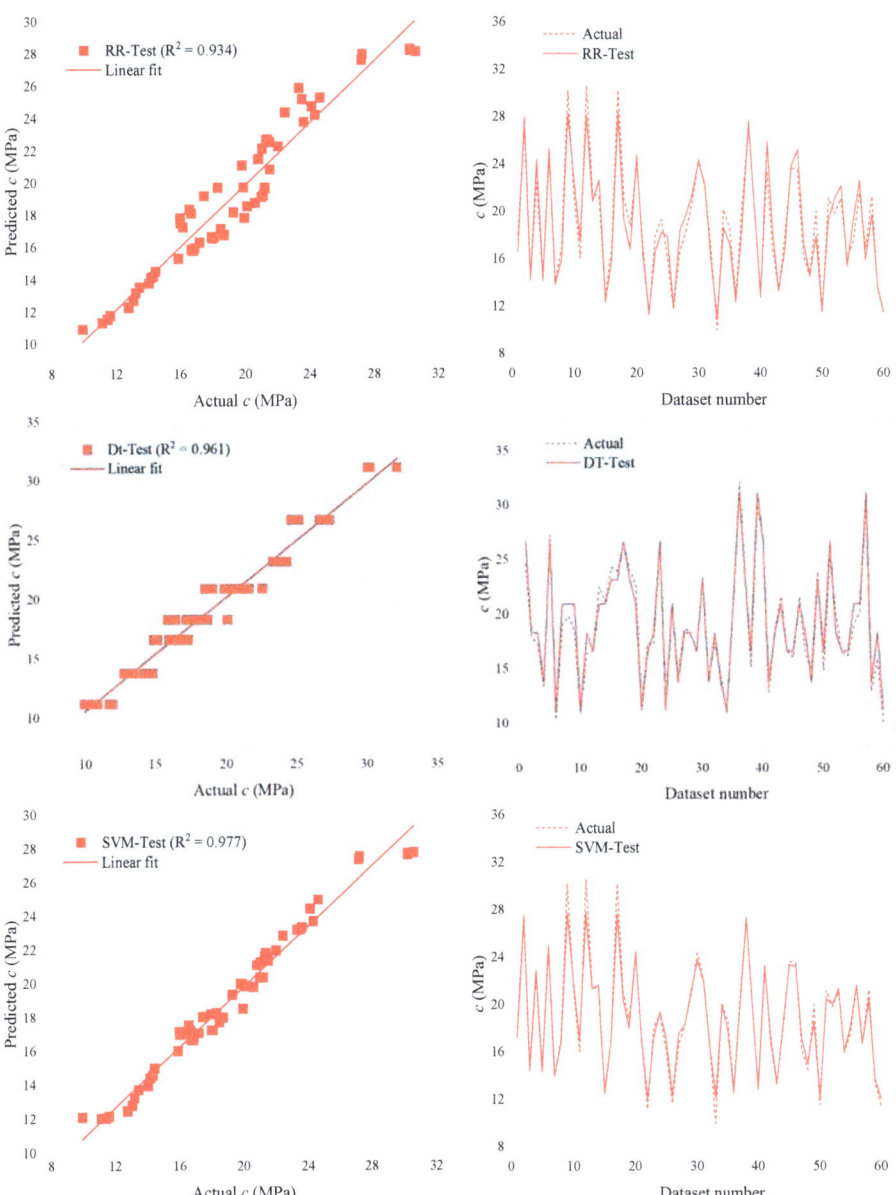

**Figure 5.** Performance plots of LR, RR, DT, and SVM models for the $c$ (MPa) at the testing level.

The data were split into two parts by DT, as shown in Figures 6 and 7. By averaging the two closest leaves, the similarity score and gain were computed, and the residuals were then transferred to the leaf with the maximum score and gain. The learning rate and maximum depth were set to 1.0 and 3.0, respectively, to prevent model complexity. Once the prediction results (residuals) were obtained, all data points were run through the model to produce h(x) and F(x) predictions.

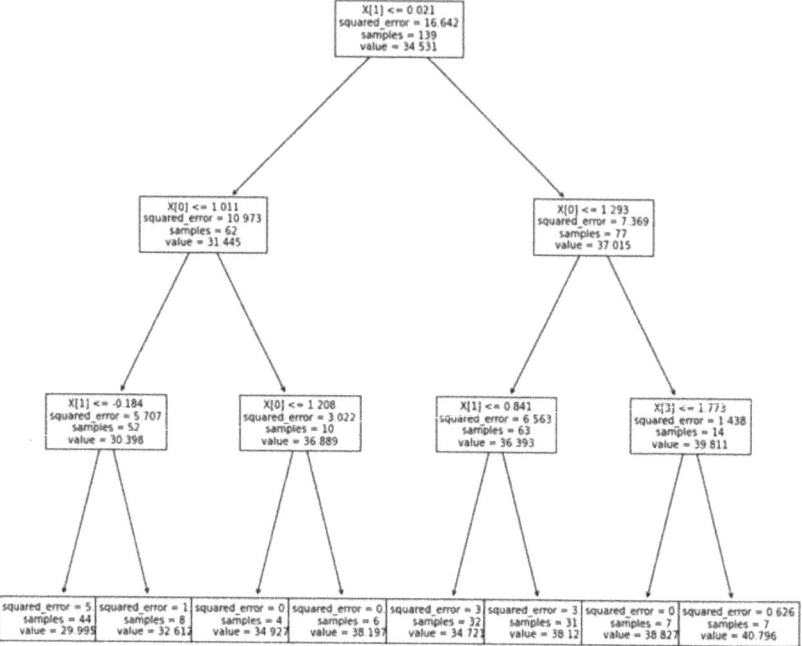

**Figure 6.** Decision tree for $\varphi$ (°).

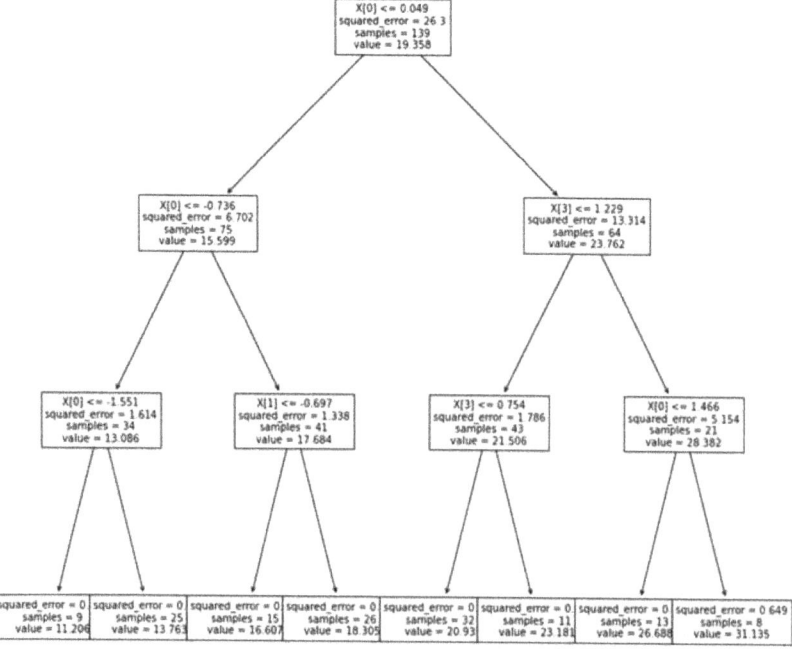

**Figure 7.** Decision tree for $c$ (MPa).

Table 3 shows the performance indices of the developed LR, RR, DT, and SVM models calculated by Equations (6)–(10). In this work, based on the developed LR, RR, DT, and SVM models, SVM outpaced other models at the testing level with $R^2$ = 0.916, MAE = 0.9094, MSE = 1.6656, RMSE = 1.2906, and a10-index = 1.00 for the $\varphi$ (°) prediction and $R^2$ = 0.977, MAE = 0.5577, MSE = 0.6811, RMSE = 0.8253, and a10-index = 1.00 for the $c$ (MPa) prediction. Therefore, SVM is an applicable ML-based intelligent approach that can be applied to accurately predict the $\varphi$ (°) and $c$ (MPa), as shown in Figure 8.

**Table 3.** Performance indices of ML-based developed models in this study.

| Model | | Training | | | | | Testing | | | | |
|---|---|---|---|---|---|---|---|---|---|---|---|
| | | $R^2$ | MAE | MSE | RMSE | a10-Index | $R^2$ | MAE | MSE | RMSE | a10-Index |
| LR | $\varphi$ (°) | 0.648 | 2.1653 | 6.9105 | 2.6288 | 1.00 | 0.606 | 2.3064 | 7.4286 | 2.7255 | 1.01 |
| | $c$ (MPa) | 0.941 | 1.2416 | 2.6128 | 1.6164 | 1.02 | 0.928 | 1.1454 | 2.2188 | 1.4896 | 1.02 |
| RR | $\varphi$ (°) | 0.65 | 2.1298 | 6.8575 | 2.6187 | 1.01 | 0.607 | 2.3003 | 7.4289 | 2.7256 | 1.00 |
| | $c$ (MPa) | 0.946 | 0.9756 | 1.5001 | 1.2248 | 1.00 | 0.934 | 1.0335 | 1.5405 | 1.2412 | 0.99 |
| DT | $\varphi$ (°) | 0.787 | 1.4562 | 3.5475 | 1.8835 | 1.00 | 0.822 | 1.7655 | 5.2730 | 2.2963 | 1.00 |
| | $c$ (MPa) | 0.976 | 0.6138 | 0.6088 | 0.7803 | 1.00 | 0.961 | 0.8389 | 1.1151 | 1.0560 | 0.99 |
| SVM | $\varphi$ (°) | 0.912 | 1.0021 | 1.7958 | 1.3401 | 1.00 | 0.916 | 0.9094 | 1.6656 | 1.2906 | 1.00 |
| | $c$ (MPa) | 0.978 | 0.6957 | 1.2308 | 1.1094 | 1.00 | 0.977 | 0.5577 | 0.6811 | 0.8253 | 1.00 |

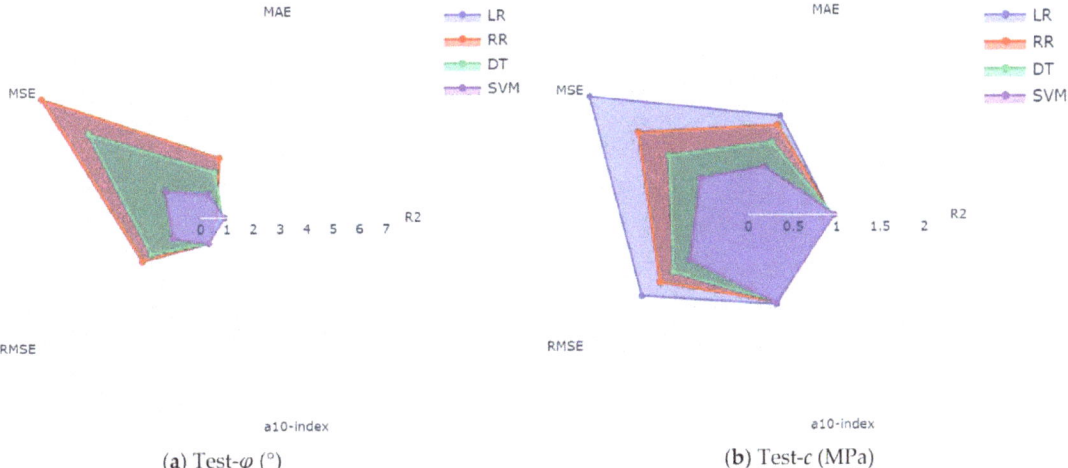

**Figure 8.** Radar plots of performance indices $R^2$, MAE, MSE, RMSE, and a10-index of the developed predictive models for the (a) $\varphi$ (°) and (b) $c$ (MPa) at the testing phase in this study.

The dataset used in this study was extracted from published literature [42] where the authors used an ANFIS and SLR to develop correlations between UCS, tensile strength, $c$ (MPa), $\varphi$ (°), and P-wave velocity. For further comprehensive comparison between intelligent approaches, we used the robust SVM model and predicted $c$ (MPa) and $\varphi$ (°), achieving the best results. Recently, few studies have used ML techniques to predict the $c$ (MPa), $\varphi$ (°); however, their results are limited to a single type of rock. Moreover, the authors neglected to evaluate the performance of robust ML approaches for different types of rocks [16,24,43,44].

## 6. Sensitivity Analysis

It is crucial to accurately analyze the most important parameters that have a considerable influence on the rock $\varphi$ (°) and $c$ (MPa), which can be problematic in the design of the rock structure. Therefore, the cosine amplitude method [67,68] is used for the relative influence of the input parameters on the output in this study.

Because of the high accuracy of the SVM model in predicting the $\varphi$ (°) and $c$ (MPa), only a sensitivity analysis was performed at the testing level. Figure 9 show the relationship between each input parameter of the developed model and output. All parameters are positively correlated, while UCS and tensile strength are the most influential parameters in predicting the $\varphi$ (°) and $c$ (MPa). Contrarily, the P-wave velocity and density are less influential parameters in predicting the $\varphi$ (°) and $c$ (MPa). The feature importance of each input parameter is given as P-wave velocity = 0.067, density = 0.066, UCS = 0.068, and tensile strength = 0.069 for the $\varphi$ (°). P-wave velocity = 0.067, density = 0.067, UCS = 0.068, and tensile strength = 0.069 for $c$ (MPa).

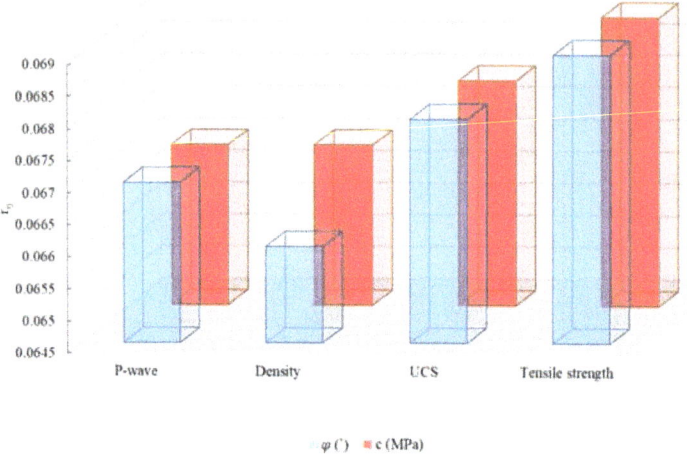

**Figure 9.** Sensitivity analysis values of $\varphi$ (°) and $c$ (MPa).

### 7. Limitations and Future Work

The performance of the SVM ML-based intelligent approach in predicting $\varphi$ (°) and $c$ (MPa) is consistent. Thus, for large-scale rock engineering projects, this work presents a sufficient basis to overcome the constraints. In order to carry out other projects, the model proposed in this study should be considered as a foundation and its results should be reanalyzed, reevaluated, and even reprocessed.

### 8. Conclusions

In this study, four ML-based intelligent models, i.e., LR, RR, DT, and SVM, were developed in order to introduce the most accurate prediction model for predicting the $\varphi$ (°) and $c$ (MPa). An identical 5-fold iterative cross-validation method was used to improve the efficiency of each model. The P-wave velocity (m/s), density (gm/cc), UCS (MPa), and tensile strength (MPa) were the selected input parameters for all developed models. Finally, the performance of each model was evaluated by $R^2$, MAE, MSE, RMSE, and a10-index values. The important conclusions drawn from this study are as follows:

1. Based on the estimated results of the developed LR, RR, DT, and SVM models, SVM outpaced other developed models at the testing level with $R^2$ = 0.916, MAE = 0.9094, MSE = 1.6656, RMSE = 1.2906, and a10-index = 1.00 for the $\varphi$ (°) prediction and $R^2$ = 0.977, MAE = 0.5577, MSE = 0.6811, RMSE = 0.8253, and a10-index = 1.00 for the $c$ (MPa) prediction.
2. According to the sensitivity analysis, UCS and tensile strength were the most influential parameters for predicting the $\varphi$ (°) and $c$ (MPa), with coefficient values of 0.068 and 0.069, respectively.

3. The findings of LR, RR, and DT are also applicable for predicting the $\varphi$ (°) and $c$ (MPa); these models can be used conditionally.

Therefore, SVM is an applicable ML-based intelligent approach that can be applied to accurately predict $\varphi$ (°) and $c$ (MPa).

**Author Contributions:** Conceptualization, N.M.S.; Data curation, N.M.S. and R.A.; Funding acquisition, M.A.E. and M.E.G.; Investigation, N.M.S.; Methodology, N.M.S.; Project administration, M.A.E. and M.E.G.; Software, K.S.S. and R.A.; Supervision, N.M.S. and B.U.; Validation, K.S.S.; Visualization, B.U.; Writing—original draft, N.M.S.; Writing—review & editing, B.U., E.M.T.-E. and F.U.H. All authors have read and agreed to the published version of the manuscript.

**Funding:** The authors extend their appreciation to the Deanship of Scientific Research at King Khalid University, Abha, Saudi Arabia, for funding this work through the Research Group Program under grant no. RGP. 2/19/43. In addition, the authors are grateful to the Deanship of Scientific Research at Umm Al-Qura University for supporting this work by grant code 22UQU4350057DSR09.

**Institutional Review Board Statement:** Not applicable.

**Informed Consent Statement:** Not applicable.

**Data Availability Statement:** Data can be made available upon request to the corresponding author.

**Conflicts of Interest:** The authors declare no conflict of interest.

# References

1. Yu, M.H. Advances in strength theories for materials under complex stress state in the 20th century. *Appl. Mech. Rev.* **2002**, *55*, 169–218. [CrossRef]
2. Alejano, L.R.; Carranza-Torres, C. An empirical approach for estimating shear strength of decomposed granites in Galicia, Spain. *Eng. Geol.* **2011**, *120*, 91–102. [CrossRef]
3. Wang, Y.; Akeju, O.V. Quantifying the cross-correlation between effective cohesion and friction angle of soil from limited site-specific data. *Soils Found.* **2016**, *56*, 1055–1070. [CrossRef]
4. Sivakugan, N.; Das, B.M.; Lovisa, J.; Patra, C.R. Determination of c and $\varphi$ of rocks from indirect tensile strength and uniaxial compression tests. *Int. J. Geotech. Eng.* **2014**, *8*, 59–65. [CrossRef]
5. Rezaei, M. Indirect measurement of the elastic modulus of intact rocks using the Mamdani fuzzy inference system. *Measurement* **2018**, *129*, 319–331. [CrossRef]
6. Wu, Y.; Huang, L.; Li, X.; Guo, Y.; Liu, H.; Wang, J. Effects of Strain Rate and Temperature on Physical Mechanical Properties and Energy Dissipation Features of Granite. *Mathematics* **2022**, *10*, 1521. [CrossRef]
7. Xiao, P.; Zhao, G.; Liu, H. Failure Transition and Validity of Brazilian Disc Test under Different Loading Configurations: A Numerical Study. *Mathematics* **2022**, *10*, 2681. [CrossRef]
8. Li, X.; Zhou, Z.; Lok, T.S.; Hong, L.; Yin, T. Innovative testing technique of rock subjected to coupled static and dynamic loads. *Int. J. Rock Mech. Min. Sci.* **2008**, *45*, 739–748. [CrossRef]
9. Zhou, Z.; Li, X.; Ye, Z.; Liu, K. Obtaining constitutive relationship for rate-dependent rock in SHPB tests. *Rock Mech. Rock Eng.* **2010**, *43*, 697–706. [CrossRef]
10. Labuz, J.F.; Zang, A. Mohr-Coulomb failure criterion. *Rock. Mech. Rock. Eng.* **2012**, *45*, 975–979. [CrossRef]
11. Singh, A.; Ayothiraman, R.; Rao, K.S. Failure Criteria for Isotropic Rocks Using a Smooth Approximation of Modified Mohr–Coulomb Failure Function. *Geotech. Geol. Eng.* **2020**, *38*, 4385–4404. [CrossRef]
12. Armaghani, D.J.; Hajihassani, M.; Bejarbaneh, B.Y.; Marto, A.; Mohamad, E.T. Indirect measure of shale shear strength parameters by means of rock index tests through an optimized artificial neural network. *Measurement* **2014**, *55*, 487–498. [CrossRef]
13. Rullière, A.; Rivard, P.; Peyras, L.; Breul, P. Influence of Roughness on the Apparent Cohesion of Rock Joints at Low Normal Stresses. *J. Geotech. Geoenvironmental Eng.* **2020**, *146*, 04020003. [CrossRef]
14. Cai, M. Practical estimates of tensile strength and Hoek–Brown strength parameter mi of brittle rocks. *Rock Mech. Rock Eng.* **2010**, *43*, 167–184. [CrossRef]
15. Beiki, M.; Majdi, A.; Givshad, A.D. Application of genetic programming to predict the uniaxial compressive strength and elastic modulus of carbonate rocks. *Int. J. Rock Mech. Min. Sci.* **2013**, *63*, 159–169. [CrossRef]
16. Shen, J.; Jimenez, R. Predicting the shear strength parameters of sandstone using genetic programming. *Bull. Eng. Geol. Environ.* **2018**, *77*, 1647–1662. [CrossRef]
17. Şahin, M.; Ulusay, R.; Karakul, H. Point Load Strength Index of Half-Cut Core Specimens and Correlation with Uniaxial Compressive Strength. *Rock Mech. Rock Eng.* **2020**, *53*, 3745–3760. [CrossRef]
18. Mohammed, D.A.; Alshkane, Y.M.; Hamaamin, Y.A. Reliability of empirical equations to predict uniaxial compressive strength of rocks using Schmidt hammer. *Georisk Assess. Manag. Risk Eng. Syst. Geohazards* **2020**, *14*, 308–319. [CrossRef]

19. Kurtulus, C.; Sertcelik, F.; Sertcelik, I. Estimation of Unconfined Uniaxial Compressive Strength Using Schmidt Hardness and Ultrasonic Pulse Velocity. *Teh. Vjesn.* **2018**, *25*, 1569–1574. [CrossRef]
20. Jing, H.; Nikafshan Rad, H.; Hasanipanah, M.; Jahed Armaghani, D.; Qasem, S.N. Design and implementation of a new tuned hybrid intelligent model to predict the uniaxial compressive strength of the rock using SFS-ANFIS. *Eng. Comput.* **2021**, *37*, 2717–2734. [CrossRef]
21. Teymen, A. Estimation of Los Angeles abrasion resistance of igneous rocks from mechanical aggregate properties. *Bull. Eng. Geol. Environ.* **2019**, *78*, 837–846. [CrossRef]
22. Farah, R. Correlations between Index Properties and Unconfined Compressive Strength of Weathered Ocala Limestone. Master's Thesis, University of North Florida School of Engineering, Jacksonville, FL, USA, 2011.
23. Karaman, K.; Cihangir, F.; Ercikdi, B.; Kesimal, A.; Demirel, S. Utilization of the Brazilian test for estimating the uniaxial compressive strength and shear strength parameters. *J. South. Afr. Inst. Min. Metall.* **2015**, *115*, 185–192. [CrossRef]
24. Mahmoodzadeh, A.; Mohammadi, M.; Salim, S.G.; Ali, H.F.H.; Ibrahim, H.H.; Abdulhamid, S.N.; Nejati, H.R.; Rashidi, S. Machine Learning Techniques to Predict Rock Strength Parameters. *Rock Mech. Rock Eng.* **2022**, *55*, 1721–1741. [CrossRef]
25. Weingarten, J.S.; Perkins, T.K. Prediction of sand production in gas wells: Methods and Gulf of Mexico case studies. *J. Pet. Technol.* **1995**, *47*, 596–600. [CrossRef]
26. Plumb, R.A. Influence of composition and texture on the failure properties of clastic rocks. In *Rock Mechanics in Petroleum Engineering*; OnePetro: Delft, The Netherlands, 1994.
27. Asquith, G.B.; Krygowski, D.; Gibson, C.R. *Basic Well Log Analysis*; American Association of Petroleum Geologists: Tulsa, OK, USA, 2004; Volume 16.
28. Jaeger, J.C.; Cook, N.G.; Zimmerman, R. *Fundamentals of Rock Mechanics*; John Wiley & Sons: Hoboken, NJ, USA, 2009.
29. Edimann, K.; Somerville, J.M.; Smart BG, D.; Hamilton, S.A.; Crawford, B.R. Predicting rock mechanical properties from wireline porosities. In *SPE/ISRM Rock Mechanics in Petroleum Engineering*; OnePetro: Trondheim, Norway, 1998. [CrossRef]
30. Abbas, A.K.; Flori, R.E.; Alsaba, M. Estimating rock mechanical properties of the Zubair shale formation using a sonic wireline log and core analysis. *J. Nat. Gas Sci. Eng.* **2018**, *53*, 359–369. [CrossRef]
31. Abbas, A.K.; Flori, R.E.; Alsaba, M.; Dahm, H.; Alkamil, E.H. Integrated approach using core analysis and wireline measurement to estimate rock mechanical properties of the Zubair Reservoir, Southern Iraq. *J. Pet. Sci. Eng.* **2018**, *166*, 406–419. [CrossRef]
32. Almalikee, H.S.; Strength, R.C. Predicting rock mechanical properties from wireline logs in Rumaila Oilfield. *South. Iraq* **2019**, *5*, 69–77.
33. Shakeri, J.; Asadizadeh, M.; Babanouri, N. The prediction of dynamic energy behavior of a Brazilian disk containing nonpersistent joints subjected to drop hammer test utilizing heuristic approaches. *Neural Comput. Appl.* **2022**, *34*, 9777–9792. [CrossRef]
34. Shahani, N.M.; Kamran, M.; Zheng, X.; Liu, C.; Guo, X. Application of gradient boosting machine learning algorithms to predict uniaxial compressive strength of soft sedimentary rocks at Thar Coalfield. *Adv. Civ. Eng.* **2021**, *2021*, 1–19. [CrossRef]
35. Asadizadeh, M.; Karimi, J.; Hossaini, M.F.; Alipour, A.; Nowak, S.; Sherizadeh, T. The effect of central flaw on the unconfined strength of rock-like specimens: An intelligent approach. *Iran. J. Sci. Technol. Trans. Civ. Eng.* **2022**, *46*, 3679–3694. [CrossRef]
36. Shahani, N.M.; Zheng, X.; Guo, X.; Wei, X. Machine Learning-Based Intelligent Prediction of Elastic Modulus of Rocks at Thar Coalfield. *Sustainability* **2022**, *14*, 3689. [CrossRef]
37. Armaghani, D.J.; Amin MF, M.; Yagiz, S.; Faradonbeh, R.S.; Abdullah, R.A. Prediction of the uniaxial compressive strength of sandstone using various modeling techniques. *Int. J. Rock Mech. Min. Sci.* **2016**, *85*, 174–186. [CrossRef]
38. Armaghani, D.J.; Safari, V.; Fahimifar, A.; Monjezi, M.; Mohammadi, M.A. Uniaxial compressive strength prediction through a new technique based on gene expression programming. *Neural Comput. Appl.* **2018**, *30*, 3523–3532. [CrossRef]
39. Armaghani, D.J.; Momeni, E.; Abad, S.V.A.N.K.; Khandelwal, M. Feasibility of ANFIS model for prediction of ground vibrations resulting from quarry blasting. *Environ. Earth Sci.* **2015**, *74*, 2845–2860. [CrossRef]
40. Shahani, N.M.; Zheng, X.; Liu, C.; Li, P.; Hassan, F.U. Application of soft computing methods to estimate uniaxial compressive strength and elastic modulus of soft sedimentary rocks. *Arab. J. Geosci.* **2022**, *15*, 1–19. [CrossRef]
41. Khandelwal, M.; Armaghani, D.J. Prediction of drillability of rocks with strength properties using a hybrid GA-ANN technique. *Geotech. Geol. Eng.* **2016**, *34*, 605–620. [CrossRef]
42. Armaghani, D.J.; Mohamad, E.T.; Narayanasamy, M.S.; Narita, N.; Yagiz, S. Development of hybrid intelligent models for predicting TBM penetration rate in hard rock condition. *Tunn. Undergr. Space Technol.* **2017**, *63*, 29–43. [CrossRef]
43. Khandelwal, M.; Marto, A.; Fatemi, S.A.; Ghoroqi, M.; Armaghani, D.J.; Singh, T.N.; Tabrizi, O. Implementing an ANN model optimized by genetic algorithm for estimating cohesion of limestone samples. *Eng. Comput.* **2018**, *34*, 307–317. [CrossRef]
44. Hiba, M.; Ibrahim, A.F.; Elkatatny, S.; Ali, A. Prediction of cohesion and friction angle from well-logging data using decision tree and random forest. *Arab. J. Geosci.* **2022**, *15*, 1–11. [CrossRef]
45. Kainthola, A.; Singh, P.K.; Verma, D.; Singh, R.; Sarkar, K.; Singh, T.N. Prediction of strength parameters of himalayan rocks: A statistical and ANFIS approach. *Geotech. Geol. Eng.* **2015**, *33*, 1255–1278. [CrossRef]
46. Wan, Z.; Xu, Y.; Šavija, B. On the use of machine learning models for prediction of compressive strength of concrete: Influence of dimensionality reduction on the model performance. *Materials* **2021**, *14*, 713. [CrossRef] [PubMed]
47. Çelik, S.B. Prediction of uniaxial compressive strength of carbonate rocks from nondestructive tests using multivariate regression and LS-SVM methods. *Arab. J. Geosci.* **2019**, *12*, 1–17. [CrossRef]

48. Suthar, M. Applying several machine learning approaches for prediction of unconfined compressive strength of stabilized pond ashes. *Neural Comput. Appl.* **2020**, *32*, 9019–9028. [CrossRef]
49. Negara, A.; Ali, S.; AlDhamen, A.; Kesserwan, H.; Jin, G. Unconfined compressive strength prediction from petrophysical properties and elemental spectroscopy using support-vector regression. In *SPE Kingdom of Saudi Arabia Annual Technical Symposium and Exhibition*; OnePetro: Dammam, Saudi Arabia, 2017.
50. Sun, J.; Zhang, J.; Gu, Y.; Huang, Y.; Sun, Y.; Ma, G. Prediction of permeability and unconfined compressive strength of pervious concrete using evolved support vector regression. *Constr. Build. Mater.* **2019**, *207*, 440–449. [CrossRef]
51. Arif, C.; Jale, T. Prediction of Compressive Strength of Recycled Aggregate Concrete using LASSO. *Civ. Eng. Res. J.* **2018**, *5*, 555654. [CrossRef]
52. Hassan, M.Y.; Arman, H. Comparison of Six Machine-Learning Methods for Predicting the Tensile Strength (Brazilian) of Evaporitic Rocks. *Appl. Sci.* **2021**, *11*, 5207. [CrossRef]
53. Bai, C.; Xue, Y. Predicting uniaxial compressive strength of rocks: Comparison of twelve machine learning-based regression models. 2020; *Preprint*. [CrossRef]
54. Santosa, F.; Symes, W.W. Linear inversion of band-limited reflection seismograms. *SIAM J. Sci. Stat. Comput.* **1986**, *7*, 1307–1330. [CrossRef]
55. Zou, H.; Hastie, T. Regularization and variable selection via the elastic net. *J. R. Stat. Soc. Ser. B* **2005**, *67*, 301–320. [CrossRef]
56. Hoerl, A.E.; Kennard, R.W. American Society for Quality Ridge Regression: Applications to Nonorthogonal Problems. 1970. Available online: http://www.jstor.orgURL:http://www.jstor.org/stable/1267352 (accessed on 28 November 2015).
57. Alpaydın, E. *Introduction to Machine Learning*; MIT Press: Cambridge, MA, USA, 2020.
58. Şeker, Ş.E. *Karar Ağacı Öğrenmesi*; 2017; pp. 1–7.
59. Vapnik, V.; Golowich, S.E.; Smola, A. Support vector method for function approximation, regression estimation, and signal processing. In *Advances in Neural Information Processing Systems 9 (NIPS 1996)*; MIT Press: Cambridge, MA, USA, 1997; pp. 281–287.
60. Xu, C.; Amar, M.N.; Ghriga, M.A.; Ouaer, H.; Zhang, X.; Hasanipanah, M. Evolving support vector regression using Grey Wolf optimization; forecasting the geomechanical properties of rock. *Eng. Comput.* **2020**, *38*, 1819–1833. [CrossRef]
61. Longjun, D.; Xibing, L.; Ming, X.; Qiyue, L. Comparisons of random forest and support vector machine for predicting blasting vibration characteristic parameters. *Procedia Eng.* **2011**, *26*, 1772–1781. [CrossRef]
62. Cortes, C.; Vapnik, V. Support-vector networks. *Mach. Learn.* **1995**, *20*, 273–297. [CrossRef]
63. Barzegar, R.; Sattarpour, M.; Nikudel, M.R.; Moghaddam, A.A. Comparative evaluation of artificial intelligence models for prediction of uniaxial compressive strength of travertine rocks, case study: Azarshahr area, NW Iran. *Model. Earth Syst. Environ.* **2016**, *2*, 76. [CrossRef]
64. Ullah, B.; Kamran, M.; Rui, Y. Predictive modeling of short-term rockburst for the stability of subsurface structures using machine learning approaches: T-SNE, K-Means clustering and XGBoost. *Mathematics* **2022**, *10*, 449. [CrossRef]
65. Shahani, N.M.; Zheng, X.; Liu, C.; Hassan, F.U.; Li, P. Developing an XGBoost Regression Model for Predicting Young's Modulus of Intact Sedimentary Rocks for the Stability of Surface and Subsurface Structures. *Front. Earth Sci.* **2021**, *9*, 761990. [CrossRef]
66. Shahani, N.M.; Kamran, M.; Zheng, X.; Liu, C. Predictive modeling of drilling rate index using machine learning approaches: LSTM, simple RNN, and RFA. *Pet. Sci. Technol.* **2022**, *40*, 534–555. [CrossRef]
67. Momeni, E.; Nazir, R.; Armaghani, D.J.; Maizir, H. Prediction of pile bearing capacity using a hybrid genetic algorithm-based ANN. *Measurement* **2014**, *57*, 122–131. [CrossRef]
68. Ji, X.; Liang, S.Y. Model-based sensitivity analysis of machining-induced residual stress under minimum quantity lubrication. *Proc. Inst. Mech. Eng. Part B J. Eng. Manuf.* **2017**, *231*, 1528–1541. [CrossRef]

*Article*

# Dynamic Tensile Mechanical Properties of Outburst Coal Considering Bedding Effect and Evolution Characteristics of Strain Energy Density

Shuang Gong [1,2,3], Chaofei Wang [1], Furui Xi [4,5,*], Yongqiang Jia [1], Lei Zhou [1], Hansong Zhang [1], Jingkuo Wang [1], Xingyang Ren [1], Shuai Wang [1], Shibin Yao [1] and Juan Liu [1]

1. School of Energy Science and Engineering, Henan Polytechnic University, Jiaozuo 454000, China
2. Henan Key Laboratory for Green and Efficient Mining & Comprehensive Utilization of Mineral Resources, Jiaozuo 454000, China
3. Collaborative Innovation Center of Coal Work Safety, Jiaozuo 454000, China
4. China Institute of Geo-Environment Monitoring, Beijing 100081, China
5. Key Laboratory of Mine Ecological Effects and Systematic Restoration, Ministry of Nature Resource, Beijing 100081, China
* Correspondence: xifurui@mail.cgs.gov.cn

**Citation:** Gong, S.; Wang, C.; Xi, F.; Jia, Y.; Zhou, L.; Zhang, H.; Wang, J.; Ren, X.; Wang, S.; Yao, S.; et al. Dynamic Tensile Mechanical Properties of Outburst Coal Considering Bedding Effect and Evolution Characteristics of Strain Energy Density. *Mathematics* **2022**, *10*, 4120. https://doi.org/10.3390/math10214120

Academic Editor: Vasily Novozhilov

Received: 30 September 2022
Accepted: 1 November 2022
Published: 4 November 2022

**Publisher's Note:** MDPI stays neutral with regard to jurisdictional claims in published maps and institutional affiliations.

**Copyright:** © 2022 by the authors. Licensee MDPI, Basel, Switzerland. This article is an open access article distributed under the terms and conditions of the Creative Commons Attribution (CC BY) license (https://creativecommons.org/licenses/by/4.0/).

**Abstract:** The evolution of strain energy density of outburst-prone coal is of great significance for analyzing the characteristics of energy accumulation and release in coal and rock masses. The dynamic mechanical properties of coal samples were tested by using the split Hopkinson pressure bar (SHPB) technique. Dynamic tensile mechanical properties, layered effect and density evolution characteristics of strain energy for coal were studied. The dynamic failure and crack propagation process of the specimen were recorded with a high-speed camera. In addition, a digital image correlation (DIC) method was used to analyze the evolution characteristics of the strain field during the deformation process of the specimen. The distribution characteristics of the particle fragments were statistically analyzed. The results show that the bedding orientation of the coal has a significant effect on its deformation and damage features. The presence of weak planes, microcracks and laminae causes its shear damage zone to behave more complex. If the crack plane coincides with the high shear stress plane, the developed shear cracks extend along the weak laminae and the shear damage zones in BD specimens are not symmetrically distributed. When the laminated surface of the coal sample is at a certain angle with the impact loading direction, the damage mode is coupled with tensile and shear damage. The percentage mass distribution of particles and fines increases with increasing bedding orientation. The effect of water on the dynamic damage of coal samples is significant. Based on the principle of pressure expansion of wing-shaped cracks, the formula for calculating the dynamic strength of water-saturated coal samples under dynamic loading was derived.

**Keywords:** dynamic tensile mechanical property; outburst coal; crack extension; strain energy density; impact loading

**MSC:** 74H45

## 1. Introduction

Engineering fields such as oil well fracturing, mining rock fracturing, protection under explosion and other catastrophic natural phenomena such as earthquakes and rock bursts are almost always related to rock fracture and stress wave propagation in rocks under impact loads. Common geological hazards such as coal and gas protrusion and coal rock instability in coal mine production also involve deformation, crack expansion, energy accumulation and release, and damage mechanism of rocks under impact loading [1]. The mechanical properties of rocks under impact loading are quite different from those under static loading. Due to the natural complexity of rocks and the inertial effect of impact loading, theoretical and experimental studies on the dynamic damage of rock materials are not yet complete. There are still many fundamental problems that need further exploration and in-depth research. In order to develop rock engineering technology and prevent the occurrence of catastrophic accidents due to rock damage caused by impact in engineering, it is necessary to understand the dynamic damage mechanisms of rocks [2]. The study of dynamic mechanical properties of rocks is of great interest to reveal the damage mechanisms of rocks and guide engineering practice.

The dynamic mechanical properties of coal rock have been studied extensively by previous scholars. Song et al. [3] studied the deformation and damage processes of rocks under different loading conditions. A rock matrix-fracture medium model for non-homogeneous and fractured coal seams was proposed by Zhang et al. [4]. Hao et al. [5] used the crack volume strain method, and acoustic emission (AE) method were used to analyze the anisotropy of the crack initiation strength, damage strength, the failure mode and the AE characteristics of coal reservoir. Li et al. [6] studied the influence of sampling directions (perpendicular to bedding planes and parallel to bedding planes) on the transient charge signals of coal. Gong [7] analyzed the crack extension process and crack distribution after damage in bituminous coal specimens. Liu et al. [8] used an acoustic emission system to experimentally investigate the mechanical properties and associated acoustic emission characteristics of loaded coal for different bedding angles, and developed an acoustic emission-based damage model. The effect of bedding angle on coal permeability was systematically investigated by Pan et al. [9–12]. Hou et al. [13] carried out Brazilian splitting tests on bedding coal and analyzed the effects of low temperature cooling fracturing and bedding orientation on the mechanical properties and fracture morphology of the coal. The effect of bed texture on the dynamic indirect tensile strength of coal was investigated by Zhao et al. [14]. Li et al. [15] established a model for the calculation of anisotropic coal permeability and analyzed the distribution pattern of permeability in arbitrary directions at different angles to the beds plane. Li et al. [16–18] investigated the effect of circumferential pressure and bedding angle on the mechanical properties of coal. Liu et al. [19,20] carried out LNMR and NMR studies of the microstructural characteristics and pore size distribution of high-grade coals with different bedding structures. Influence of bedding on the fracture pattern of the coal mass during blasting was investigated Zhao et al. [21]. Yuan et al. [22] revealed the influence of primary fractures and the bed angle of the coal on its deformation and damage characteristics. Huang et al. [23,24] used the double-exposure holographic interference method to observe the evolution of strain field of barite before destruction. This method uses a pulsed laser as the light source to record the interference fringes of a pair of images superimposed on a photographic dry plate at very short intervals. However, it can only measure transient processes, not continuous dynamic processes. Regarding the study of photomechanical methods, the digital scatter correlation method (DSCM) based on image recording has obvious advantages in the measurement of deformation fields of rock specimens [25]. In the early 1980s, DSCM was proposed as an image processing method by Peters et al. [26] and by Yamaguchi [27]. Skurtveit et al. [28–31] used scattering interference and digital scattering correlation methods to analyze the fracture evolution of inhomogeneous rocks. Song et al. [32–34] used the white-light digital scattering correlation method as an observation tool to study the deformation field and stress evolution during rock damage under uniaxial compression. The geological formation process of coal rocks determines the complex composition, structure and tectonics of coal rocks. Primary structures such as undulating laminae, linear laminae, lenticular laminae, and secondary structures such as joints, are widely present in coal rocks [35,36]. Rocks are quasi-brittle materials with basic mechanical parameters such as tensile strength, compressive strength and fracture toughness. Since the tensile strength of rocks is much lower than the compressive strength, tensile damage often occurs first when they are subjected to external loads. As a common main damage mode of rocks, the study of dynamic tensile deformation damage of rocks is essential for further understanding of dynamic mechanical properties of rocks.

In our study, the dynamic mechanical properties of coal samples were tested by using the SHPB technique. Dynamic tensile mechanical properties, layered effect and density evolution characteristics of strain energy for coal were studied. The dynamic failure and crack propagation process of the specimen were recorded with a high-speed camera. In addition, the DIC method was used to analyze the evolution characteristics of the strain field during the deformation process of the specimen. The distribution characteristics of the particle fragments were statistically analyzed.

## 2. Experimental Setup

### 2.1. Specimen Preparation

The coal specimens used in the test were selected from the $7_1 35$ return air roadway of Pingmei Shenma coal mine (see Figure 1). The coal type is long bituminous coal. To make the experimental results comparable, the coal specimens used for the experiments were obtained from relatively intact bulk coal specimens. The dimensions of the disc specimens were based on those recommended by the International Society of Rock Mechanics. The size of coal specimen was $\Phi 50$ mm $\times$ 25 mm. A total of 90 specimens were selected from the processed disc specimens. The average diameter was 49.29 mm and the average thickness was 25.27 mm. The dimensional error was within $\pm 1$ mm. The two-end face was polished, and the unevenness was $\pm 0.05$ mm. The maximum deviation of the vertical axis was not more than $0.25°$. Figure 2 shows the prepared coal specimens with different bedding angles. In this study, the bituminous coal of Pingdingshan mine was selected and the bituminous coal samples were tested by X-ray diffractometer produced by Japan Science Electric Co., Ltd., which is located in Tokyo Port, Japan. XRD test results of bituminous coal are shown in Figure 3. All specimens were divided into three groups of 0.45, 0.47 and 0.49 MPa according to the emission pressure. The specimens were divided into five groups of 15 each according to the bedding angle ($0°$, $22.5°$, $45°$, $67.5°$ and $90°$). Table 1 shows the grouping of coal samples. There were three specimens used in equivalent test conditions.

Table 1. Grouping of coal samples.

| Water Saturated State | | Natural Grouping | | | | | Water Saturation Grouping | | | | |
|---|---|---|---|---|---|---|---|---|---|---|---|
| Bedding Angle | | 0° | 22.5° | 45° | 67.5° | 90° | 0° | 22.5° | 45° | 67.5° | 90° |
| Emission pressure | 0.45 MPa | 1-1-1 | 1-2-1 | 1-6-1 | 1-6-4 | 1-4-1 | 3-1-1 | 1-3-1 | 3-4-1 | 3-7-1 | 3-7-2 |
| | | 1-1-2 | 1-2-2 | 1-6-2 | 1-6-5 | 1-4-2 | 3-2-1 | 1-7-1 | 3-5-1 | 3-8-1 | 3-9-1 |
| | | 1-1-3 | 1-2-3 | 1-6-3 | 1-5-1 | 1-4-3 | 3-3-1 | 1-7-2 | 3-5-2 | 3-8-2 | 3-9-2 |
| | 0.47 MPa | 2-1-1 | 2-3-1 | 3-4-1 | 3-6-1 | 4-1-1 | 3-4-1 | 3-4-2 | 2-4-1 | 4-3-2 | 4-6-1 |
| | | 2-1-2 | 2-3-2 | 3-4-2 | 3-6-2 | 4-1-2 | 3-4-2 | 2-2-1 | 2-4-2 | 4-4-1 | 4-6-2 |
| | | 2-1-3 | 2-3-3 | 3-4-3 | 3-6-3 | 4-1-3 | 3-4-3 | 2-2-2 | 4-3-1 | 4-4-2 | 4-8-4 |
| | 0.49 MPa | 4-2-1 | 4-5-1 | 4-7-1 | 4-8-1 | 4-9-1 | 5-1-1 | 5-2-1 | 5-3-1 | 6-1-1 | 6-2-1 |
| | | 4-2-2 | 4-5-2 | 4-7-2 | 4-8-2 | 4-9-2 | 5-1-2 | 5-2-2 | 5-3-2 | 6-1-2 | 6-7-2 |
| | | 4-2-3 | 4-5-3 | 4-7-3 | 4-8-3 | 4-9-3 | 5-1-3 | 5-2-3 | 5-4-1 | 6-7-3 | 6-2-3 |

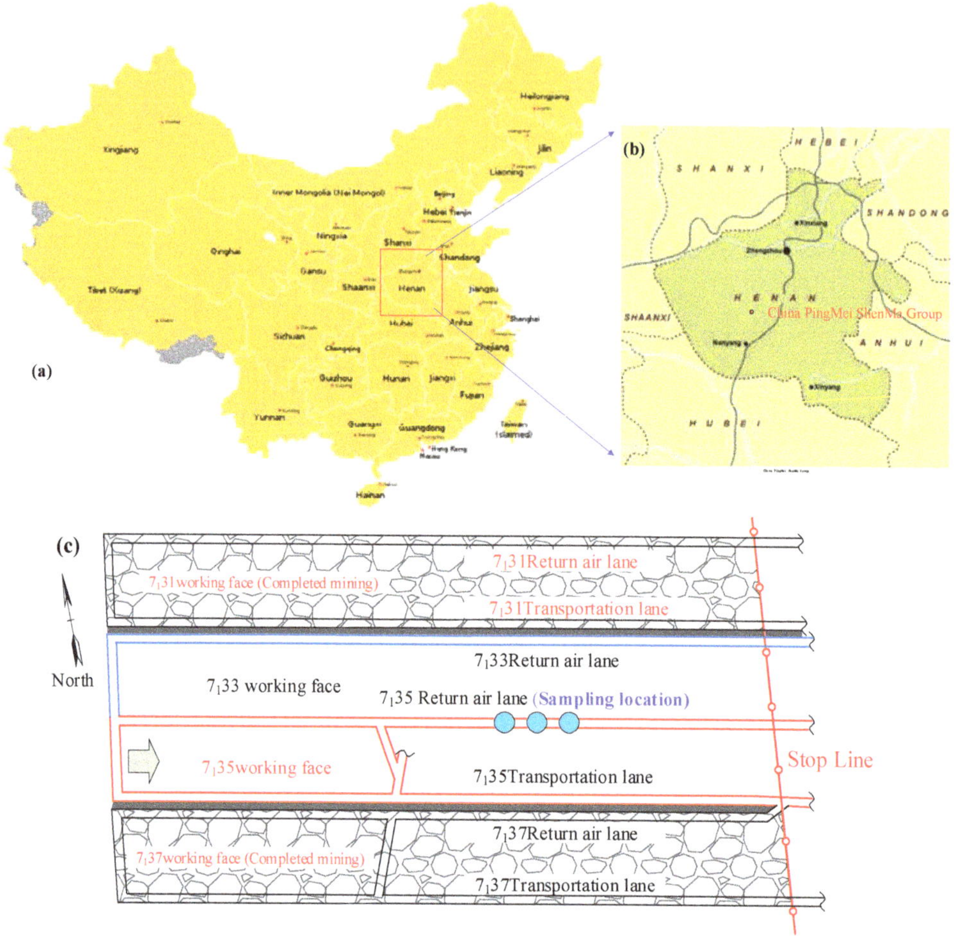

Mathematics 2022, 10, 4120

**Figure 1.** Location of outburst coal sampling. (**a**) The location of Pingmei Shenma Coal Mine in China. (**b**) Location of rock sample collection. (**c**) The coal rock sample was collected at $7_1 35$ return air lane.

**Figure 2.** Actual photos of prepared coal specimens.

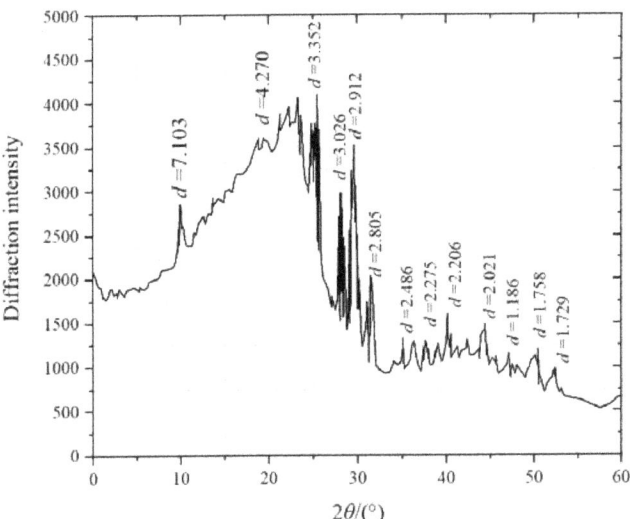

**Figure 3.** X-ray diffraction pattern of outburst proneness coal.

### 2.2. Laboratory Devices

Figure 4 shows the structure of the SHPB loading device. Under a certain air pressure, the punch collides with the incident bar at a certain speed. A stress pulse is generated at the end of the incident bar. According to the homogenisation condition of the SHPB device, the stresses and strains at the two interfaces become balanced after several reflections. The mean stress $\sigma$, strain $\varepsilon$ and strain rate $\dot{\varepsilon}(t)$ of the specimen can be derived as a function of time, i.e.,

$$\sigma(t) = \frac{[\sigma_I(t) - \sigma_R(t) + \sigma_T(t)]A_e}{2A_S} \quad (1)$$

$$\varepsilon(t) = \frac{1}{\rho_e C_e L_s} \int_0^t [\sigma_I(t) + \sigma_R(t) - \sigma_T(t)]dt \quad (2)$$

$$\dot{\varepsilon}(t) = \frac{\sigma_I(t) + \sigma_R(t) - \sigma_T(t)}{\rho_e C_e L_s} \quad (3)$$

where, $\sigma_I(t)$, $\sigma_R(t)$ and $\sigma_T(t)$ are the incident, reflected and transmitted stresses at time $t$ respectively, $\rho_e C_e$ is the wave impedance of the elastic rod, $L_s$ is the length of the specimen, and $A_e$, $A_s$ are the cross-sectional areas of the elastic rod and the specimen, respectively.

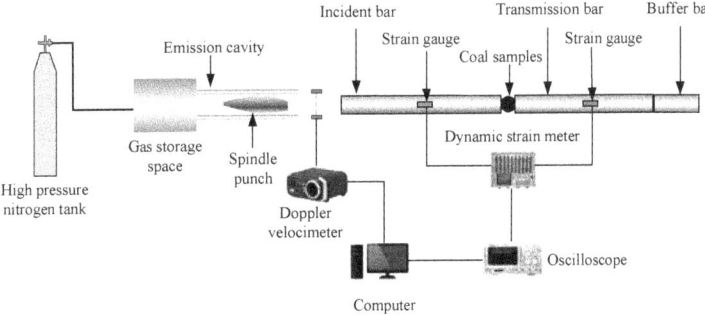

**Figure 4.** Dynamic loading device.

Equations (4) and (5) can be derived from one-dimensional stress wave theory [37]. The load and displacement at the two end faces of the specimen are

$$p_1(t) = EA[\varepsilon_I(t) + \varepsilon_R(t)] \tag{4}$$

$$p_2(t) = EA\varepsilon_T(t) \tag{5}$$

$$u_1(t) = c_0 \int_0^t [\varepsilon_I(t) - \varepsilon_R(t)]dt \tag{6}$$

$$u_2(t) = c_0 \int_0^t \varepsilon_T(t)dt \tag{7}$$

where subscript 1 denotes the left end face of the specimen. Subscript 2 denotes the right end face of the specimen, $I$ is the incident wave initial, $R$ is the reflected wave initial, and $T$ is the transmitted wave initials.

From Equations (4)–(7), the following equations can be obtained

$$\varepsilon_s(t) = \frac{u_1(t) - u_2(t)}{l_s} = \frac{c_0}{l_s}\int_0^t [\varepsilon_I(t) - \varepsilon_R(t) - \varepsilon_T(t)]dt \tag{8}$$

$$\dot{\varepsilon}_s(t) = \frac{d\varepsilon_s(t)}{dt} = \frac{c_0}{l_s}[\varepsilon_I(t) - \varepsilon_R(t) - \varepsilon_T(t)] \tag{9}$$

$$\sigma_s(t) = \frac{p_1(t) + p_2(t)}{2A_s} = \frac{EA}{2A_s}[\varepsilon_I(t) + \varepsilon_R(t) + \varepsilon_T(t)] \tag{10}$$

In addition,

$$\varepsilon_I(t) + \varepsilon_R(t) = \varepsilon_T(t) \tag{11}$$

Substituting Equation (11) into the three Equations (8)–(10), the following equations can be obtained

$$\varepsilon_s(t) = \frac{u_1(t) - u_2(t)}{l_s} = \frac{-2c_0}{l_s}\int_0^t \varepsilon_R(t)dt \tag{12}$$

$$\dot{\varepsilon}_s(t) = \frac{d\varepsilon_s(t)}{dt} = \frac{-2c_0\varepsilon_R(t)}{l_s} \tag{13}$$

$$\sigma_s(t) = \frac{p_1(t) + p_2(t)}{2A_s} = \frac{EA\varepsilon_T(t)}{A_s} \tag{14}$$

The DSCM method was used to observe the variation of strain field on the surface of the specimen. Figure 5 shows the principle of digital speckle method. It is necessary to determine a reasonable method to calculate the correlation coefficient. The standardized covariance correlation method is the most widely used method in calculating correlation formula, as shown in the following equation.

$$S = \frac{\sum_{i=-M}^{M}\sum_{j=-M}^{M}(F(x,y) - \bar{F}) * (G(x^*,y^*) - \bar{G})}{\sqrt{\sum_{i=-M}^{M}\sum_{j=-M}^{M}\left[F(x_i,y_i) - \bar{F}\right]^2 * \sum_{i=-M}^{M}\sum_{j=-M}^{M}\left[G(x_i^*,y_i^*) - \bar{G}\right]^2}} \tag{15}$$

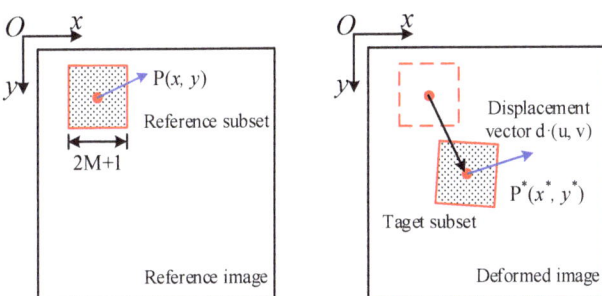

**Figure 5.** The principle of Digital Speckle Correlation Method (DSCM).

### 2.3. Stress Distribution Analysis in Brazilian Disk

The stress components inside and around the Brazilian disk were calculated, as shown in Figures 6 and 7. From Figure 8, for any point $M$ in the Brazilian disk, it is known that the stress component at point $M$ is

$$\begin{cases} \sigma_{xx} = \frac{1}{2}\sigma_{rr} + \frac{1}{2}\sigma_{rr}\cos 2\theta = \sigma_{rr}\cos^2\theta \\ \sigma_{yy} = \frac{1}{2}\sigma_{rr} - \frac{1}{2}\sigma_{rr}\cos 2\theta = \sigma_{rr}\sin^2\theta \\ \tau_{xy} = \frac{1}{2}\sigma_{rr}\sin 2\theta = \sigma_{rr}\sin\theta\cos\theta \end{cases} \quad (16)$$

when the point $M$ is on the right side of the force, both $\theta_1$ and $\theta_2$ take positive values, and both take negative values when on the left side. There is the following relationship in $\triangle OMN$

$$r_2^2 = r_1^2 + D^2 - 2r_1 D \cos\theta_1 \quad (17)$$

$$\cos\theta_2 = \frac{D^2 + r_2^2 - r_1^2}{2r_2 D} = \frac{D - r_1\cos\theta_1}{r_2} \quad (18)$$

$$\sin\theta_2 = \sqrt{1 - \cos\theta_2} = \frac{r_1 \sin\theta_1}{r_2} \quad (19)$$

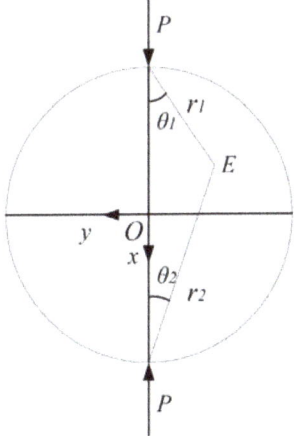

**Figure 6.** Force state of Brazil disc test.

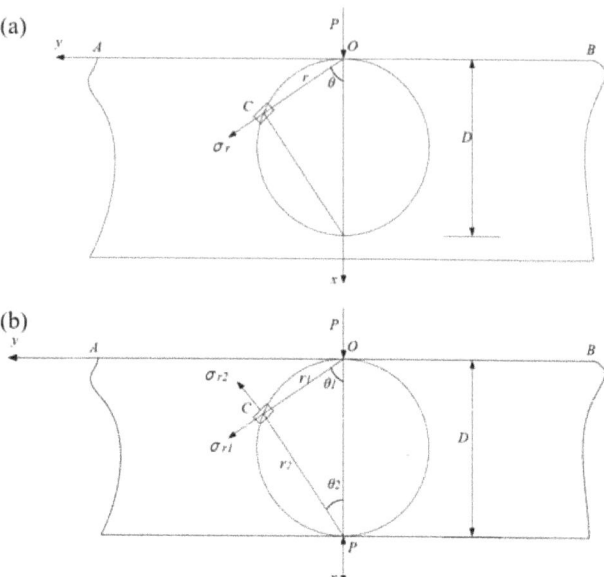

**Figure 7.** Force analysis of the disc. (**a**) Half plane of infinite plate on the role of $P$ in the level of vertical load on the boundary AB. (**b**) The plates on both sides are infinitely long, the width is $D$, and the thickness of the plate is $l$, which is affected by a pair of symmetrical line load $P$.

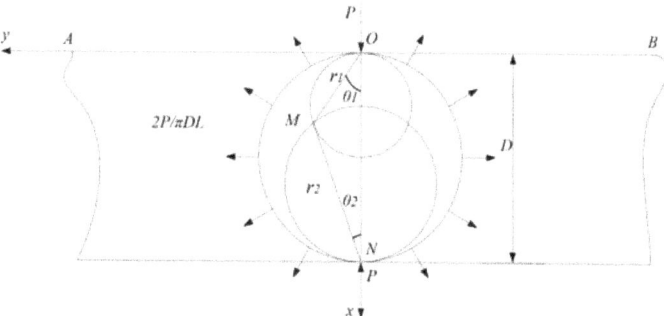

**Figure 8.** Force state of the Brazil disc.

Substituting Equations (17)–(19) into Equation (16) yields

$$\begin{cases} \sigma_{xx} = \frac{2P}{\pi l}\left[\frac{\cos^3\theta_1}{r_1} + \frac{(D-r_1\cos\theta_1)^3}{(r_1^2+D^2-2r_1 D\cos\theta_1)^2} - \frac{1}{D}\right] \\ \sigma_{yy} = \frac{2P}{\pi l}\left[\frac{\cos\theta_1 \sin^2\theta_1}{r_1} + \frac{(D-r_1\cos\theta_1)r_1^2\sin^2\theta_1}{(r_1^2+D^2-2r_1 D\cos\theta_1)^2} - \frac{1}{D}\right] \\ \tau_{xy} = \frac{2P}{\pi l}\left[\frac{\cos^2\theta_1 \sin\theta_1}{r_1} - \frac{(D-r_1\cos\theta_1)^2 r_1^2 \sin\theta_1}{(r_1^2+D^2-2r_1 D\cos\theta_1)^2}\right] \end{cases} \quad (20)$$

To further simplify, a coordinate translation is performed. The origin $O$ of the $Oxy$ coordinate system is translated to the center of the disc.

$$\begin{cases} x = r_1\cos\theta_1 - \frac{D}{2} \\ y = r_1\sin\theta_1 \end{cases} \rightarrow \begin{cases} r_1 = \sqrt{\left(x+\frac{D}{2}\right)^2 + y^2} \\ \cos\theta_1 = \frac{x+\frac{D}{2}}{r_1}, \sin\theta_1 = \frac{y}{r_1} \end{cases} \quad (21)$$

Substituting Equation (21) into Equation (20) yields,

$$\begin{cases} \sigma_{xx} = \frac{2P}{\pi l} \left\{ \frac{(x+D/2)^3}{\left[(x+D/2)^2+y^2\right]^2} + \frac{(D/2-x)^3}{\left[(x-D/2)^2+y^2\right]^2} - \frac{1}{D} \right\} \\ \sigma_{yy} = \frac{2P}{\pi l} \left\{ \frac{(x+D/2)y^2}{\left[(x+D/2)^2+y^2\right]^2} + \frac{(D/2-x)y^2}{\left[(x-D/2)^2+y^2\right]^2} - \frac{1}{D} \right\} \\ \tau_{xy} = \frac{2P}{\pi l} \left\{ \frac{(x+D/2)^2 y}{\left[(x+D/2)^2+y^2\right]^2} - \frac{(D/2-x)^2 y}{\left[(x-D/2)^2+y^2\right]^2} \right\} \end{cases} \quad (22)$$

From Equation (22), when $y = 0$ and $x = 0$, the stress components on the diameter ON are

$$\begin{aligned} \sigma_{xx} &= \frac{2P}{\pi Dl} \left( \frac{4D^2}{D^2-4x^2} - 1 \right) \\ \sigma_{yy} &= -\frac{2P}{\pi Dl} \\ \tau_{xy} &= 0 \end{aligned} \quad (23)$$

The stress component perpendicular to the diameter ON is given by

$$\begin{aligned} \sigma_{xx} &= \frac{2P}{\pi Dl} \left[ \frac{4D^2}{(D^2+4y^2)} - 1 \right] \\ \sigma_{yy} &= \frac{2P}{\pi Dl} \left[ \frac{16D^2 y^2}{(D^2+4y^2)} - 1 \right] \\ \tau_{xy} &= 0 \end{aligned} \quad (24)$$

The above represents the analytical solution of the stress state at any point inside the Brazilian disk based on the Airy stress function and the linear elasticity superposition principle. Figure 9 shows the internal stress distribution of the Brazilian disc.

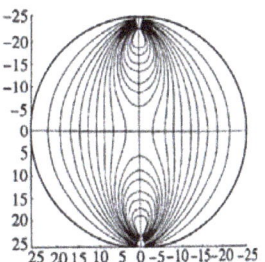 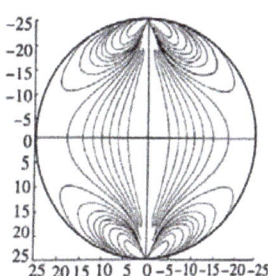 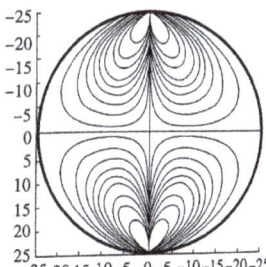

**Figure 9.** Distribution of stress in Brazil disc.

In Figure 10, on the diameter ON, $y = 0$ and the tensile stress $\sigma_{yy}$ is a constant. Therefore, under critical conditions, when the load at the time of damage is $P_c$, the tensile strength $T_0$ of the material can be obtained as

$$T_0 = -\frac{2P_c}{\pi Dl} \quad (25)$$

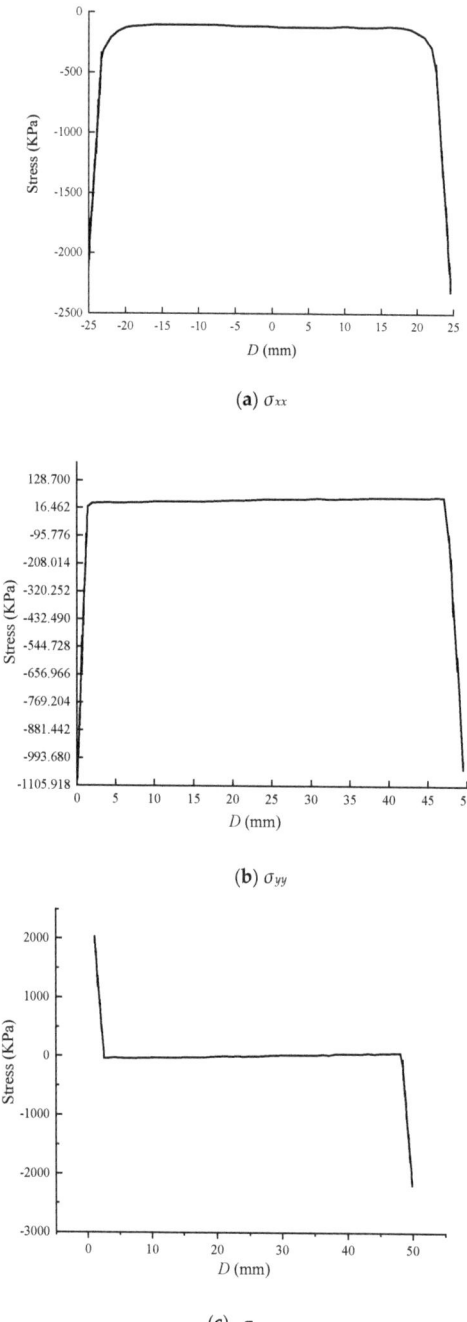

(a) $\sigma_{xx}$

(b) $\sigma_{yy}$

(c) $\tau_{xy}$

**Figure 10.** Stress component on the diameter $ON$.

## 3. Experimental Results and Discussion

### 3.1. Debris Characterisation

Specimens of equal water saturation were analyzed for comparison. The saturation of the coal specimens was 100%. Figure 11 shows the corresponding histograms of the mass distribution of coal rock debris particle size groupings. The specimens in each group had the same water saturation state and were subjected to various velocities of impact loading. The mass percentages of the debris particle size distribution for each group of specimens were compared according to the bedding orientation of the specimens. As can be seen in Figure 11a, the specimens with a bedding orientation of 45° had the lowest percentage mass distribution of particles and fines. As the bedding orientation increased or decreased from 45°, the percentage mass distribution of particles and fines increased. In Figure 11b,c, the particle and fines chip size mass distribution increase and then decrease as the laminate orientation changes from 0 to 90°. This means that the percentage mass distribution of particulate and fines debris was smallest for both sets of specimens when the lamination orientation is 0 and 90°. When the lamination orientation was 22.5, 45 and 67.5°, the percentage mass distribution of particles and fines was higher than the percentage mass distribution of debris at the previous two bedding orientations. For the specimens in Figure 11d,e, except for coal samples with bedding angle of 90°, the percentage mass distribution of particles and fines increased with increasing bedding orientation.

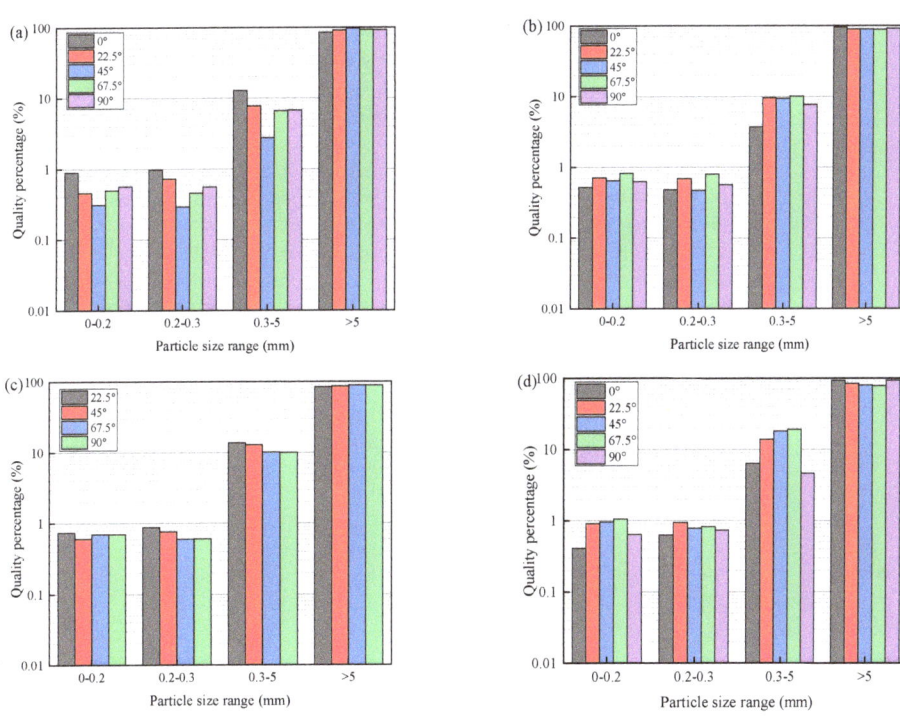

**Figure 11.** *Cont.*

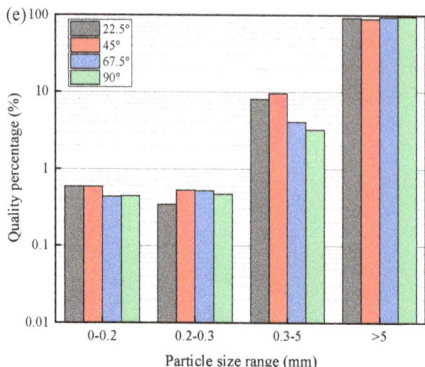

**Figure 11.** Percentage mass distribution of debris particle size at different lamination angles. (**a**) $v = 1.737$ m/s, (**b**) $v = 2.351$ m/s, (**c**) $v = 2.728$ m/s, (**d**) $v = 3.309$ m/s, and (**e**) $v = 4.008$ m/s.

For coal rock fragments with a particle size greater than 5 mm, the fragment scale ratio distribution is shown in Figure 12. In Figure 12a, for the specimen with the bedding orientation of 0°, the length-to-thickness ratio of the debris basically ranged from 1.3 to 6.3, with an average value of 2.64. It was concentrated in the range of 2 to 3.5, mainly in the form of lumpy debris, including some plate debris, with a representative size of $L:W:D = 3:2:1$ ($L$, $W$ and $D$ are the length, width and density of the debris, respectively). In Figure 12b, for the specimen with the bedding orientation of 22.5°, the length-to-thickness ratio of the debris ranged from 1 to 5.7, with an average value of 2.54. It was mostly in the form of lumpy debris, with a representative size of $L:W:D = 2.0:1.8:1.0$. The specimen with a bedding orientation of 45° in Figure 12c had a length-to-thickness ratio of 1.7 to 5, with an average value of 3.08, with the largest number of plate debris and a slightly smaller number of block debris, and a representative size of $L:W:D = 3:2:1$. The specimen with a bedding orientation of 67.5° in Figure 12d had a length-to-thickness ratio of 1.7 to 5, with an average value of 3.08. The specimen with a bedding orientation of 67.5°, the length to thickness ratio of the debris was mainly concentrated in the range of 1~3, with an average value of 1.99. It basically consisted of blocky debris, containing some plate debris, with a representative dimension of $L:W:D = 2.0:1.5:1.0$. The specimen with a bedding orientation of 90° in Figure 12e, the length to thickness ratio of the debris ranged from 1.3~5.2, with an average value of 2.66. It mainly consisted of blocky debris, containing some plate debris, with a representative dimension of $L:W:D = 2.0:1.5:1.0$. In addition, it contained plate debris with dimensions of $L:W:D = 2.5:1.3:1.0$.

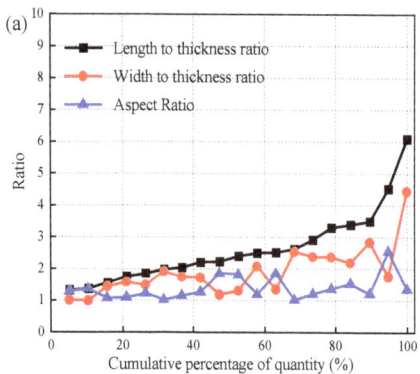

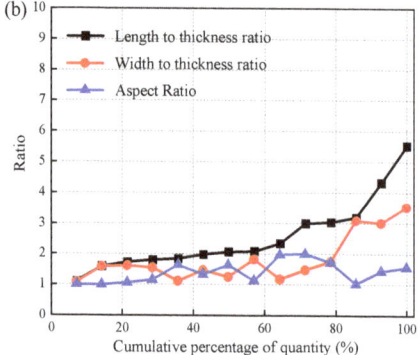

**Figure 12.** *Cont.*

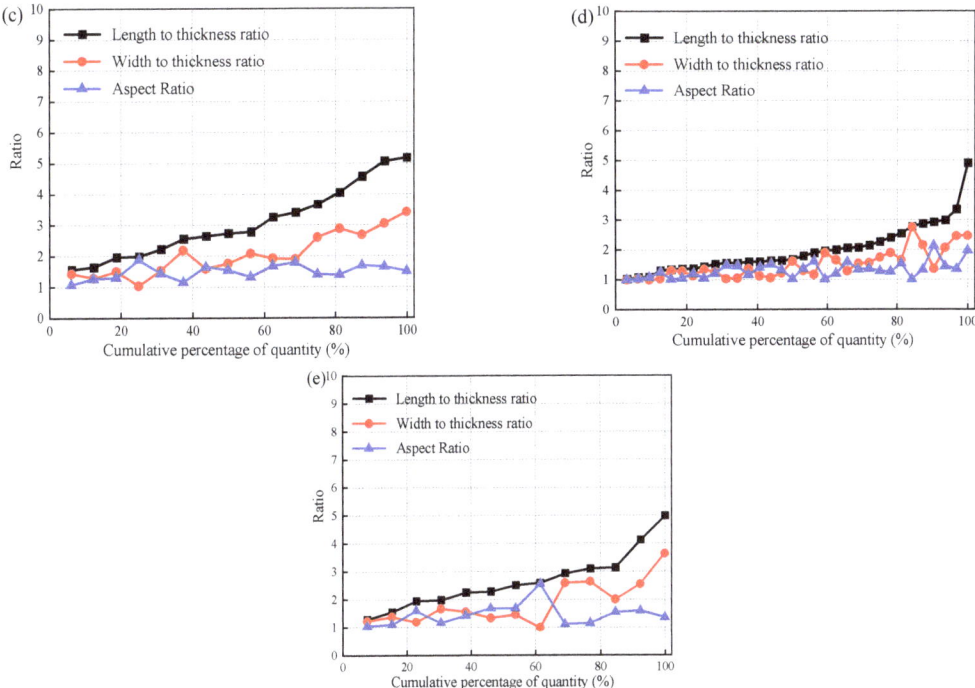

**Figure 12.** Debris scale ratio distribution of coal rock specimens with different laminar orientations. (**a**) $\theta = 0°$, $v = 3.221$ m/s, (**b**) $\theta = 22.5°$, $v = 3.233$ m/s, (**c**) $\theta = 45°$, $v = 3.308$ m/s, (**d**) $\theta = 67.5°$, $v = 3.363$ m/s, and (**e**) $\theta = 90°$, $v = 3.15$ m/s.

### 3.2. Evolution Characteristics of Strain Energy Density

Figure 13 shows the crack propagation process and fragment distribution in representative outburst-prone coal. When the bedding orientation was 0°, the coal and rock specimens underwent complete tensile failure. The failure mode of the coal rock specimen was mainly tensile failure. For example, in the second row, a tensile crack first occurred in the radial direction of the specimen, and finally the crack ran through the entire specimen. Figure 14 shows the evolution of the strain field in the dynamic tensile process of representative outburst proneness coal. In addition to tensile strain localization in the radial direction, the coal specimens with different bedding orientation also showed strain localization in other regions. In the second row, tensile strain occurred in the direction of the bedding of the specimen. In the fifth row, tensile strain localization occurred in both radial and bedding directions. The size of the strain localization area in the bedding direction was much more modest than in the radial dimension. When the quantity of the localized area of the disk specimen surged, i.e., when macroscopic failure occurred, the localized phenomenon on both sides of the localized zone disappeared immediately.

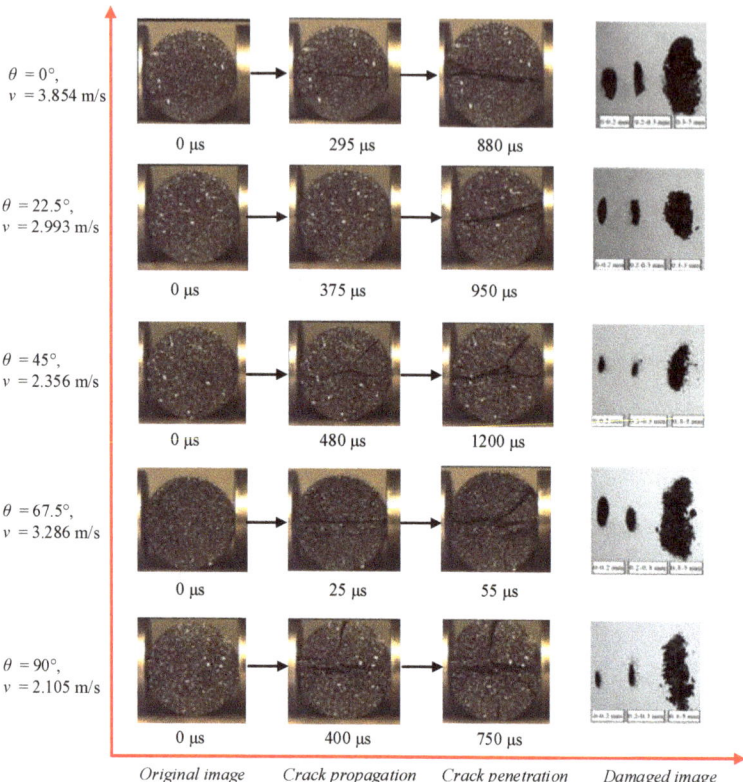

**Figure 13.** Crack propagation process and fragment distribution in representative outburst-prone coal.

In the SHPB test results, the damage modes of BD specimens mainly included shear and tensile failure. When the BD disc specimen was homogeneous and isotropic, the tensile damage crack started at the middle of the disc and expanded in a direction parallel to the impact loading, as shown in Figure 15a. The tensile crack rapidly expanded and divided the BD disc specimen into two half discs. At this point, the specimen was no longer intact, resulting in a redistribution of stress around the contact surface at both ends of the specimen. As the loading continued and the stresses at both ends of the specimen were redistributed, shear damage zones appeared at both ends of the specimen. Since the specimen was homogeneous and isotropic, the shear damage zone was basically symmetrical in distribution. However, for anisotropic coal rocks that were non-homogeneous and contained laminae, the damage mode of their BD specimens was more complicated, as shown in Figure 15b. The tensile breakage mode was still the main damage mode of the specimen, due to the higher tensile stress to which the coal sample was subjected and its own lower tensile strength. However, the presence of weak planes, microcracks and laminae caused its shear damage zone to behave in a more complex fashion. If the crack plane coincided with the high shear stress plane, the developed shear cracks extended along the weak laminae and the shear damage zones in BD specimens were not symmetrically distributed, as shown in Figure 15b. The above experimental results confirm our hypothesis, as shown in the second, third and fourth rows of Figure 14, where the presence of asymmetric shear damage zones at both ends of the specimen can be observed in the final damage pattern of the specimen.

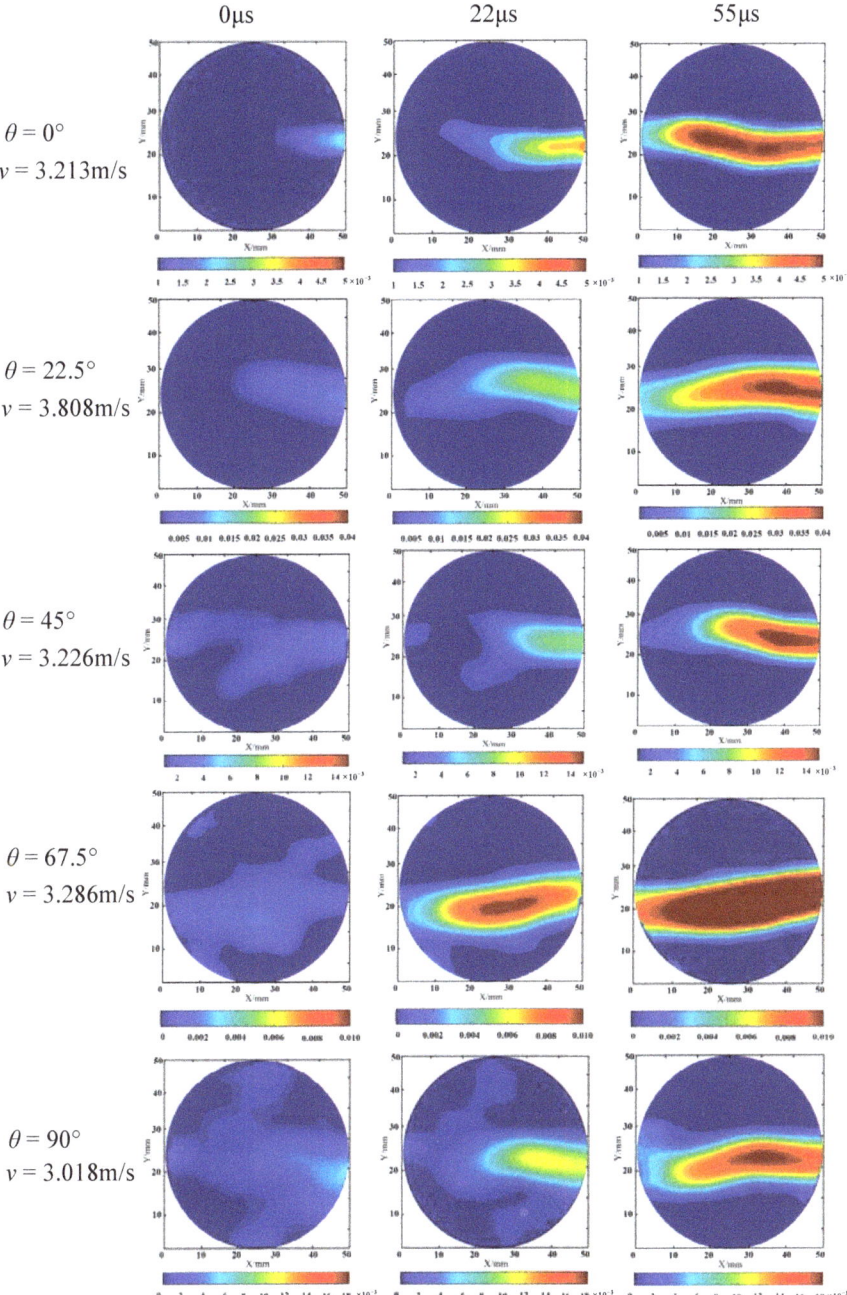

**Figure 14.** Evolution of strain field in dynamic tensile process of representative outburst-prone coal.

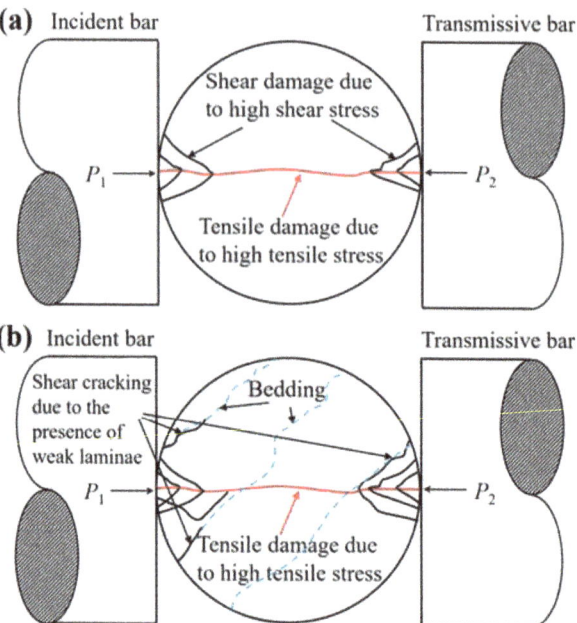

**Figure 15.** Comparison of loading and failure modes of layered rock. (**a**) Homogeneous and isotropic rocks. (**b**) Non-homogeneous and anisotropic coal rocks.

Deformation energy evolution was analyzed quantitatively. Based on the final damage mode of the specimen and the strain field before damage, the calculated deformation field was divided into the deformation localisation zone and the area outside the deformation localisation zone. As shown in Figure 16a, the energy analysis area was divided into zone 1 and zone 2 outside the deformation localisation zone (strain energy density was calculated separately for each region). The elastic deformation energy density formula could be used to derive the deformation energy density $U$ in the area outside the deformation localisation zone of the rock specimen

$$U = \frac{E}{2(1-v^2)}(\varepsilon_1^2 + \varepsilon_2^2 - 2v\varepsilon_1\varepsilon_2) \tag{26}$$

where, $E$ and $v$ are the modulus of elasticity and Poisson's ratio of the coal rock specimen, respectively. $\varepsilon_1$ and $\varepsilon_2$ are the principal strains at the surface of the rock specimen.

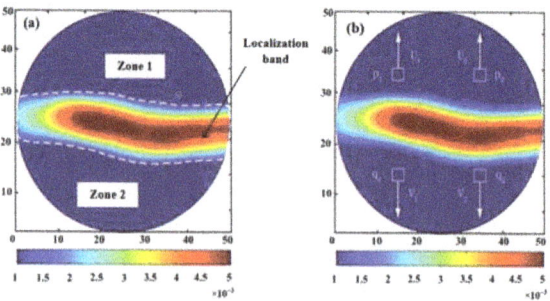

**Figure 16.** Characteristics of deformation localization zone of coal with outburst proneness. (**a**) Schematic diagram of energy analysis area. (**b**) Relative tensile displacement.

Figure 16b shows a schematic diagram of the relative tensile displacement analysis of the deformation localisation zone of the coal rock specimen. Figures 17–19 show the energy evolution curves and tensile displacement evolution curves of coal and rock specimens. As can be seen from Figure 17, when the impact velocity was 1.303 m/s, the maximum deformation energy density in the two regions of the specimen was $750 \times 10^6$ J/m$^3$ and $580 \times 10^6$ J/m$^3$, respectively. The relative tensile displacements of the two sets of measurement points increased simultaneously with the beginning of the peak in zone 1. When the impact velocity was 2.112 m/s, the peak values of zone 1 and zone 2 were close to $470 \times 10^6$ J/m$^3$ and $310 \times 10^6$ J/m$^3$. When the energy density began to increase, the relative tensile displacement of the two groups of measuring points also increased at a relatively stable rate. When the time was increased to 200 μs, the displacement of the two groups of measurement points had a difference of about 0.05 mm. The relative tensile displacement increases rapidly as the energy on either side of the specimen positioning zone reached its peak.

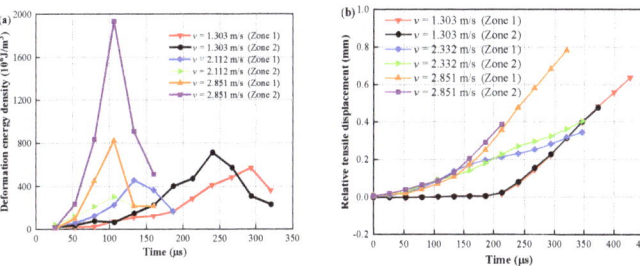

**Figure 17.** Deformation energy density and tensile displacement characteristics of coal specimens with bedding orientation of 0°. (**a**) Deformation energy density. (**b**) Relative tensile displacement.

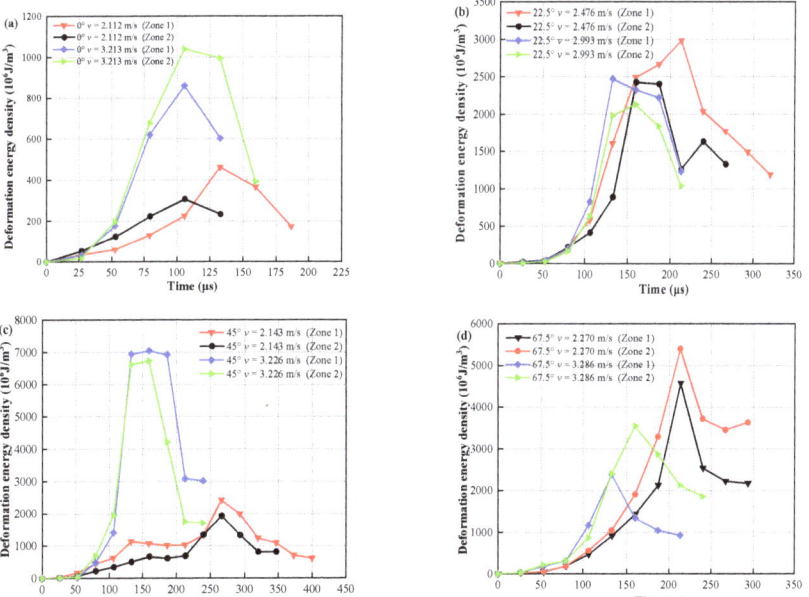

**Figure 18.** *Cont.*

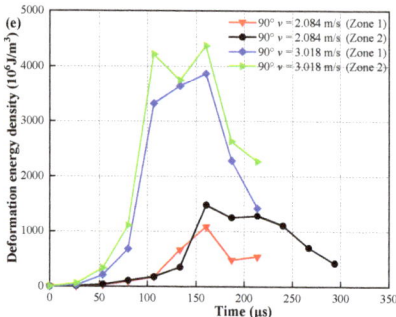

**Figure 18.** Deformation energy density evolution curves of coal specimens. (**a**) 0°, (**b**) 22.5°, (**c**) 45°, (**d**) 67.5°, (**e**) 90°.

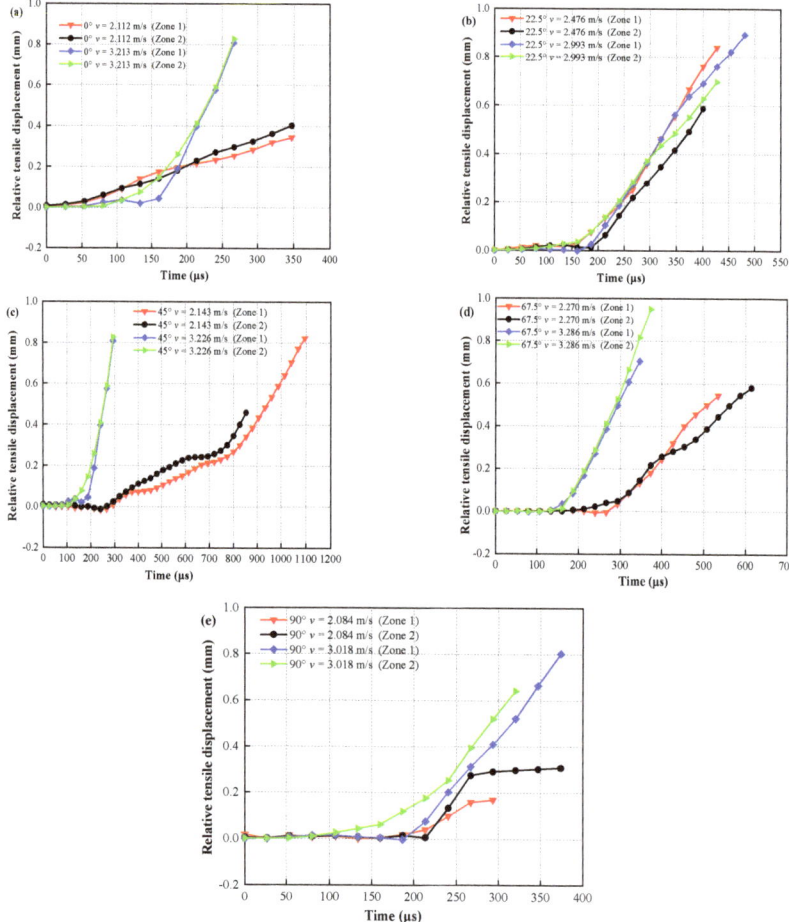

**Figure 19.** Relative tensile displacement evolution of outburst coal specimens. (**a**) 0°, (**b**) 22.5°, (**c**) 45°, (**d**) 67.5°, (**e**) 90°.

It can be seen from Figure 18 that when the bedding orientation was 45°, the peak deformation energy density in area 1 and area 2 of the specimen reached $7000 \times 10^6$ J/m$^3$, which was the largest among the five specimens. When the bedding orientation was 90°, the peak deformation energy density was about $4000 \times 10^6$ J/m$^3$. The time taken for the specimen to reach peak energy was essentially 100–130 μs.

When the peak of the deformation energy density fell ($\theta = 0°$), the peak deformation energy density differed by a factor of 5–7, influenced by the velocity of the impact load on the specimen. It is speculated that when the bedding orientation is 0°, because the cohesion between radial bedding is weak, microcracks would develop rapidly in the coal rock along the bedding surface. However, the microcracks in other areas of the coal rock would not be fully developed, so the deformation degree of the specimen would not be large, resulting in too little energy accumulation. When the bedding orientation gradually increases, the microcracks would fully develop, the deformation would be significant, and the accumulated deformation energy would be greater than that when the bedding orientation was 0°.

When the bedding direction was 0°, the relative tensile displacement of the two sets of measurement points began to increase as the energy began to accumulate (Figure 19). The relative tensile displacements of the two groups of measurement points in the localized zone were basically unchanged until the deformation energy density reaches its peak. When the energy density of zone 1 reached a peak, the relative tensile displacements of the two groups of measurement points started to grow at the same time. When the energy density started to grow, the relative tensile displacement of the two groups of measurement points also started to grow at a relatively stable rate. When the time increased to 200 μs, the displacement of the two groups of measurement points generated a difference of about 0.05 mm. The relative tensile displacement of the two groups of measurement points started to grow relatively slowly, and when the energy density in the area on both sides of the localized zone reached its peak, the growth of the relative displacement tensile amount became large rapidly. From Figure 19b it can be seen that, the tensile displacements of the measured points in the two regions of the specimen started to increase when the energy density decreased from the peak. There was a difference of about 0.02 mm between the displacements of the two sets of measurement points at the beginning of the growth. As the displacement increased, the difference gradually decreased. The relative tensile displacements of the measurement points bifurcated after the growth started. The difference decreased briefly in the middle and then continued to increase again. The difference of about 0.1 mm between the tensile displacements of the two measurement points was maintained throughout the growth process. The relative tensile displacement of the measurement points started to increase after the energy density reached its maximum value (Figure 19c). The relative tensile displacements of the two groups of measurement points, on the other hand, started to grow only when the energy density reached the second peak, and there was a difference of about 0.02~0.03 mm. At 160 μs, the displacement of the original group of measurement points with larger displacement decreased by 0.05 mm compared to the other group of measurement points. The coal samples with a laminar angle of 67.5 degrees had a different time for the relative tensile displacement to start growing in the region, which was influenced by the impact velocity. The higher the impact velocity, the earlier the growth time. The increasing trend of tensile displacement at different impact velocities was similar in both regions when the laminar angle is 90 degrees.

### 3.3. Distribution Characteristics of Coal Specimen Fragments

The residual debris of coal rock was collected and analyzed, and the debris in the range of 0~0.2 mm, 0.2~0.3 mm and 0.3~5 mm were collected and weighed. The classification method of rockburst debris is shown in Table 2. The mass percentage of particle sizes of broken coal specimens are shown in Figure 20. Since the mass percentage distribution range of each particle size after crushing of coal specimens was large, in order to better reflect its distribution characteristics, semi-log coordinates are used in the figure. Combined with the scale characteristics of semi-log coordinates, the percentages of fragment mass of natural or water-saturated coal specimens in the size range of 0–0.2 mm can be seen to vary little with increasing impact velocity (0.4489~0.776%). For natural or saturated coal specimens with chip particle sizes of 0.2 to 5 mm, however, the percentage chip mass was significantly increased with increasing impact velocity (3.533~11.879%). The percentage mass of saturated coal specimens with chip sizes of 0.2 to 5 mm was less than that of natural coal specimens, except for the coal specimens in which the bedding angle was 45 degrees, according to the results in Table 2 and Figure 20. This conclusion, therefore, proves the benefits of water injection for dust removal.

**Table 2.** Classification criteria and analysis method of rockburst debris.

| Rock Debris Classification | Range of Particle Size (mm) | Methodology | Result |
| --- | --- | --- | --- |
| Particle | <0.075 | Laser particle size analyzer | Grain fraction curve |
| Fine grain | 0.075~0.250<br>0.250~0.500<br>0.500~1.000<br>1.000~2.000<br>2.000~5.000 | Sieving method | Fractal results of mass distribution |
| Medium grain | 5.000~30.000 | SEM, Scale measurement, 3D topography scanning | Fractal results of size distribution |
| Coarse grain | >30.000 | Scale measurement, 3D topography scanning | Fractal result of reconstructed image |

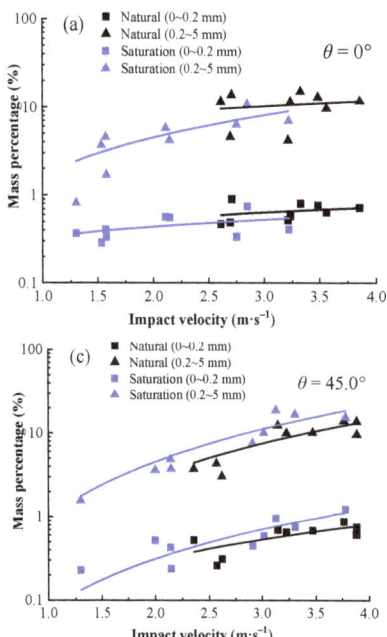
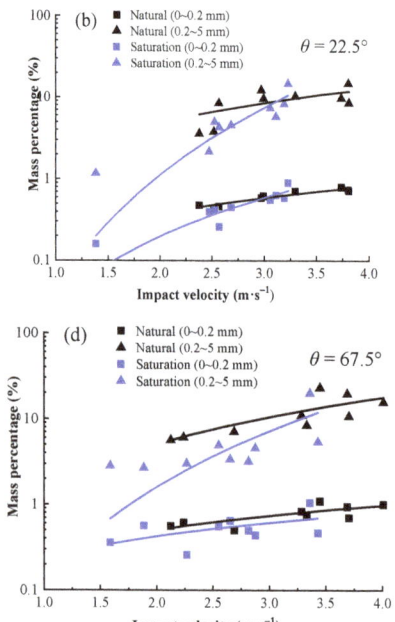

**Figure 20.** *Cont.*

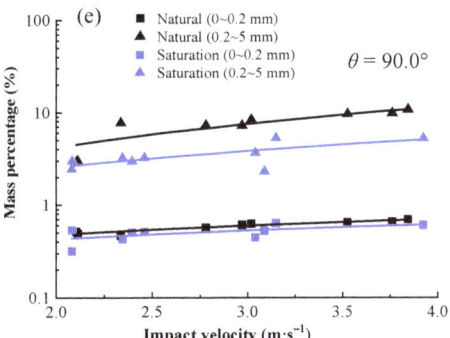

**Figure 20.** Statistical mass percentage of particle size of broken coal specimens. (**a**) 0°, (**b**) 22.5°, (**c**) 45°, (**d**) 67.5°, (**e**) 90°.

## 4. Numerical Simulation

### 4.1. CDEM and Criteria

CDEM has evolved based on the Lagrangian system. It combines the advantages of both continuous and discrete simulation methods. It can simulate the whole process of material deformation to cracking. The numerical model in CDEM is shown in Figure 21a. This numerical model consists of blocks and interfaces. CDEM contains different node types such as continuous, discrete and hybrid node types, as shown in Figure 21b. One of the finite element types is shown in Figure 21c.

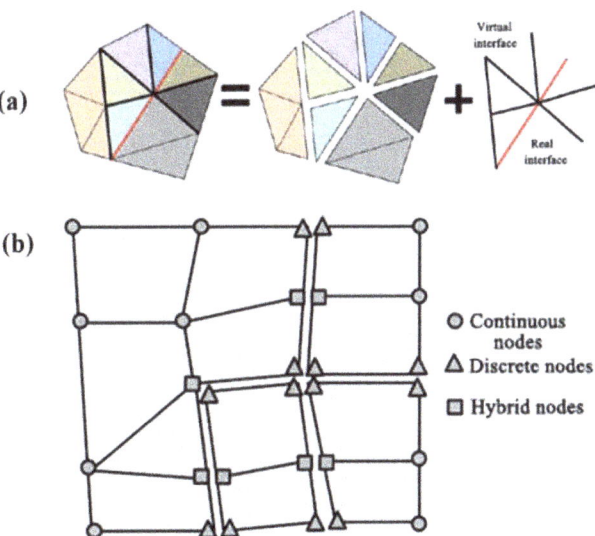

**Figure 21.** *Cont.*

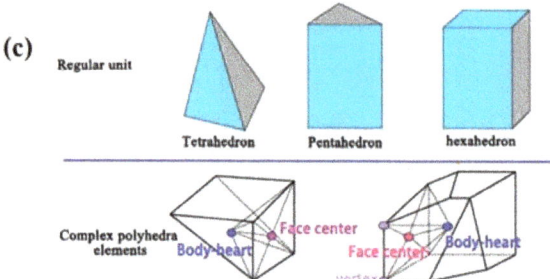

**Figure 21.** Schematic diagram of CDEM method and principle. (a) The structure of the numerical model in CDEM. (b) Node type in CDEM. (c) The element of finite element in CDEM.

CDEM can monitor the contact force, the type of microcracks and the number of microcracks at various points within the specimen during the test, while the development of cracks on the surface of the specimen and the displacement of the specimen as a whole can be observed on a macroscopic level. In CDEM, when the particles are subjected to an external load, the particles move and change the bonding force between them. When the bonding force exceeds the bonding strength of the particles, microscopic cracks are created, and adjacent cracks overlap to form macroscopic visible cracks.

The input parameters used were a uniaxial compressive strength of 27.64 MPa, a tensile strength of 1.75 MPa, a cohesion of 7.85 MPa, an internal friction angle of 32.64°, a damping factor of 0.7, a modulus of elasticity of 2.29 GPa, and Poisson's ratio of 0.24 obtained from the tests. The continuous-discontinuous element method establishes the control equations through a Lagrangian energy system [38–40]. The expressions are as follows

$$\frac{d}{dt}\left(\frac{\partial L}{\partial \dot{u}_i}\right) - \frac{\partial L}{\partial u_i} = Q_i \tag{27}$$

In the formula, $Q_i$ is the nonconservative force of the system, and $L$ is the Lagrangian function, which can be written as

$$L = \prod_m + \prod_e + \prod_f \tag{28}$$

where, $\prod_m$, $\prod_e$ and $\prod_f$ are the work of system kinetic energy, elastic energy and conservative force.

The energy functional of the unit is

$$L = \frac{1}{2}\int_V \rho \dot{u}_i^2 dV + \int_V \frac{1}{4}\sigma_{ij}(u_{i,j} + u_{j,i})dV - \int_V f_i u_i dV \tag{29}$$

The damping force and the boundary external force are

$$Q_\mu = \int_V \mu \dot{u}_i dV, \quad Q_{\overline{T}} = -\int_S \overline{T}_i dS \tag{30}$$

where, $\mu$ is the damping factor and $\overline{T}_i$ is the surface force on the cell boundary.
From Equations (28)–(30), Equation (27) can be written as

$$-\left(\int_V \rho \ddot{u}_i dV + \int_V \sigma_{ij}\frac{\partial u_{i,j}}{\partial u_i}dV - \int_V f_i dV\right) = \int_V \mu \dot{u}_i dV - \int_S \overline{T}_i dS \tag{31}$$

Using the integral by parts, we get

$$\int_V \sigma_{ij}\frac{\partial u_{i,j}}{\partial u_i}dV = \int_S \sigma_{ij}n_j dS - \int_V \sigma_{ij,j}dV \tag{32}$$

The Lagrangian equation is simplified as

$$\int_V (\sigma_{ij,j} + f_i - \rho\ddot{u}_i - \mu\dot{u}_i)dV + \int_S (\overline{T}_i - \sigma_{ij}n_j)dS = 0 \tag{33}$$

In addition

$$F_i^e = \frac{\partial \Pi_e}{\partial u_i} = K_{ij}^e u_j \tag{34}$$

Then the Lagrangian equation can be written as

$$\int_V \rho\ddot{u}_i dV + \int_V \mu\dot{u}_i dV + F_i^e = \int_V f_i dV + \int_V \overline{T}_i dS \tag{35}$$

When the unit rupture occurs, the above equation can be written as

$$\int_{V_1} \rho\ddot{u}_i dV_1 + \int_{V_1} \mu\dot{u}_i dV_1 + F_i^{e_1} = \int_{V_1} f_i dV_1 + \int_S \overline{T}_i dS - \int_{S_b} \overline{T}_{ib} dS \tag{36}$$

and

$$\int_{V_2} \rho\ddot{u}_i dV_2 + \int_{V_2} \mu\dot{u}_i dV_2 + F_i^{e_1} = \int_{V_2} f_i dV_2 + \int_S \overline{T}_i dS + \int_{S_b} \overline{T}_{ib} dS_b \tag{37}$$

The final equation is

$$M\ddot{u}(t) + C\dot{u}(t) + Ku(t) = F(t) \tag{38}$$

Solving Equation (38) is the core of CDEM operations. First seeking the elastic force

$$\begin{bmatrix} K_{1,1} & K_{1,2} & \cdots & K_{1,n} \\ K_{2,1} & K_{2,2} & \cdots & K_{2,n} \\ \cdots & \cdots & \cdots & \cdots \\ K_{n,1} & K_{n,2} & \cdots & K_{n,n} \end{bmatrix} \begin{bmatrix} u_1 \\ u_2 \\ \cdots \\ u_n \end{bmatrix} = \begin{bmatrix} f_1 \\ f_2 \\ \cdots \\ f_n \end{bmatrix} \tag{39}$$

Seeking damping force

$$\begin{bmatrix} C_{1,1} & C_{1,2} & \cdots & C_{1,n} \\ C_{2,1} & C_{2,2} & \cdots & C_{2,n} \\ \cdots & \cdots & \cdots & \cdots \\ C_{n,1} & C_{n,2} & \cdots & C_{n,n} \end{bmatrix} \begin{bmatrix} v_1 \\ v_2 \\ \cdots \\ v_n \end{bmatrix} = \begin{bmatrix} f_1' \\ f_2' \\ \cdots \\ f_n' \end{bmatrix} \tag{40}$$

The motion equation is

$$\begin{cases} a_i = (f_i + f_i' + f_i^{out})/m_i \\ v_i = v_i^{t-1} + a_i t \\ u_i = u_i^{t-1} + v_i t \end{cases} \tag{41}$$

For solving CDEM arithmetic problems using Euler forward interpolation methods, two steps are included in each time step, namely the finite element solution and the discrete element solution. Throughout the calculation, the degree of equilibrium of the system is represented by the unbalanced rate.

CDEM uses a time-based dynamic relaxation technique for explicit iterative calculation. Figure 22 shows the calculation flow.

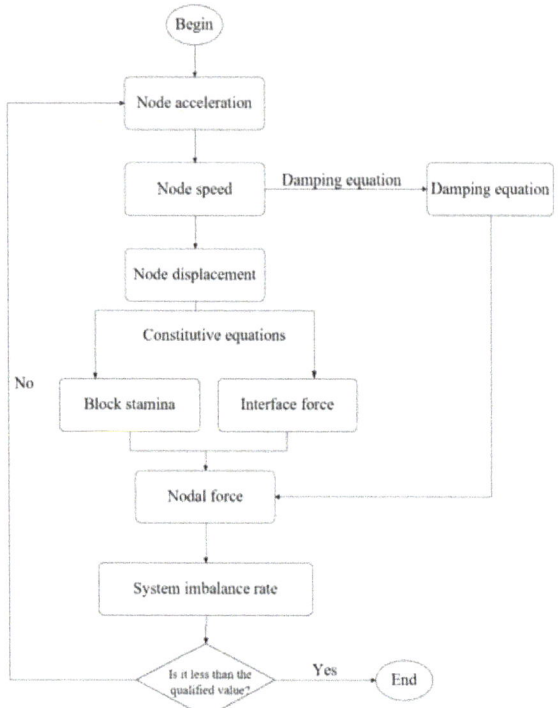

**Figure 22.** Flow chart of CDEM calculation steps.

### 4.2. Analysis of Dynamic Tensile Characteristics of Coal Based on CDEM

Figure 23 shows the experimental model. The stratification angles are set in five groups of 0°, 22.5°, 45°, 67.5° and 90°. The whole model consists of 10,429 nodes and 20,544 triangular unit blocks. The substrate and laminar mechanical properties in the model are shown in Table 3.

**Table 3.** Parameters of coal specimens involved in numerical calculation.

| Medium | Parameter | Symbol | Numerical Value |
|---|---|---|---|
| Coal matrix | material density | $P\ [kg/m^3]$ | 1301 |
| | elasticity modulus | $E\ [GPa]$ | 2.29 |
| | Poisson's ratio | $v\ [-]$ | 0.24 |
| | cohesion | $c\ [MPa]$ | 7.85 |
| | tensile strength | $T\ [MPa]$ | 1.75 |
| | internal friction angle | $\varphi\ [°]$ | 32.64 |
| | dilation angle | $\Phi\ [°]$ | 15 |
| Bedding structure | normal stiffness | $n\ [GPa/m]$ | 10 |
| | shear stiffness | $s\ [GPa/m]$ | 10 |
| | internal friction angle | $\varphi\ [°]$ | 30 |
| | cohesion | $c\ [MPa]$ | 7 |
| | tensile strength | $T\ [MPa]$ | 1.5 |

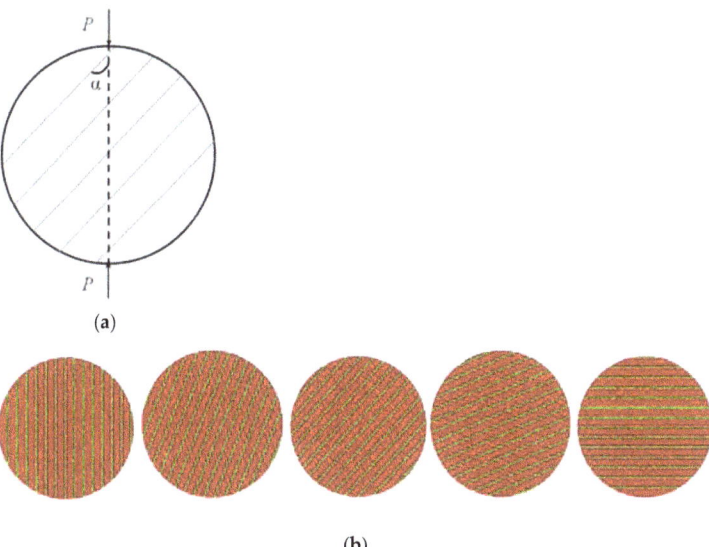

**Figure 23.** Numerical model of Brazilian disk coal specimen with different bedding angles. (**a**) The angle between the bedding plane and the loading direction is the bedding angle. (**b**) Models with bedding angles of 0°, 22.5°, 45°, 67.5° and 90° respectively.

When applying a velocity load at the upper loading point of the specimen to characterize the applied dynamic load, its loading parameters are

$$v(t) = \begin{cases} vt/t_0, & (t \leq t_0) \\ v, & (t > t_0) \end{cases} \tag{42}$$

In the above equation, $v$ is the applied dynamic velocity load, m/s, and $t_0$ is the time required for the rate load to go from 0 to a given value. Here, the model is uniformly taken as 60 μs. This rise time is generally taken as the time required for the stress wave to make five round trips within the specimen, with different loading rates corresponding to different strain rates.

Figure 24 shows the evolution of the dynamic splitting stress field in the specimen, and the propagation of the stress waves. In the Figure, the impact velocity $v = 4$ m/s and the coal specimen lamination angle $\theta = 45°$. After the impact load was applied, the stress wave started to propagate from the upper loading point to the lower boundary, and reached the lower loading point at 60 μs. Then, the stress waves were reflected from the loading point below. The overall stress field was symmetrically distributed at 120 μs, and this distribution pattern was consistent with the theoretical solution above. Stress concentrations in the middle of the specimen became more concentrated with the superimposed effect of the stress waves. Crack initiation occurred in the middle of the Brazilian disc specimen at 210 μs. The cracks then continued to expand to the loading boundaries of the upper and lower layers. Some secondary cracking occurred at the loading point. Cracks of 320 μs penetrated and the specimen was damaged. Figure 25 shows the displacement field change and crack extension process for the same specimen. From the evolution of the displacement field, the characteristics of the stress wave in the specimen can be seen. In contrast, the middle of the specimen cracked at 210 μs.

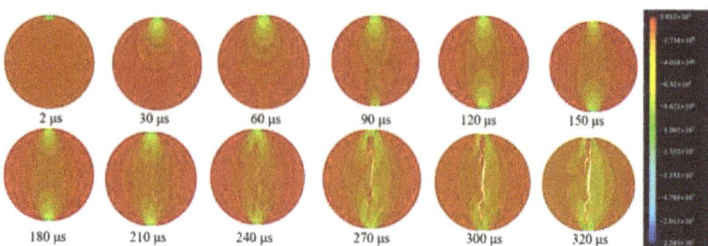

**Figure 24.** Dynamic splitting stress field evolution of a typical Brazil disk coal specimen under impact load.

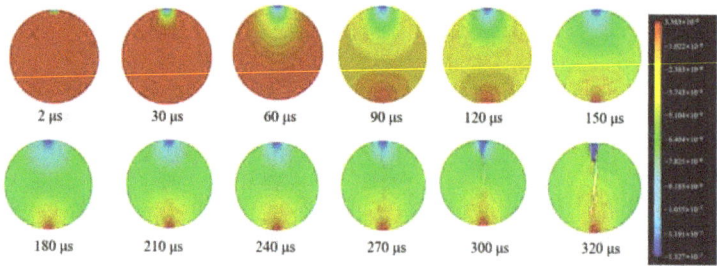

**Figure 25.** Dynamic splitting displacement field evolution of a typical Brazil disk coal specimen under impact load.

Figure 26 shows the crack expansion process of coal specimens with impact velocity $v = 4$ m/s and bedding angles of 0°, 22.5°, 45°, 67.5°, and 90°. The cracks in the coal specimen first started in the center part along the stratification plane ($\theta = 0°$), because this weak surface is prone to stress concentration and subsequent crack expansion occurred along the stratification plane at the upper and lower loading boundaries. Eventually crack penetration damage occurred in the specimen. The specimen damage mode was typical of tensile damage. The specimens exhibited certain shear damage characteristics along the lamina surface ($\theta = 22.5°, 45°, 67.5°$) but the main damage mode was still tensile damage. When the stratified planes were perpendicular to the direction of loading ($\theta = 90°$), the specimen still exhibited tensile damage characteristics. Simultaneous tensile and shear damage occurred at an angle to the direction of loading at the split level. The results of this numerical simulation are consistent with the conclusions obtained from the experiments carried out. In addition, in the numerical simulations, we also observed some secondary cracks along the weak surface of the lamina. This was due to the additional shear damage caused by the laminar surface. This result is consistent with the phenomenon depicted in Figure 14.

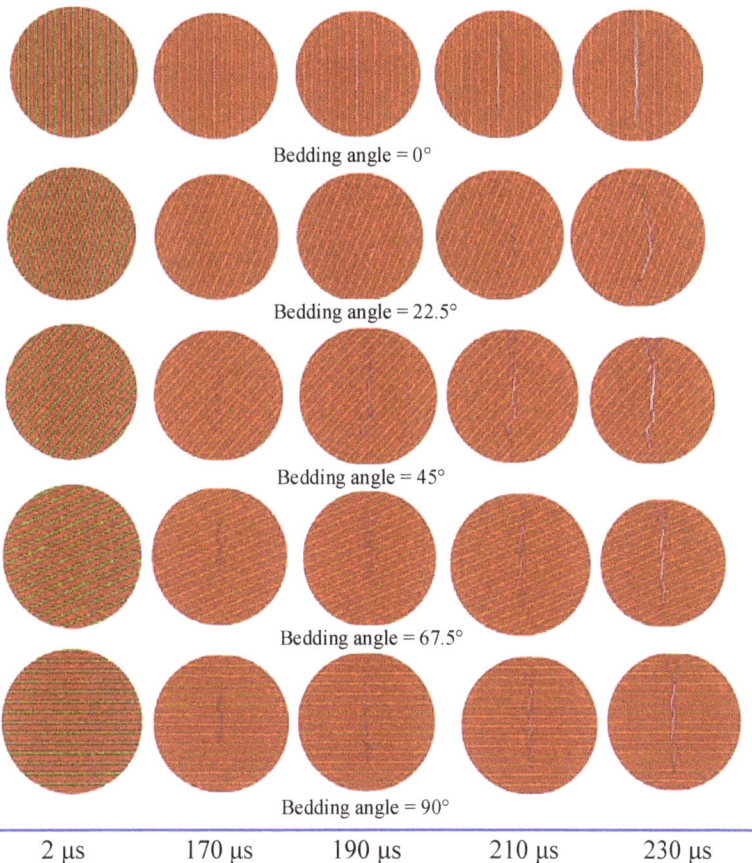

**Figure 26.** Dynamic crack initiation process.

Figure 27 shows comparisons between the numerical simulation results of CDEM and the experimental results. It can be seen that the damage patterns of the specimens obtained from the numerical simulations are in good agreement with the experiments. The failure modes are all standard Brazilian disc failure modes with cracking along the center of the specimen. The main cracks are tensile cracks and show a tensile-shear compound fracture pattern at the end of the specimens. It is noteworthy that the simulated 22.5° bedding angle coal sample had a more obvious shear effect along the bedding plane, which is consistent with the experimental primary crack pattern. Figure 28 illustrates the comparison of the impact velocity-dynamic tensile strength curves obtained from the experimental and CDEM simulations. It can be noted that the numerical simulation can calculate a larger range of impact velocities, and the dynamic tensile strength test dispersion of coal samples with different bedding angles was greater than that of the experiment. However, in general, the trend that the dynamic tensile strength obtained from the simulation increased approximately linearly with the increase of impact velocity, and is consistent with the experimental findings. Both methods show the rate effect of dynamic tensile strength.

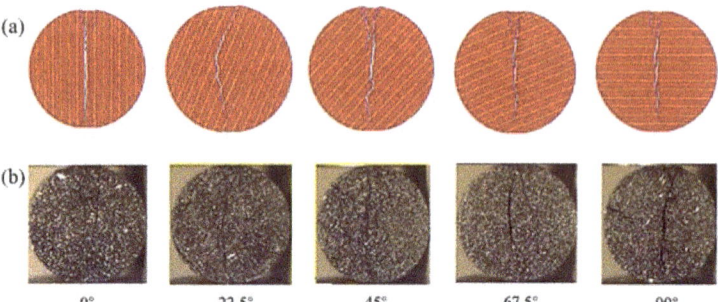

**Figure 27.** Comparison of numerical simulation and experimental results. (**a**) Failure models of coal specimen with different bedding angles. (**b**) SHPB test.

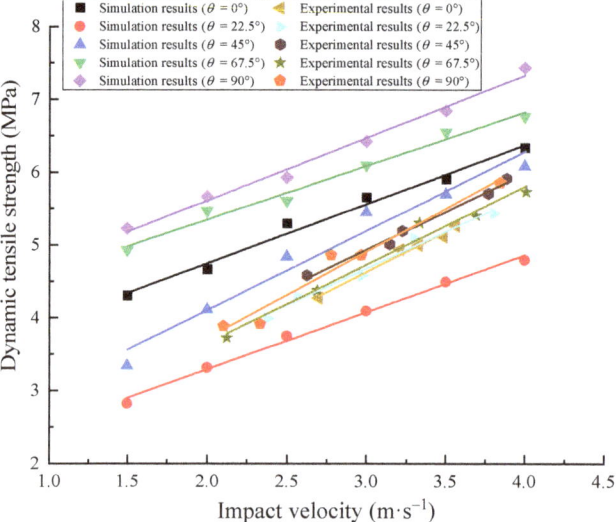

**Figure 28.** Comparative plots between the impact velocity and dynamic tensile strength curves obtained from experiments and numerical simulations.

The results of the CDEM simulation show the evolution of the dynamic splitting stress and strain fields of the Brazilian disc coal sample under impact loading, and the propagation, reflection and superposition characteristics of the stress waves in the coal rock specimen, which are in good agreement with the experimental results. This compensates for the incomplete recording of the crack initiation and extension process due to the limited frequency of the high-speed camera.

## 5. Discussion

Figure 29a shows a diagram of the Stefan effect. It is also known as the Stefan-Reynolds equation. It was first derived by Stefan when analysing the external forces required to separate two discs immersed in a viscous fluid at a given speed with a small distance between them. The Stefan effect is a physical phenomenon. When thin discs immersed in a viscous fluid are separated from each other, a hydrostatic pressure gradient is created between the discs due to the viscous flow, creating a viscous drag force that prevents the discs from separating from each other. The understanding of the Stefan effect is not limited to disc separation. It is clear that any change in the volume of fluid between the discs would cause a change in the hydrostatic pressure of the fluid between the discs, which would cause a viscous fluid to flow, creating a resistance to the movement of the discs [41]. Thus, coal can be considered as a series of micro-disc systems containing free water (viscous fluid). When the coal is subjected to dynamic loading, the Stefan effect occurs during the deformation of the pores due to the presence of free water in the coal micro-pores. This is shown in Figure 29b. Water does not easily reach the pore tips when dynamically loaded.

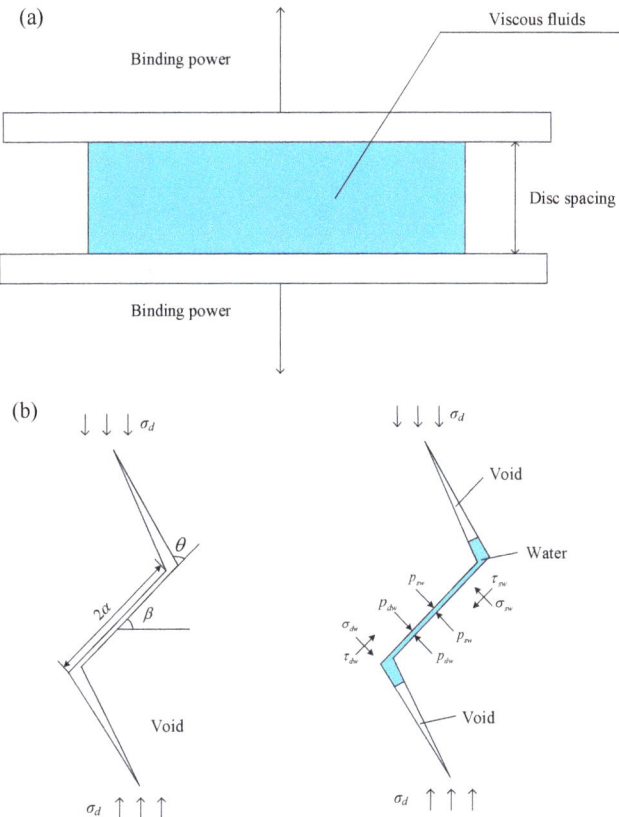

**Figure 29.** Schematic representation of the effect of water on the dynamic expansion characteristics of cracks in coal. (**a**) Schematic of the Stefan effect. (**b**) Dynamically loaded free water forces on fracture surfaces.

The single dynamic load, the cohesive force $F$ due to the free water surface tension of the fissure, and the resistance $F'$ due to the Stefan effect, prevent the fissure from expanding and fracturing. The force preventing fracture of the fracture is $p_{dw}$:

$$p_{dw} = (F + F')/M = \left( \frac{VK}{2\delta^2 \cos \varphi} + \frac{3\eta r^4}{2\pi h^3} \frac{dv_{dw}}{dt} \right)/M \qquad (43)$$

where $V$ is the volume of the liquid, $K$ is the surface energy, $\varphi$ is the wetting angle, $\delta$ is the radius of the curved surface of the water, $\eta$ is the viscosity of the liquid, $r$ is the radius of two parallel circular plates filled with incompressible viscous liquid in the middle, $v_{dw}$ is the relative velocity of the separation of the two circular plates, $h$ is the distance between the two circular plates, and $M$ is the area of the fissure containing water.

The shear stress $\tau_{d\text{-}sw}$ and the normal stress $\sigma_{d\text{-}sw}$ at the main fracture face of the winged fissure containing pore free water are expressed in Equations (44) and (45) as shown in Figure 29b:

$$\tau_{d-sw} = \sigma_d \sin\beta \cos\beta - f_{d-sw}\left[\sigma_d \cos^2\beta - p_{sw} + p_{dw}\right] \quad (44)$$

$$\sigma_{d-sw} = \sigma_d \cos^2(\beta + \theta) - p_{sw} + p_{dw} \quad (45)$$

where, $f_{d\text{-}sw}$ is the friction factor of the fracture surface under dynamic water content conditions.

We found that the dynamic tensile strength, breaking strain and peak deformation energy density of coal rock specimens in the water-saturated state were higher than those in the natural state when the lamina orientation was the same and the impact velocities were similar. When the lamina orientation was 0° and the impact velocity was less than 3 m/s, the tensile strength of the water-saturated specimens was basically the same as that of the specimens in the natural state. After the impact velocity exceeded 3 m/s, the growth rate of the former gradually increased compared with the latter. The difference between the tensile strength of the water-saturated specimens and the natural state of the coal rock specimens reached 0.3~0.4 MPa when the lamination orientation was 22.5° and the impact velocity was greater than 2.5 m/s. When the lamination orientation was 45° and the impact velocity was 3 m/s, and the strength of the water-saturated specimens was about 0.1 MPa higher. When the lamination orientation was 67.5°, the data obtained from the water-saturated specimens were less and the strengths were slightly lower than those of the natural state by 0.1~0.2 MPa. When the lamination orientation was 90°, the tensile strengths of the water-saturated specimens were higher than those of the natural state by 0.1 MPa after the impact velocity was greater than 3 m/s.

The peak energy density of the water-saturated coal rock specimens was higher than that of the natural state coal rock specimens, with the former being 1.5 to 2 times higher than the latter. The energy density of the water-saturated specimens reached its peak at a time period 10–20% later than that of the natural coal rock specimens. Our preliminary analysis suggests that this is due to the fact that the crack expansion under impact loading is much faster than the expansion rate during static loading. The free water in the rock pores is unable to diffuse into the expanding fracture in an instant, while the effect of surface tension begins to emerge. The water creates a cohesive force F at the crack face that prevents crack expansion, resulting in an increase in the stress value when the rock is ruptured in a water-saturated state. This phenomenon can be explained by the Stefan effect in physics: when parallel circular flat plates separate at a relative velocity $dv/dt$, the viscous fluid generates a counter force $F'$ to prevent the separation between the plates. The resistance produced by the Stefan effect can be expressed as Equation (43), $\eta$ being the viscosity of the liquid ($Pa\cdot s$). Coal rock specimens in the water-saturated state have higher values of $\eta$ than specimens in the natural state. The stress values of coal rock specimens in the saturated water state are greater than those of coal rock specimens in the natural state for similar impact velocities. Due to the presence of water, the crack expansion rate in the coal rock specimens is suppressed. Therefore, the saturated water specimens have higher peak stress and peak deformation energy density.

## 6. Conclusions

In this work, the dynamic tensile properties and evolution characteristics of strain energy density for coal were investigated using both the SHPB and CDEM methods. The following conclusions are drawn.

(1) When the laminated surface of the coal sample is at a certain angle with the impact loading direction, the damage mode is coupled with tensile and shear damage. For the natural or saturated coal samples with debris particle sizes of 0~0.2 mm, the percentage of debris mass does not change much with the increase of impact velocity. In addition, the percentage of fragment mass increases significantly with the increase

of impact velocity for the natural or water-saturated coal samples with the fragment size of 0.2~5 mm.
(2) The presence of weak planes, microcracks and laminae cause the shear damage zone to behave in a more complex manner. If the crack plane coincides with the high shear stress plane, the developed shear cracks extend along the weak laminae and the shear damage zones in BD specimens are not symmetrically distributed.
(3) Changes in the difference between the relative tensile displacements of two groups of measurement points on the localization zone also reflect the evolution of deformation localization of the specimen. When the deformation localization begins in the center of the specimen, the displacements of the two groups of measurement points are relatively consistent at the beginning of the growth, and the difference between them generally begins to increase in the middle.
(4) The energy accumulated inside the coal rock specimen that causes damage of the specimen increases with the increase of impact velocity. For medium-grained debris with a particle size >5 mm, the scale ratio characteristics show that the range of variation of the scale ratio of coal rock debris is relatively large when the impact velocity is small. Plate fragments with a length-thickness ratio range of 3~6 are predominant. When the impact velocity gradually increases, the variation range of coal rock debris scale ratio gradually decreases, the debris scale characteristics tend to be stable, and the blocky debris with the length-to-thickness ratio lower than 3 predominates.

**Author Contributions:** Conceptualization, S.G. and C.W.; Methodology, L.Z.; Software, Y.J. and L.Z.; Validation, S.G., C.W. and F.X.; Formal analysis, H.Z.; Investigation, J.W. and X.R.; Resources, S.W.; Data curation, S.Y.; Writing—original draft preparation, S.G., C.W. and L.Z.; Writing—review and editing, S.G.; Visualization, J.L.; Supervision, S.G. and F.X.; Project administration, F.X.; Funding acquisition, S.G. All authors have read and agreed to the published version of the manuscript.

**Funding:** This work was financially supported by the Fundamental Research Funds for the Universities of Henan Province (grant no. NSFRF200332), China Postdoctoral Science Foundation (grant no. 2021M701100), Key Research and Development and Promotion of Special (Science and Technology) Project of Henan Province (grant nos. 212102310379 and 212102310603), National Natural Science Foundation of China (grant nos. 41907402 and 51604093), the Key Scientific Research Project Fund of Colleges and Universities in Henan Province (grant nos. 21A610005 and 20B440001), and the Doctoral Foundation of Henan Polytechnic University (grant no. B2019-22).

**Data Availability Statement:** Data will be made available on request.

**Conflicts of Interest:** The authors declare no conflict of interest.

# References

1. Lu, J.; Zhang, D.; Huang, G.; Li, X.; Gao, H.; Yin, G. Effects of loading rate on the compound dynamic disaster in deep underground coal mine under true triaxial stress. *Int. J. Rock Mech. Min. Sci.* **2020**, *134*, 104453. [CrossRef]
2. Li, J.; Zhao, J.; Gong, S.Y.; Wang, H.C.; Ju, M.H.; Du, K.; Zhang, Q.B. Mechanical anisotropy of coal under coupled biaxial static and dynamic loads. *Int. J. Rock Mech. Min. Sci.* **2021**, *143*, 104807. [CrossRef]
3. Song, H.; Zhang, H.; Fu, D.; Yang, Y.; Huang, G.; Qu, C.; Cai, Z. Experimental study on damage evolution of rock under uniform and concentrated loading conditions using digital image correlation. *Fatigue Fract. Eng. Mater. Struct.* **2013**, *36*, 760–768. [CrossRef]
4. Zhang, C.; Yu, G.; Zhang, C. Rock matrix-fractured media model for heterogeneous and fractured coal bed. *Trans. Nonferrous Met. Soc. China* **2011**, *21*, 621–625. [CrossRef]
5. Hao, X.; Wei, Y.; Yang, K.; Su, J.; Sun, Y.; Zhu, G.; Wang, S.; Chen, H.; Sun, Z. Anisotropy of crack initiation strength and damage strength of coal reservoirs. *Petrol. Explor. Dev.* **2021**, *48*, 243–255. [CrossRef]
6. Li, J.; Guan, C.; Han, K.; Wang, Z. Characteristics of transient charge on Datong coal sample surfaces with different cracking propagation. *PLoS ONE* **2020**, *15*, 0229824. [CrossRef]
7. Gong, S. Investigation of tensile and fracture mechanical properties of bituminous coal at different strain rates. *J. Mater. Res. Technol.* **2021**, *15*, 834–845. [CrossRef]
8. Liu, J.; Yang, M.; Wang, D.; Zhang, J. Different bedding loaded coal mechanics properties and acoustic emission. *Environ. Earth Sci.* **2018**, *77*, 322–332. [CrossRef]

9. Pan, R.; Fu, D.; Yu, M.; Lei, C. Directivity effect of unloading bedding coal induced fracture evolution and its application. *Int. J. Min. Sci. Technol.* **2017**, *27*, 825–829.
10. Tian, K.; Wei, E. Gas seepage model and experiment based on bedding effect of fractured coal body. *Math. Probl. Eng.* **2022**, *2022*, 3863267. [CrossRef]
11. Dai, J.; Liu, C.; Li, M.; Song, Z. Influence of principal stress effect on deformation and permeability of coal containing beddings under true triaxial stress conditions. *R. Soc. Open Sci.* **2019**, *6*, 181483. [CrossRef]
12. Liu, C.; Yin, G.; Li, M.; Shang, D.; Deng, B.; Song, Z. Deformation and permeability evolution of coals considering the effect of beddings. *Int. J. Rock Mech. Min. Sci.* **2019**, *117*, 49–62. [CrossRef]
13. Hou, P.; Xue, Y.; Gao, F.; Dou, F.; Su, S.; Cai, C.; Zhu, C. Effect of liquid nitrogen cooling on mechanical characteristics and fracture morphology of layer coal under Brazilian splitting test. *Int. J. Rock Mech. Min. Sci.* **2022**, *151*, 105026. [CrossRef]
14. Zhao, Y.; Zhao, G.; Jiang, Y.; Elswoth, D.; Huang, Y. Effects of bedding on the dynamic indirect tensile strength of coal: Laboratory experiments and numerical simulation. *Int. J. Coal Geol.* **2014**, *132*, 81–93. [CrossRef]
15. Li, M.; Liang, W.; Yue, G.; Yue, J.; Zheng, X. Experiment and modeling of permeability under different impact loads in a structural anisotropic coal body. *ACS Omega* **2020**, *5*, 9957–9968. [CrossRef]
16. Li, Y.; Zhao, B.; Yang, J.; Sun, J.; Huang, W.; Li, Z.; Wang, B. Experimental study on the influence of confining pressure and bedding angles on mechanical properties in coal. *Minerals* **2022**, *12*, 345. [CrossRef]
17. Zhong, K.; Zhao, W.; Qin, C.; Chen, W. Experimental study on the mechanical behavior and failure characteristics of layered coal at medium strain rates. *Energies* **2021**, *14*, 6616. [CrossRef]
18. Yang, R.; Zhou, Y.; Ma, D. Failure mechanism and acoustic emission precursors of coal samples considering bedding effect under triaxial unloading condition. *Geofluids* **2022**, *2022*, 8083443. [CrossRef]
19. Liu, J.; Hu, J.; Shen, M.; Yang, M.; Fang, Y. LNMR study on microstructure characteristics and pore size distribution of high-rank coals with different bedding. *Adv. Civil Eng.* **2021**, *2021*, 8542630. [CrossRef]
20. Liu, J.; Jia, G.; Gao, J.; Hu, J.; Chen, S. NMR study on pore structure and permeability of different layers of deep low-rank coal. *Energy Sour. Part A Recovery Util. Environ. Eff.* **2020**, *2020*, 1742254. [CrossRef]
21. Zhao, J.; Zhang, Y.; Ranjith, P.G. Numerical simulation of blasting-induced fracture expansion in coal masses. *Int. J. Rock Mech. Min. Sci.* **2017**, *100*, 28–39. [CrossRef]
22. Tao, Y.; Yuanlong, W.; Shiwan, C.; Liu, W.; Zhao, L.; Zhang, X. Study on mechanical properties and crack propagation of raw coal with different bedding angles based on CT scanning. *ACS Omega* **2022**, *7*, 27185–27195.
23. Huang, J.; Cheng, G.; Zhao, Y.; Ren, W. An experimental study of the strain fields development prior to failure of a marble plate under compression. *Tectonophysics* **1990**, *175*, 269–284.
24. Liu, D.; Cai, M.; Zhou, Y.; Chen, Z.Y. A study on dynamic monitoring of rock crack extension process. *J. Rock Mech. Eng.* **2006**, *25*, 467–472.
25. Sutton, M.A.; Mingqi, C.; Peters, W.H.; Chao, Y.J.; McNeill, S.R. Application of an optimized digital correlation method to planar deformation analysis. *Image Vis. Comput.* **1986**, *4*, 143–150. [CrossRef]
26. Peters, W.H.; Ranson, W.F. Digital imaging techniques in experimental stress analysis. *Opt. Eng.* **1982**, *21*, 427–431. [CrossRef]
27. Yamaguchi, I. A laser-speckle strain gauge. *J. Phys. E Sci. Instrum.* **1981**, *14*, 1270. [CrossRef]
28. Skurtveit, E.; Torabi, A.; Gabrielsen, R.H.; Zoback, M.D. Experimental investigation of deformation mechanisms during shear-enhanced compaction in poorly lithified sandstone and sand. *J. Geophys. Res. Solid Earth* **2013**, *118*, 4083–4100. [CrossRef]
29. Sun, Q.; Cai, C.; Zhang, S.; Tian, S.; Li, B.; Xia, L. Study of localized deformation in geopolymer cemented coal gangue-fly ash backfill based on the digital speckle correlation method. *Construct. Build. Mater.* **2019**, *215*, 321–331. [CrossRef]
30. Ma, S.; Xu, X.; Zhao, Y. The GEO-DSCM system and its application to the deformation measurement of rock materials. *Int. J. Rock Mech. Min. Sci.* **2004**, *41*, 292–297. [CrossRef]
31. Yuan, C.; Yuan, Z.; Wang, Y.; Li, C.-M. Analysis of the diffusion process of mining overburden separation strata based on the digital speckle correlation coefficient field. *Int. J. Rock Mech. Min. Sci.* **2019**, *119*, 13–21. [CrossRef]
32. Song, Y.; Ren, H.; Xu, H.; Chen, Z.; Dong, A. Study on synergistic system of energy-absorbing yielding anti-impact supporting structure and surrounding rock. *Sci. Rep.* **2022**, *12*, 1–9. [CrossRef]
33. Zhang, Z.; Xie, H.; Zhang, R.; Guo, X.; Chen, Z.; Dong, A. Deformation damage and energy evolution characteristics of coal at different depths. *Rock Mech. Rock Eng.* **2019**, *52*, 1491–1503. [CrossRef]
34. Meng, Q.; Zhang, M.; Han, L.; Pu, H.; Nie, T. Effects of acoustic emission and energy evolution of rock specimens under the uniaxial cyclic loading and unloading compression. *Rock Mech. Rock Eng.* **2016**, *49*, 3873–3886. [CrossRef]
35. Wold, M.B.; Connell, L.D.; Choi, S.K. The role of spatial variability in coal seam parameters on gas outburst behaviour during coal mining. *Int. J. Coal Geol.* **2008**, *75*, 1–14. [CrossRef]
36. Chen, Y.; Zhang, Y.; Li, X. Experimental study on influence of bedding angle on gas permeability in coal. *J. Petrol. Sci. Eng.* **2019**, *179*, 173–179. [CrossRef]
37. Xibing, L. *Rock Dynamics Fundamentals and Applications*; Science Press: Beijing, China, 2014.
38. Fan, Y.; Li, S.; Hou, Y.; Kim, M.-S.; Yun, S. A study of the failure mechanism of rock and soil associate under different boundary conditions. *Hydrogeol. Eng. Geol.* **2013**, *40*, 47–48.
39. Fan, Y.; Adewuyi, O.I.; Feng, C. Strength characteristics of soil rock mixture under equal stress and cyclic loading conditions. *Geosyst. Eng.* **2015**, *18*, 73–77.

40. Feng, C.; Li, S.; Liu, X.; Zhang, Y. A semi-spring and semi-edge combined contact model in CDEM and its application to analysis of Jiweishan landslide. *J. Rock Mech. Geotech. Eng.* **2014**, *6*, 26–35. [CrossRef]
41. Zheng, D.; Li, Q. An explanation for rate effect of concrete strength based on fracture toughness including free water viscosity. *Eng. Fract. Mech.* **2004**, *71*, 2319–2327. [CrossRef]

MDPI  
St. Alban-Anlage 66  
4052 Basel  
Switzerland  
Tel. +41 61 683 77 34  
Fax +41 61 302 89 18  
www.mdpi.com

*Mathematics* Editorial Office  
E-mail: mathematics@mdpi.com  
www.mdpi.com/journal/mathematics